FANTASTIC ARCHAEOLOGY

FANTASTIC

THE WILD SIDE OF

ARCHAEOLOGY

NORTH AMERICAN PREHISTORY

STEPHEN WILLIAMS

UNIVERSITY OF PENNSYLVANIA PRESS
Philadelphia

Library of Congress Cataloging-in-Publication Data
Williams, Stephen, 1926–
   Fantastic archaeology : the wild side of North American prehistory
   Stephen Williams.
     p.   cm.
   Includes bibliographical references and index.
   ISBN 0-8122-8238-8 (cloth). — ISBN 0-8122-1312-2
   1. Archaeology—North America—History.   2. North America—
Antiquities.   I. Title.
CC125.N7W55   1991
973.1—dc20   90-29189
                                                  CIP

Second paperback printing 1991

TO THE MEMORY OF
LOIS AND CLYDE
who long ago sparked my interest in the Past
AND
WITH LOVE TO
EUNICE, JOHN, and TIMOTHY
who have helped me now appreciate the Present

Contents

viii   Contents

List of Illustrations

Introduction

A first encounter with any grand fantastic theory, not political or
economic, delights me.

J. B. PRIESTLEY, 1949

Looking back at my youth, I realize that I, like many other Americans, first
learned about archaeology as an intellectual pursuit from its wild side, from
what I call "Fantastic Archaeology"—that is, archaeology based on fantasy
rather than on carefully recovered prehistoric evidence.

I can still remember that fall day nearly fifty years ago when I went into
the familiar but still imposing oak-paneled library at my country day school
and took down a copy of James Churchward's *Lost Continent of Mu*. It was
indeed a fateful day. I wish I could recall who suggested that title to me; the
quiet but always helpful librarian, Miss Hiniker, may have been the one.
Perhaps I asked for a book on archaeology and got that instead. Or it could
have been on the suggestion of the headmaster, a devoted believer in
Atlantis, but I seem to recall learning of that quirk in this otherwise
scholarly gentleman at a later date, when I myself was deeply hooked on the
mysteries of Mu.

In retrospect I can even see a certain fatal inevitability about my
involvement with what I now call Fantastic Archaeology. After all, some
years later I would inherit an armful of autographed works of that exuberant transplanted Minnesota politician turned Atlantis/Shakespeare scholar,
Ignatius Donnelly, as a result of familial ties to close friends of the "Sage of
Nininger." Of course, I was growing up in Minnesota, a land inhabited by
Norsemen, almost all of whom were firm Kensington Rune Stone believers. So it seems that I could not escape my ultimate fate.

Looking today at my own copy of Churchward's *Mu*—the same 1926
edition that I had seen in my school library—I wonder that I could have
been so easily co-opted. Would you feel confident about a book written by a
British fop, who appears on the frontispiece with a rose in his lapel and the
florid self-advertisement on the title page "Colonel," late of the Bengal
Lancers? But taken in I was, hook, line, and sinker. It got so bad that I was
importuning family friends and pouring out the thrilling Mu story—as

James Churchward

purportedly read from the mysterious clay tablets, now forever lost somewhere in the wastelands of India—to all who would listen. There was no one to warn me to check the evidence. Even the headmaster had never heard of Mu or Churchward and was very interested to learn about this new continent lost in the Pacific. Surely it was the only vaguely intellectual discussion I ever had with that formidable man during my seven years at his school.

So there it was—Mu and Atlantis, with a bit of Viking derring-do mixed in to add local spice. I cannot, mercifully, recall exactly when I fell from the true faith with regard to Mu, but by my graduate student days at Yale I was prepared to write a debunking paper on the Kensington Rune Stone, after doing some original research at the Minnesota Historical Society. From then on, I never looked back.

The 1950s, when I entered the archaeological profession, were an exciting period for popular archaeological literature. C. W. Ceram's excellent blockbuster Book-of-the-Month Club selection *Gods, Graves and Scholars* made for good cocktail-hour conversation, but it vied for readers' attention with the exciting account of high-seas adventure on the *Kon-Tiki* raft by Thor Heyerdahl. The raft voyage was remarkable, but the archaeological

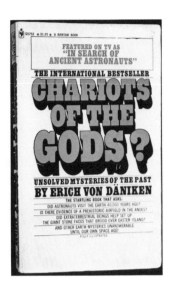

Von Däniken's
Chariots of the Gods?

thesis that it tried to support was very weak. There was also a bulky but untrustworthy compilation by Paul Hermann, *They All Discovered America,* which had the Vikings showing up at Chichén Itzá. Another flawed contender was Hjalmar Holand's pro-Kensington-Rune-Stone narrative *Westward to Vinland*. No wonder the public didn't know what to believe then and still doesn't.

I had always valued truth, and this playing fast and loose with archaeological facts would upset me as I began teaching anthropology to Harvard undergraduates in the late 1950s. In Sophomore Tutorial I used Heyerdahl's works and that glorious spoof of Harold Gladwin's *Men Out of Asia,* as exemplars of how to recognize *imperfect* archaeological interpretation. One of my older colleagues saw my assignment sheet with Gladwin's saga of Pacific migrations on it, and he raised serious objections to its use at Harvard. He felt that the students were too immature to be exposed to such dangerous nonsense. I refused his advice and continued to discuss such works as a heuristic device until I was wooed away to the even more exciting tales of Erich von Däniken's extraterrestrial workers and their connections with most of the world's great archaeological mysteries.

One should now consider the current state of popular knowledge of archaeology. Although there have been no recent runaway best-sellers like Ceram's volume, fictionalized accounts on archaeological topics, such as

James Michener's *The Source,* have done well. Of great recent interest has been the well-done Earth's Children series by Jean M. Auel: *The Clan of the Cave Bear, The Valley of Horses, The Mammoth Hunters,* and *The Plains of Passage,* which present believable recreations of European prehistoric cultures in a responsible manner. Auel has been a guest speaker at several major archaeological conferences.

Current science-oriented magazines such as *Discovery* and *Smithsonian* have all dealt frequently with the more "interesting" aspects of archaeology, taking off from *Scientific American*'s excellent long-term commitment to the field and that of the less well-known, but excellent, *Natural History. Omni* magazine was not included in that list for good reason; it has chosen an orientation to the weird and the wild side, and its contribution has been mainly to the fantastic aspect of archaeology.

Of course, the *National Geographic Magazine* has long had a special role in the field, in publishing a great number of important finds, in making Leakey a household word, and in supporting archaeological research via its own research grants program. Its well-illustrated books, *Clues to America's Past* and *Discovering Man's Past in the Americas,* have been best-selling hardcover volumes in the field, very fairly priced because of their huge print runs (in excess of two hundred thousand copies). The most recent of these volumes is the almost gaudy *Adventure of Archaeology* (1985) by Brian Fagan, with a very strong title page and excellent pictures and text. The *Geographic* movies have made their mark as well. The profession's own popular journal, *ARCHAEOLOGY,* has recently been restyled and upgraded. It has a bit of an Old World emphasis; it has gained substantially in circulation in recent years and now tops one hundred thousand subscribers.

Television coverage has been spotty in America, with a two-year stint on PBS by Michael Ambrosino's "Odyssey" series (1979–80) being the brightest long-term commitment. The "Odyssey" shows, now available as educational films and tapes, won good audience support but were too costly to continue because of diminishing federal support. Other specials, such as Richard Leakey's "Origins," have provided a small window on the archaeological world. "Nova," originated by Michael Ambrosino, continues to confront some archaeological trouble spots—its debunking of von Däniken was excellent. Unfortunately, in the same show there was a treatment of the Sirius B astronomical problem, wherein the Dogon of Africa are said to know of the existence of this mysterious star via extraterrestrials. British television has a much stronger track record of concern and careful treatment of archaeological questions, including the mysteries of Stonehenge and other megalithic structures. In contrast, the United States–based "In Search of" series, with the indefatigable Leonard Nimoy as narrator, provided mainly fodder for the far-out fringe.

Movies made for box office consumption have not been a very positive force for public education in archaeology. For example, the space fantasy *2001: A Space Odyssey* provided only a brief glimpse of the "cultural" activities of Early Man. The most recent of this ilk, *Quest for Fire,* was also the most believable; it was best on technological developments such as fire, of course, and procreation. Nonetheless, it did not get much support from the profession or at the box office.

The most forceful impact on archaeology came from Steven Spielberg's classic *Raiders of the Lost Ark* and its less successful sequel, *Temple of Doom.* The end of the trilogy, *The Last Crusade,* recovers some of the lost style. Harrison Ford as a role model for young diggers has made Indiana Jones, with his bullwhip and felt hat, very memorable indeed. I have not noticed a great increase in archaeology majors, however. Whatever else the *Raiders* series did, it made Fantastic Archaeology (the course) very exciting. I have regularly shown some of these films as a crowd-pleasing finale to my class on this topic, just before the exam. To keep the record straight, there really are some archaeologists, of rather that persuasion, searching now for the "true" Ark, not to mention Noah's Ark, as well.

Popularizing archaeology, especially the North American variety, has never been a high priority for most professionals. Whereas there are now quite a few excellent introductions to the Meso-American field, the archaeology of the rest of the hemisphere, Peru excepted, is virtually untouched by readable popular volumes. The well-known British-based series "Peoples and Places," which now numbers more than one hundred volumes, has devoted less than ten to New World subjects.

Until this general situation changes, it seems that popular archaeological interests in America are being served more and more by quite another fare—what I call Fantastic Archaeology. There are plenty of books on that subject!

My colleague Glyn Daniel has said:

> But while I strongly support the popularisation of archaeology in all possible ways, I have no illusions that it is easy to get across the newer archaeology to our learned colleagues or the general public—that scholarly mob who read and alas! write bad and sad archaeological books—the only too many people who lurk in the lush lunatic fringes around the fairway of true archaeology. (Daniel, 1976: 29)

Harrison Ford as Professor Indiana Jones

He continued in a lecture, which had the archaeologically knowledgeable Prince Charles in the audience (and he *was* amused), as follows: "Nowhere, alas, does bullshit and bang-me-arse archaeology flourish so well these days as in America where foolish fantasies pour from the press every month and sell like hotcakes."[1]

It is this phenomenon that is the cause and focus of this volume. Perhaps this explicit terminology by my British colleague will make it apparent why I have chosen less argumentative phrasing. Other American colleagues have called it "pseudoarchaeology," but that also suggests that there are easily defined limits—what is *real* archaeology and what is "pseudo"?

Although that is usually not too difficult a choice, I prefer my own terminology.

Therefore I have for a number of years used the term "Fantastic Archaeology," because it has a less pejorative effect. Science does require the use of imagination and fantasy, in reasonable amounts, as I will describe in a later chapter. Then, too, something in this outer realm of archaeology may make its way toward the center of the field on the basis of new information. Thus I do not wish to banish any topic. For archaeologists do change their minds based on new data. We must not forget the way that geologists recently have had to rethink plate tectonics and continental drift. So *Fantastic* Archaeology it is.

It is probably not unreasonable to ask, even at this juncture, Why study this fringe area of archaeology at all? If one considers it worthless, lacking in veracity, won't discussing it give it more credibility than it deserves? If we ignore it, perhaps it will go away.

Such disdain for these wilder alternative explanations of archaeology has in the past been a common practice by members of the profession, but that attitude appears to be changing. As we will see, the phenomenon is not new—it is a century and a half old when viewed from the American scene; Fantastic Archaeology even had a golden age in the nineteenth century. Some scholars see it having a cyclical pattern, rising in interest and then becoming much less prominent. Others feel that these more extraordinary explanations are amusing—they capture the interest of outsiders and help to popularize the field, so they think. Fortunately, this latter position is not widely held.

A review of eight introductory archaeology texts indicates that the authors are about evenly split in their responses to the subject. Four ignore it, taking the view that it does not exist, or at least it is best not to tell newly interested students about that wild aspect of the field. But the students have all probably seen *Raiders* and have their own stereotypes of the field and those who work in it anyway. Interestingly, one text mentioned the topic of "Psychic Archaeology" in its first edition but dropped it from the next.

The remaining three texts, by Brian Fagan, by William Rathje and Michael Schiffer, and by Robert Sharer and Wendy Ashmore, treat Fantastic Archaeology as a serious problem. They all also use Atlantis and von Däniken as prime examples. Fagan, a well-published popular writer as well as a Ph.D.-burdened university professor, stresses the need for modern archaeologists to establish credibility by communicating their results in "intelligible and enjoyable terms." Rathje and Schiffer debunk von Däniken in very specific terms, but they also feel that the natural fascination with the mysteries of the past must be carefully translated into a concern for conservation of the records of the past. Sharer and Ashmore go so far as to call pseudoarchaeology one of the two greatest challenges to contemporary archaeologists—the other being the destruction of archaeological remains. They feel that "archaeology has a responsibility to prevent pseudoarchaeologists from robbing humanity of the real achievements of past cultures."[2]

How do we prevent this robbery? Not by pretending that the theft is not happening, but also not by preventing the publication of this floodtide of Fantastic Archaeology. Daniel has further insisted that these books should be reviewed. I trust we have learned our lesson well in that area. For example, the Establishment attacks on Immanuel Velikovsky (some especially strong ones came from my own institution), which caused a shift of publishers for *Worlds in Collision,* only added fuel to the fire. As George Bernard Shaw said, "Martyrdom, sir, is what these people like: it is the only way in which a man can become famous without ability."[3]

Although I cannot offer a very constructive solution here, I must say that many publishers in America do rush into print any volume that they feel will attract attention, without ever submitting the text to any review, much less by peers. It is as if to say, We don't really care about the content, just be sure it will sell. The unsightly rush to publish the now-exposed fake Hitler diaries, without checking them at all, represents journalistic greed at its very worst.

So there is, I feel, a responsibility to condemn nonsense, to show that some Fantastic archaeologists have as scant a garment of real data as did the Emperor with his new vestments. But also there is a need to promote public awareness of the really exciting discoveries made in archaeology each year. If we can do that, progress can be made in balancing public knowledge of the field.

Make no mistake, the publishing of Fantastic Archaeology is big business and the growth rate is now amazing. The golden oldies persist; Erich von Däniken's tenth book has come out: *Did I Get It Wrong?* The dust jacket of an earlier volume tells us that more than 45 million copies of his books have been sold. That old master of the rhetorical question just keeps rolling along. People still believe that he is an archaeologist. This "gold rush" spawned a huge number of imitators—even of the jacket design on the paperbacks—and they are selling too.

Obviously, one positive reaction, from a personal point of view, is to write a book on the other side; that is the "why" of this volume. I value truth, and it really bothers me to see fakes and frauds masquerading as genuine archaeological objects. So too do alternative views on archaeological facts that expeditiously employ mysterious and miraculous explanations, rather than carefully reasoned attempts to deal with what all would have to admit are enigmatic problems of the past. Most archaeologists, however, are willing to say that they do not know the answers to such questions, and I am one of that number.

There are some real difficulties in coming to grips with such widely differing views of past events. These ideas are very deeply held; they almost seem to fill some essential need: a view of the past that sees "fair Atlantis with its joyful population of citizen scholars," for example. Certainly scorn and invective are not a suitable mode of persuasion toward a new perspective on these long-held notions. I will, perforce, use terms such as *pseudoscience, crank scientist,* and *fake* or *fraud*—they are part of the regular vocabulary of other scholars such as Martin Gardner and Sprague de Camp, whose work in this general field I esteem and hope to emulate in this treatment of archaeological subjects.

To provide a foundation for the topics in this volume I will critically discuss the background, credentials, quality of data analysis, and nature of the presentation of the various individuals involved. And I hope to approach this academic task in the sanguine style of the late Robert Wauchope, whose tone in *Lost Tribes and Sunken Continents* I deeply admire.

When a piece of data has been carefully studied and evaluated, such as the Kensington Rune Stone or the Davenport Tablets, its fraudulent nature must then be clearly stated. Some materials and cases will still remain enigmatic, objects in a "fantastic" realm we cannot yet fully explain. This uncertainty principle is true in all of archaeology, but it is often misunderstood by the lay public with the following retort, "If *you,* the expert, don't know the answer, then my explanation is obviously just as good as yours." That problem will be addressed in an ongoing discussion of how one evaluates archaeological evidence in general.

In this volume I hope to explain a number of interesting cases of Fantastic Archaeology, to show how archaeology really works to unravel the fascinating story of America's past, and finally to indicate where I feel the truly fantastic past exists: in the hard-won knowledge of the first inhabitants of North America, from a dim period of exploration and expansion into the New World at the end of the Pleistocene epoch to the final unforgiving confrontation with the European explorers at the end of the sixteenth century. That is a unique and fantastic tale, unknown, unfortunately, to most of the inhabitants of what we now proudly call the United States of America.

So with some archaeological tools, precepts of study at hand and in mind, we will begin our wayfaring trip through the wild side of archaeology as seen in America. It will not be an easy journey, for many pitfalls lie along the winding path, such as the gaudy seductions of the fantastic theories that so delighted Priestley, but the pilgrim, I trust, will make progress.

1

The Byways and Forgotten Pathways of Fantastic Archaeology

There may be something in it, you know.
GLYN DANIEL, 1962

The thud of the newspaper on the driveway just before 7 A.M. heralds the arrival of our daily recommended dose of bad news—rape in the dark streets, political scandal in the mayor's office, rising taxes on the state and local levels, and child abuse at the day-care center. But this particular issue brings good news too. The media have seen fit to devote a spread to the story of an exciting discovery in Lowell, Massachusetts, of a new mini-Stonehenge just north of Boston. The discoverer, an English teacher at a local college, feels sure that this rude circle of standing stones "is perhaps the most significant of all the pre-Columbian sites in New England." He would date it to the fourth or fifth century A.D. Yet he has done no excavations, there are no telltale Bronze or Iron Age artifacts lying around, and he has not even done historical research in the area to see if it might be the work of a nineteenth-century landscape architect. "It might be a folly, yes," he is quoted as saying, "but I'd be very surprised if this doesn't turn out to be the real thing."

This is classic Fantastic Archaeology: the hopes outrun the evidence from the very start, no explanations are offered as to how and why fourth-century Britons would be in this part of New England, let alone construct a possible astronomical monument. The facts are merely that these strange stones seem to cry out for an archaeological interpretation. Our worthy scholar is ready to provide it, although the Establishment archaeologists interviewed by the media discount his views. As the British archaeologist Glyn Daniel has so aptly put it:

We know only too well that all over the world, from wayward undergraduate to B.B.C. producer to publisher's reader there are people, otherwise sensible and sane, people who would not believe in six-headed cats and blood-curdling spectral monsters, who yet read some folly about Noah's ark or Atlantis or cataclysmic world-tides, and say, with a contented sigh, "There may be something in it, you know." (Daniel, 1962: 167)

I have said earlier that this is a volume about Fantastic Archaeology, but what does that broad term mean to me? What is the gamut of the field, so defined? Fantastic Archaeology covers those alternative views of the past that use data and interpretations that will not stand close scrutiny. It does not subsume all that is wonderful and amazing in our knowledge of the past. Surely that tremendous sense of wonder about the miracles of the past is the very reason why many archaeologists, myself included, are drawn into the field. No, the past is not simple, and I do not mean to suggest that all archaeologists agree on all explanations of the past. That simply is not true, and they do seem to change their minds all too frequently. What I am saying is that there is an ever-growing body of fanciful archaeological interpretations that have been tested and found wanting.

We can start with the familiar notion that there are sunken continents beneath both the major oceans, the Atlantic and the Pacific, known as Atlantis and Mu, that supported great civilizations thousands of years ago. Then there are those who yearly search for the remains of Noah's Ark, still thought to be parked somewhere on Mount Ararat. In Central America there are lost cities with giant pyramids that were built with the necessary aid of either overseas voyagers or extraterrestrials.

There is a plethora of fakes, frauds, and misinterpreted cracks in rocks; even American Indian rock carvings (petroglyphs) all across America are seen by some as inscriptions in Hebrew, Egyptian hieroglyphs, Kufi Arabic, and Ogam, to mention only a sample of the assorted literature waiting for ardent readers. There are Viking rune stones from Maine to Oklahoma, and a Viking longboat was sighted just a little off course in the middle of the California desert. There are Aztecs in Ohio and a Jewish-Roman community in the Sun Belt at A.D. 700.

The presumed megalithic monuments in New England are an unordered mess compared to those in Britain. There, stone monuments and sacred spots, such as those now with cathedrals atop them, are seen by some to be beautifully set up in neat, orderly arrangements. Indeed, they are a bit like microwave transmitters to which, remarkably, they have been closely compared by some, since they are felt to be emitting powerful messages from the past.

In the field of Fantastic Archaeology every mystery is solved, every unread script from Easter Island to the Indus is easily deciphered. Fantastic archaeologists have an explanation for everything; the real mystery for them is why it took so long. The professionals, with their time-consuming putterings, might just as well "pack it in."

What causes this phenomenon? What allows such unfortunate misconceptions about the field of prehistory to persist? Perhaps it is because archaeology is seen by many as a game that all can play; no special training is needed. Thus perception is the key to the matter, and I mean perception from the most basic level on up. "Seeing is believing" is a very common-sense feeling. Yet when we archaeologists look at an object, how do we know what it is?

Every archaeologist knows the problem. You are at your desk at the museum, a phone call comes from the front desk, and you are asked to come down and help a visitor who has found a strange rock in the backyard. Very often it is nothing—nothing archaeological, that is. It merely looks like an artifact, but it is hard to convince the visitor of that. This same problem can arise in the field with amateur collectors who have lots of real artifacts but also some "special ones"—not like any of the others and thus deeply cherished. It is difficult to tell them that those *special* ones are often not artifacts at all.

This ability to make the determination of artifact or no is essential to all practicing archaeologists, and it is not easily learned. The first stumbling steps one makes in that learning process are hard. I well remember when I was at my first archaeological field school in Arizona and was showing a stone "thing" I had found to an older student. I asked rather hesitantly, "What is it?" and was given a very brief answer: "A used flake." Almost immediately I was asking, "How do you know that?" Believe me, the answers can be taught and learned.

So one must learn to see archaeologically; it is part of the basic challenge to knowing that keeps us going. The University of Pennsylvania scholar Loren Eiseley, with a touch of the poet that he was, has said it better and with a bit of sadness:

A man who has once looked with the archaeological eye will never see quite normally. He will be wounded by what other men call trifles. It is possible to refine the sense of time until an old shoe in the bunch grass or a pile of nineteenth-century beer bottles in an abandoned mining town tolls in one's head like a hall clock. This is the price one pays from learning to read time from surfaces other than an illuminated dial. It is the melancholy secret of the artifact, the humanly touched thing. (Eiseley, 1971: 81)

Nonetheless, the torrent of Fantastic Archaeology continues. Those of us in the field can get a bit paranoid. We ask, Why us? Are we the only ones who have to suffer from this onslaught of wild interpretations? Does no other field suffer from such gross exaggerations or oversimplifications, which pass for truths? In fact, we are not alone. Yes, we have certainly had more than our share of fakes and frauds, but so have history, fine arts, literature, and even other sciences. Martin Gardner's classic volume *Fads and Fallacies in the Name of Science* and his more recent volume *Science: Good, Bad and Bogus* provide wonderful insights into the range and depth of what is termed by all as pseudoscience. It is a glittering expanse of "might be's" and "can't be's." But before we look at antiscience, we should explore the nature of the scientific method itself.

The question, What is science? and its answer are indeed the subject of numerous books and articles. There are, of course, many ways to view the matter, but I happen to like the discussion of the topic by Kenneth Boulding in his Presidential Address to the American Association for the Advancement of Science entitled "Science: Our Common Heritage." He stressed three aspects of the subject: Curiosity, Testing, and Veracity. He suggests that in the 1500s in Europe a high value began to be placed on *Curiosity.* The questioning of established "truths," such as biblical authority, was joined by the opportunity to say "what if" this might be true instead; asking what, at that time, could be termed "fantastic questions." But with those questions came the understanding that there was a real world out there that would respond to inquiry—*Testing.* Boulding says: "Without fantasy, science would have nothing to test; without testing, fantasy would be unchallenged."[1] This testing would be done by logic and with organized input from outsiders, with data from our own senses, and from the trustworthy records of others. So finally we come to *Veracity.* Trust in the records of others is essential. Science has always placed a high value on this trait—*on not telling lies.* Boulding feels that "in the scientific culture, it is central."

Veracity is a very touchy topic, and as a result it has not often been widely discussed. Textbooks in archaeology, for example, do not have a section devoted to it; recently, however, a danger flag has been raised in other scientific fields that cannot be ignored. William Broad and Nicholas Wade have written *Betrayers of the Truth,* which details the many, far too many, betrayals of truth in the hard sciences. They focused mainly on medicine, a field in which, especially in the labs of many famous universities, including Harvard, faked data had been published with fudged numbers and too-perfect results. They saw the pressure to publish as a major cause and felt there was an epidemic in the loss of veracity. I see a problem in other branches of inquiry too; that Sigma Xi, a scientific honor society, published a handbook on the subject indicates the immediacy of the situation. Recent incidents, including cases of plagiarism, have struck both the presidential primaries and high officials in venerable hospitals. One wonders if the epidemic is spreading.

Boulding, in his discussion of scientific methods, further emphasizes the importance of careful records of observations, including details of space and time. Such record keeping is well demonstrated in the field of archaeology, Boulding notes. In discussing cases in Fantastic Archaeology, we will see how very crucial this aspect is and how often these precise data are missing when we need them most. In terms of logic, the familiar use of Occam's razor is recommended. That logician's rule states that the simplest explanation is the best. Boulding concludes that there is, however, a dangerous illusion about science: that there is a *single* scientific method—"a touchstone that can distinguish what is scientific from what is not." That touchstone does not exist; there are a series of scientific methods (plural) that can be applied in different circumstances and fields.

If Boulding is correct, and I think he is, then how do we distinguish pseudoscience, since he has robbed us of our little black "detector box"? The answer is, "not easily, but it can be done." One of the difficulties is that pseudoscience writings often have some of the trappings of science. The archaeologist John Cole recently reviewed a volume explaining New World archaeology in fantastic terms by Jeffrey Goodman and specifically mentioned that one dangerous aspect of the volume is that it "looked like the real thing." The format may be right—even von Däniken's most recent book has a fairly complete bibliography for a change—but the content is not.

In these works there is always a strong dose of the Curiosity that Boulding recommended, but there is little Testing. This lack is a common failing, and the volumes are often short on Veracity too. That is why hoaxes and frauds are so important to this present inquiry. After all, a hoax or a fake is nothing but a *lie,* to state it very bluntly! Unfortunately, these fraudulent artifacts often continue to be used in Fantastic Archaeology long after they have been thoroughly discredited. Finally, there is a lack of the use of logic; often Occam's razor does apply for very complex explanations which are often used although a much simpler solution will do the work.

Daisie and Michael Radner have recently written a little-known classic on pseudoscience entitled *Science and Unreason.* In it they have carefully delineated the "marks of pseudoscience," sort of a birdwatcher's guide to the identification of the species. Their list includes everything from anachronistic thinking to the use of mysteries and myths as hard data. Other marks include a grab-bag approach to evidence, the use of irrefutable hypotheses, and argument from spurious similarity. All this is done with a lighthearted touch—especially the anecdote in which a pet dog is proved innocent of eating his dead master thanks to a psychic who interviewed the dog and exonerated "Prince" via ESP. Prince found the suggestion distasteful.

But Radner and Radner have tackled the other aspect of the field as well—the *person* who practices pseudoscience. They use the term *crank,* as have many others (Martin Gardner, Sprague de Camp), and I will use it as well. The *Oxford English Dictionary* defines *crank* as "a person with a mental twist, an eccentric; especially a monomaniac." Certainly that description fits many of those engaged in Fantastic Archaeology. Martin Gardner says that "if a man persists in advancing views that are contradicted by all available evidence, and which offer no reasonable grounds for serious consideration, he will rightfully be dubbed a *crank* by his colleagues."[2] All in all, it is a term that I am less than happy with despite its widespread use, but I am at a loss to offer a better alternative, so *crank* it is.

However one chooses to refer to the purveyors of pseudoscience, they do have a similar personal profile. They often work in almost total isolation from professional colleagues, and they exhibit a tendency to paranoia. They consider themselves geniuses and view their professional colleagues as ignorant blockheads. They feel that they suffer unjust persecution and are discriminated against, especially when they try to publish in professional journals. In selecting targets for their work, they often pick great scientists and their theories. When they write up their work, they often use complex jargon. This profile was put together by Martin Gardner, but others, like Radner and Radner, also see similar characteristics in their appraisals of cranks. As with any generalization, the profile does not fit everyone in the group, but the rather uniform pattern of behavior in whatever field one chooses to investigate is amazing.

Turning to a somewhat happier side of the question, one is met by the fact that common myths tend to intersect with what I have called pseudoscience. Herein lies some rather testing mind-stretching: you may well ask, Are you going to let me cling to some very comfortable little myths, ones that I grew up with, or are you—in your destructive onslaught of right thinking—going to destroy water dowsing, sea serpents, seances, UFOs, *and* the Abominable Snowman in one fell swoop?

I think you know the answer. What can I say to help make the loss less severe? Well, for one thing, there usually is some real basis for the belief, a foundation in an observed phenomenon that first leads one to accept the idea. For example, water dowsing, especially in areas where there is lots of groundwater (which is where the practice is most common), does usually work—water *is* found by dowsers. Isn't that proof enough?

Then, too, there is a worldwide belief in humanlike monsters, often lurking in the unknown woods. As anthropologist Michael Ames has said, "If monsters did not exist, we would invent them." Serious study of the Big Foot–Sasquatch–Yeti–Abominable Snowman question indicates to me that that is exactly what has happened—we've got them everywhere we want them—but conveniently they don't take up much space and seem to eat very little. Sea serpents and their inland cohorts, Nessie, Champ, and so on, are equally widespread and have a long and distinguished history of appearing to the many that seek them—similar to humanlike monsters, they are very difficult to capture physically or on photographic film. Even underwater radar has not definitively caught their images yet.

So what and whom do you believe, and why? In our youth we are taught not to believe everything we read in the newspapers; but how many of us really accept that caution? We read and accept, until it hits home. We read in a local paper some nonsense about ourselves or someone we know well, and we are properly outraged. "That isn't right. That's not what I said! That person isn't like that at all." But then we continue to read and continue to believe.

What about what we see? Visual images are even stronger data to our senses; our children watch television and believe almost all that they see. They discriminate a bit with cartoon figures and the like, but what about pseudoscience and other such nonsense? There is no warning label that ingestion of this image may damage your thought process about that subject.

Psychologist Paul Kurtz has said that he feels that critical judgment is being perverted and polluted by television, that watching the tube is replacing analysis, and that people can no longer tell what the truth is. For example, if one were to ask children after watching a docudrama if they had *actually* seen such and such event, I am sure that the answer would be yes, they had really witnessed it. How can they be expected to tell the difference between a news clip of actual footage from Vietnam and the exploits of Rambo? Does it matter? It does, if you value truth.

But the will to believe, even in the face of contrary evidence, is strong as well. One cannot just tell people that a fact is not true and expect them to

Spiderman—Atlantis: Legend or Truth?

believe it; at least that is what the writer H. L. Mencken found out to his chagrin. Bergen Evans has told this sad/happy story of a journalistic spoof that went much too far. In a "Tale of the Tub," Evans relates that Mencken wrote in his newspaper column in 1917 about the use of the first bathtub in America by a gentleman in Cincinnati some seventy-five years before. He elaborated on how there had been strong opposition to this new idea even from the medical profession, but the day had been carried when President Millard Fillmore took up the practice in a tub he had installed in the White House.

There was not a jot of historical fact behind a word of this story, but for reasons far outweighing the nature of the pronouncement or its writer, the story became enshrined as a *fact* of American history and was widely quoted from editorial mastheads to local pulpits. About ten years later Mencken grew weary of the charade and confessed publicly that the story about the bathtub and its history was a hoax. The retraction was widely published, but the tale would not die. He published a second retraction with no success and even received rebukes for his attempts to destroy this myth. As Evans has said, "Five minutes in any library would be enough to refute it, but it has ceased to be a question of fact and has become an article of faith."[3] So myths, like old soldiers, never die; perhaps my task is impossible.

Nevertheless, I will persist. I feel that if I can show how archaeologists view their evidence and what biases we bring to the analysis, then my case can be made. Archaeologists usually consider their evidence to have three dimensions: *Form, Space,* and *Time.* These dimensions are, for the most part, perceptible with the use of our own senses and some instrumentation that aids those senses, such as microscopes or surveying equipment. *Form* is the easiest dimension to deal with: if it is an artifact, we can measure it, weigh it, and so forth. We will look at it and determine what it is made of, what the source of that material was, how it was made, and finally, and with more difficulty, how it was used. Our formal analysis will be to compare the artifact to like materials and ultimately to set up a covering typology. This same method would be used if we were dealing with house structures, mounds, or archaeological sites themselves.

Space is a rather easy dimension to deal with *if* we have discovered the artifact ourselves. We carefully record its location; if in an excavation, we would like a three-dimensional fix on it because depth can be crucial. If our artifact has left its original context, we must depend on the records of others to pinpoint these essential bits of information. Another aspect of the spatial dimension that is most significant is that of *context*. With what other items was the artifact found? In a simple case like a burial, what were the conditions of the burial location and what other things were found with it? King Tut's tomb is a good example. Next in our analysis we would want to compare the distribution of this form in space—map the finds of similar artifacts and look for a pattern of distribution.

Finally, we turn to the *Time* dimension. This aspect is the most difficult to deal with. Unless we have a dated coin or inscription, we must get our position in time from other sources. Formal analysis can often help—most of us can roughly date the cars we pass on the streets, at least to the decade if not exact year; remember the tail fins on the 1950s Cadillac?

Forms do change. We recognize this temporal shift in most other categories of our culture, from clothes to beverage containers. Thus too in archaeology we can get, as a result of finely calibrated formal divisions, the chronology of many artifacts from form alone, as Eiseley remarked. We are also aided in this endeavor by outside dating methods that can be applied to cultures as a whole—here we are dealing with some of the more sophisticated devices for dating such as carbon 14, potassium argon, and tree rings.

Although these methods are often referred to as "Absolute Dating Techniques," one must be assured that this terminology is used in contrast to "Relative Dating" such as that derived from change in forms. None of these dating techniques is absolutely right—for example, carbon 14 can be used on things that once were alive, such as bone, wood, and plant materials, but stone and pottery cannot be dated by this technique. We date the life span of the tree that produced the wood. We know when it died, with a small error of perhaps plus or minus a hundred years. The basic question is always, How does that piece of wood, so dated, relate to the archaeological context within which it was found? If we are dealing with charcoal from a hearth, especially in an arid environment, we must be concerned about how old the tree limb was when it was burned. Or if found in an island situation, was that "old" driftwood that has been burned? These examples sound like nit-picking of the worst sort, but many cases of both such errors in dating are known to have occurred.

Potassium argon dating has been the most important adjunct to early hominid studies in Africa. At Olduvai Gorge, for instance, it has allowed for the dating of deposits in spans of millions of years, far beyond the range of carbon 14, which cannot go much beyond fifty thousand years. This dating is based on the analysis of volcanic materials, which fortunately are prevalent in this part of Africa; but, again, what is dated is a geological deposit, not the artifacts or the sites themselves.

Also, all such dates are subject to physical errors—bad samples, errors in treatment of the sample, errors in the dating devices themselves. It is a standard of archaeological procedure to try to get several dates, from several laboratories and from several methods of dating, to establish securely a date for a layer or a culture. A single date is just that; it is lonely and afraid in a world that it never made. Yes, some archaeologists go out on a long limb with a single date—it is very enticing to have the "earliest" occurrence of agriculture, the oldest known structure, or the first evidence of fire—but if the statement is based on a single date rather than a series of dates, BEWARE.

Once we have finished with our three basic dimensions—Form, Space, and Time—then and only then should we proceed to interpretations and conclusions. That is the ideal pattern. That this sequence is not always followed is part of our story in this volume. Even the most righteous archaeologists obviously have ideas about where and how the archaeological data they are recovering fit into some overall story of cultural history. But they must let the evidence point the way, not allow the answer to lead the excavations. As I have noted, perception is not objective—our vision can be severely limited or directed by our own wishes, hopes, and dreams. If we expect to find evidence to support our conclusions, then our interpretations will lead us to the site and, consequently, color our findings.

What, then, are my biases? What special way of seeing am I burdened with? My viewpoint is *archaeological*, as I have already noted, but it is more than that. It is based on experience and background. I have alluded to my heritage in Minnesota; I was educated there and at Yale and the University of Michigan. My field experience in archaeology ranges from Minnesota to Arizona and in the southeastern United States, where I have specialized for the last thirty-five years, from South Carolina and Georgia to the Lower Mississippi Valley (Missouri to Louisiana). I have also visited archaeological sites in Europe, East Africa, and Mexico.

My academic training was in anthropology, as it was for most American-trained archaeologists of my generation. That means that I was required to have a basic competence in the three other fields of anthropology—biological anthropology, linguistics, and ethnography—with a little geology thrown in on the side. Thus I was introduced to everything from human osteology, phonetic analysis of Potawatomi, to Australian kinship and African art—a little bit about a lot of things. I have also *seen* many things. Having lived in anthropological museums all my professional career, I have been surrounded by specimens.

This experience is the basis for the comparative approach that is fundamental to all anthropology. Thus I come by my introduction to *formal* analysis very naturally. One must, however, learn to make comparable classes of artifacts. Perceptions can blur, and all things that look alike are not the same. The problem of the argument from "spurious similarity" rears its ugly head here. Pyramids in Egypt, Cambodia, and Yucatán are not the same, despite general similarities in shape. Their histories and functions are quite different.

In *spatial* analysis we go from direct perception of the artifacts to their distribution in space. We know a lot about this dimension—we deal with it all the time—distance, maps, and such. But in terms of the spread of traits, how far can we logically take our studies? Continentwide, certainly—we must not be bound by a notion that peoples in the past were stay-at-homes. Certainly we must avoid a parochial viewpoint, but, as we approach the seven seas, we do tend to lose track of our data. The wake of a raft is gone in a few minutes, and there are no midocean signposts.

Can we object to transoceanic connections purely on the basis of logic alone? No; in fact, recent anthropological data from the once-great continent of New Guinea–Australia (it was a single land mass fifty thousand years ago) indicate that humans spread out of Southeast Asia and made their way into that old continent across some watery straits more than fifty kilometers wide. Thus boats or similar transport were available very early; the newest dates from Australia indicate first human occupation there nearly fifty thousand years ago. That is Fantastic, with a capital F!

We continue to have trouble with the *temporal* dimension, not just because it is hard to come by, but because our own understanding of the units of time is so limited. Yes, we know inches, feet, and miles; we also know seconds, minutes, days, and years. But take one hundred years—few experience that period of time, but centuries are one of our basic measuring sticks in archaeology. Sometimes we can cut it finer than that, but not too often. I have just casually referred to fifty thousand years—what does that really mean? We know what $50,000 will buy, or used to, but that many years is a blur—a segment of time that is unfathomable. We must stretch our minds to take in these huge spans of time and also the rates of change over these awesome periods of years.

It is all too easy to slip into very old ways of thinking about time. For example, in the 1930s, when American scholars were working on Mayan archaeology in the Yucatán, they did some estimates as to the time required by the Maya to build the impressive stone-faced pyramids that dot the landscape there. They came up with estimates of many hundreds of years. The archaeologists even used some analogies to show how persevering the Maya had been in building these great religious monuments; quite like our own medieval ancestors in Europe and their great Gothic cathedrals, they said.

New research, with time-motion studies of stone-cutting and construction experiments, showed the original estimates to be much too long. The earlier scholars thought highly of the Maya and wished to give them characteristics they admired. No wonder that they were referred to at this time as "New World Greeks" by Sir Eric Thompson, a British scholar with strong classical training. Obviously it is not difficult for a good archaeologist to be led astray in the areas of interpretations and conclusions by preconditioning.

With all those caveats, I have to state that my own priorities lie in the direction of humanism rather than science. Here I mean what some archaeologists refer to as the Science of Archaeology—that the only way to look at these data is with a very strong scientific slant. I am not a number-cruncher or a staunch advocate of logico-hypothetico-deductive analysis. In this I may be seen as a bit of an old conservative, and the New Archaeology, a tag for a mini-revolution in archaeological thinking in the late 1960s and 1970s, may seem to have passed many of us by, but not without changing some of our vocabulary and some of our priorities. Of course, as any student of archaeological history can tell you, there was also a New Archaeology in the 1880s, and there will be others in the future. Therefore I hope to balance the new with the old.

I am committed to an anthropological view of the past. I see it as a quest to recover bits of the "past as it was" and turn them into the "past as known." It is not an easy task, but my basic methodology is *comparative,* with a scope that is worldwide and with an unlimited temporal framework; *egalitarian,* believing that all cultures have equal aptitudes for development of technologies; and finally *explanatory,* seeking to discover cultural behavior and functions that have a basis in known lifeways both past and present—no using extraterrestrials to do human work.

Throughout this volume we will encounter many other foundations of belief, some of them well known, others less so. They are, by natural selection, rather different belief systems from those that I or most other archaeologists employ as the underpinning of our intellectual world. Therefore, I disagree with them as useful foundations upon which to build explanations for archaeological facts. I think I know the reasons for their use, and I hope that I can be charitable to these different ways of viewing the world of archaeology: they are what I have subsumed under the heading of Fantastic Archaeology.

One of the most obvious kinds of archaeology in the Fantastic field is that backed by a strong appeal to nationalism. Familiar cases are the Kensington Rune Stone of Minnesota dated to A.D. 1362 and a number of other evidences, such as the Newport Tower in Rhode Island, which purport to prove that the Vikings were in America long before the arrival of Columbus. That general notion is very likely the truth, but as I will develop later, most of the evidence put forward, often with a strong bias in favor of the Vikings, does not support their case.

Other cases of ethnic pride deal with the so-called America Firsters such as the Welsh, the Ten Lost Tribes of Israel, and so on. There was a strong nationalistic force behind the well-known Piltdown forgery case, and there is a strong undercurrent of this feeling in many other attempts to rewrite archaeological history. It is probably no surprise to anyone that totalitarian groups such as the Nazis and the Stalinists have created their own versions of the past to fit their nationalistic needs.

Somewhat related but of a different stripe is the use of racism as the foundation for archaeological interpretations in America. It was fundamental to the Nazi case, of course, but I will not deal with that here. In the study of American prehistory racism has a long history. The nineteenth-century Myth of the Moundbuilder was for many of its adherents a way of softening the racist notion that the Indians were nothing but savages who were residing on lands of greater value to others. It was thought that the Native Americans could not really "own" the lands because it was suggested that they had only recently taken them away from the Moundbuilders, probably a fair-skinned race. It was also evident to many that the Moundbuilders were capable of cultural achievements that no mere Indian could have attained. We will look at that case in detail later.

In more recent times, the hyper-diffusionist views of marine biologist Barry Fell and others suggest that the Indians would not have achieved what they did in America without the aid of visitors from across the Atlantic. These purported pre-Columbian trans-Atlantic voyagers are ethnically stereotyped; arriving Celts, for example, are copper miners.

A commentator on Fantastic Archaeology, John Cole, has participated in a number of meetings of true believers and has used the term Cult Archaeology to characterize the strong belief systems that some adherents maintain, despite attempts by outsiders to provide other explanations for these notions. Good examples are to be found among the Theosophists, a group that began in the nineteenth century under the leadership of an extraordinary woman, Helena Blavatsky, a sometime holder of seances. The Theosophists became deeply entangled in the quest for lost Atlantis; the group still remains today a viable mélange of archaeology, astrology, health food diets, and other curing practices. Atlanteans come in a variety of guises, not all under the Theosophy banner, and they remain today one of the largest groups. Many gathered at the feet of the late Edgar Cayce, who regularly gave personal readings which identified the adherent as a former resident of the now-vanished Atlantis. There is a huge Cayce research operation in Virginia Beach, but more of both Blavatsky and Cayce in later chapters.

For such groups, belief is paramount over evidence. After all these years there still have not been any significant archaeological finds to support the case for sunken Atlantis, but that really does not matter. It bears a great similarity to the belief in Big Foot, the humanlike monster of North America. There is no physical evidence to speak of despite more than a thousand sightings, but try to dissuade the true believer!

Religion is, of course, a major belief system that serves as the philosophical and moral foundation for most cultures. My concern here is only for the point at which religion and archaeology intersect. Biblical Archaeology is a separate segment of the profession, and I will not discuss it to any extent. I might note, however, that there even exists a modern (1943) Papal Encyclical letter that supports strongly "the exploration and investigation of the monuments of antiquity" for their ability to contribute "to the solution of questions hitherto obscure."[4]

The Mormon religion, that of the Church of the Latter Day Saints, is an American-based faith that has deep roots in what must be called the "archaeological discoveries" in 1827 by Joseph Smith in New York State. The Mormon Bible, the text of which Smith read from a group of golden tablets, recounts a series of historic events that must be weighed against current knowledge of the prehistory of America. Thus I will treat this topic, while leaving, somewhat reluctantly, other aspects of the intersection of religion and archaeology—such as authenticity of the Shroud of Turin and even Creationism and dinosaurs—for others to debate.

Finally, we have a series of archaeological hypotheses that are either a mixture of some of the above or just so far out that they fall beyond the limits of classification; I call them Fantasy. Erich von Däniken's works are in this latter category. Although most of his data, thankfully, come from outside North America, one cannot discuss Fantastic Archaeology without dealing with the current leader of the pack. His ancient astronauts have influenced a generation or more, and his copycat friends continue to pour out further adventures. One of them has a four-hundred-thousand-year chronology for cultures on this planet. And so it goes; much earlier, Harold Gladwin proposed a maritime connection via remnants of Alexander's fleet across the Pacific to bring culture to Middle America. He presented no data; I believe it was a spoof. But now some take him seriously, as we will see later.

Fantasy, religion, cult belief, racism, or nationalism—all can be the basis for the origin of new hypotheses about cultural events. We do have to ask, Where do biases begin? We all have them—show me a person who says he's unbiased, and I'll show you a deeply uninformed person, even about himself. How do we deal with some new evidence? Let me present some new data.

Some years ago a well-trained U.S. Geological Survey scientist, assigned to the Boston area, stumbled across some strange-looking rocks on a wharf at a lumberyard in South Boston. The stones certainly did not look like any materials from New England that he knew about. In search of an answer, he decided to show the materials to the Peabody Museum's specialist on Old World archaeology, who recognized the materials right away as being from England and very likely Thames River gravels. They were very nice rocks—just the sort that have been made into fine flint tools in Great Britain for two hundred thousand years or more. Fortunately for us, none of these were fashioned into artifacts, but then, how did British flints get to Boston in considerable quantity? Did some prehistoric English artisan, possibly the builder of the mini-Stonehenge in Lowell, transport them to our shores? After all, there are no really good toolmaking flints or cherts of this quality anywhere in New England so that would be reason enough.

We can think of many other reasons, but let's use Occam's razor and look for the simplest answer, *after* first looking at the context and, second, doing just a bit of historical research. The rocks are all alone—there is nothing else with them. Second, we know that in the middle of the nineteenth century there were many old sailing ships coming across the Atlantic, even as steam took over. Sail was on the way out, and these tired old three-masters were given the heavy, low-cost loads. Because of a shipping imbalance, they often came to America quite empty to pick up finished lumber here; therefore they needed ballast when they left the ports of England. So they scooped up river gravels for the trans-Atlantic voyage and dumped the stones in America. Indeed, today these ballast rock cargoes are being studied from Maine to Florida—Caribbean coral turns up in Down East Maine ports!

In the South, along the Georgia coast, I have seen whole islands built of this ballast rock, since in the 1870s the down-and-out South ravaged its forests for much needed cash and supplied lumber to build Victorian England. And guess what, some archaeology *has* come along with that ballast rock. At least reputable scholars in South Carolina have explained sherds of true Roman pottery found in Charleston harbor in this manner.

What a field day some of the hyper-diffusionists would have had if among those Thames River pebbles from the Boston wharf there had been a veritable Paleolithic hand ax or two—not an improbable find. Would we then have had tales of Paleolithic voyagers on rafts of ice pulled by a matched pair of whales leaving Southampton for South Boston to see if they could beat the Irish to Southie?

We see, therefore, where new data can or might lead us. We have to continue to ask ourselves slightly outrageous questions, or at the very least respond to new data as they are presented to us. We do not want to say, Don't show it to me, I've already made up my mind on that. We must continue to be skeptical inquirers after knowledge and relentless foes of fraud and unreason. For, as the literary critic Bergen Evans has said, "No error is harmless. . . . the harm that may result from forming an opinion without evidence, or from distorting evidence to support an opinion, is incalculable." He states further: "The civilized man has a moral obligation to be skeptical. . . . An honorable man will not be bullied by a hypothesis. For in the last analysis all tyranny rests on fraud. . . . any man who for one moment abandons the questioning spirit has for that moment betrayed humanity."[5]

Thank goodness such questioning spirits still exist, for there was a follow-up on "Druids in Lowell," the story of the mini-Stonehenge in the old mill town northwest of Boston. The local public television station (WGBH) has an internship for young reporters, and one of them heard of ongoing archaeological excavations at this strange "megalithic" site. Doing a nice bit of investigative reporting, he filmed the dig and interviewed the participants. Fortunately, there was a rather satisfactory conclusion to this "mysterious circle of standing stones."

A bit of historic research by the excavators showed that a tuberculosis sanatorium had stood on "Druid Hill" about 1914; it was torn down in the 1930s. The excavations around and under the stones produced *only* artifacts that dated to the early part of this century. An elderly gentleman, who owned the adjoining property, remembered seeing the stones lying about the field in his youth before the construction of the hospital swimming pool that generated the earth used as a foundation for the circle of stones. Thus the circle, or "folly," was of fairly recent construction; no trans-Atlantic crossing by the contractors was required.

So we may write "solved" on that problem, as even the once eager English professor affirmed the conclusion of a modern date; interestingly enough, a small minority of dig participants did not. One, a "true believer," felt that only more digging would prove the true age of the monument, and the geologist kept insisting that "the rocks are very old." That is true—the stones were geologically aged, but their special alignment, a human config-uration, was not. We might wish that all the mysteries that lie ahead will be so satisfactorily addressed and answered.

2
American Curiosity and the American Indian

Great question has arisen from whence came those aboriginal inhabitants of America?

THOMAS JEFFERSON, 1787

The long and costly War of Independence was finally over; never again
would America be so free—with a face to the west, for nearly eighty years
(1783–1860) it would grow unabated. A minor war (1812–14) would briefly
intervene, but otherwise it was an exciting time of movement and growth.
The restless and the adventurous would head west, which was, for most,
the Ohio country. Leaving many vacant New England farms and their
rocky fields behind, these willing pioneers were unknowingly laying the
seeds for some fantastic tales of ancient megalithic builders which would
sprout there nearly two centuries later.

The pioneers went to the Ohio Territory, where a galaxy of presidents
and other high government officials would take a surprisingly detailed
interest in the findings there: Thomas Jefferson, William Henry Harrison,
Albert Gallatin, and Benjamin Franklin. It was, indeed, a great time of
discovery, geographically, but also of the self and other mysteries. Lewis
and Clark would be waiting in the wings to trek even to the distant Pacific.
The intrepid Meriwether Lewis honed his observational skills in the Ohio
country, so the area served many important functions.

The way to the Ohio Territory took most travelers west across the
mountains from Philadelphia to Pittsburgh and into the Ohio River drainage. One of the amazing sights on the Ohio was a great earthen mound on
the east bank south of Wheeling. It was early termed the Grave Creek
Mound; Lewis saw and described it in 1805. We will return to its surprising
contents later. Further south, where the Muskingum River joins the Ohio,
was a large cluster of mounds that were to become the sine qua non of all

Great Mound at Marietta, Ohio

the numerous prehistoric monuments that dotted the Ohio Valley as far south as Cincinnati. For it was at this very favorable location that the second Ohio Company landed in 1788 and established the settlement of Marietta, across the river from the earlier Fort Harmar.

Marietta was to become briefly the capital of the Northwest Territory; this pattern of European settlement on the site of aboriginal occupation was typical throughout the entire colonization of America. The "First Americans" had picked the best locations for habitation, and thus many major prehistoric sites throughout this country were doomed to be destroyed from the start. At Marietta, however, early efforts were made to preserve some of these Indian structures as public places, and they remain so today. Few American towns have such a long and honorable record of preservation.

What happened at Marietta was unusual, but the persons involved were unusual too. Much of what happened in the Ohio country is a direct result of the nature of the people involved in this new American adventure. Many were college-trained New Englanders, including the expedition leader, Rufus Putnam. Putnam, born in Sutton, Massachusetts, and a Revolutionary War General, led the Ohio Company west, obtaining rights to the land from the government and selling it to the settlers.

The Putnam name would remain connected with Ohio archaeology forever because Rufus is buried at the foot of the largest mound at Marietta. His collateral relative, Frederic Ward Putnam, would in the 1880s lead the

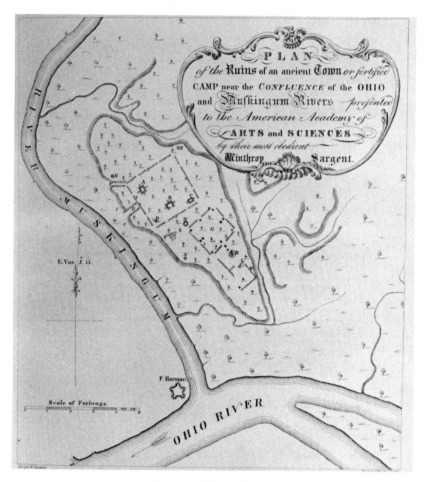

Sargent's Map of Ruins

Peabody Museum's lengthy excavations in Ohio, as well as preserve the Serpent Mound (now a state park) from destruction.

The Ohio Company expedition of 1788 to Marietta was a very New England undertaking. The boat carrying the first group of company settlers was named the *Ohio Mayflower*, and one of Rufus Putnam's chief aides was Winthrop Sargent, also from Massachusetts. Putnam became deeply interested in the earthen monuments among which they had disembarked, and he drew a crude map of the prehistoric "works," which survives to this day.

These constructions were much more than just a few earthen mounds;

they were complex earthworks, with geometric enclosures laid out with great precision. This extraordinary archaeological site at Marietta would be mapped and remapped for almost a century. These sites and their contents were truly amazing, and they sparked an outpouring of interest that made Ohio archaeology the major focus for American archaeology for the entire century 1780–1880.

As John Jakle in his valuable *Images of the Ohio Valley* has pointed out, the valley was seen as an ideal laboratory for studies of natural history. "[The Valley] shall draw men of science to trace and investigate the various phenomena which this country exhibits,"[1] said Gilbert Imlay in 1793, and it was made use of in that way by a veritable Who's Who of American science in the nineteenth century. It drew some of the best and the brightest: John James Audubon, John Heckewelder, Meriwether Lewis, Henry R. Schoolcraft, and British scholars George W. Featherstonhaugh and Charles Lyell—not to mention Constantine Rafinesque, whom we will investigate later at great length.

The pressure of progress, the civilizing of the area, proceeded with the founding of new towns throughout the territory, and as a result new archaeological remains were unearthed. Not only were mounds and burials discovered, but artifacts as well. They called out for interpretation: were these the remains of the American Indians and their cultures, or were they materials left behind by much more civilized races? Who were the American Indians anyway? To answer those questions in historical perspective we must go back much before the 1790s, for it had been a matter of some concern for centuries. In going back to the period of discovery, we will also discover the roots of some of the myths that will dog us throughout this volume: Atlantis, the Lost Tribes, Carthaginians, and others of that ilk, including even the Welsh Prince Madoc.

We must start with Columbus, for although he and his shipmates probably were *not* the first Europeans to visit the New World, all others have failed to provide any direct evidence of their views on the question at hand. We can only speculate on how the Vikings must have felt at first contact; the "skraelings" of the sagas were probably Eskimos. We do know that the first Spanish explorers were searching for Asians, and that is what they found—the occupants of the *West* Indies were obviously Indians. By 1521, however, with the Magellan expedition's successful circumnavigation of the globe, the true and separate nature of the New World was established once and for all. There was a real problem, therefore, as to who and what these people were.

The Spaniards were not sure how to regard the native peoples of the Americas; one must confess that in some cases they treated them not like savages but like animals. After due consideration, however, Pope Paul III declared them "truly men" in 1537 and capable of being Christians. If this were so, then what was their origin?

Although many answers were given during the sixteenth century, the best synthesis of the problem was written by the Jesuit scholar Joseph [Jose] de Acosta (1540–1600), who had solid firsthand experience with American Indians, having spent seventeen years in the Indies. He started off in Peru in 1570 and was in Mexico in 1586. He completed his book *Historia natural y moral de las Indias* in 1590; it was written first in Latin, then in Spanish, but by 1604 it had also appeared in English so that it had a wide audience quite early.

Acosta took a very objective approach to the question of the Indians' origins. After considering all possibilities, he decided that the only feasible answer was that the Indians had arrived in the Americas through slow migration via a land bridge from the Old World. This notion was rather original because geographic knowledge was so limited at the time of his writing that the Bering Strait was not even known to exist. He dismissed two other possible origins that had been suggested: (1) Atlantis or (2) Jewish or Lost Tribes of Israel. Acosta felt that the first arrivals came as primitive hunters, later developed agriculture, and finally attained the civilizations that he had noted in Peru and Mexico. He also suggested that there might have been some latecomers.

Overall Acosta's was an astounding piece of work. He had a minimum of data, but he very perceptively dealt with possible alternative hypotheses in a most scientific way. Would that later scholars (even those of today) had followed his lead. It is regrettable that this insightful contribution to the question of American Indian origins is not better known today, despite its availability via early translation in many languages. It does seem to have had an impact at first, but a different view was soon to come from a very similar source.

Gregorio Garcia was also a Catholic scholar, of the Dominican order. He too had spent time in the New World—nine years in Peru. In 1607 he published *Origen de los Indios del Nuevo Mundo*. It focused solely on the topic of origins, whereas the bulk of Acosta's work, in two volumes, was on natural and moral history. Garcia, even more systematically than Acosta, discussed some eleven major options as to Indian origin. He found reasons to support each and every one, including Carthaginians, the Lost Tribes, Atlantis, and East Asians.

Unlike Acosta, Garcia seemed unable to make critical judgments, and he included a considerable amount of misinformation as a result. He cited a very long list of sources, but strangely one name is missing: Jose de Acosta. There seems to be little question that his colleague's seminal work was available and known to him while Garcia was preparing his own volume. Garcia can now be seen as the spiritual father, if not the actual predecessor, to dozens of equally uncritical mélanges of myths and half-truths about New World cultural origins.

And so the battle was joined. This argument was thoroughly reviewed by Lee Huddleston. For some the question would never be seriously in doubt ("the Acostan Tradition," Huddleston calls it)—the First Americans were immigrants from Asia who had come across the Bering Strait (discovered in 1728), gradually filled the entire hemisphere, and developed indigenously the cultures that were found archaeologically. The contemporary Indians were their descendants. An autocthonous development—a brilliant new concept.

But this view was a minority opinion in the eighteenth and nineteenth centuries, especially if one were to take a simple popularity poll. American curiosity and scholarship definitely saw the origins of Native Americans as a major question, and for many (labeled by Huddleston "the Garcia tradition") the answers were less clear. For example, the local North American Indians were seen as one group, but the Aztecs and other "high culture" groups were viewed as another. Hence the strange question, Were the makers of the mounds in the eastern United States Aztecs or Indians? The answer was no, but yes, because the Aztecs of Mexico were just as Indian physically as were those "savages" roaming the woodlands of North America. Perhaps, the Garcians suggested, two separate origins or migrations were involved.

The question, too, would be asked with a large body of information that was not *archaeological*: that is, from the skeletal remains, from languages the natives spoke, and from the Indians' own history of their past as recorded in migration stories. Thus the question was truly *anthropological*, although this breadth of scope was not clearly recognized even by such innovative inquirers as Acosta. Although he did use classical sources as well as the Bible, some native myths, and just a tiny bit of archaeology, Acosta made no important use of the biological aspect of the question; he used no racial speculations in answering it.

Of course, this curiosity about the inhabitants of the New World can also be seen in a much broader context, that growing out of the Age of Discovery in general. Natural history was a major part of Acosta's treatise in the 1580s, for example. Those involved in world exploration came back with written comments and collections from peoples and places that had never been seen before. Plants, animals, and people were all subject to new scrutiny. Although travelers' tales were not always the most trustworthy sources for new information, they were often seized on by hungry writers, and thus anthropology was burdened from the start with a veritable mishmash of evidence. Wild tales of manlike apes or apelike men were interspersed with well-recorded strange new customs and ideas. It has taken some time to sort them out; some still reappear in fantastic modern accounts supporting the existence of the Abominable Snowman and the like.

Investigation of archaeological remains in North America began, according to Mourt's *Relation* (1622), with the Pilgrims digging up an Indian burial site on Cape Cod in 1620, soon after they landed. So Puritan or not, anything was fair game to this new curiosity. And soon this inquisitive nature and its discoveries would be placed in a new context—a scientific appraisal of the meaning of the new discoveries. It was slow at the start; in the 1730s and 1740s people such as Benjamin Franklin and others in Philadelphia began to form scientific societies to promote intellectual activities, but it was not until the end of 1768 that the American Philosophical Society united several such organizations and real progress was made.

Although other similar groups were forming at this time, I have focused on activities in Philadelphia, for it was the American Philosophical Society that began the first really organized movement to collect data on American antiquities. The moving force behind this program was, of course, Thomas Jefferson, who did not let a higher calling interfere too much with his leadership of the American Philosophical Society.

The breadth of Jefferson's scientific interests is well known, and many branches of science are wont to claim him as their founder—American archaeology certainly has a good case in this regard. Beginning with his famous *Notes on Virginia* in 1787, in which he describes the excavation of an Indian burial mound on his property in Virginia, to his establishment of a Standing Committee on Antiquities at the American Philosophical Society at the first meeting at which he presided, Jefferson had deep concern for research in such matters.

In the Acosta/Garcia argument, Jefferson clearly sided with Acosta and supported the Asian migration hypothesis. He even used evidence of linguistic diversity to "prove" that the Indians had been on this continent for a long time. Under the term *antiquities* he included, besides archaeology, what we would today call the fields of paleontology, historical geology, and ethnography. The American Philosophical Society committee was anxious to learn about new antiquarian discoveries and sent out a form letter of scientific inquiry.

I suppose that Jefferson felt that since just such a letter from the French government had sparked his long reply, which later became *Notes on Virginia,* a similar inquiry might be as successful within America. I know of no direct records of the results, but the *Transactions* and *Proceedings* of the society between 1797 and 1820 do contain some very important archaeological articles. Some Indian artifacts also came to Philadelphia, where they still reside. Their survival is a fine testimony to the ofttimes steadfast nature of museum curators and the care they take of their collections.

After Jefferson, there would be one more White House tenant, William Henry Harrison, who would have a strong interest in archaeology; he wrote of his youthful viewing of Indian mounds in Cincinnati. Since then there has been a long, long drought. Few archaeology buffs have shown up at the cabinet level since the mid-nineteenth century; if there, they must have been of the closet variety. It is said that President Jimmy Carter had an interest in Georgia arrowheads, but I have little evidence to confirm or deny that suggestion.

After this long detour, we return at last to the Ohio River Valley and the opening of the Northwest Territory with the settlement at Marietta in 1788 by Rufus Putnam and the Ohio Company. His assistant, Winthrop Sargent, who later became secretary of the territory, drew a very creditable map of the elaborate earthworks on the high river terrace upon which the first settlement was located. A few years before the actual settlement (1786), Sargent, who was charged with surveying the lands for the government, had met up with some idle army officers at Fort Harmar, whom he had known in the service. They looked at the antiquities across the river, and one of them took the trouble to write the presidents of Harvard and Yale about his interesting discoveries. These letters from General Samuel H. Parsons and the map by Captain Jonathan Heart were published in 1793 and started the basic corpus of Ohio archaeology. Sargent's map, made at this same time, would not be published until much later (1850). These careful on-site records, however, were to play an important role in the Mound-builder arguments that lay ahead. One cannot cease to be amazed at what levels archaeological discourse was then carried on: first the White House and now the offices of university presidents—it is seldom that way today.

Winthrop Sargent (1753–1820) is the sort of character one only rarely expects to meet in archaeological research. Massachusetts-born, he at-

Winthrop Sargent

tended Harvard at the ripe old age of thirteen and was sent down for a year for "behavior unbecoming a gentleman" during his senior year. In the Revolution, he served with distinction, despite a little Madeira-inspired gout, and then went off to the Ohio country, where he married Rowena Tupper, the daughter of Putnam's Ohio Company founding partner General Benjamin Tupper. Before going west, Sargent had visited in Philadelphia, where he met Franklin and became a member of the American Philosophical Society.

As territorial secretary of Ohio, the first assistant to the governor, he moved to Cincinnati, where Rowena died in childbirth, as did his son. While Sargent was living in Cincinnati, an Indian mound near his home was dug into during road work in 1795, and artifacts of copper, hematite, and other minerals were discovered. Sargent recovered these distinctive and elaborate relics, had them drawn, and wrote a brief description that was published in 1799 in the Philosophical Society *Transactions*. The objects are easily recognizable today as typical Hopewellian artifacts dating from about A.D. 100. I recently saw most of them at the University Museum of the University of Pennsylvania, where many of the Society's archaeological treasures have ended up.

Sargent's career then took him further afield; he always sought higher political status and was named the first governor of the Mississippi Territory in 1798. It was an unsuccessful move from a political standpoint, and he was soon removed from the position because of some ugly disagreements

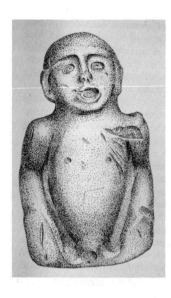

Natchez Idol

over policy. Never one to lose time over amenities, however, he married a rich widow in Natchez before his first year in the territory was up. Sargent then lived very handsomely on his "Gloster" Plantation until his demise in 1820.

One last archaeological note: while in Natchez, Sargent met a local planter with a fine piece of stone sculpture—a human figure, possibly an idol from an Indian temple. By means not revealed, Sargent obtained the artifact and shipped it to the American Antiquarian Society in Worcester, Massachusetts, of which he was also a member, and this artifact graced the society's first archaeological publication, authored by Caleb Atwater, of whom much more later. Sargent, with his Marietta map, the Cincinnati artifacts—the first *excavated* archaeological finds published in the United States, to my knowledge—and the Natchez idol, is a very important but little-known contributor to the fledgling field of American archaeology.

Now, one can rightly ask what was the drive behind this American curiosity, exemplified by scientific societies and their wonderfully broad-gauged "amateur" scientists? One answer is surely a very natural nationalism growing out of the final success of the Revolution. Daniel Boorstin has spoken of a "Quest for a National Past"[2] and has looked at the question from the standpoint of growth of historical views of the United States. But there was more to it than that—there was a deeply felt need to prove the quality of America, to defend it from rather scurrilous attacks from abroad.

A good example is to be found in Jefferson's deep interest in the fossils of large animals that were being found in the Ohio Valley, particularly at Big Bone Lick, Kentucky. Jefferson personally funded one such collecting trip. The front hall at Monticello housed some of these paleontological finds along with Indian relics. The genesis of this concern for large fossil mammals was the statement by the French scholar George-Louis Buffon that all such forms of life found in America were smaller than those found in Europe. The fossil "mammoths" and sloths found in Kentucky were large enough to help put that argument to rest, at least on this side of the Atlantic.

Charles Willson Peale of Philadelphia began in 1800 to excavate some "mammoths" in New York State—they were really mastodons in modern terminology—and was aided by the American Philosophical Society in this venture. Also at this time Peale was allowed to move his museum into the society's building and became de facto curator of the collections. One of the mastodons was mounted for exhibit and, shortly afterward, an Old World elephant skeleton was placed beside it. The American mastodon was larger. How's that for the comparative approach to prove a point? I'm sure Jefferson was pleased.

But the contest between Old and New Worlds was fought on geological and archaeological grounds as well: "Our mountains are as old, if not older, than yours!" Henry Steele Commager has appropriately referred to this venture as the "Search for a Usable Past." Henry M. Brackenridge in a letter in 1813 to Jefferson published by the Society said it very well:

> The philosophers of Europe, with a narrowness and selfishness of mind, have endeavored to depreciate every thing which relates to it. They have called it the *New World,* as though its formation was posterior to the rest of the habitable globe. A few facts suffice to repel this idea;—the antiquity of her mountains, the remains of volcanoes, the alluvial tracts, the wearing away of cataracts, etc. and the number of primitive languages, greater perhaps than in all the rest of the world besides . . . I question much whether before those periods, comparatively recent [in the Old World], there existed or could exist, nations more civilized than the Mexicans or Peruvians. (Brackenridge, 1818: 158–59)

Brackenridge (1786–1871) was born in the frontier village of Pittsburgh and was tutored at home by his Princeton-educated father. He first studied law and then, more important for our interests, went west to the Mississippi Valley in 1810–14. There he wrote his well-known *Views of Louisiana,* which contains some of the best early descriptions of the great mounds near St. Louis and further south.

Henry M. Brackenridge

Curiosity, driven by many objectives, regarding a national past was not confined to Philadelphia. The first half of the nineteenth century, from an archaeological vantage point, is the story of the founding of several institutions with such scientific purposes. As any historian knows, one has difficulty separating the history of an institution from that of its major personalities—as with Jefferson and the American Philosophical Society. Unless one adheres to a "great man" theory of history, this difficulty generates problems of cause and effect. The very foundation of an institution creates a situation like that of a magnet drawing interest and support, while the leadership of a strong personality can be read in deeds and documents.

An important case in point is Isaiah Thomas and the American Antiquarian Society. Thomas (1749–1831) was a self-educated Bostonian, who became a wealthy printer and publisher in Worcester after a heroic career during the Revolution as printer of the *Massachusetts Spy* and as a Minute Man at Lexington and Concord. He published a wide variety of materials: Bibles, law books, novels, and even Mother Goose. His financial successes were such that he became a generous philanthropist and, because of his interest in the history of America, founded the American Antiquarian Society in 1812 to help preserve materials relating to that history.

Thomas was well connected with the men of learning of this period and took a strong interest in the antiquities of the Ohio Valley. He commissioned work there by a young Massachusetts-born lawyer named Caleb Atwater (1778–1867), who had moved in 1815 to Circleville, Ohio, which was named for the prehistoric monument upon which it was built.

Although college-trained at Williams, Atwater does not seem to have had any special bent toward archaeology in his prior training; he had only a brief fling at the ministry before studying the law. But the results of his work, *Description of the Antiquities Discovered in the State of Ohio and Other Western States,* were outstanding, especially in the careful delineation of the numerous earthen structures that he measured and mapped, in his "spare time," or so it is said. He was aided in surveying sites by a dozen local men who joined him "to promote the good of our beloved country." About his own objectives, he said, "It has been my most anxious endeavour to collect and convey FACTS, which may be of some use to the Philosophers, the Historians, the Antiquarians and Divines of future times."[3]

Atwater's treatise was the first book-length treatment of American antiquities; recent information indicates that Isaiah Thomas had a hand in "editing" this work as well. The first ninety pages are a careful description of the prehistoric works with eleven well-drawn maps, beginning, of course, with the familiar group at Marietta. There follow some sixty pages of conjectures "respecting the origin and history of the ancient works in Ohio." These pages are graced with a number of illustrations, mostly of artifacts, but also a skull or two. The contribution ends with a sixteen-page Appendix extracted from Alexander von Humboldt's *Views of the Cordilleras* to "shew the correspondence which exists between the Teocalli [pyramids] of the Mexicans and the tumuli of the North Americans"—the comparative approach again.

Most of the sites described by Atwater are ones that he personally visited in Ohio, although he does throw in a few comparisons such as the Grave Creek Mound of [West] Virginia and some of those described by Brackenridge in the Mississippi Valley. He sees connections down to the Gulf of Mexico and even to South America. He gives but small space to functional interpretations beyond that of the mounds as "places of sepulture [burial] and worship." He does not strongly suggest that the works had a defensive aspect and even posits that some, especially those with parallel walls, may have been places of "Diversion."

So far, so good. Atwater's section "Conjectures" is another matter entirely. The first paragraph is a list of "who, whence, when, and how long"—perfectly appropriate questions. He rightly indicates that these are questions that cannot be answered with "proofs amounting to mathematical certainty." Reasonable ones, however, can be obtained from a study of the geology and botany of the land, by a study of the skeletons, and by an examination of their artifacts and sites. He describes this evidence as "these fragments of history, as Bacon would say, which have been saved from the deluge of time."[4] We must compare these fragments with those materials found now or heretofore on any part of the globe, certainly a broad view.

He starts with the Bible, plunges into pre-Roman Britain, and then is off to Egypt. About twenty pages later, he has his conclusions in hand—the builders of the American tumuli were not American Indians ("mere hunters") but "Hindoos" from India: shepherds and husbandmen, who built sacred places on the banks of rivers, like those on the Indus and the Ganges, although he mentions Tartars as well. How did he go so wrong? He says: "If the coincidences between the worship of our people [of the Ohio Valley], and that of the Hindoos and southern Tartars, furnish no evidence of a common origin, then I [Atwater] am no judge of the nature and the weight of testimony."[5]

We can only hope that he was a better lawyer than he was as a scholar of comparative cultures. Once on this trail, he sees all the artifacts as having a Hindoo cast, including the stone idol from Natchez sent north by Winthrop Sargent. This artifact resides presently in my Peabody Museum office, where I give it a daily inspection for Hindoo traits.

What are Atwater's basic arguments? I must confess I find them a bit difficult to follow. He starts with "high towers" from the Bible and the Middle East, then moves from mounds in Britain to burial mounds in general throughout the Old World, concluding that these ancient works, which are similar to those found in the Ohio Valley, prove that "all men sprung from one common origin." He then looks at the Ohio data and stresses the quality of the constructions, the metal artifacts, and even the skeletons; they are not from "our Indians."

Apparently one artifact made up Atwater's mind—the so-called Triune idol, a ceramic vessel found on Cany Fork of the Cumberland River in Tennessee. It had three heads joined together, with an ascending carafe neck, and some painted colors were still present on some of the faces. He was sure it represented "the three chief gods of India, Brahma, Vishnoo and Siva." With some irony as seen from our perspective, Atwater concluded that "unless his mind is formed differently from mine, he will see in this idol, one proof at least, that the people who raised our ancient works . . . worshipped gods resembling the three principal deities of India."[6] As I emphasized earlier, perception plays a very important role in archaeological interpretation. Thus Atwater's conjectures are just that. Nonetheless, we can gratefully keep his facts; the descriptive portion is his great contribution, which cannot be denied.

Triune Vessel

Atwater was to do no more archaeology. He soon joined the ranks of minor politicians in the state legislature with sound populist tendencies, promoting canals, highways, and popular education. He made a trip west to Wisconsin as Indian treaty commissioner in 1829 and wrote about that journey and later a history of the state of Ohio. A final *Essay on Education* in 1841 was "the best thing he ever wrote." Whether the old pioneer still held to his Hindoo theory at the time of his death in 1867 is not known. A lot had happened in the archaeology of Ohio by then.

How did Isaiah Thomas feel about Caleb Atwater's contribution? I know of no specific response although he did refer to the original manuscript as rather a mess. Atwater mentioned in his monograph the possibility of carrying on the archaeological survey in other areas but in tones that indicated he did not expect that to happen, and it did not. His work appeared in the very first volume published by the then eight-year-old American Antiquarian Society and was entitled *Archaeologia Americana,* and quite properly so because the entire volume, some 436 pages, is devoted to that general topic, with the exception of introductory matter concerning the organization itself. It was a successful piece of work as a whole and would be a major building block of American archaeology for a generation at least.

Atwater's Hindoo connection or point of origin for the American Indians was not idiosyncratic. Dr. Hugh Williamson had advocated the same doctrine in 1811–12, as did John Clifford of Lexington, Kentucky, who provided Atwater with the drawing of the "triune" vessel. After all, it was in the Acostan tradition, with no multiple origins or wayward immigrants from Atlantis. Thus the volume presented a somewhat acceptable hypothesis in its final conjectures.

This period was one of great change in America; by 1820 all the states in the Northwest Territory were in place, and the same was true for the South, with the exception of Florida. Canals, which were the interstate highways of the period, were being built at a rapid pace. The great Erie Canal was finished with a flourish by De Witt Clinton in 1825, and a youngster growing up alongside it would see fossils (trilobites) revealed by the excavations and make paleontology his life work. This youth, Othniel C. Marsh, ultimately the great dinosaur hunter from the Yale Peabody Museum, was also to make some important archaeological contributions. These widespread canal excavations would do some damage to the Ohio Valley antiquities, too, as it was not all to science's benefit.

This period, from 1825 to 1840, would also be a crushing time of change for most of the American Indians residing in these newly formed states. President James Monroe proposed their removal in 1825, but it was Andrew Jackson who enforced that policy. Removal began in earnest in 1830, and by 1835 the deed was done via the devastating "Trail of Tears"—actually it should be trails (plural) because several routes leading out of the Southeast to the Indian Territory (Oklahoma) were taken, none much better than the other. In terms of large population aggregates, only some of the Iroquois tribes in the North, some renegade Cherokee in the Appalachians, and the Seminole in Florida were left. The Myth of the Moundbuilder could grow happily without too many tawdry reminders of the dispossessed.

The eastern populace developed a weird combination of feelings at this time—most favored removal, and the need for more land was a paramount good, despite the toll of human life and suffering—after all, they were only Indians, and pretty woebegone savages at that. Some Indians, however, were thought to be noble, romantic, and interesting to look at—the ones in the West, not those underfoot—so that Indian painters such as George Catlin and others would have successful art shows in the East Coast cities, and the somewhat opportunistic McKenney & Hall would publish (1836–44) their great volumes of Indian portraits at this otherwise dark moment.

Archaeology continued to expand during this period with work in the Natchez area by a visiting doctor from Philadelphia named Montroville Dickeson in 1837–41. Dickeson did outstanding fieldwork, little of it yet published, and he toured with one of the great Mississippi Valley painted panoramas giving illustrated lectures. With the name Montroville he sounds like a prime candidate for fakery and flummery, but he was no fantastic archaeologist. His records and collections are still preserved at the University Museum in Philadelphia and are amazing in their quality and

Ephraim G. Squier and Edwin H. Davis

depth of analysis. He named his stone projectile point types, just as we do today. Some large, heavy ones he called Bull Dozers, a strange term for the 1840s, but at that time the term referred to a heavy pistol.

Important work continued in the Ohio Valley too, where a pair of workers took up Atwater's task and, in 1848, produced the first real archaeological landmark of America. Ephraim George Squier (1821–88) and Dr. Edwin Hamilton Davis (1811–88) were an odd couple. Davis was a native of Ohio, a Kenyon College graduate, a medical doctor, and a collector of Indian relics. Squier, a self-educated New Yorker, was but twenty-four when he went to Chillicothe, Ohio, to publish the *Scioto Gazette*. He became interested in the prehistoric monuments and soon met Davis, then a prominent physician. Together they decided to study the earthworks and publish their findings.

Squier went back east to raise some money. He met such important people as the historian William Prescott, Albert Gallatin of the American Ethnological Society, and Professor Benjamin Silliman of Yale, one of the most distinguished scholars of the period. As William Stanton put it, "Intensely ambitious and not a little vain, Squier returned much gratified with his reception by the scientific men of the East."[7]

Squier and Davis worked quickly and, with good professional surveyors at their service, produced some extraordinary maps of the Ohio mounds and complex earthworks. Their accuracy exceeded that of Atwater by some measure. The perfection of the geometry of many of the earthworks was early thought to be the work of the contemporary surveyors, not that of the ancients, but aerial photography and test excavations have shown this not to be true. The Moundbuilders were just fine architects and engineers.

As did Atwater, Squier and Davis took some of their examples from outside the Ohio Valley, indicating that they expected Dickeson's work on the Natchez area to fill out the coverage of the region. They also made use of the work of others, specifically the drawings by the somewhat erratic botanist Constantine Rafinesque, whose Moundbuilder materials had come to rest in other hands following his death in 1840.

Once completed, the manuscript was sent, in 1847, to the American Ethnological Society for publication. It was a large undertaking, and old Albert Gallatin (1761–1849), then head of the Society and no stranger to Washington, turned to the newly founded (1846) Smithsonian Institution and its Secretary, Joseph Henry, with the suggestion that it should be the inaugural volume in the publication series Smithsonian Contributions to Knowledge. It was accepted, after a little hemming and hawing, and the 306-page monograph came off the presses in 1848.

It was an impressive volume with 47 lithographic plates and 207 wood engravings. It provided a view of America's past that would, in some ways, never be eclipsed. Today many of the sites are gone, destroyed by agriculture and urban sprawl. But the splendor of these complex earthworks, rendered in fine detail—sections through the earthen walls and overall plots showing the relationships of one site to another over distances encompassing many square miles—remains. It was a *succès fou*.

Squier and Davis had achieved much more than a fine description of the "Ancient Monuments of the Mississippi Valley," as their work was titled. First, they had made a functional classification of the works: Enclosures for Defense, Sacred Enclosures, Mounds of Sacrifice, Temple Mounds, Mounds of Sepulture, and so on. Many of the mounds are shown in section so that the methods of construction are clearly revealed—this is a real first. Jefferson's excavation of his burial mound is often cited very favorably, but no drawing of the excavated sections was made, although the strata were described and interpreted.

There are eight chapters covering the materials that had been recovered from the sites; most are from Davis's own collection. The illustrations are of very fine quality. Many of these artifacts are still extant and compare very favorably with the representations figured in the monograph. This careful delineation was not always the case, either before or after this important publication. Even minor details are revealed; in one case a lowly

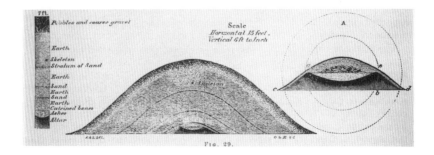

Section of Mound 1 and Its Altar

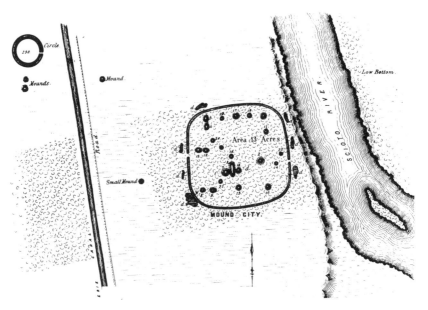

Squier & Davis's Map of Mound City, Ohio

Moundbuilder Pottery

potsherd, a broken pottery fragment, is illustrated well enough so that its ceramic type can be identified.

But what does it all mean? There are but six pages in the "Concluding Observations." The project's supporters had feared that heresies would be offered in the explanatory section; instead there was great caution, almost too much. The presentation of so few definitive conclusions at the end of such a magnum opus is a distinct disappointment. One can almost see Squier calculating what sources he could safely cite in the final chapter: Albert Gallatin, President Harrison, and then James McCulloh, "a writer of distinction," according to Squier.

Who, then, were the Moundbuilders? According to Squier and Davis, they were an extinct race, possibly connected in some way to the semi-civilized nations of Mexico and Peru. They could also be characterized as "a numerous, stationary, and an agricultural people." Early in the volume Squier and Davis pointed out that the resident Indians sometimes used the mounds for burials, but those burials could easily be seen as relatively recent and at times even included European trade materials.

How old were the mounds? Squier and Davis believed that they were of immense antiquity as shown by geology, the state of decay of bones in the burials, and the age of the trees that surrounded and covered the works. Only one thing was perfectly clear: the contemporary Indians were not related to the Moundbuilders. Even the slight amount of physical anthropological data presented in the volume (a handful of skulls) supported that view. The skeletal analysis was the work of Samuel G. Morton, about whom more later. Squier and Davis's collective fame, which was great, would not be based on the strength of their conclusions.

Following this strong beginning with the Squier and Davis volume, the Smithsonian Institution continued to publish important archaeological works during the next decade. One was a fine descriptive work on the interesting effigy mounds of Wisconsin (1855), a project whose fieldwork by Increase Lapham (1811–75) was sponsored by the American Antiquarian Society. The volume provided more spectacular maps of these earthen constructions in a great variety of shapes and sizes. But Lapham, an engineer who started his career with work on the Erie Canal before going west, was loath to say much about their chronology. He did believe that the Moundbuilders were the ancestors of modern Indians; he might have found out much more if he had been less cautious and asked the right people, or so it seems. Although Lapham did use data from many previous workers, he seems to have been mercifully ignorant of William Pidgeon's fieldwork, such as it was, in the Prairie du Chien region of Wisconsin, which I will discuss later.

In 1856 the Smithsonian published another volume that had a tie to Worcester, Massachusetts, and the Antiquarian Society, *Archaeology of the United States* by Samuel F. Haven (1806–81). Haven was the Librarian of the Society and one of its most distinguished scholars. The main title of the book is pretentious; its long subtitle is more informative: *Sketches, Historical and Bibliographical, of the Progress of Information and Opinion Respecting Vestiges of Antiquity in the United States*. It really was a careful review of the development of American archaeology, giving the evidence a thorough scrutiny unusual even in the century and more that has followed its publication. Sad to say, Haven's work has remained relatively unknown to later generations of archaeologists, as Gordon Willey pointed out in his introduction to the reprint edition in 1973.

Haven produced a richly documented monograph of some 168 pages that covered first "General Opinions respecting the origin of population in the New World." Herein he displays his breadth of knowledge in a most extraordinary manner, handling Atlantis, Noah's descendants, and the Ten Lost Tribes of Israel with references to the ancient classics and sixteenth-century literature as well. He concludes that the analogies used as evidence for such intercontinental connections are "superficial resemblances"— none of these hypotheses is proven, and they "have left the questions in their original perplexity." He suggests that more detailed studies in the areas of physical anthropology and linguistics may provide more productive conclusions, as we well know to be true today.

Samuel F. Haven

The second and most lengthy chapter of Haven's book is entitled "Progress of Investigation in the United States" and is an impressive history of research in the area to 1850. Haven does not restrict the evidence to archaeology but devotes long sections to ethnography, physical anthropology, and linguistics—a truly anthropological approach. He even anticipates Fantastic Archaeology in his section entitled "Vagaries," and we will soon turn to that aspect of the nineteenth-century scene.

Haven's conclusions are brief and to the point: the evidence was not yet sufficient to prove that human occupation in America was of really great antiquity despite possible associations with extinct fauna. Haven argued that some of these extinct forms may have persisted in America until fairly recent times. He suggests that there may have been casual and accidental contacts across both oceans but that these voyagers did not have a permanent effect on the culture of the aboriginal inhabitants. He firmly states that the Moundbuilders were the ancestors of the contemporary American Indians.

Haven further noted that the region composed of the states bordering the Ohio River contained a great center of ancient habitation but that it was deserted at the time of European contact. This "Dark and Bloody Ground" was empty of permanent inhabitants. "What mighty cause of destruction anticipated by a few centuries the mission of the whites [European expansion] it is not easy to conjecture," said Haven.[8] That most of these elaborate sites were vacant of recent Indian occupation certainly had strengthened the Moundbuilder Myth; the explanation for its exact cause remains a very pertinent question even today.

Haven ends his conclusions with a very prudent statement: "We desire to stop where evidence ceases; and offer no speculations as to the direction from which the authors of the vestiges of antiquity in the United States entered the country, or from whence their arts were derived."[9] One must understand that he is referring to questions of contact from Mexico and the South; he is strong in affirming their ultimate source: "With all their characteristics[,] affinities are found in the early condition of Asiatic races; and a channel of communication [Bering Strait] is pointed out through which they might have poured into this continent."[10]

So, like Acosta centuries before, Samuel Haven had it right by the middle of the nineteenth century; not only was he right but he had argued the case with a strong hand of data and with an open mind as to the outcome of the investigation. As with Acosta, it is discouraging to note how seldom his wise judgments were invoked in the remaining decades of that century.

In terms of our fundamental dimensions of archaeology—Form, Space, and Time—the workers on the problem of the Moundbuilders had, up to the 1850s, been fairly good in formal analysis. They set up typologies of mounds and sites; they did not have too many other artifacts to deal with. In spatial analysis they were outstanding, mapping sites carefully and plotting their distribution. Temporal analysis was their weakest area—only the tentative use of tree rings to say that the mounds were more than four hundred years old and the observation of some geological aspects that suggested considerable age. They did recognize the intrusion of European trade goods as marking the coming of the white man: the Historic Period. They fared the worst in overall interpretation, but, as has been pointed out by Irving Hallowell, they did not have any good European models to follow in archaeology; both geology and linguistic analysis had more advanced methodologies at that time.

Hallowell has suggested that the period before the Civil War was a high point of public interest in archaeology. One sure sign of this popularity was the sale of books on the topic, which Haven called "vagaries" and which I now class as some of the earliest examples of Fantastic Archaeology in America. The first example was written by Judge John Haywood of Tennessee and published in 1823, with the scholarly title *The Natural and Aboriginal History of Tennessee*.

The volume, one of a pair by Haywood, is a strange mélange of archaeological and natural history anecdotes. It is a veritable hodgepodge of ideas, some from Atwater (Hindoos and the "triune idol"), mixed with notions of a race of conquering giants and accounts of pygmies whose burial sites were found in great numbers in Tennessee. The claim for the pygmies was firmly and fairly destroyed by local researchers by the 1870s, only to reappear as fact in Barry Fell's most recent volume—these ideas are immortal!

Like many good writers of this genre, Haywood was concerned that some of his readers might consider his findings somewhat conjectural; he avowed that "it will *soon be converted* into real history" (emphasis added).[11] To be fair to the judge, whose second volume, on the political history of Tennessee, is much less controversial, he did improve on Atwater in his handling of some rather difficult data: ancient coins. Even at this early time (1823) some Roman coins had been found in various parts of the state. Rather than suggest that these might be veritable evidence of ancient voyagers, as did Atwater, Haywood felt that they were recent losses by persons with antiquarian interests. Overall, therefore, Haywood was not a charlatan, just a bit uncritical of some of his sources. Haven agreed.

But for a runaway best-seller one must turn to the inimitable Josiah Priest (1788–1851). A New Yorker born and bred, he raised a family of ten children mainly in the Albany area, to which he moved in 1819. We know nothing of his educational background except that his family was from New England, and one can presume some basic primary and secondary schooling. Some of his children were college educated; one son became a minister, another a doctor.

His first trade was that of a coach "trimmer" and then a saddler and harness maker. While still in the Albany area, however, in 1825 he turned to a very different way of life—a literary career. As one of his not-too-kind critics has said: "When Priest turned to making books for a living, he stitched together whatever scraps were at hand, much as he must have done in crafting the equipage of the Albany gentry."[12] He put together these volumes of strange phenomena and stirring historical adventures using materials extracted from a variety of sources.

If the cases that are known in detail serve as any example, Priest was not too careful either about the rights to use the material he borrowed or about its veracity. His historical adventures included tales about Indian captivity which often contained much sordid detail of methods of torture. The nature of the volumes can best be seen in the fact that seven out of ten full-page plates in his first book show scenes of torture and gory sacrifice.

In 1827 he got into the Millennium business with a volume predicting that "six thousand years of sorrow have well nigh fulfilled their tardy and desastrous [sic] course." This prophecy of doom went through seven editions, the last one in 1839. The buying public was apparently not too concerned about the apparent tardiness in the arrival of Priest's millennium.

His greatest successes, however, were historical pamphlets dealing with heroes of the American Revolution. One commentator, who suggested that Priest "embellished and adorned" these tales with "certain exaggerated picturesque features" to appeal to the popular fancy, had to admit that his story of a backwoods romance involving George Washington and an Irish girl, his first love, was pure fiction. But as today's scandal sheets know only too well, these pamphlets sold and sold. Joel Munsell, a well-known Albany publisher who profited from Priest's handiwork, called him "the greatest *inventor* of ancient history and biography of his time" (emphasis added).[13]

One can only guess what turned Josiah Priest to his next effort except that he knew his market and his stories about Indians had been successful before. In 1833 he published *American Antiquities, and Discoveries in the West*. It was a four-hundred-page volume that would go through some five editions and sell more than twenty-two thousand copies. The last edition was published in 1841 and differed from the original mainly in the addition of some half dozen illustrations.

The contents are hard to describe. There are sixty-one separate articles, and their arrangement can only be generously called confused; for example, on page 40 we meet the Romans at Marietta, but our next direct encounter with them is on page 385. In between we meet the Lost Tribes, some wandering Danes, traces of Egyptians in Kentucky, Norwegians and Welch (sic) in America 800 to 900 years ago, Mongol (sic) Tartars landing on the West Coast, voyagers from Italy and Africa to the continent of America, and resemblances of western Indians to ancient Greeks. That list encompasses about three-quarters of the hypotheses that have found their way into Fantastic Archaeology in the last 150 years—what a source book!

But that's not all—in his preface Priest states very clearly some other hypotheses: "We have also attempted to show that America was peopled before the flood; that it was the country of Noah, and the place where the ark was erected."[14] He states that "as aids in maturing this volume" he consulted the works of many scholars, but "the subject has proved as difficult as mysterious: any disorder and inaccuracies, therefore, in point of inferences which we have made, we beg may not become the subjects of the severities of criticism." That is as fine an escape clause as I have ever read.

Priest concludes his preface with a hopeful wish: "If, however, we should succeed in awakening a desire to a farther investigation of this curious subject, and should have the singular happiness of securing any degree of public respect, and of giving the subscriber an equivalent for his patronage, the utmost desires of the author will be realized." In other words, his real goal was to encourage interest in American antiquities, not to worry about accuracy and the orderly presentation of facts. Von Däniken has stated almost the same goals and with equal financial success.

One must ask how much of this is Josiah Priest and how much the work of others. Some of his material, specific chapters, do bear the names of other authors, but he was not too careful in this aspect. One scholar, Constantine Rafinesque, took direct exception to what he considered to be Priest's unfair and incorrect use of his written materials. One writer even suggests that Rafinesque may have accosted Priest in person in Albany; at any rate, Priest did drop some of the items that he had "barrowed." Rafinesque was so upset by some of Priest's views that he challenged him to a public debate on such matters as the Lost Tribes' ties to the American Indian and the final resting place of Noah's Ark, but he got no taker.

In one of his rare mistakes, the fine scholar Samuel Haven felt that Rafinesque was wrong in saying that Priest believed that of Noah's three sons one was white, one red, and one black. My own reading of Priest indicates that this time Rafinesque was correct.

As with many popular books, and there is no question that Priest's *American Antiquities* was just that, it is difficult to judge the immediate effect of this strange volume. It is clear that a generation or more later, some of the data in this very untrustworthy volume would be seriously cited as evidence for one fantastic belief after another. Sometimes apparently the sheer age of a volume brought to investigators a sense of veracity that unfortunately went unchallenged. Such is surely the case of our next stop in our survey of "vagaries" in nineteenth-century archaeology, as Haven termed these works.

Curiosity about the mounds and their builders during the first decades of the century was strong and recruited many to the search for answers. One of the more energetic and widely traveled recruits was a gentleman named William Pidgeon. His only major publication was *Traditions of De-Coo-Dah and Antiquarian Researchers* (1852). We know little of him except from his own hand. He began digging in stone mounds in Frederic County,

William Pidgeon

Virginia, in 1812; forty years later he had excavated 124 mounds and done a partial examination of more than 400 earthworks. These are Pidgeon's own figures, and, as will devolve later, some caution should be used in accepting their accuracy.

In 1826 he visited South America with a major interest in tumuli. Those that he recorded in Venezuela were certainly interesting—few have seen anything like them there since. The most spectacular was the so-called Battle Mound with four tiers, figured in his foldout frontispiece. The lower terraces were crowded with warriors, "while the feeble and the women and children, on safe heights, view the doubtful battle from the summit. But the flood of battle slowly rises from terrace to terrace, till the last blow is struck."[15] This is forceful writing and shows great imagination. These fictive battle mounds, first seen by Pidgeon in South America, are found throughout the hemisphere but are scarcely known north of the mouth of the Ohio, according to the redoubtable Pidgeon. No one has seen such mounds in North America either.

Our traveler then turns up in the Miami River Valley in southern Ohio in 1829. Pidgeon lived near the great archaeological site called Fort Ancient, which includes impressive earthen enclosures and numerous conical burial mounds that were mapped and described by Atwater. There he met local antiquarians and traveled to see many other sites in nearby parts of the Ohio Valley. He was inculcated with the standard belief that these were Indian mounds and cemeteries, "the sacred tombs of the ancient fathers of the aborigines." As we have seen, this is *not* the most common belief that he could have learned in the 1830s given Atwater's then recent findings.

But Pidgeon is nothing if not a peripatetic soul, and the years 1837–39 found him visiting the Upper Mississippi Valley, presumably that stretch of river north of St. Louis. There he saw a number of mounds that were "freaks of fancy" unlike any he had seen before, and he decided to make a tour of exploration of the "unfrequented wilds of the west" to study these mounds in more detail. In 1840, by his own account, he set forth from St. Louis and made his base of operations at Prairie du Chien, on the east bank of the Mississippi, Wisconsin Territory. He became quite well acquainted with the local Indians and learned something of their language.

The next incident was to be crucial for Pidgeon: at this point he met his primary informant, an old Indian named De-coo-dah, who was said to have extensive knowledge about the mounds. He was a treasure trove for Pidgeon, who spent almost two years mining this source. De-coo-dah seemed to have an answer for almost every one of Pidgeon's questions. When shown maps of sites in Ohio that Pidgeon had visited, the old sage knew their names and their function—the bones of his fathers rested there. Indeed, his knowledge was encyclopedic; when told of the stone mounds in Virginia on Pidgeon's father's farm, he says, "That was the resting place of some great war-chief or chiefs, placed by national order, to be honored with a funeral pile, in anticipation of leaving the country."[16]

De-coo-dah was the last member of the Elk Nation, according to his own testimony. Exactly what this meant is a bit hard to explain. In Pidgeon's rendering it sounds like pretty standard Moundbuilder mythology: "The primitive Elk nation, originally a branch or tribe of the ancient American, had become mingled and amalgamated with the race of red men from the south."[17] De-coo-dah's ancestors once held sway over most of the East, hence the ties to the Ohio mounds, but internal wars ensued, and they stopped raising their monumental commemorations (the mounds), some of which had hieroglyphic meaning (the emblematic ones). Pidgeon himself is sure that there was "a plurality of nations anterior to the occupation of North America by the modern Indian race"[18] and that they waged war for many ages. It is typical Moundbuilder fare espoused by many other early nineteenth-century authors.

Pidgeon's volume is unique in that no other author had a direct native source for much of the interpretations, and few other books are so confusing. The illustrations are a good example; there are some 75 engravings scattered through the 325-page text, but these engravings have four different numbering systems and virtually no internal order. Other peculiarities include topical construction, such as Chapter XXX, which begins with the

DE-COO-DAH.

"De-coo-dah"

heading "Egyptian Sanctuary"—this is a cave in Indiana on the banks of the Ohio, but nothing in the text ties it to Egypt; indeed that word does not appear in the chapter, most of which deals with "Earthen walls of Ohio" and "Mounds of Migration," which Pidgeon investigated in Wisconsin during the autumn of 1842.

The volume is truly a potpourri of tidbits about Pidgeon's "Antiquarian Researches"—its subtitle. The last three short chapters give us some generalizations: (1) the Egyptians were here; (2) the extinction of some of the Moundbuilders was probably caused by a great flood; (3) racial mixture causes national degeneration and "total extinction assumes the attitude of sovereign reality among the mound-builders."[19]

The final question is, How much of this can we believe? Robert Silverberg has called it "a crazy masterpiece of pseudoscience," a characterization with which I agree. He further points out that some "authorities" in the 1870s and 1880s used Pidgeon's work without criticism. Unfortunately, Haven does not mention him, presumably because his manuscript was completed just prior to Pidgeon's.

Mercifully, however, unlike so many other cases, someone did test Pidgeon's claims. The fieldwork of Theodore H. Lewis of Minnesota, who was an investigator with excellent credentials, formed the backbone of

N. H. Winchell's monumental *Aborigines of Minnesota* (1911), and Lewis carried out excavations as far south as Natchez. His investigations, published in 1886, showed that Pidgeon's mound descriptions were gross exaggerations. Lewis interviewed old settlers who had known Pidgeon and came to the conclusion that "the Elk nation and its last prophet De-coo-dah are modern myths."[20]

But that is not the end. Myths and books about those myths live on. A 1983 volume by the English author John Michell, entitled *The New View over Atlantis,* uses and reprints Pidgeon's mound data as verifying the worldwide distribution of certain monumental constructions. Perhaps he did not bother to read the accompanying text.

If one reviews the state of American archaeology by the mid-1850s in terms of data collection, analysis, and interpretation, one sees that good progress had been made in the first area. Atwater and Squier and Davis, for example, had gone into the field and done fine field recording: they were good at data collection. Analysis of these data was progressing too. Similar categories of artifacts—sites, pipes, and pots—were being classified and compared, and typologies were being set up. Interpretation, however, was lagging behind. The data were hard to classify chronologically, and guesses and myths were deemed equally useful as facts. In terms of our other science trilogy, there was plenty of curiosity, a small amount of testing—tree-ring counting for dating—and unfortunately, much lack of veracity, as we shall see shortly in Chapter 4, "The American Humbug."

How does this situation compare with European archaeology of the 1850s? Were the "colonies" really that far behind? The answer is a non-chauvinistic no. There is no question that in many areas science was forging ahead across the water in Europe; Americans looked in that direction for new ideas and techniques as in analytical chemistry. That was not the case in archaeology, though the situation would change markedly in just a few years. A revolution in knowledge and understanding (our old friend perception) took place during the first sixty years of the nineteenth century in European archaeology and geology.

Four major events contributed to this change: (1) advances in geology which provided a new understanding of time and process: millions of years and change without the Flood or other catastrophes; (2) recognition of man-made tools in association with extinct animals; (3) the invention of a Three-Age system of chronology (Stone, Bronze, and Iron); and (4) the discovery of fossil man.

At the turn of the century, 1799, some tantalizing discoveries were made: Napoleon's Egyptian adventure provided the impetus for the discovery of the Rosetta stone, which would lead in 1821 to the deciphering of the Egyptian hieroglyphs. At the same time, in England, John Frere observed Acheulian hand axes in a gravel pit at Hoxne, near Diss, and he felt there was evidence associating these stone tools with extinct fauna. He published his findings in 1800, but they were not accepted until May 1869. His direct descendant Mary Leakey was to have better luck in East Africa a century and a half later.

Although the Biblical chronology of the origin of the earth was not taken as the final word by many scientists at this time, it was certainly the work of the English geologist Charles Lyell that set the stage for broad acceptance of a long chronology. Lyell's *Principles of Geology,* published in 1830–33, built on the earlier work of James Hutton and William "Strata" Smith. Lyell's explanations of geological processes made use of mechanisms that were currently visible on the globe. Lyell suggested that given sufficient *time,* even mountains would wear down. The existence of the fossil record was also quite well understood at this time, similar fossils from disparate parts of Europe were seen as showing synchrony. Geological time was greatly expanding.

In Denmark at the National Museum, C. J. Thomsen, following the departure of Rasmus Nyerup, began in 1816 to organize the Royal collection of artifacts—the King's Cabinet. The museum was opened in 1819 with its rooms of artifacts from the Stone, Bronze, and Iron Ages. In 1836 Thomsen published a small volume indicating the use of a Three-Age system of classification of these archaeological materials: stone, bronze, and iron. This method was derived logically from the materials, with history rather than detailed stratigraphy, giving proof to the order. J. A. Worsaae, also working at the National Museum, later followed up Thomsen's work and in the 1850s spread the concept to England. The idea of time had been introduced into later prehistory.

At the other end of the chronological scale, a French customs official at Abbeville named Boucher de Perthes had, as early as 1837, been digging in the gravels of the Somme River. He published five volumes on the materials he found there, trying to convince his readers that these hand axes were the tools of Early Man. These findings were not readily accepted. His opponents used the weapon of disdain, but he persevered, even having to overcome the planting of some fakes in his excavations. Then a group of noted English geologists, including Hugh Falconer and James Prestwich, visited his site, viewed his artifacts, and finally, in 1859, accepted them as tools in ancient geological contexts, the glacial gravels of the Somme terraces.

The other needed data then seemed to come in a rush: in 1857 there was the discovery of a Neanderthal skeleton near Düsseldorf in Germany—it was seen as an ancient *human* ancestor. Finally, in 1858, a Cornish man named William Pengelly, digging at Kent's Cavern in Brixham, near where others had worked before, showed to everyone's satisfaction at last that ancient tools were surely associated with extinct fauna; they were found together beneath a stalagmite layer. Here there was no chance for mixed context, which had been the basis of earlier objections.

Then, too, there was a quiet gentleman, once a world traveler, working away in Down, Kent, who would rush into print on November 24, 1859, with *The Origin of Species*. Charles Darwin would add the last piece to the puzzle—it all came together in what has been called by some "1859—Annus Mirabilis." It was such indeed. What had happened was a whole new way of looking at the data: perception had been changed.

Frere was not the only one to find those hand axes. All through the eighteenth century, they had been picked up and called "thunder stones," but now they could be recognized as human artifacts, not nature-facts. Geoffrey Bibby has called it "The Discovery of Time," and now, in both geology and archaeology, there was room enough on the time scale for many things to happen. Man's activities on this planet were no longer crowded into a tight timetable from 4004 B.C. to the present.

The archaeology that would come out of this new way of looking at the world would be based on an interplay between the natural sciences and the prehistoric data. In 1865 John Lubbock published his *Prehistoric Times* and said that "a new science had been formed." He saw archaeology as forming the link between geology and history and in this volume coined the terms "Paleolithic" and "Neolithic" that would help sort out the Stone Age data into useful categories. The book was a best-seller.

What have these Old World activities to do with North American archaeology? Everything and nothing. The Darwinian revolution would challenge American scientists forever. Some of Darwin's most vocal critics would appear early in Cambridge: Louis Agassiz, for example. American perceptions of man's early beginnings would follow those of Europe and, indeed, attempt to follow them too closely in the next decades. But American archaeology would, in the main, follow a different path that it had, perhaps unknowingly, already started down. It would be an archaeology linked to the study of the American Indian and thus based more directly on anthropology than on the natural sciences. That is where the answer to the main question we have been following, Who were the Moundbuilders? would be found, but only after many a troubled turning.

3

The Golden Age:
The Myth Destroyed

For more than a century the ghosts of a vanished nation have am-
buscaded in the vast solitudes of the continent.
JOHN W. POWELL, 1894

The Search for a Usable Past with which the new republic began the
century would come to a crashing halt when the nation's condition forced a
focus on more pressing problems: Fort Sumter and all that followed. The
year 1860 would be an *Annus Mirabilis* of a very different sort for this
country. Perceptions and conditions would, indeed, be changed forever,
but not on the level of science or archaeological interpretation. The impact
on the nation of the Civil War (1861–65) was great, and an essentially new
entity would emerge by 1870—the Gilded Age. Some things persisted: the
Smithsonian continued to print its useful Annual Reports, but many of the
figures in postwar American archaeology were *who* they were or *where* they
were because of the bloody War Between the States. A major shift in focus
took place too—no longer was the Ohio Valley to be the center of all
archaeology; first the Southeast and then in turn, the Southwest claimed
center stage.

That the Myth of the Moundbuilder should survive the war was
perhaps no surprise. Like so many myths, it was capable of being finely
embroidered by each believer following his own pattern and shading, with
no nasty little facts blocking its progress. As the myth was laid to rest near
the close of the century (1894), John Wesley Powell characterized its appeal
as follows:

> It is difficult to exaggerate the prevalence of this romantic fallacy, or the
> force with which the hypothetic "lost races" had taken possession of the
> imaginations of men. For more than a century the ghosts of a vanished nation
> have ambuscaded in the vast solitudes of the continent, and the forest-covered

mounds have been usually regarded as the mysterious sepulchres of its kings and nobles. It was an alluring conjecture that a powerful people, superior to the Indians, once occupied the valley of the Ohio and the Appalachian ranges, their empire stretching from Hudson bay to the Gulf, with its flanks on the western prairies and the eastern ocean; a people with a confederated government, a chief ruler, a great central capital, a highly developed religion, with homes and husbandry and advanced textile, fictile, and ductile arts, with a language, perhaps with letters, all swept away before an invasion of copper-hued Huns from some unknown region of the earth, prior to the landing of Columbus. These hypothetic semicivilized autochthons, imagined to have been thus rudely exterminated or expelled, have been variously identified by ethnologists with the ancestors of the Aztecs or the Toltecs, the Mayas, the Colhuas, the Chicimecs, or the Pueblos, who have left no signs of their existence save the rude and feeble fortifications into which they fled from their foes, and the silent and obscure elevations in which their nobles found interment. (Powell, 1894: xli)

The major outline of the myth was that the builders of the mounds and earthworks of the eastern states—now known from as far west as Minnesota and as far south as Florida—were a group called the Moundbuilders, whose culture was more advanced in technology and art than that of the Native Americans who occupied the area more recently. The Moundbuilders were sedentary agriculturalists, who knew how to craft artifacts of copper and silver, and their art, particularly in sculpture of both stone and pottery, exceeded that of any known group of Indians. Certain inscriptions, such as that from the Grave Creek Mound, gave evidence that they probably also had a written language, which was unknown to the native tribes.

Attempts to prove that the Moundbuilders were a completely separate race had not been too successful. Samuel G. Morton was probably the most authoritative scholar on the physical remains of the Moundbuilders. Squier and Davis had used his work in their famous tome. But Morton's data were not clear. Working in the 1840s, he purported to show by craniometric measurements that the Indians were inferior and that this was obvious merely by looking at the capacity of their skulls. Stephen Jay Gould has recently reviewed this work in a book entitled *The Mis-Measure of Man*. Gould feels that Morton subjectively misread the data to support his prejudice but that he did not consciously manipulate it. Indeed, Morton did publish *all* his data; hence Gould had the opportunity to study it. As an aside, Morton's work was embraced by special interests in the South, as the Negro grouping, based on these measurements, was at the very bottom of his list.

When tackling the Moundbuilder problem, however, Morton did not find any very significant differences among American Indian skulls, including those designated specifically as Moundbuilders. He did not sort out a Moundbuilder race; instead he put forward the notion of two separate kinds of Indians: Toltecans, who were semicivilized, and Barbarous for all the rest. The Moundbuilders were surely Toltecans—the southern origin was redolent and obvious in the name; it was the favored place of their origin by many others as well.

Could the archaeology of the post–Civil War period put this myth to rest? It could and it did, but to understand how this final act was accomplished we must first understand the background of the major actors and their institutional platforms.

As we have seen, it was thanks mainly to a series of local organizations, like the American Philosophical Society and the American Antiquarian Society, with their volunteer leadership and self-motivated members, that organized approaches were first taken toward the varied archaeological situations. By 1846–48, with the founding of the Smithsonian and its quasi-governmental status and the major impetus of government-sponsored expeditions to the West, official activities with paid staffs and research budgets entered the archaeological scene. During the Mexican War (1846–47), military officers began to report on archaeological sites from Pecos to Chaco Canyon and even Mesa Verde. Southwestern archaeology was coming into view; the earlier Spanish sightings of some of these same ruins were unknown to most American scholars at this time.

What had begun as primarily military operations in the 1840s and 1850s became major scientific explorations in the late 1860s and 1870s, as economic expansion that focused on California and the building of railroads took place in the West. These postwar surveys were to be the training grounds for some of the major figures in American archaeology, although there was very little emphasis on prehistory in these basically topographic and geological explorations. Any archaeology that was recorded was almost accidental except for the work of F. W. Putnam with the Wheeler Survey.

The leaders of these expeditions, such as George M. Wheeler and F. V. Hayden, were tough and ambitious men, vying for fame, if not fortune, in the vast new frontier. A rather unlikely winner in this competitive game was a former Army Major named John Wesley Powell (1834–1902). Powell came from a midwestern minister's family and had little formal education, but he had a keen interest in the mounds near where he had grown up in Ohio and Illinois. Powell came up through the ranks during the War and lost an arm

John Wesley Powell

at Shiloh. He seemed to have a basic political sense from early on, manip-
ulating his U.S. Army situation to get leave in the middle of the conflict to
get married and having his wife nearby, even at Shiloh. His epic trips of
discovery down the Colorado River, begun with an institutional base at a
small Illinois college, hit the national limelight by 1870.

Powell began a media campaign with the excellent photographs he had
managed to have taken during these challenging trips. By 1879 he had
become Director of the U.S. Geological Survey, a very ripe political plum,
and also Director of the newly founded Bureau of Ethnology. The next
decade would see him at the height of his powers; 1894 was his high-water
mark in archaeology with the publication of twelfth Annual Report of the
Bureau of American Ethnology (BAE) from the Foreword of which the
stirring Moundbuilder passage quoted above was taken. But fame is fleet-
ing, as Powell found out to his sorrow. What political power can give, it can
also take away. His last decade would be one of sad scenes and a tattered
reputation.

But all was golden back in 1879 as Powell stepped to the helm of his
new Bureau of Ethnology. Powell brought on to his staff two veterans of
the western surveys: one an aging entomologist and former college professor, Cyrus Thomas; the other a startlingly fine artist famous for his
panoramic drawings of geological exposures in the vast western canyons,
William Henry Holmes. This unlikely pair would be the myth-destroyers
par excellence.

Powell had had an early interest in Indian mounds; in 1858–60 he had actually dug into some in Illinois and nearby states. Even during the war he examined mounds in the Nashville region. There was time during the War, apparently, for many things other than martial activities. But when he took charge of the bureau, ethnology was his major interest, and he was to make a very significant personal contribution to the field of American Indian linguistics using materials collected by many other fieldworkers. In archaeology, there had been some attempts to collect important data on the mounds from Jefferson's time on. In 1858, the American Association for the Advancement of Science (AAAS) set up a special committee to survey the mounds, but very little activity took place and the committee's short report in 1869 was not significant.

Thus the field was still open for a large government-sponsored program, and after some early bungling by Wills de Hass, who had had a hand in the AAAS project, Powell set out to have a proper Mound Survey done in 1881, apparently, at least for the record, with some reluctance. The purpose of the survey was to settle the Moundbuilder question once and for all. Powell knew the answer—the Indians *were* the Moundbuilders—but he also knew that new data would have to be carefully collected to test and prove this conclusion.

Powell put Cyrus Thomas in charge, gave him a small budget, and off they went. Thomas ran the project from his Washington office, making only a few field inspections, but he was a stern taskmaster to his rather motley field crew. Thomas gave them quite clear instructions and expected and got very good results, in the main. They tested sites across the whole area, avoiding only a few regions where their work would have been redundant because of the excavations of others, such as Putnam's then-current work in Tennessee. The data were fine, but Powell was, I believe, a bit disappointed that there was no flood of museum-quality specimens to be installed in the newly created National Museum, as he was always looking for ways to get more Washington support.

Although the facts are not clear on the matter, it seems that Thomas approached the question of the Moundbuilders with a fairly open mind. Powell, his boss, knew the answer, but Thomas began to attack the problem in what would today be called the Direct Historical approach: did any of the known Indian tribes actually build mounds? The answer, especially from the Southeast, was definitely in the affirmative. Haven and others had pointed that out long ago. It was in the Ohio Valley, where the focus of archaeology had been, that these data were most obscure. Moundbuilding

Cyrus Thomas

and mounds used as platforms for important structures had been recorded firsthand among the Southeastern Indians by Hernando De Soto's chroniclers in the 1540s and as late as the 1750s by William Bartram. There really wasn't any mystery there.

The dirt archaeology done by Thomas's fieldworkers showed that the remains in the mounds were quite compatible with known Indian artifacts. They also found, as others had before them, indications that there were intrusive burials in the mounds made by Indians who had obtained trade goods from Europeans, providing evidence for continuity of mound use into historic times. All this was seen against a much larger data base, for while Thomas was dealing with the mounds directly, William H. Holmes, he of the artistic bent, was looking in detail at the artifacts of the Moundbuilders—especially those made from shell and pottery. Not surprisingly, these were some of the most aesthetically pleasing objects, and Holmes treated them with respect and care. His studies of these artifacts were to have been coordinate volumes with those produced by Thomas, but given the exigencies of government research and distractions of other projects, it was not until after Powell's death in 1902 that all Holmes's volumes were published.

Holmes's studies were both anthropological and aesthetic in approach. He compared the objects broadly with those of similar character in the New World, he classified them by shape and decoration, and he gave an appreciation of their artistic and technological achievement. His ceramic

William H. Holmes

groupings of the eastern United States pottery have remained basic even to modern-day analysis. He used essentially a single time frame set of categories, but the geographic units he set up still hang together, now that chronology has become a part of our system.

Indeed, time remained a major problem for both Thomas and Holmes. There was no sure way to discover the temporal dimension of these earthen monuments; Thomas even felt that trees and their rings gave uncertain results. This temporal problem would haunt Eastern archaeologists for decades more. We know now that the building of these mounds spans more than twenty-five hundred years so it is no wonder there were problems of interpretation then. It was clear that most of the mound constructions were prehistoric, but beyond that generalization there was little more chronology to hang on to. Another major Moundbuilder problem was the perceived difference in the level of culture between North American and Middle American (Mexican) Indians. Also, what was the temporal relationship between the agricultural and thus sedentary groups of the south and the nonagricultural hunters of the north? Obviously, the influence of Lewis Henry Morgan and other contemporary cultural evolutionists was being felt in these questions.

Cyrus Thomas's work, published in the twelfth Annual Report of the Bureau of American Ethnology (1894), was a masterful review of the subject, including an exhaustive treatment of the positive evidence for extensive corn agriculture by the Indian tribes of the eastern United States. I especially like the way Thomas treated the supposed Moundbuilder inscriptions; he called them "anomalous waifs." Overall, the conclusion was very clear: the Indians were the Moundbuilders—the myth was dead. It had been killed by a clear look at hard evidence. But just because the government said it was so did not make it so.

Of course, there were some other important individuals and institutions working on the Moundbuilder problem as well. One of the most significant was the Peabody Museum of American Archaeology and Ethnology at Harvard University. It was founded in 1866 by George Peabody, and a main thrust of its charter, that "in view of the gradual obliteration or destruction of the works and remains of the ancient races of this continent, the labor of exploration be commenced at as early a day as practicable,"[1] essentially addressed the Moundbuilder question. Its first Director, Jeffries Wyman, was like so many scholars of that day, a brilliant but modest generalist—one for whom *Naturalist* was a term of approbation. He could and did turn from sea shells to potsherds with ease and insight.

Wyman's archaeological focus was on mounds, too, not the fancy Ohio earthworks but the more utilitarian shell "heaps" of Florida, where he carried on research in the winter for health reasons. Wyman worked on these Florida shell heaps as early as 1859 but did his most important work there while he was Director of the Peabody (1867–74). This focus on shell heaps was an important American link to the archaeology of the Old World: the "kitchen middens" of Scandinavia were important sources of data on late Stone Age cultures, noted in the 1850s by Thomsen and others. An article by A. von Morlot on the subject was translated and published in the Smithsonian Annual Report for 1860, and as a result shell heaps from Nova Scotia to Florida were soon under investigation.

The American work proved that most of the sites were not preceramic as they were in Europe and thus not as old, alas. But Wyman's posthumous monograph (1875) on the Shell Mounds of the St. Johns River in Florida was a virtuoso performance, with methods of analysis of the pottery in terms of technology and decoration that were not to be matched for nearly one hundred years. What Wyman could not know was that he was dealing with the earliest ceramics in North America; we now know that they date to nearly 2500 B.C. Wyman did not need any mysterious moundbuilders to create the material that he so brilliantly studied.

Wyman died in 1874 and was temporarily succeeded at the Peabody by Asa Gray as interim head. Frederic Ward Putnam, the full-time successor to Wyman in 1875, was also trained as a naturalist. Fish had been his major interest when Putnam, a Massachusetts native, was a student at Harvard under the energetic Swiss-born scholar Louis Agassiz. But he had an early

Jeffries Wyman   Frederic W. Putnam

interest in archaeology too, picking up some sherds in Toronto while at a AAAS meeting in 1857. Putnam, like Agassiz, was a museum man and thus an excellent choice as the next director of the Peabody. He would go on to found other anthropological museums at the American Museum of Natural History in New York, at the Field Museum in Chicago, and at the University of California at Berkeley, all the while still running the Peabody in Cambridge.

Putnam liked archaeological fieldwork, but he saw his function as that of overseer rather than field director. Thus he soon had a small group of fieldworkers in various parts of the East, particularly Ohio, but also in Tennessee and Arkansas. These were the areas that Thomas pretty much avoided with his own BAE field parties. Putnam, like Thomas, was a great correspondent, and the archives of both institutions are filled with letters to and from the field. Even his somewhat illiterate digger, Edwin Curtis, kept notes on every burial, drew maps of his sites, and carefully packed the materials for shipment back to Cambridge. Those artifacts can still be put back in their original burial context through the use of the catalogs and field notes. Even the lowly potsherds were cataloged, though often with the noncommittal location "General Diggings"; actually keeping broken sherds and animal bones was not a common practice in the 1870s, even in Europe.

The results of the Peabody excavations in Tennessee and Arkansas, as well as collections that were purchased from Missouri, allowed Putnam to see that there were important similarities and differences among what we now call "Mississippian" ceramics, using a terminology first applied by Holmes in his study of pottery at the National Museum. The similarities between the Tennessee and Missouri materials led Putnam to indicate ties between these two areas, but the Arkansas materials were different, thus he felt that they were not from a single tribe but a number of different groups. In other words, there was not a homogeneous culture that had a single origin—they were Indians, yes, but not one tribal unit. Thomas could—and did—accept this interpretation. It is important to underline this agreement, for there is little question that there was a strong rivalry between the Smithsonian and the Peabody, the two major archaeological centers in America in 1880. On many questions they were in complete agreement, as further case histories will show.

In the case of Early Man studies, however, the two institutions differed considerably. By the 1890s as the Moundbuilder question wound down, Putnam became more involved in the search for the chimera of the earliest evidence of occupation in America. It had been so easy in Europe: within a decade of the *Annus Mirabilis* (1859), it was all wrapped up. The work of Edouard Lartet and Henry Christy in the Dordogne region of France was especially important. There was good stratigraphy in the French caves and rock shelters; separate stone tool assemblages in association with extinct faunas had been discovered. Even distinct chronological periods had been named and exhibited in some detail at the Paris Exhibition of 1867. But this was not the case in America.

It was clear what was needed: hand axes directly associated with extinct animals and probably found in caves. The solution seemed simple enough to the investigators—dig some caves and surely the artifacts would be there. And so they believed until well after the turn of the century, even after dozens of unsuccessful excavations. Some extinct animals, mastodons and the like, were found but no hand axes. Still they tried; oh, how they tried. They looked on river terraces and in glacial gravels from New Jersey to Minnesota. They found a few crude stone tools but no veritable hand axes. Putnam was sure that the Indians were not latecomers to this hemisphere, that they had been here for thousands of years, and as a result he let his hopes bend his perception to admit some rather tenuous materials.

On the Smithsonian side, it was none other than the artist-turned-archaeologist William H. Holmes who led the opposition. Holmes had grown into his archaeological position and was a very good fieldworker by the turn of the century. He felt that man was a recent entrant into the New World. He did some digging near Washington, D.C., and showed quite clearly that some of the crude tools that proponents like Putnam had been likening to Paleolithic artifacts were nothing but unfinished tools of a much later period. In other words, their crudity was a stage in their manufacture, not a sign of great age. As it turned out, both Putnam and Holmes were right *and* wrong: Putnam was right that Native Americans were ancient inhabitants of the New World but wrong about the data he was using to prove his point; Holmes was right that the artifacts that had been found were not in fact very old but wrong in thinking that the Indians were recent arrivals.

Although so far in discussing the post–Civil War period I have mentioned the contributions of what passed for professionals with staff positions at major research institutions, I do not want to give the impression that archaeology had become professionalized by this time. It would be the turn of the century before any Ph.D.s would appear. Putnam at Peabody and Powell, Thomas, and Holmes at the Smithsonian were very dependent on the work of amateurs, and there were dozens of them anxious to help. Letters poured into both institutions with photographs of interesting specimens that had turned up in local mounds or even village sites. These individuals were not trying to sell them, although some of that was going on; mainly they wanted opinions about what they had found, and both institutions were happy to respond. Often a relationship would be formed, and the collections would ultimately be donated to the museum, often with notes and maps of where they had been found.

This period, especially that of Grant's presidency, has often been referred to by historians as the Gilded Age, but in archaeology it was truly a *Golden Age*. From 1870 until nearly the turn of the century, there was a tremendously strong interest in North American archaeology and dozens of books were published on the subject. Local historical societies and many Academies of Science, in Chicago, St. Louis, and even Davenport, Iowa, were publishing the results of the work of amateurs and garnering collections of great size that would put terrible pressure on curatorial support for decades to come.

Who was involved in this search for knowledge about the prehistoric Indian remains? They were, in the main, well-educated and often affluent members of local communities—doctors, lawyers, and merchants. Typically, they would do some digging in nearby sites and become acquainted with the pertinent literature that was mercifully small at that time: the Smithsonian and Peabody reports, Henry Rowe Schoolcraft's six volumes on the American Indians, and a few others. Then these gentlemen would write books on the subject. They would copy the illustrations from one of the above, add a few of their own, and the book would come rolling off the presses. Many were not trivial; descriptive archaeological data are always valuable, in spite of the often naive interpretations.

Some of these works became major classics—one thinks, for example, of William H. Potter's *Archaeology of Missouri* (1880), which Putnam helped to get published. The map therein, showing in fine detail the patterns of settlement on Sikeston Ridge in the southeastern part of the state, has never been surpassed; the study of Settlement Patterns would be rediscovered by New World archaeologists about seventy years later. Gates P. Thruston, a northern soldier who never left Nashville after the War, published his comprehensive *Antiquities of Tennessee* in 1890, based on his extensive collections from the Nashville area. One way or another, he managed to illustrate artifacts characteristic of all the major cultural periods now recognized in the state, although he did not know that when he put his book together.

The Jones brothers, one a doctor in Tennessee, the other writing from Georgia, made very substantive contributions. Charles C., the one from Georgia, was well read on the subject, and some of his interpretative sections, using history and ethnography, were especially fine. And there were dozens more. The South did rise again, at least archaeologically.

Rise, indeed, and even surpass the Ohio Valley finds with the materials such as those that turned up at the amazing Etowah site near Cartersville, Georgia, just north of Atlanta. Etowah was a large mound site known since 1820 at least, but the 1880s Smithsonian excavations by the Bureau of American Ethnology crew and the artifacts gathered earlier by Charles Jones showed qualities of excellence in technology (especially native copper) and art (embossing on copper and engravings on shell) that were stunning to the locals and those in Washington as well.

With all these exciting new discoveries of the 1870s and 1880s, the Moundbuilder question was still very much alive. One aspect of it that I have not touched on in detail, and it is a fairly recently broached topic, is that of the rather virulent racism inherent in much of the argument against the American Indians as being the authors of these mounds, earthworks, and elaborate artifacts. The stereotype of the lazy and ignorant Indian, incapable of such technical feats, was much too prominent in this period not to get an appropriate airing here. Some of the most blatant remarks come from a person who should have known better: John Wells Foster (1815–73), of Chicago, a geologist and a former President of the American Association for the Advancement of Science and President of the Chicago Academy of Sciences.

In 1869 Foster published a scientifically titled volume, *The Physical Geography of the Mississippi Valley*. This topic would seem harmless concerning the Moundbuilder/Indian question, but not so. Foster was a convinced environmental determinist. As an example, he noted that because the climate of the North was so invigorating, both physically and morally, the outcome of the recent southern Rebellion had been sealed before it began. Later he turned to a discussion of the Indians as differentiated from the Moundbuilders. He repeated many of the negative stereotypes about the Indians and then moved to the question of what to do with them.

After all, they had been in the way, Foster pointed out, since the first European settlements and were still causing the same problems despite the Trail of Tears. They took up too much room and therefore should be moved, experimentally, to reservations. Should this suggestion prove harmful to their health, Foster said, one must remember that extinction is what happens to less vigorous species—the Darwin effect. He did allow that it would be too bad to lose the Cherokee; after all, they had shown the ability to rise from Barbarism with their use of the written symbols (Sequoya's Syllabary) and might be fit for survival. Having finished off the Indians, he then spent many more pages recounting the prowess of the Moundbuilders—who grow paler on every page.

Foster's best-known book was published four years later in 1873—*Pre-Historic Races of the United States of America*—and it was often cited in the years that followed. Knowing what we know of Foster, it would be easy to dislike and discount this second volume; it is, however, as an archaeological contribution, a hard book *not* to admire. It is full of original data, and I have checked it for accuracy carefully. He knows the literature with a breadth of coverage exceeded by only a few. Most of his illustrations are original; when he has borrowed from others, he properly cites the source.

Yet Foster still holds a strong line against the Indians. As to the Moundbuilders and their origins, it depends on which page you read: on page 338 we find them coming from Brazil at a very remote time, not from Siberia. On page 341, he apparently agrees with the wild French scholar Brasseur de Bourbourg that the Toltecs are identical with the Moundbuilders. Then on page 351 we find the Moundbuilders being expelled from the Mississippi Valley, only to take refuge in Central America, where they develop their admirable civilization. The one certain conclusion, according to Foster, is that the American Indian was not the Moundbuilder.

In other areas, Foster's critical ability stands him in much better stead. In his Appendix he first deals with early writers on the "condition" of the Indians—their life-styles. But then he turns to much more controversial topics such as the "Atlantic Theory"—he does not believe in Atlantis. More than that, he scores almost a perfect 10 on "Ante-Columbian Discoveries," in which he carefully debunks the runes on Dighton Rock, the Grave Creek and Newark Holy Stone inscriptions, the Newport Tower, and Welsh-speaking Indians. All told, it is an effective effort. The one thing missing from this volume covering all the United States is any mention of Southwestern archaeology, but remember, this book was published in 1873.

By 1876 Cliff Palace at Mesa Verde was first sighted by a wandering cowboy. By 1880 any volume on American Archaeology would have to discuss the second American mystery: who were the Cliff Dwellers? That question did not take anywhere near as much time to answer as had the Moundbuilder debate; after all, the Pueblo Indians were sitting right there. Maybe you could not find anyone who claimed to have an ancestor who lived in the Cliff Dwellings, but the Pueblos were all over the Southwest. Also, their current lifeways were much like those of the people who had disappeared from places like Mesa Verde; for example, they still had underground ceremonial structures (*Stoufas,* or Kivas in current terms); they made the same sort of pottery and other crafts. How could the media make a real question of this? They couldn't, and they soon gave up on it. The Pueblo Indians were the descendants of the Cliff Dwellers.

When the Smithsonian published Cyrus Thomas's great report of the Mound Survey in 1894, it for all intents and purposes shut the door from a scientific standpoint on the Moundbuilder question. John Wesley Powell had therefore won his great battle against the myth, but he was not as fortunate in his other Washington contests. Before he had headed the Geological Survey, he had drawn together a report titled "The Lands of the Arid Regions of the United States" in 1879—an innocent enough topic, one would have thought, but that was not the case. Powell was never one to shrink from the facts and what they seemed to tell. He saw clearly that these western lands were more Great American Desert, as the area had originally been characterized, than a farmer's paradise as they began to be sold by energetic opportunists, and he said so. He felt that only a small percentage of the area could be reclaimed for agriculture and that the water supply would have to be centrally controlled for the public good.

For more than a decade (1881–92) Powell led the Geological Survey brilliantly and with strong support from Capitol Hill. But outside pressures from landowners and cattlemen who opposed his views on the western arid lands brought him down, and in 1894 he resigned as head of the Geological Survey. He stayed on at the Bureau of American Ethnology, but his last eight years there were very unhappy.

Powell's old war injury, which had given him much pain for years, grew worse after a supposedly corrective operation; he was a sick man. He had begun to write a long series of articles on Science and Philosophy that have not stood the critical test of time too well. Meanwhile, he summered in Haven, Maine, where he puttered about in some nearby Indian shell mounds. He died there in September 1902. The questions of water and land use in the West, which long concerned Powell to his detriment, have still not been answered. One thinks today of the Californian program, just now getting underway, to "borrow" water from Powell's beloved Colorado, for example. When will that problem be solved?

But are the Moundbuilders really gone? Well, not exactly; if you had done fieldwork in the backcountry of Missouri in the 1950s, as I did, you would have found them alive and well—still standing as much as seven feet tall and still very mysterious. The myth lives on and is constantly regenerated. After doing some excavations in rural Mississippi (1958–60), I returned some years later to hear stories about the seven-foot skeletons that I had uncovered in my excavations. The largest male we dug up was well under six feet in height, but what is one to do? And I just received an announcement flyer for a new *Dictionary on North American Indians;* one of the main headings in the Archaeological Index is "Moundbuilder Period." Who knows when it will end?

In the final decade of the nineteenth century, a major event took place in Chicago—the 1893 World's Columbian Exhibition. F. W. Putnam from Peabody, who seemed to have plenty of time on his hands as usual, was made head of the anthropology exhibits at the World's Fair. He sent out teams to collect archaeological and ethnological specimens for the Hall of Anthropology, and they produced an archaeological treasure trove, especially from Ohio and Peru. Putnam even brought in some Native American peoples and groups from other parts of the world to "show their different cultures" to the visitors. As suspect as this venture might sound in dealing with the personal feelings of these peoples, documents show that Putnam realized the dangers inherent in such an arrangement but felt it could be done without harm to them. Putnam's crowning achievement, and one that was to have long-lasting effect, was to hold an International Congress of Anthropology, using that term for the first time in an inclusive, generalizing manner. He had speakers representing Physical Anthropology, Archaeology, Ethnology, and Linguistics. This meeting, although very critically reviewed by Holmes, his "friend" from the Smithsonian, signaled the professionalization of the field of anthropology.

This landmark event did not, however, signal the end of nonprofessional contributions to the field of American Archaeology. Indeed, the contributions of amateurs remain very significant to this day, although they do not now carry on their work with quite the panache that Clarence B. Moore of Philadelphia did. Moore was a Harvard graduate (1873), who may have had a short field season with Jeffries Wyman in Florida while still an undergraduate. Moore had chosen his parents well; his father owned a successful paper company, thus enabling C.B. to spend a few years on a world tour that took him not only to Europe, the Mediterranean, and Egypt but also to Java (Borabadur) and over the Andes and down the Amazon. Then it was back to Philadelphia and the family business.

Moore kept hard at work for nearly two decades but then tired of his commercial labors and returned to Florida and began a career in archaeology. He dug mounds and the like. He forged some ties with two institutions: the Academy of Natural Sciences at home in Philadelphia and Peabody at Harvard, and he quietly helped Putnam with his yearly expenses— a modest $500 at a time, but very helpful nonetheless.

Moore would continue his own researches in the Southeast and their publication in lavishly illustrated volumes until the 1920s. His contribution would be large, not just for the excavation and description of so much interesting material but because he continued to ask questions, such as the nature of the copper artifacts he had exhumed. He sought and got excellent quantitative chemical examinations of these artifacts, proving they were of native, not European, manufacture, as some had thought.

So we have seen the field of American archaeology grow from a rather parochial curiosity about some mounds in the Ohio Valley to a soon-to-be professional field of scientific inquiry with good scholars and wise students and amateurs investigating prehistoric remains from one side of the continent to the other. But in the transition the mystery was gone and the myth had been destroyed—the Moundbuilders had pulled up stakes and moved out of the river valleys for good, and there were some who mourned their passing. Now the story of American archaeology was the story of the American Indian, for better or for worse. As long and as broad as that tale might be, it would never, it seemed to some, have quite the same fascination. Where had the fantasy gone?

4

The American Humbug: They'll Believe Almost Anything!

"Humbug" consists in putting on glittering appearances . . . by
which to suddenly arrest public attention.
P. T. BARNUM, 1865

We have now surveyed the general development of the archaeology of
North America from discovery until the beginning of the twentieth century. By 1900 the field had become professionalized, and archaeology was
making great strides in both the American Southwest and Mesoamerica.
These two areas were considered to be more interesting, more challenging,
and more rewarding than the East, where so much of the foundation for the
profession had been laid. The Eastern United States was definitely "out,"
the Southwest was "in," and that was where all the bright lads went. After
all, with the Moundbuilders gone, what was left in Eastern archaeology was
pretty dull and drab, or so it seemed.

Now we will turn to a series of case studies in Fantastic Archaeology,
set against the nineteenth-century archaeological scene we have just reviewed. By the 1820s, America was self-confident. The young Republic had
been playing "Add-a-State" since 1812, and half a dozen states were added to
the fold by now in a manner in which no other democratic government had
ever operated. There was freedom of expression in the state constitutions,
yet added national power as well, as far west as the Mississippi.

Some important economic pathways were being constructed, such as
the Erie Canal between Buffalo and Albany. The epic-making canal was
started in 1817 and completed in 1825, when a triumphant Governor De Witt
Clinton, riding a flag-draped ship, presided over ceremonies joining the
waters of the east and the west. There were even a few token Indians on

board, despite Clinton's published view that the mounds were really built by Scandinavians.

Of course, this young nation was not without it critics, and some of the most strident voices came from the British homeland. I noted earlier that settlers in the Ohio Valley at this time sought inspiration and good fortune; why else did Mrs. Frances Trollope end up running a bazaar in Cincinnati in 1829? Her critical remarks may have been slightly tinged by her economic problems in this new world. But others with less of an ax to grind still found America pretentious and, more important, given to "humbug," or perhaps even humbuggery, a well-used term, of some age (1751), meaning to hoax, fraud, or delude. It was a favorite of Charles Dickens, as we all know well from Mr. Scrooge's lips.

What was American Humbug? Everything from outright land swindles to just overbearing boosterism for the seemingly obvious treasures of this new land. There were some straightforward hoaxes, too, as we will see. The association of the term *humbug* with Connecticut-born Phineas T. Barnum is no accident—he was a past master of the art and even wrote a book on the subject in 1865. He began his career as a showman in 1835 when, playing on the emotions of a willing audience, he produced a black woman, Joice Heth, said to have been the nurse of George Washington and then 160 years old. She was a success—the public would indeed believe anything. Later evidence showed Joice Heth to be not more than 70 years old.

Like many characters I will discuss, Barnum is easy to stereotype; we think of him as the "king of humbug" and little more. A reading of his own book on the subject, *The Humbugs of the World* (1865), gives quite another view. He is capable of critical evaluation and does a fine job debunking the then-prevalant Spiritualists. He presents well-documented case studies of deceptions such as the "Moon-Hoax," a newspaper fraud of 1835. So Phineas Taylor Barnum was much more than a huckster with an opera singer on one arm and a grizzly bear on the other. He was a man of his times, according to his biographer, Neil Harris; another commentator said, "He never befooled the public to its injury," and I believe that.

We will return to Mr. Barnum's later activities, but first let us see why archaeology of this period was to be so successfully exploited by various practitioners of humbuggery, who had less skill than old P.T. In reviewing the development of the field, I have noted that there were no professional archaeologists at this time: Atwater and Squier and Davis were self-taught. There were a few Geologists, and Linguistics as a general field was developing out of classical studies of Greek and Latin and, of course, Sanskrit.

P. T. Barnum

But archaeology was open to anyone, and the data could be inter-preted almost any way and, as we have seen with the likes of Josiah Priest, usually was. The lack of systematic knowledge of the materials that were being found archaeologically had led to conclusions such as calling Paleo-lithic hand axes "thunder stones." Ceramics were a bit better understood; the properties of tempered clay in the Indian vessels were recognized early, even to distinguishing correctly between grit and shell inclusions, for example. There was no problem with materials from the Historic Period—they were from the investigators' own culture, after all. The rest were still quite mysterious and thus subject to many interpretations.

The nineteenth century was a time for frauds in general; not just archaeology was affected. Indeed, one commentator on fine arts has said, "Forgery became really rampant during the nineteenth century, first owing to the Gothic revival and then because of renewed interest in the works of art of the Renaissance."[1] Most of the objects that we will investigate unfortunately lack the artistic qualities of the specimens that author has mentioned. Indeed, they must be seen to be believed; that is, how can one believe that intelligent individuals once actually thought them to be gen-uine documents of the prehistoric past?

Indeed, archaeological hoaxes were so common at this time that they were at least twice used as literary devices by some well-known writers: Charles Dickens and James Russell Lowell. Dickens involved old Sam Pickwick and the Pickwick Club in just such activities in 1837. Mr. Pickwick, while on a stroll, chanced on an engraved stone; he became enchanted with its mysterious message and gained notoriety and membership in numerous scientific organizations as a result of his writings on the subject. It soon became clear to some that the inscription was not Roman or the like and could be read as a simple statement of ownership, "BILL STUMPS HIS MARK," rather than a message from the distant past. Pickwick remained firm in his original belief, and tempers rose. Mr. Blotton, a Pickwick Club member, said it was a *humbug,* to strong cries by loyal supporters of "No, No." Archaeology was full of funny hoaxes, especially as related to inscriptions, or so some writers seemed to think; I will discuss Lowell's contribution to this genre later.

We begin our tour of American humbugs, not surprisingly, in the Ohio Valley. As the travelers left Pittsburgh on their way west, they could hardly avoid seeing, a dozen miles south of Wheeling, the great mound on the banks of Grave Creek, not more than a quarter of a mile from the river. It was in present-day Moundsville, West Virginia, then in western Virginia, where in 1775 Nicholas Creswell saw the mound and said it was one hundred feet high. There was a ditch around the base; Meriwether Lewis, in 1805, said a tree on the mound was at least three hundred years old. In 1820 Atwater was to remark that the large mound, said to be ninety feet high by his informant, was part of a larger works "laid out with taste." The mound is really *seventy* feet tall and is now preserved in a small park.

The Tomlinson family owned the property; in 1819 they allowed only sufficient investigation to reveal that "this lofty and venerable tumulus . . . contains many thousands of human skeletons, but no farther." Joseph Tomlinson was praised for his preservation, but two decades later in 1838 Abelard B. Tomlinson took a very different view of the matter. He felt that major excavations could provide the public with something worth viewing. A shaft was sunk from the top and a "drift" or side tunnel from ground level. The investigators did not strike the multitude of burials forecast in 1819, but what they did find was remarkable: a timber-lined vault covered with rocks, if we can believe the reports.

Actually, we now know that such tombs are often found in such mounds so we can accept those data as well as the information that the tomb contained two skeletons, shell beads, and a bone ornament. A second

Grave Creek Mound (view)

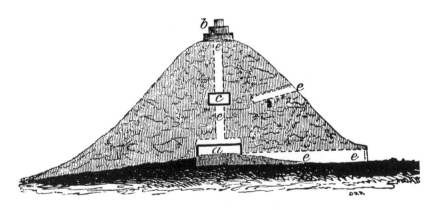

Grave Creek Mound (section)

tomb was found about thirty-four feet above the lower vault and contained a single occupant with a profusion of shell beads (more than 2,000), copper bracelets, and more than 250 pieces of cut mica. When the entrance tunnel was enlarged to accommodate visitors, a mass burial of ten skeletons was uncovered.

John W. Foster, in interpreting these finds, felt that the major burial was that of a "royal personage." He called upon Herodotus's description of a Scythian burial and one more recently excavated at Kertch to explain this burial ritual that may have included "retainer" burial (the mass of ten). This explanation was not too farfetched for Foster, whom we have met before. The same questions are still being asked today of these Adena burials, as we now call them; they date from about 400 B.C. and are found quite frequently in this part of the Ohio Valley.

But the burials alone were not what caused all the interest in the Grave Creek finds of Abelard Tomlinson; about five years after the excavations, Henry Rowe Schoolcraft, a noteworthy scholar, visited the site and "found this curious relic lying unprotected among broken implements of stone, pieces of antique pottery, and other like articles"[2] in the building that had been erected to house the artifacts from the excavations. The "curious relic" that came to Schoolcraft's hand was the now-famous Grave Creek Stone, containing three lines of inscription.

According to Foster, writing much later, the stone was first shown about two years after the excavations had taken place and was said to have been one of the relics taken from the mound. It is not clear from which tomb it came, but it was probably taken out of the mound in a wheelbarrow load of dirt and found in that dirt. I wish I could give more precise contextual data, but the truth is that there are none. What does exist is a series of conflicting statements by witnesses asked to recall the circumstances of the discovery nearly forty years after the find. I will unravel that aspect of this strange dig after we see what was on the stone that made it so curious.

The first major supporter of the Grave Creek Stone and its inscription was Schoolcraft (1793–1864), who was a unique figure in the pioneer days of American anthropology. He was more of an ethnographer than anything else, beginning his career in the 1820s as an Indian Agent at Sault Ste. Marie. In 1832 he discovered the true source of the Mississippi at Lake Itasca in Minnesota. He had an in-depth understanding of the Great Lakes Indians; his first wife was an educated woman of mixed blood. He first focused on native tales, Indian folklore, and concluded his work in anthro-

Henry R. Schoolcraft

pology with a huge six-volume encyclopedia on the Indian tribes. Midway in his career, as he moved from detailed fieldwork to more general topics, Schoolcraft got involved with the strange finds at Grave Creek.

His conclusions, published in 1845, were that the inscription of some twenty-five characters was alphabetic but not from a single language; instead he compared them to characters from a number of different alphabets, all from the Old World. It was a strange inscription, to say the least. Other European scholars took their shots at deciphering, one finding it Lybian, another Numidian. Schoolcraft ultimately termed it an "Intrusive Antiquity," meaning that it was not of Indian origin.

Of course, much of the interest in the inscription lay in the possibility of proving that the Moundbuilders had a written language and thus a claim to Civilization, unlike the lowly Indians. That was surely not Schoolcraft's intention, for he was a steadfast and early believer that the Indians had built the mounds. Thus the Grave Creek Stone would instead show him outside influences, not unlike the then-recent and controversial discoveries of the golden tablets by Joseph Smith in New York State upon which the Mormon Church was founded.

The Grave Creek controversy raged for some years; perhaps its best feature was the eccentric elegance of the translations of the twenty-five characters. Also, we should remember the scale of this inscription upon which so much attention is focused. The artifact is an oval, water-worn pebble of sandstone one and three-quarter inches in length, not a very monumental tablet for such high-sounding words as the various decipher-

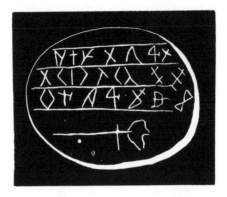

Grave Creek Stone

ers read it: "The Chief of Emigration who reached these places has fixed these statutes forever," or "The Grave of one who was assassinated here. May God to avenge him strike his murderer, cutting off the hand of his existence." That is a big message to get on a skipping stone. A final translation, with true French flair, was "What thou sayest, thou dost impose it, thou shinest in thy impetuous clan and rapid chamois."[3] Do you think it lost a little in the second translation? Of course, the early nineteenth century was a great time for decipherments: Babylonian fell to the experts in 1802, and Champollion unraveled the Egyptian hieroglyphs in 1821; no wonder every one wanted to participate in this one.

What did the archaeological experts say? In 1856 dour old Sam Haven was not amused: "If genuine, it is at least unique, and is unsupported by any similar or analogous relic."[4] He then proceeded to shred other would-be inscriptions that had come to hand. Even earlier, E. G. Squier (1846 and 1848) had voted no, saying that there was no good reason to support the notion of Moundbuilder writing. John Foster was very forthright in 1873: "It is a stupid forgery." Charles Whittlesey from Ohio, in an incisive article on archaeological frauds in 1879, studied the Grave Creek find in some detail and found it less than credible.

How did they reach these conclusions? Early on I discussed Kenneth Boulding's trio: curiosity, testing, and veracity. We find that Haven tried to test the Grave Creek Stone by comparing it to others like it and found it wanting—it was, he said, "unique." Foster obviously felt that it was also wanting in veracity—a fake. Haven had said that the case stood on the assertion that the stone was found in the heart of the tumulus, a statement weakened by the time that purportedly elapsed between its discovery and the announcement of the find. Whittlesey had also sought by correspondence to get better data on the engraved stone's context and time of discovery, with no great success. The problem of a time delay is a common thread running through a number of Fantastic Archaeology cases.

In 1877 an Ohio geologist with some legal training, Matthew Canfield Read, took the case, as it were. He had been associated with several colleges and had also been involved with the state's archaeological exhibit at the Centennial Exposition at Philadelphia in 1876. He was appointed to a committee of the Ohio State Archaeological Society to investigate the authenticity of the Grave Creek Inscribed Stone, and, by his own statement, he "undertook to divest himself of all pre-conceived opinions, to investigate the matter *de noco* [sic], and with judicial impartiality."[5] He set out four questions: (1) Is it alphabetical? (2) If alphabetical, does it represent a known alphabet? (3) Is it an authentic find? (4) If alphabetical and authentic, what does it indicate?

First, Read needed some information about the discovery, and he set out to gather it thirty-nine years after the fact. He wrote and wrote again to the major participants: to Abelard Tomlinson, the owner of the site; to Colonel Wharton, who was said to have witnessed the discovery, although this was denied by Tomlinson; and to P. B. Catlett, who claimed to have found the stone (also denied by Tomlinson). Catlett and Wharton were in accord; one must also remember that by then Tomlinson was nearly seventy years old and living in California. Also, Tomlinson's description of the way the shaft and drift were dug does not accord with any of the statements made by any of the observers of the excavations. We must conclude, as Read did, that Wharton's and Catlett's testimony was nearest to the truth. Thus it appears clear that the inscribed stone was not seen in its original context within the mound but was discovered in the dirt pile after having been dumped there from the wheelbarrow. That is its find spot! Exactly where it came from can never be known.

Read next attacked the problem of the inscription: was it alphabetical? He decided on an interesting test; he asked four individuals (a teacher, a schoolgirl, a druggist, and a college professor) to write down twenty or more arbitrary symbols, not resembling any characters known to them and using only straight lines. "In every case an inscription was produced presenting as many indications of being alphabetical as the one under discussion [Grave Creek]."[6] All four of the tests also had characters that could be pronounced Cypriotic or Phoenician; some were also recognizable in English, as are some on the stone in question. Also recognizable were characters of Pelasgian, Coptic, Gothic, and Runic, to name a few, some of which had been identified on the stone by the "experts."

Read was left with the strong conclusion that "there is nothing in the form of the characters [on the stone] which requires us to decide that they are old, that they are alphabetical, or if alphabetical that they are derived from any known alphabet."[7] This is a lesson that some modern-day decipherers could well learn by heart. Read does not come right out and say who did it; instead he says: "It [the inscription] is precisely of such character as would be the result of an ordinary attempt to manufacture an inscription" and that any of the laborers could have made it. Read's well-structured and careful testing should have laid the question of the Grave Creek inscription to rest. Unfortunately, his excellent piece of work, which was published in 1879 in an archaeological journal (*American Antiquarian*), is not well known; even well-read scholars of today seem unaware of it. But debunking literature is often ignored.

Cyrus Thomas at the Smithsonian, however, as he wound down his great Mound Survey volume for Powell in 1894, covered much of the controversial data on the Moundbuilders and took a very strong, almost sarcastic, stance toward the Grave Creek Stone and Schoolcraft's support of it. Indeed, all the Smithsonian scholars would take a very hard line in many of the upcoming cases.

I do not disagree with their positions, but the individuals in Washington seemed to have lacked a sensitivity to the national role they were seen as playing. Their affect was not always productive in furthering knowledge and promoting important interchanges between the growing ranks of the true professionals and the enthusiastic amateurs to whom they owed some appropriate responses.

Certainly you know the next line—yes, the Grave Creek Stone still lives. Indeed, the busy Barry Fell published in 1976 a fourth translation: he sees it as an Iberian inscription; the language is Phoenician written in an alphabet used in Spain during the first millennium B.C. It reads as follows (from right to left): "The mound raised-on-high for Tasach / This tile / (His) queen caused-to-be-made."[8] This royal commemoration seems like a low-budget affair when they got to the purchase of the "tile." Recall that the artifact is pocket-sized, all of one and three-quarter inches in length.

So the problem persists. Another twentieth-century revelation might tell us even more. According to Curtis MacDougall, in his classic work *Hoaxes,* "One day in 1930 Andrew Price, president of the West Virginia

Historical Society, accidentally solved its riddle. . . . A casual side glance at the inscription caused part of it to form the figures, '1838.'"9 With this clue he used his printer's knowledge of type to translate the whole as "Bill Stump's Stone. October 14, 1838." The stone, found a year after the publication of Dickens's *Pickwick Papers,* was, according to Price, the work of someone merely attempting to amuse himself, or so says MacDougall. Having read Price's little monograph on the subject, I am not convinced of that solution. The work by Price has all the earmarks of a spoof. It is written in a jocular fashion and contains a "history" of the builders of the mound and tomb that would do credit to Rafinesque and other wild-eyed writers such as William Pidgeon. My verdict is that the riddle was not solved by Andrew Price; still, I say, "Bah, humbug, Mr. Tomlinson."

I have already characterized the period following the Civil War as one of great popular developments in archaeology. Our next case is not exactly what I had in mind, but since some have called it the "greatest hoax of all times," I can hardly pass it by. The Cardiff Giant was big and bold and very popular. George Hull succeeded beyond his wildest dreams with this hoax. This is a case in which the mystery is not who did it but why this particular brand of the American humbug was so successful. Was there a special naiveté among the populace that made them especially susceptible to this very blatant hoax? One has to admit that some noted savants in Cambridge were willing believers too—not just those country bumpkins who were pushed through the tented excavation at a handsome admission price.

The great stone figure was "discovered" by some well-diggers in central New York on the Newell farm in the Onondaga valley near Cardiff on October 16, 1869. It caused a great sensation. The local papers loved it; a tent was put up and the crowds came in great numbers—by train to Syracuse and then by carriage or stage to Cardiff. The crowds were spellbound by the sight. Here was a fossil man of truly giant proportions. Other fossils had been found in the area, and so this giant was just another example, albeit an unusual one in that the soft parts of the body had turned to stone. The "petrifactionists" saw that unusual aspect as no great obstacle to belief because under the proper conditions, anything was possible. The opposition said that it was not a fossil but a statue—possibly of great age. There was great local support; four doctors said it was a fossil man. The controversy raged, and business in Cardiff had never been better.

Farmer William C. Newell and his relative George Hull, who had taken over the running of the enterprise, were doing very well from the sale of admissions, food and drink, pamphlets, and so on. All this happened in

The Cardiff Giant

just a few weeks—and then some local citizens offered to buy a three-quarter interest in the Giant for $37,500. The Giant was syndicated and moved to Syracuse for exhibition there—quite a task as it was more than ten feet long and weighed nearly three thousand pounds. But by early November the handbills were up at the Bastable Arcade and the crowds came pouring in, skeptics and believers alike.

What did men of science say? Andrew D. White, the president of Cornell University and a geologist, said it was a hoax; O. C. Marsh, a paleontologist from Yale, said it was neither a fossil nor a good piece of art; and Benjamin Silliman, his colleague in chemistry, agreed. But there was not agreement even among educators; James Hall of the New York State Museum, also a paleontologist, intoned that the Giant was "the most remarkable object yet brought to light in this country." Somewhat later (1872) it was taken up very positively by a Yale divinity student, Alexander McWhorter, who saw the sculpture as a Phoenician god, with pictorial inscriptions on it, which he alone could see; he then proceeded to translate them. President White, a strong commentator on many subjects, said that Dickens and his Pickwick Club had "never conceived anything more funny" than McWhorter's scholarly constructions.

As things proceeded on their merry way, there were mutterings about certain activities by George Hull and carryings-on at the Newell farm the previous year that made an outright hoax probable. By December 1869, just three short months after the "discovery," George Hull was prepared to admit his guilt, and by the following February the whole tale was told. George Hull had purchased a block of gypsum in Fort Dodge, Iowa, had it crafted in Chicago, treated and aged there, and shipped by train to New York State, and then brought overland by heavy wagons, to be buried in the dead of night by the Newell barn in November 1868, a year before its discovery. Hull's expenses were said to have been $2,200. Thus a quick profit had surely been made. Hull said that his motive had been to win an argument with an evangelist in Iowa about a biblical statement concerning giants in the earth. I would have to say that Hull won the argument.

Even Hull's admission of the fraud and the nay-saying by the scientists did not stop the cash flow; recall Mencken's problem with his bathtub tale. None other than P. T. Barnum, now making a very successful comeback from some earlier reverses, offered $60,000 for a three-month lease of the Giant, a handsome sum in those days. He was turned down but, never daunted, Barnum had his own copy of the Cardiff Giant fashioned and put it on exhibit in New York City as the *real* giant. It was not long before New Yorkers had two giants to choose between because Hull's original came to town as well. Sad to say, Barnum won the crowds, and Hull's Cardiff Giant moved briefly to New England. In Boston it met with great success—men of discriminating taste and education gave it a thorough inspection. Oliver Wendell Holmes drilled a hole near its ear and said the giant's anatomical development was wonderful; Ralph Waldo Emerson was enthralled with its antiquity, and a local sculptor said it was definitely not a humbug. So much for Bostonian wisdom.

The original Giant spent some more years wandering about New England, ending up in storage in Fitchburg, Massachusetts. It did make a brief sortie to the Buffalo Pan-American Exposition in 1901 before going back for a long stay in Iowa from whence its gypsum had come. After that demeaning residence in a publisher's recreation room, the Giant came ceremonially to its final resting place at the Farmer's Museum in Coopers-town, New York, where it is the property of the New York Historical Association. Although it is now best seen as a piece of nineteenth-century folk art, the Cardiff Giant did have a wonderful career on the stage of American gullibility.

The will to believe in the face of specific evidence to the contrary—it wasn't really a very good fake petrified man, and the hoaxer confessed after three months—just proves that people wanted to believe very strongly. Some have said that George Hull had the wisdom to give the people exactly what they wanted, but I think that is an overstatement. Post–Civil War America seems to have been ready for fantastic discoveries—the Cardiff Giant was big, unexpected, and pretty mysterious. That was enough.

We turn now from this rather harmless tale to a story of personal intrigue and very destructive behavior that pitted reputable amateur scientists against government specialists in a nasty little affair that would embitter the participants and confuse two important aspects of American archaeology for decades. One author has called it the "Davenport Conspiracy." We go back to Iowa—not for gypsum but on the trail of the Moundbuilders. It was the winter of 1877, and the Reverend Jacob Gass, a fairly recent émigré from Switzerland, was digging in some small burial mounds on the Cook farm, not far from Davenport. While investigating a tomb in Mound 3, he came upon, in some loose soil where bones were scattered, two slate tablets with rather exciting designs engraved on them. It seemed logical that they were Moundbuilder hieroglyphics.

To understand the context of Gass's finds we must look at the total setting. Davenport, Iowa, was a bustling Mississippi River town in the post–Civil War years. As early as 1867 a small group of interested amateur scientists came together to discuss their mutual interest in natural history.

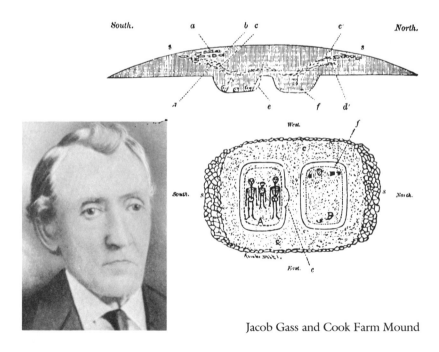

Jacob Gass and Cook Farm Mound

Copper Axe from Iowa

The Davenport Academy of Natural Sciences arose out of this common concern, just as many similar institutions had begun across the country at this time. The membership was drawn mainly from the educated and professional levels of society but was not exclusive. Anyone with a sincere and proven devotion to these matters could contribute.

Thus it was a matter of some interest to the Davenport Academy members and possibly with just a little envy that they investigated the Reverend Gass's earlier finds in 1874 at the Cook farm. He had found some extraordinary materials, very unusual for Iowa at least. At Mound 3, which was about five feet high, Gass had gotten into a well-preserved burial chamber and found nicely sculpted stone pipes and some fine copper axes with their enclosing cloth bags preserved by the copper salts.

In 1875 and 1876 Dr. Robert J. Farquharson wrote up these finds for the academy's *Proceedings*. Photos of these very interesting specimens were sent to scientific institutions, including the Harvard Peabody Museum. These artifacts were very like materials that had been found in the Ohio mounds, which we now call Hopewellian and which date about A.D. 100. They were very scarce in Iowa then and reman so today; thus Gass had made a significant find, one of national importance.

He was asked to join the Academy, although this move was not approved by all. After all, Gass did not speak or write English fluently—

German was his native language, and he regularly preached in that tongue. Nonetheless, the Academy was justly proud of these finds, even if its members (the Establishment) had not been directly involved. The publication indicates that Gass had done quite a careful excavation and documented it very well.

In the winter of 1877, the Reverend Gass returned to work at Mound 3 because the property was changing hands and he wanted to salvage anything left in the mound. January was a strange time to go digging in Iowa, as any Minnesotan can testify. The mound was complex in its stratigraphy—there were later intrusive burials with historic artifacts as well as the earlier stone chambers where the axes were found. The diggers worked with unseemly haste; they pierced the frozen ground and found another historic burial. Then in loose soil inside Chamber B they found the extraordinary slate tablets described above. All in one day's work! One can imagine that note-taking was a little hurried at 5 P.M. on that cold January day. What is the archaeological context of these bizarre tablets? We know that Gass recovered them under salvage conditions from Mound 3; he gives sufficient details to make their discovery within the mound credible. That is about all the information there is. What is incredible are the tablets themselves.

Dr. Farquharson was then President of the Academy and, speaking for that institution, indicated that "we are, in a measure, astonished at the unexpectedness of our discovery, and also somewhat embarrassed with its richness."[10] But from the beginning the academy members were convinced of the genuineness of these inscriptions. They were amazing—one was called the Calendar Stone and had concentric circles scribed around a central dot; the other, somewhat larger, had a scene drawn on each side with animals, mounds, and Indians crudely delimited. There were lines of symbols on one side that were not immediately deciphered, but not for long. The Calendar Stone also had some marks that could be glyphs within the perfect circles; was it an astrological chart?

This treasure trove was almost more than the academy could handle, but the bounty would not stop. In January 1878, obviously Gass's favorite digging season, he returned to the Cook farm with several Academy members as assistants. This time they invaded Mound 11 and met with equal success. Instead of shale/slate, they found a painted limestone tablet with elaborate engravings on it. Strange to say, when they found this tablet it was in an "open" area, not filled in with dirt, and the paint was very fresh looking. The preservation was amazing, indeed.

Two stone effigy pipes were found with the tablet. But if that wasn't

Davenport Tablets

enough, the Reverend Gass acquired another stone effigy pipe; unlike the others, which portray local animals such as ducks, birds, and mammals, this new pipe, "found" by a local farmer, had an elephant. In 1880, Gass and his brother-in-law dug up another elephant pipe at the supposed site of the first find.

It seems that they couldn't leave well enough alone. They had unearthed prime data on two of the most crucial questions facing American archaeology: first, the Moundbuilder was shown to be civilized and able to make written inscriptions; second, man was shown to be contemporary with elephants or mammoths.

From the very beginning, with the publications by Farquharson, the Davenport Academy had tried to act in a scientific manner toward these finds. One of Farquharson's early statements would, however, come back to haunt him; quoting from a letter from the esteemed Samuel Haven, he says, "Science and civilization do not leave solitary monuments"—a great statement supporting the comparative approach. But sad to say, good comparative data would be very hard to locate for the remarkable Davenport finds.

The originals were sent to the Smithsonian for careful examination, and at first there were some favorable comments. Spencer Baird, the Secretary of the Smithsonian, was quite impressed, but then the tide turned. The Smithsonian scholars began to go on the attack. They saw the inscriptions and the pipes clearly as fakes. The most devastating comments were by an ornithologist, Henry Henshaw, in 1883. He attacked the elephant pipes in particular; there is a purported elephant or tapir on one of the tablets, as well. Henshaw was not restrained in his strong comments; as a result, a veritable storm of protest was raised, more over his manner of comment than its content.

It was hard not to side with the Academy against this outspoken member of the Establishment. Jacob Gass was the main unnamed victim of the attack. The response by the Academy was written by Charles E. Putnam, a wealthy local businessman with a special commitment both to the Academy, which he supported and had formerly led as President, and to Gass's discoveries. Putnam's young son Duncan, who had been only a sometime student at Harvard because of ill health, was a strong supporter of Gass's finds until his untimely death in 1881. Charles Putnam, probably a collateral kinsman of both Rufus and Frederic Ward, wrote a masterful response to Henshaw. Without a doubt, Charles Putnam believed in these archaeological discoveries with all his heart and soul.

Needless to say, translators and interpreters for these purported prehistoric documents came forward from every side. Noah and the Ark and Hittite hieroglyphics were just some of the answers given. But the battle about authenticity, the central question, continued to escalate. Cyrus Thomas was now the Smithsonian spokesman, and the battle was no longer fought in the minor journals; the columns of *Science* were now filled with articles on the Davenport finds, pro and con. Finally, if that term can be used in a moderate way, the end of the debate seemed to come in the twelfth Annual Report of the Smithsonian (1894), the Mound Survey volume by Thomas. The tablets and the pipes were discussed in detail and found to be not genuine. They were more "anomalous waifs" without a single support-ing piece of comparative data; Samuel Haven's statement about solitary monuments was seen as correct again.

It seems clear that the Reverend Gass had nothing to do with the tablets. Indeed, the best evidence brought forward by Marshall McKusick, the most recent reviewer of the affair, would seem to implicate Academy members in planting the frauds in the mounds for Gass to find as an ill-advised joke. Evidence was produced, however, to suggest that the good Reverend Gass had been known to trade in fakes, including stone pipes, some of which he gave to the Academy. The elephant pipes seem to have come to hand only when either Gass or his brother-in-law was around. The Putnams and Farquharson seem to have been outside all this—innocent bystanders dragged into the nasty business by their own concern for the Academy and its scientific standing.

How does the actual evidence look from this perspective? The major objects, the tablets, verge on the absurd. The Calendar Stone was obviously done with a compass on a slate from a building near the museum—the two nail holes are there for all to see. The scenic drawings are pathetic—it is denigrating to suggest that they are the work of Indian craftsmen. The work is like that of a grade schooler, and not a very skilled one at that. The limestone tablet is a real joke, with red paint and inset stone eyes in the figure.

The inscriptions are not even as believable as those on the Grave Creek Stone. As I have tried to indicate in the description of the find spots, the contexts are not too believable either. How could the limestone slab have remained buried for many years and not have *any* dirt adhering to it? Why is the context of the tablets in Mound 3 so different from that of the pipes and axes found there earlier? The elephant pipes have virtually no context at all.

So we are left with the artifacts. They are like nothing else that had ever been found there, and they remain unique today. I wish I could say that with Marshall McKusick's lengthy debunking volume (1970), using origi-nal documents and even oral history, the Davenport Tablets have been laid to rest along with the Cardiff Giant. No such luck—Barry Fell is now producing new translations of the tablets as if they were true records of the past; he blithely dismisses all the contrary evidence. In his eyes, "it seems clear that Iberian and Punic speakers were living in Iowa in the ninth century B.C., making use of a stone calendar regulator whose Egyptian hieroglyphs could apparently be read. The settlers had presumably sailed up the Mississippi River to colonize the Davenport area."[11] Never mind that the mounds are Hopewellian, dating to the time of Christ, and that the actual settlements of these Iberian and Punic speakers have never been found.

What can we learn from these hoaxes? Specialists on the topic have discussed the rationale of these occurrences in terms of the reasons why. There are two aspects. First, why we don't disbelieve: here, indifference, ignorance and superstition, suggestion, and prestige play important roles. In the Cardiff case, ignorance was an important part of its success. Suggestion and prestige had a lot to do with both Grave Creek and Davenport. Second, what are the incentives to believe: financial gain, vanity, a cause, chauvinism and prejudices, thrills, and finally, cultural climate. As an anthropologist I have stressed the cultural climate, but a cause, supported by his ailing son, swayed Charles Putnam at Davenport. Financial gain amply rewarded farmer Newell and George Hull with the Cardiff Giant and even Abelard Tomlinson at Grave Creek. Plenty of adherents lined up for the Davenport Tablets as a result of the prejudices stirred up by Henry Henshaw. Intellectual vanity may well have been Mr. Pickwick's fatal flaw.

How do we handle hoaxes? Henshaw showed us the worst-case scenario—sarcasm and put-down will raise an army of supporters for the very hoax one is trying to debunk. But what about dealing with it on a professional level? Frederic Ward Putnam stayed out of the Davenport case by making no published statements as far as I can determine, although in 1883 he did write a brief note in *Science* about other "Archaeological Frauds." But photos of the tablets in the Peabody Archives carried the notations "frauds" in his handwriting, and he wrote of that opinion to Farquharson. F. W. Putnam would find many other opportunities to be drawn directly into contact with frauds, as we will soon see.

The harshness of the Davenport fight, it seems to me, had a very long-term effect on how the archaeological profession dealt with hoaxes. About the turn of the century, there were two articles in the national journals—Professor A. E. Jenks detailing some fake stone tools being made in the Midwest and Professor Francis W. Kelsey on the fake inscriptions from Michigan. Since then there has been a resounding silence.

In my graduate training, fakes were never mentioned. Although I did graduate work in Ann Arbor, I never was shown the classic Soper frauds Kelsey had debunked. There was no training in recognizing fakes, which makes up such an important aspect of fine arts graduate instruction. Fakes and frauds were left alone—perhaps it was thought that the topic was best treated with silence. There was no point, apparently, in wasting valuable journal space on the subject either.

But that situation has changed somewhat; perhaps we can credit discovery of the Piltdown Forgery with that breakthrough. Fakes are much more openly discussed and written about. It is all to the good because the topic is large and dangerous. The unwary can use fraudulent data without realizing it or sometimes without wanting to know better. All archaeological frauds are not "Pickwickian" in nature; they sometimes go to the very centrality of understanding of a field. As Barnum suggested, "humbugs" can, indeed, dazzle the beholder. We must be ever vigilant.

5

The Walam Olum:
Where Did the Delaware Go?

Time renders justice to all at last.
C. RAFINESQUE, 1836

In this pursuit of truth about the past, I have already made some strong judgments about a number of the participants, such as George Hull and the Reverend Jacob Gass. Hull engineered the Cardiff Giant hoax, but since that fraud was not too serious, my comments are benign. I am prepared to find Gass innocent of making the Davenport Tablets but am still concerned about his possible involvement with some of those fraudulent exotic pipes. I have even urged understanding of the "king of humbug," P. T. Barnum. In historical writing one must always face the problem of dealing with personalities now long dead, whose profiles are mainly the remnant quirks and postures of once lively individuals with all the complexities of one's current friends and colleagues.

With the next major character, Constantine Rafinesque, we must weigh the personal evidence very carefully. We must also try to avoid accepting stereotypical characterizations and let the data draw the picture if we can. It remains difficult to render justice to Rafinesque 150 years after the death of this complex individual.

Constantine Samuel Rafinesque-Schmaltz was, indeed, a character. Born in Galata, a suburb of Constantinople, on October 22, 1783, he died in Philadelphia of cancer of the stomach on September 18, 1840. Chronology is the easiest part of his life; what went on between those two dates is the stuff biographers would kill for. There are some biographies of Rafinesque but none that does this extraordinary person justice, if that is possible.

Constantine Rafinesque was a legend in his own time. Descriptive words that leap to mind are *eccentric, egocentric, erratic*. Almost everyone who has ever written about Rafinesque has used and overused those epi-

Constantine S. Rafinesque

thets; I did, too, until I got to know him better. It is very easy to pick up these stereotypical phrases, and everyone uses the same incidents to prove their points. That is hard to avoid when they include John James Audubon telling tales of a midnight bat attack by his house guest, Rafinesque, who is clouting and collecting bats in his bedroom, running about naked and using Audubon's favorite violin as the collecting instrument. One would have to admit that he was a colorful character.

But what he was really like is hard to tell. His appearance was remarkable, but was he large or small? Some say he was small, others give his height as 5 feet 10 inches; certainly he looks diminutive in his portraits. His dress was remarkable—he had a flair for the unconventional, possibly more for financial reasons than for extravagant taste. He was perennially out of pocket and probably wore what he could lay his hands on or was given. But the one sure thing about him was his personal commitment to his intellectual pursuits—he was in perpetual motion, gathering data, writing, always writing, and he had a genuine mania for publication. His bibliography contains more than nine hundred items, but sheer numbers are not an honest measure. Many of these publications are brief notices, a few paragraphs in length, or republications of earlier materials.

What is really important to know about Rafinesque is that he was a very talented human being; he wrote his articles in four languages, and his works ranged from short love poems to 248-page epics, from brief historical notices to lengthy and scholarly monographs. They covered economics, history, and most of the field then called natural history—botany, zoology, and geology—as well as archaeology. He initiated, edited, wrote, and published half a dozen journals, short-lived though they were. He originated more new species names than Linnaeus, collected thousands of specimens, mostly botanical, and drove many of his friends and acquaintances away from him with his tireless seeking for knowledge in three different directions all at the same time. He was not easy to work with; his only substantial position in America was at Transylvania University in Lexington, Kentucky, where he taught from 1819 to 1826, until he resigned as a result of disputes with the administration. Rafinesque was both erratic and difficult, to be sure; but he probably also had a special genius—certainly he was not insane, as some have suggested.

Rafinesque had early evidenced strong interest in natural history and, through family travels, was exposed to a broad range of such experiences: natural history and travel were ever to be his life. He spent most of his youth in Italy and France, where he seemed to get most of his broad education through self-directed readings. In 1802 he and his brother first came to America and landed in Philadelphia. He arrived with letters of introduction and spent about two years in the States, variously working for a merchant in Philadelphia, traveling and collecting natural history specimens in the East, and meeting important people, including President Jefferson. The Philadelphia merchant was John Clifford; that connection would later turn out to be very significant.

In 1805 Rafinesque returned to the Mediterranean and spent a decade in Sicily before returning to America in 1815. His return did not have an auspicious beginning as his vessel was shipwrecked at its landfall near New York and all his collections, books, and manuscripts were lost. Disconsolate and in dire straits, he got help from friends. Soon he began his scientific ramblings in America again that were to characterize his life, meeting new people and seeing new sights, seemingly without end.

But why are we interested in Constantine Rafinesque in this volume? That part of his story begins when he finally ends up at Transylvania University in Lexington, Kentucky. The university was the first institution of higher learning west of the Alleghanies, headed by President Horace Holley. Rafinesque came in the midsummer of 1819 as the Professor of Botany and Natural History, with Modern Languages added later. He got the position through the help of his old acquaintance John Clifford, formerly of Philadelphia, but then a Lexington resident.

It was during a stay that would last seven years in this post that Rafinesque was to do most of his work with the American Indians and related antiquities. Transylvania had a very fine library so his scholarship was not held back by his being in the "boondocks." Rafinesque had seen his "first Indians or ancient natives," as he put it, in 1802 during his initial visit to America. He thought the natives of North America had a "Tartar or Siberian origin," while those of Mexico and South America were "chiefly of oriental or atlantic origin," but this is getting ahead of the story. "It was near Chillicothe [in 1818] that I saw the first great monuments and pyramids or altars, of the ancient nations of N. America; they struck me with astonishment and induced me to study them."[1]

While in Lexington, Rafinesque found plenty of opportunity to continue this interest in the Indian mounds, not the least of which was that his friend Clifford was interested in the subject too. Clifford started a monthly magazine, the *Western Review,* the very summer (1819) that Rafinesque arrived in Lexington. Therefore, Rafinesque had for the first and last time in his life easy access to unlimited publication; he was like a child left alone in a candy store. He wrote and wrote and wrote: poems, weather reports, a three-hundred-page monograph entitled Fishes of the Ohio River, some archaeology, and more. What a wonderful time for Rafinesque.

His friend John Clifford was really that—the best friend he ever had; Clifford was also in touch with the major archaeologists of the period, including Caleb Atwater, so that Rafinesque had important intellectual contacts in this area. It sounds too good to be true. Unfortunately, the full exposition of the Lexington archaeological group is another story for another place, but the sad ending was that John Clifford died May 8, 1820, and the *Western Review* died with him. Clifford was just in his forties, as was Rafinesque, and this was a crushing blow to Constantine.

But to return to Rafinesque and his archaeology. In a letter to a friend in 1823 Rafinesque listed his accomplishments in archaeology as quite significant, including descriptions and maps of about one hundred monuments in Kentucky and fifty elsewhere; enumeration of all ancient sites in North America, about five hundred; the ancient history and chronology of North America with a short history of each Indian nation; a history of the invasion of North America by the Spaniards, plus the discovery of Tennessee, Kentucky, Missouri, and Arkansas; and comparative vocabularies of all North American Indian languages to prove their affiliations.

These data were set forth in a manuscript, but he indicated that the American Antiquarian Society had turned down the opportunity to publish it. I do know that Rafinesque corresponded with Isaiah Thomas, but I have no details of this contact. Never daunted, Rafinesque published it all privately, in somewhat abbreviated form we must assume, as *Ancient History, or Annals of Kentucky* (1824).

I am fortunate to have a copy at hand, and it is typical of Rafinesque's work. It is not a book; it is a forty-page pamphlet. The title page includes a subtitle that tells us there is a "Tabular View of the Principal Languages and Primitive Nations of the whole Earth." I like that lowercase "whole"— Rafinesque was no braggart. He lists the author as having an A.M., and a Ph.D. The A.M. he did get from Transylvania; the Ph.D. is a little more difficult to locate—it may be a slight transposition of letters from a foreign degree that was bestowed on him. He then lists his academic position and follows with his membership in thirteen learned societies that may not be a complete listing as he concludes with three "&c's." All that was pretty standard for the period, but what of the content?

Annals of Kentucky is a bit of everything Rafinesque had said he had done on this topic in his letter to the friend, and it is vintage Rafinesque. As one commentator has said about the prehistoric reconstructions, "Most amazing [is] the *certainty* with which he works out the movements of past tribes and the names of their rulers, down from the time of invasion."[2] It is a most exciting story covering the whole history of the earth from creation until A.D. 1774 in thirty-one short pages—that would even make the *Reader's Digest* condensed books blush. The geological portion focuses on Kentucky and the surrounding countryside and carries us swiftly through six periods—man is created in Eden in the highlands of Asia in Period 4, followed, of course, by Noah's Flood and finally Period 6 and Peleg's Flood. It is during the latter (for Peleg, see Priest's book) that the huge animals roam Kentucky and end up as the fossils at Big Bone Lick, from which Jefferson sought data.

In Part II Rafinesque's *Annals* gets complicated with another six "chapters" that cover the history of mankind as it relates to Kentucky. During his first period following the "Noachian revolution," America is discovered for the first time, and it keeps being rediscovered ever after. Thus New World prehistory must be seen from a global perspective, and Rafinesque gives us just that. The story is told with a complexity of national and tribal names that boggles the mind. Rafinesque was noted in his biological work for an ability to name species; he certainly wins the gold medal in prehistory. It is hard enough to spell all the names, much less pronounce them. Because he always used local, and one presumes inexpensive, printers, many of his works are flawed by terrible typesetting. This particular work does not seem to have this problem, although how can one know whether tribes with names such as "Apalans, Timalans, Pocons, Popolocas, and Wocons" are misspelled?

Among all these many names, one jumps off the page: the *Talegas,* afterward known as the Talegawes. They were a powerful tribe in the Ohio Valley, and we will meet them again shortly. Meanwhile, far away in another land, the Oghuzian Empire fell, and the battered remnants were driven "to the north-east corner of Asia, came in sight of America and crossing Behring Strait on the ice, at various times, they reached North America."[3] You thought I was jesting, but there you have the arrival of the stalwart heroes of our tale on center stage in Rafinesque's own words. The *Lenaps* (Lenape or Delaware Indians) are one group of those Oghuzian refugees, who, after their northern journey, seek milder climes and finally run headfirst into the powerful *Talegas* as they push eastward across the Mississippi. But they persevere against all odds and fight many other tribes until they end up happily with some of their number east of the Alleghanies, not far from Delaware Bay, where it seems they were headed in the first place.

Why all this interest in the *Lenaps,* anyway? Rafinesque provides more detail on them than any other tribe, especially their wonderful transcontinental journey. It is just happenstance, I guess, but then again maybe not. And why does it capture my interest? The migration story of the Lenape happens to be at the heart of Constantine Rafinesque's most controversial contribution to American anthropology. During his last years, while residing in Philadelphia and enjoying better financial times than ever before, Rafinesque published a veritable flood of words. In 1836, along with his autobiographical *A Life of Travels,* his 248-page poem "Instability," and some botanical works, he published Volume One, in two parts, of a projected series entitled The American Nations.

Tucked away in this volume was a forty-page chapter entitled "Original Annals and Historical Traditions of the Linapis, from the creation to the flood, passages and settlements in America, as far as the Atlantic Ocean &c., till 1820 &c." This chapter included a translation of the Walam Olum, the Migration Legend of the Lenni Lenape. Walam Olum can be interpreted as "red score" or "painted sticks," and it is this part of the saga that is most interesting, for Rafinesque said he obtained a bundle of sticks with Lenape pictographs on them. Each pictograph stood for a verse of the chronicle. Later he obtained, presumably from a Delaware, the "songs" that went along with these pictographs. From these songs, which he translated, he wrote down the migration legend.

Although some demotic sign language of North American Indians was known to exist, nothing like these mnemonic ideographs had appeared before, especially not with a text to go with them. Right from the beginning even Rafinesque knew that there would be doubters, and he cites the work of Loskiel and Heckewelder as supporting evidence for the authenticity of this document and its translation.

Before we get any deeper in this story, let us do a little backtracking. Rafinesque published his translation in 1836, but he completed it in 1833 (the date is written on the manuscript). Where did he get this amazing material? His own statements, short as they are, are ambiguous. He says that he got the pictographic record from the late Dr. Ward of Indiana in 1820, and two years later he obtained the songs in the Lenape language from another individual, name and place unreported. All this took place during his tenure as professor at Transylvania.

We know quite a bit about this interval (1819–25), unlike some periods of his life; indeed, Rafinesque devotes a single chapter of autobiography to his stay in Lexington, and many letters of this period are preserved, especially those to his friend Collins in Philadelphia. There are also the mixed memories of some of his students and other acquaintances at Transylvania. This was a very productive period, yet in all this documentation there is not a single word about his fascinating discovery of a *written* language for the Indians.

Indeed, fourteen years passed between the time Rafinesque acquired the songs and his publication of the Walam Olum. We do know that he was very concerned about people stealing his data. He felt that he had been the victim of intellectual robbery many times; perhaps he was hiding this important find until he could publish it properly. But why did he not gloat over it in his own life story published that same year? It seems very strange.

He left Transylvania in 1825 with mixed feelings; he had had troubles with the President, of a personal nature, and his friend John Clifford was dead. But when he wrote his friend Collins in Philadelphia, he said he was leaving because great financial opportunities were opening up in that city. He was probably covering up his unhappiness with new and somewhat grandiose hopes for the future.

Once in Philadelphia, he began to study the Delaware language. Rafinesque says that he made use of the works "of Zeisberger, Heckewelder and a manuscript dictionary." The translation of the Walam Olum was completed only in 1833, eight years later. "The contents [of the songs] were totally unknown to me in 1824, when I published my 'Annals of Kentucky,' "[4] he tells us in the text that accompanies the published translation in 1836. Why did Rafinesque bring up that subject: a possible connection to his *Annals*? No one else has in the next 150 years. But let's look at the Migration Myth of the Lenapes as translated from these weird pictographs with the aid of dictionaries using the text of the songs obtained by Rafinesque in 1822 from that unnamed source, located we know not where.

The Migration tale starts, as it should, with the beginning of the world by the God Creator (Rafinesque's translation). He quickly takes care of making the land, water, sun, sky, and so on. From then on things go much slower. There are five "books" or songs in all with 183 verses. In Book One we meet the Lenape; they are hunters and gatherers and get along pretty well despite bad weather and evil snakes. Book Two takes us through the flood with the help of Nanabush, a grandfather figure in a canoe.

By Book Three the Lenape have started from Asia, passing over cold and frozen water, which they soon leave behind in a major migration, ten thousand strong, to the eastern land. By Book Four individually named chiefs have appeared; there is dissension as they cross the Great Plains. They go "From the Missouri to the Mississippi," according to Rafinesque's song headings; in the song the river is called "the fish river *Nemasipi*"; its name is hard to read in the original translation because of Rafinesque's overwriting, but it seems to start with an "M" and ends "-issipi."

It is here at the great river that the *Talegas* are found; the Delaware word is *Talligewi*. That is the name of the powerful tribe in the Ohio Valley that the Lenape run into in Rafinesque's 1824 *Annals* story. But he has just taken pains to tell the reader that he could not have known what the Walam Olum contained at that time because he had not deciphered it yet. It seems like an amazing coincidence.

In Book Five things quiet down, peace reigns in Talega land, and they have become farmers. Still, they are pulled to go east, and by verse 37 they reach the seacoast, which Rafinesque identifies as the New Jersey shore. The story ends with the white people coming in big ships.

But that is just the tale in the Walam Olum proper—trust Rafinesque to get the whole story. The next source that he translates is just as enigmatic as the first. He appends a "Fragment" that carries the story forward from A.D. 1600, when the Walam Olum closes, to about 1820. It is translated from the "Linapi" by John Burns. This time Rafinesque skips the Delaware and writes down the story in his own firm hand. But who is John Burns and where did he get this important additional "history" of the Delaware? No one knows. On the original manuscript Rafinesque wrote "This Mpt.

[manuscript] and the wooden original was procured in 1822 in Kentucky";
that is all we have. But didn't he say *1820* and from *Indiana* in the published
version? It is said that "a foolish consistency is the hobgoblin of little
minds," but one might think that Rafinesque would at least have tried to
keep the story consistent.

One might also rightly ask why anyone cares about the Walam Olum
now, what with all these questions and Rafinesque's rather shaky reputation. The answer is that they just could not let it go. "They" includes none
other than Ephriam G. Squier, the energetic Ohio Valley archaeologist,
who had a more opportunistic side to him than I presented earlier. He was a
go-getter. Squier knew of Rafinesque's work in Kentucky, but whether they
ever met I do not know. Squier was much too young to have run into
Rafinesque during his Kentucky days. After Rafinesque's death, his personal papers were sold at auction, and his archaeological notes and plans
came into the possession of Brantz Mayer of Baltimore. Squier "borrowed"
them from Mayer in 1846 and quickly made good use of them; he published
six site plans from Rafinesque in the famous *Ancient Monuments* volume in
1848.

Squier gave a paper with a new presentation of the Walam Olum the
same year. It was published in 1849. Although it does present the pictorial
symbols for the first time, since apparently Rafinesque could not afford to
have them copied in his version, the text is carelessly done. There are
omissions, and some pictographs are turned upside down. Squier's version
includes only two books given in translation and that taken directly from
Rafinesque; the rest is a free translation only. It is not too useful. But by
virtue of its uniqueness, Squier's version was reprinted twice in the century.

Squier also published the short *Monograph of the Ancient Monuments of
the State of Kentucky* in 1849; thus he obviously made much use of Rafinesque's data he had so fortunately acquired. After a diplomatic career in
Middle America and Peru, a bit more archaeology and exploration, and a
stormy marriage, Squier tragically ended his busy life in and out of a mental
asylum on Long Island. Perhaps that was justice for Rafinesque.

The next person to tackle the Walam Olum was quite a different sort:
Daniel Garrison Brinton (1837–99) was a scholar and a gentleman. He had a
medical degree and, at the time he studied Rafinesque's little mystery, was a
scholar at the Academy of Natural Science in Philadelphia. He would later
hold the first professorship in anthropology at the University of Pennsylvania. He was certainly in the right place and at the right time to tackle the
problematic Walam Olum.

Walam Olum Symbols

The papers Squier had so swiftly borrowed and used were nearly a decade in being returned to Mayer in Baltimore. Brinton purchased the Rafinesque documents, papers, and maps, including the Walam Olum, from the Mayer family following Brantz Mayer's death in 1879 and later deposited them in the University Museum, where they still remain.

Brinton, considered along with a handful of scholars such as Putnam, Powell, and Lewis Henry Morgan to be one of the founding fathers of American anthropology, was broad-gauged in his approach to the field. He made contributions in all aspects of anthropology, including pioneering shell heap archaeology in Florida (1856–59), where he preceded Jeffries Wyman, and he even made a few efforts in physical anthropology. His most important contributions were those in linguistics; thus it is no wonder that he should tackle the Walam Olum.

The Delaware homeland was close at hand, and Rafinesque's unhappy ghost must still have prowled the streets. Brinton's book *The Lenape and Their Legends* was published in 1885 so he must have turned to these researchers soon after he got the materials from the Mayer family. He attacked the problem head-on: the subtitle of the volume he produced included the phrase "an Inquiry into Its Authenticity."

Brinton was not unfamiliar with linguistic frauds; that very year he was involved in the exposure of a hoax of the Taensa language, in which two young Frenchmen made up documents for this American Indian tribe in the Mississippi Valley and fooled a number of French scholars for some time. They had created an impressive series of materials, including a grammar and some native songs. It even took in Albert Gatschet, by then an aged scholar at the Bureau of American Ethnology. Brinton's exposé was courageous and correct. He pointed out that the French had done this sort of thing before—made up a language out of whole cloth. It is too bad he seemed to forget about Rafinesque's national heritage, for Brinton came out strongly in favor of the authenticity of the Walam Olum.

He started his inquiry of Rafinesque with a brief biographical sketch; it would be a decade before the first full-scale treatment of Rafinesque's life was published. Brinton critically reviewed Rafinesque's work in natural history and often found it wanting, citing expert testimony in that vein. In archaeology he mentioned Samuel Haven's critical views; he called *Ancient Annals of Kentucky* "an absurd production, a reconstruction of alleged history on the flimsiest foundation."[5] Rafinesque's later work *The American Nations* got the same treatment from Brinton; he said: "Its pages are filled with extravagant theories and baseless analogies."[6]

With critical comments like that, one might think that the Walam Olum would get similar treatment. Not at all; Brinton traced Rafinesque's interest in signs and pictographs, a topic that often popped up as a concern. For example, in *Annals* Rafinesque stated that the "Atalans," who built the circular earthworks in the Ohio Valley before the Peleg Flood, "knew geometry, architecture, astronomy, *glyphic signs,* or *writing;* the use of metals, [and] agriculture" (emphasis added).[7] With the exception of the writing, this description is not too far off our current views of the Hopewellian culture that was responsible for all the elaborate earthworks discussed earlier. And this was in 1824, before the Grave Creek find.

In Rafinesque's last major archaeological publication, *The Ancient Monuments of North and South America,* which he produced in 1838 and to which I have not previously referred, he spoke about the writing abilities of the prehistoric peoples. The pamphlet was not unlike *Annals* in its broad coverage and its nonstop discussion of diverse topics through its twenty-eight pages. He did manage to get in a nice jab at Josiah Priest, whom he had rightly accused of stealing from his works for inclusion in his *American Antiquities.*

As usual, his historical reconstructions in *Ancient Monuments* were based on worldwide connections. I am surprised that Rafinesque has not been a favorite of the latter-day hyper-diffusionists, but perhaps his eccentric reputation has tainted his data even for them. But the strangest aspect of this work, published two years *after* the Walam Olum translation, is that although Rafinesque frequently mentioned "inscriptions" and even said, "Several nations of North America had a language of signs made or written; although known sometimes to but few, these signs or symbols . . . were used as records, in coloured strings or knots [the Peruvian "Quipu"], wampums, belts, collars."[8] Then he said, "Painted symbols or hieroglyphies, were used . . . in North America, from Florida to New Mexico," but he still made no direct mention of the significance of his Walam Olum discoveries.

The one important contribution of the work is his explanation, found on the very last page, of just how he operated intellectually, and I repeat it in full:

> In my work on Historical Palingenesy [a brand new word] or the restoration of ancient nations and languages presumed lost, I have been able to restore many of all the parts of the world (but chiefly America and Europe) in the same manner as I once did for the Haytian nation and language, whereby many historical links will be evolved and traced. My process is similar to that of

Cuvier and modern Paleontologists, who restore extinct animals by fragments of their bones. I do the same with extinct languages by fragments of their words and elements, discovered and put together. (Rafinesque, 1838, 28)

This may well be the first anthropological use of the "toe bone to whole dinosaur" analogy that haunts us even today. Like many myths, it has some scientific truth; with a definitive enough fossil part one can recognize and properly identify the whole animal; the same is true of some archaeologically derived specimens, but unfortunately the detailed comparative background to accomplish this feat is not easily acquired. Georges Cuvier, Rafinesque's model, was, of course, one of Europe's most noted scientists and not a shabby person to compare oneself with. At least we do see, however, how Rafinesque felt he could safely go from a few linguistic comparisons to the whole history of a nation, absurd as that method was. Surely Brinton understood this situation too. Why, then, did Brinton accept the Walam Olum, which even its own author would not tout given the best of all chances to do so?

Brinton did face the problem squarely: "Was the WALAM OLUM a forgery by Rafinesque?" he asked.[9] He felt early on that Rafinesque's own assertions were "insufficient warranty for the authenticity of this document." He had tried to find the elusive Dr. Ward, but to no avail. He said that it was not enough to prove that the text was in Lenape dialect; "with Zeisberger and Heckewelder at hand . . . it was easy to string together Lenape words." He had the syntax checked by Horatio Hale, a noted linguist, and also by a bilingual Delaware. The latter thought it was "a genuine *oral* composition of a Delaware Indian." There were, however, mistakes, according to Brinton: terminal inflections omitted, forms that were not "Mission Delaware," and some absurdly incorrect translations. All these blunders Brinton saw as evidence that Rafinesque did not forge the document—the errors proved the validity of his story.

But even Brinton had some nagging doubts: "It is true that a goodly share of the words in the earlier chants occur in Zeisberger [the manuscript used by Loskiel cited before]." Brinton found Rafinesque using four superlatives that are in Zeisberger's dictionary and thought that suspicious, but then he found that Heckewelder said that these forms were used by the Delawares in addressing the Supreme Being and was relieved because this was the way the Walam Olum used them. But why should he have been relieved? Rafinesque, too, had Heckewelder's volume; did Brinton make the mistake of misjudging Rafinesque's intelligence and his linguistic ability?

There was another similarity, this time to Heckewelder, that Brinton did not note because he did not discuss the "Fragment" of recent Delaware history translated for Rafinesque by the undiscovered John Burns. A modern scholar has pointed out that this brief concluding portion of the Lenape story offered by Rafinesque contains a historical error concerning the killing of Chief Tatemy—*strangely* (my word), Heckewelder makes the same error.[10] Could use of this same source have caused the unidentified Mr. Burns to make the same mistake?

Brinton's final conclusion was directly stated: the Walam Olum "is a genuine native production, which was repeated orally to some one indifferently conversant with the Delaware language, who wrote it down to the best of his ability."[11]

With Brinton's cachet upon the Walam Olum, it became a standard part of the anthropological data base. In 1907, when the authoritative *Handbook of North American Indians* came out of the Smithsonian, the entry told of the Walam Olum's checkered career at the hands of Rafinesque and Squier but concluded with a lengthy positive quote from Brinton.

The Walam Olum would then lie pretty dormant for nearly half a century, with very little use or major citation in the anthropological literature. Actually, the study of the Indians of eastern North America (ethnography) suffered a decline in this period because interest moved to the "real" Indians in the Southwest and even abroad as with Margaret Mead's studies in the Pacific so that the lack of interest in the Walam Olum is understandable.

Its next proponent came from a very unlikely direction—not from Philadelphia and not an anthropologist—but Eli Lilly of Indiana, a member of the midwestern drug manufacturing family, whose interest was born of the purported locale of the Walam Olum's original find spot, as Rafinesque told it. The mysterious Dr. Ward was from *Indiana,* and the tribal location was from a Delaware group on the White River in the southern part of that state. Eli Lilly was a devoted Hoosier; he was interested in Indiana history, Indiana archaeology, and Indiana Indians. He strongly supported the Indiana Historical Society, and it was through that agency that work on the Walam Olum began.

Eastern archaeology had suffered a decline similar to that of ethnography in the early part of the century, but the situation was changing in the 1930s. By 1937 local Indiana archaeology was primarily in the hands of Glenn Black, a quite well-trained amateur, whose work Lilly was supporting. Other Ohio Valley workers at this time included James B. Griffin, an archaeologist at the University of Michigan; Paul Weer, from the Indiana Historical Society; Carl and Erminie Voegelin, linguists studying American Indian languages; and George Neumann, a physical anthropologist. All would ultimately be caught up in the interdisciplinary study of the Walam Olum.

Jobs and research funds were scarce in those Depression days, although one positive outgrowth of the hard times was the commitment of government funds to archaeology through excavations carried out primarily in the Southeast with labor and direction from Works Progress Administration (WPA) funds. This research, beginning in 1933 and at first especially focused on the Tennessee Valley Authority dam sites of the Tennessee River, was to revolutionize our understanding of the magnitude and chronology of the prehistory of the American Southeast. No longer would it be the poor stepsister to the elegant and exciting Pueblo/Cliff Dweller archaeology of the romantic and colorful Southwest.

Eli Lilly was the catalyst in 1937, and the Walam Olum was the object of study, but the project was conceived in the broadest terms. At this point, it is hard to say whether this conception was Lilly's view or that of the opportunistic researchers who wished to study the area first and then solve the Walam Olum problem, if that was possible. Lilly was a willing donor, whatever the case may have been. Archaeology was carried on as far east as New York and Pennsylvania; the Voegelins' linguistics touched on Siouans and Iroquois as well as the Delaware, Algonkin speakers.

By 1945 Lilly was happy with the research program and agreed to another short round of excavations and more research, which was completed by about 1950. The magnum opus was published by the Indiana Historical Society in 1954. Its title was long enough to satisfy even Rafinesque: *Walam Olum or Red Score: The Migration Legend of the Lenni Lenape or Delaware Indians. A New Translation, Interpreted by Linguistic, Historical, Archaeological, Ethnological, and Physical Anthropological Studies.* It included an excellent photographic copy of Rafinesque's manuscript, pictographs and all, borrowed from the University Museum in Philadelphia.

How did the anthropological jury that Lilly had assembled and supported find for the Walam Olum? Well, the flesh is weak and the duty strong—it was authenticated again, or at least strongly supported from many different angles. Actually, the question of authenticity was not dealt with as directly as Brinton had done. It fell to Paul Weer to review the historical background of the painted records, Rafinesque's discovery of the Red Score, and the manuscript that told the migration legend. He did no better than Brinton in tracking down the elusive Dr. Ward, and he threw off the unknown John Burns with a shrug. Not that he didn't try. His efforts are convincing, and he is a good scholar, but he found no more skeletons in Rafinesque's closet. He let Brinton's general conclusions stand without further testing.

The linguistic analysis is the most crucial and in some ways the most disappointing. The Voegelins keep telling us that it is in Lenni Lenape, but no one has ever doubted that. How good is the Delaware? They don't ever really tell us. They correct Rafinesque's translation, removing some of his localisms like "New Jersey Shore," and their version is a bit stiffer and more "traditional." They also comment on the pictographic content in some detail: these tend to be such simple drawings—stick figures and the like—that nothing very creative can be said. They, like so many before them, do quite thoroughly compare the language of the Walam Olum to contemporary speakers and dialects with a success level they feel is satisfactory. But in all candor, there is a mushiness in this work that does not inspire all the confidence one would like to have. It is a bit too close to what one feels the donor would want to hear.

There is a rather detailed and somewhat embarrassing Pictograph Concordance by Lilly himself. The embarrassment is over some of the simple comparisons between the Walam Olum pictographs and symbols used by the early Chinese. I would not call it a happy use of the comparative technique. Lilly's other contribution is on the chronology of the migration of the Lenape based on the Walam Olum, and it is flawed as well. Even by the mid-1930s the overall chronology of the North American Indians was beginning to expand considerably. By the 1950s, when radiocarbon dating arrived, this expansion had become a flood. Eastern prehistory stopped taking a backseat to the West; preceramic cultures were known to have time depths of thousands of years. Lilly's own chronology would have the Lenape cross Bering Strait in A.D. 366 and the Mississippi River about A.D. 1000. Such dates are so far from our best efforts at dating today, or even in 1954, that they bear no possible relation to reality. James B. Griffin, one of Lilly's researchers, said just that in a subsequent book review, carefully and kindly worded, so as not to offend.

Such a chronological position left Glenn Black, who was close personally to Eli Lilly, with very little to say positively about the relationship of archaeology to the Walam Olum. After all, it was Black who had started the quest. He gives us nearly forty pages of prehistory, little of which, by his own admission, has anything to do with the topic at hand. Also, the field of

Historic Archaeology had not been adequately developed at that time to help in fine-tuning the last historic movements of the Delaware; the very early movements were clearly mythical.

After all, what was the purpose of the whole venture? It was to validate tribal history, as Squier stated in his 1849 publication; and Brinton could still try to make the tie between history and legend because in 1885 they were still searching for chronology in the prehistoric past any way they could get it. But such was certainly not the case in 1954. The Bering Strait crossing was then thought to have occurred ten thousand to twenty-five thousand years ago. They did not need carbon 14 to tell them that; geological dating—fossil animals and all that—gave them the order of magnitude in a perfectly acceptable fashion.

So by the time Lilly's Walam Olum study project was completed, the major pursuit had already achieved, or rather, been set aside as no longer a very significant question. It is not very important now to test the historicity of the Delaware migration myth. It was just fun and games as to whether old Rafinesque had been pulling a fast one. As I write, another *Handbook of North American Indians* is being published by the Smithsonian. How does it treat the Walam Olum? The Delaware are discussed at some length without a single historic or nostalgic reference to the Walam Olum; that is a bit too much of an antihistorical bias, I would say.

But neglecting to mention the Walam Olum is not an isolated action taken by the Smithsonian. There are four major biographical sources on Rafinesque dating from 1894 to 1949; not one of them mentions the apparently unmentionable Walam Olum. Why? One answer has to be that all four focus on Rafinesque's botanical and natural science contributions, although some of them do, at least, recognize his archaeological work; still not a mention is made of the significance of the Walam Olum. Did they feel that they knew something unfortunate about it and therefore did not want to expose their biographies to further scorn? I don't think that likely in all four cases; maybe the work did not seem that important to them. There are three post-Lilly discussions of the Walam Olum: by John Witthoft (1955), con; C. A. Weslager (1972), pro; and Regna Darnell (1988), con. The battle continues.

We've spent enough time on it—Rafinesque is a "crazy" guy. How do I vote on this case? I think there was a Delaware migration myth. I think Rafinesque may have found someone to "sing" it for him; on the other hand, he was very facile with languages, and Heckewelder's version was a good foundation to build on. I do not think that the red score (the painted sticks) ever existed, and I do think that Rafinesque created the pictographs.

So we return to our familiar trio: Curiosity, Testing, and Veracity, and the greatest of these is veracity. We apparently cannot get the final answer except from that eternal "blithe spirit" whose mortal remains are now apparently enshrined in a crypt at Transylvania College. Rafinesque's body was exhumed from his modest grave in Philadelphia in 1924 with the aid of Henry Chapman Mercer. But there are those who doubt that the right bones were, in fact, moved to Kentucky. Rest well, Constantine Rafinesque, wherever you are; your final reward is yet to come.

6

The Earliest Americans:
The Elusive Prize

. . . and also, that, in the event of the discovery in America of human
remains or implements of an earlier geological period than the present, especial attention be given to their study.
GEORGE PEABODY, 1866

If the tracing of Native American migration myths is now seen as quaint
nineteenth-century antiquarianism, our next encounters are with a topic
that remains at the top of America's "Most Significant Question" list:
EARLY MAN IN AMERICA. In our continuing search for new evidence, we
do not have to leave the Philadelphia area, broadly considered, because
important work took place at the Abbott farm near Trenton, New Jersey,
which is just across the river. It was here in the Delaware River Valley that
the Peabody Museum's Frederic Ward Putnam was bent on showing that
Paleolithic-like stone tools could be found in glacial gravels of Pleistocene
age.

I mentioned earlier Putnam's involvement in this important question.
The Peabody Museum's work at this site grew out of Putnam's use of local
amateurs, who usually contacted him with news of their finds. Such was the
case with Dr. Charles C. Abbott, a dedicated antiquarian, who first contacted Putnam in 1876. Their archaeological relationship would last well
into the new century, with Ernest Volk overseeing much of the actual
digging for the Peabody Museum, which continued as late as 1910. The
search for Early Man was almost an obsession with Putnam.

Abbott had discovered crude artifacts that had eroded out of the
riverbank; the archaeological challenge was to find them in stratigraphic
context—deeply buried within the old gravels, with no chance that they
had slipped into this position from a later occupation. It was here that the
battle would be joined between the Harvard believers and the Smithsonian

skeptics, including William H. Holmes. But there was to be one individual who would straddle the fence in a most peculiar fashion; he was Henry Chapman Mercer (1856–1930). Born in Doylestown, Bucks County, Pennsylvania, of an old and well-to-do family, he graduated from Harvard in the class of 1879, where his classmates termed him "a man of unusual character and imagination, handsome, winning, interesting—and odd." This characterization would also have fitted his friend Clarence B. Moore, of the class of 1873, who lived in nearby Philadelphia, for he shared Mercer's avocational interest in American archaeology; both were to be lifelong bachelors.

Mercer gave the law a brief try, but in 1880 at the age of twenty-four and just a year out of Harvard (he had spent a couple of years in Europe before attending college) he became a founding member of the Bucks County Historical Society, which remained a focus of interest for the rest of his life. Just about this time some interesting "Indian rocks" were turning up on the Hansell farm right in Bucks County. Picked up from the plowed fields as early as 1872, these artifacts included, besides the commonplace chipped stone arrowheads, some ground stone objects. One well-made piece had two holes drilled in it. The artifact had been broken in two, but "remarkably" the separate pieces were recovered and rejoined; the last part was found in 1882. The young farm lad who found them sold the whole lot,

Charles C. Abbott   Henry Chapman Mercer

arrowheads and all, to a collector friend of Mercer's named Henry D. Paxson.

These objects were of great interest to some of the Bucks County populace, especially the broken two-hole gorget. The amazing thing about this ground stone gorget, now whole, was that it had rather elaborate pictures incised on both sides. One side contained some twenty small pictographs: animals, fish, and objects; the other side was even more startling for it showed a scene of a large elephantlike creature raising havoc with the resident Indians, even trampling one poor wretch underfoot. How do we know they are Indians? Well, who else goes around with feathers in their hair and bow and arrows at hand, and there were their tepees in the woods nearby. Sure they were Indians, and this artifact, soon to be christened the Lenape Stone, proved once and for all that Man and Mammoth coexisted in this area.

Who should take up the cause of this "great" object, some four and a half inches long and made of slate but Henry Mercer. By 1885 he had published a handsome little book, *The Lenape Stone; or The Indian and the Mammoth*. It was a well-researched volume, and he received important help from the work of Rafinesque. According to Mercer, the twenty pictographs were a condensed version of the Migration Myth of the Lenape. Granted, one had to skip about the stone from one selected drawing to the next in no apparent order, unless one "knew" the story it told. Mercer consulted with his mentor, Putnam, at Harvard about this "reading" of the stone and was advised to use restraint in his more elaborate interpretations of the pictographs. But impetuous youth won out, unfortunately; this was Mercer's first book.

Students are like that; Putnam apparently did not strike out strongly against the Man and Mammoth association, perhaps because he would have liked to have such data to help his case for Early Man, but his correspondence has not been thoroughly searched on this topic. The truth is that Putnam never used the Lenape Stone data in his published arguments in support of his position, which indicates that he must have felt less than confident about the quality of the information.

It would be unfair to skip over Mercer's study of the Lenape Stone too quickly for it is quite a remarkable little volume. Mercer, unlike so many others we will encounter in our review of Fantastic Archaeology, truly presents an impartial treatment of the artifact. He points out (1) its uniqueness, (2) that no scientific observer was present at the discovery, (3) that it has been too well cleaned to allow for proper tests for authenticity, and (4) that many archaeological frauds have been perpetrated recently.

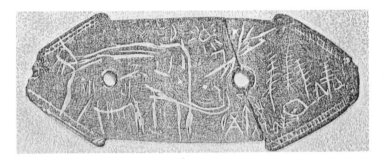

Lenape Stone (back and front)

Mercer's comparative sections are thorough, both in American and in European archaeology, including France. The interpretative sections are impressive in their selections and coverage. His Appendix details the circumstances of the finding with sworn statements and the like. He also got specialists to look at the stone and the engravings. Most felt that the lines looked very fresh. Putnam, as I said, equivocated; he first thought it was a fraud, but later he was not so sure. Brinton, turning his hand to archaeology, made short work of it—it was a fake. But remember, Mercer did print the negative votes, an uncommon practice.

But he went too far; to our sorrow, he got some more engraved rocks from the site. There are three of these, the last one found when Mercer had an excavation made on the site. All three discoveries were made by Bernard Hansell, who had found the original Lenape Stone. I say *sorrow* because, as a unique find, it had a special quality, fake or not, but all three new stones have exactly the same sort of drawings, made, I dare say, by the same hand. The last one has water, bows and arrows, and wigwams engraved on it just like the Lenape Stone. I would like to have suggested to Bernard that this was simply too much!

The new inscribed stones were all probably genuine prehistoric artifacts; one is a bannerstone or atlatl weight of familiar form, but the engravings are all quite new. The contextual data that may still be recoverable are the other surface-collected artifacts from the Hansell farm, the arrowheads and such. We know the typology and chronology of such artifacts well enough today so we can readily date the collection and see what the real prehistoric occupation of the locality was like. None of the artifacts dates to a period contemporary with the mammoth.

Even though Mercer made a good case for his rather outrageous artifact, it got very little notice either then or now. No one even mentions the other three "associated" finds. Today, we can look critically at the artifact and have to restrain a guffaw. We know that this familiar type of ground stone gorget with two holes dates no earlier than 1000 B.C. and had its greatest popularity in early ceramic times just before the time of Christ, thousands of years after the mammoth became extinct.

A careful examination, as even Mercer noted, shows that the incised decorations do *not* cross the break in the artifact, clearly indicating that the lines were drawn *after* the fracture occurred, and thus they are not contemporary with its use as a complete artifact. The scene that appears on the gorget is so full of stereotypical symbols that one does not know where to begin: the tepee and the calumet, for starters, but why go on? It is a fraud, and so were the other incised artifacts that were quickly "discovered" at the Hansell farm, but Henry Mercer believed in the lot of them for decades.

That fact is part of the "peculiar posture of Mercer" that I referred to before. He was bamboozled by the Lenape Stone, and then in the decade after 1890 he produced quality excavations described in his 1897 volume *Researches upon the Antiquity of Man,* which showed quite clearly that the data Putnam and Abbott were pushing in the Trenton gravels were not proof of Pleistocene man in the Delaware Valley.

Unfortunately, this impressive work, published by the University of Pennsylvania, where Mercer was then Curator at the University Museum's Department of American and Prehistoric Archaeology, has had little impact on discussions of this important argument. Perhaps his association with that strange artifact the Lenape Stone blocked acceptance of the clear stratigraphy at the site of Lower Black's Eddy, where he suggested there was possibly a preceramic early level in a well-excavated stratigraphic section. He was right. Similar stratified finds would not be made and accepted in the area for decades.

How did all this take place? In an appropriate but heartrending switch, Mercer had in 1894 replaced his old friend Charles C. Abbott as Curator at the University of Pennsylvania Museum. Abbott, Putnam's protégé and Mercer's field companion, had always yearned for a professional post, but he turned out to be unable to cope with the daily responsibilities the curatorship entailed. Mercer, in his curator's post at Penn, had been following carefully W. H. Holmes's pioneering work in the Washington, D.C., area. He scouted out some quarry sites, such as Holmes had dug, as well as a nearby domestic site, and proceeded to do some excellent fieldwork there. Mercer, therefore, who had been a student of Putnam's and a field survey buddy of Abbott's, was also able to stay in close touch with Holmes. He alone seemed able to bridge the Early Man chasm between Cambridge and the Smithsonian.

Unfortunately for the field, Mercer actually stayed with archaeology only for that decade (1890–1900); by the turn of the century he was well off in another career direction. He had taken up pottery as a folk industry, after seeing some Yucatecan potters at work in Mexico. The rest of his life would be devoted to folk culture. He built an extraordinary concrete mansion called Fonthill in his beloved Bucks County, filled it with farm tools, Conestoga wagons, and the like, and ran a successful pottery and tile works. It remains as a museum today.

Maybe his Cambridge classmates were right; Henry Mercer was not your typical Harvard graduate, but he accomplished much, and he did care. A Henry Mercer discovered and placed a marker on Rafinesque's unmarked grave in 1919, and the same Henry Mercer arranged for those mortal remains to make the final ceremonial trip to Kentucky. Perhaps Mercer, moneyed but a lifelong bachelor, felt a kinship for that much misunderstood and lonely man, whose Walam Olum, "the great national song" as Mercer called it, had helped him "decipher" *his* Lenape Stone.

Coincidence: how does one tell the difference between chance occurrences and those that are arranged? Of course, there are statistical ways to test such happenings, if the sample is large enough and such, but what about our more solitary historical happenings? Is it just coincidence that in many of the cases I study in Fantastic Archaeology long periods of time pass between a momentous discovery and its revelation to the public? Why did Rafinesque hold back so long on the Walam Olum? How hard did he try from 1824 to 1833 to find someone to help him translate his Delaware text? In our next Philadelphia-area case, the coincidence problem occurs in spades with both time lag and some extraordinary similarities of form. Is just coincidence involved? We'll see.

Late in the meeting of the Boston Society of Natural History on

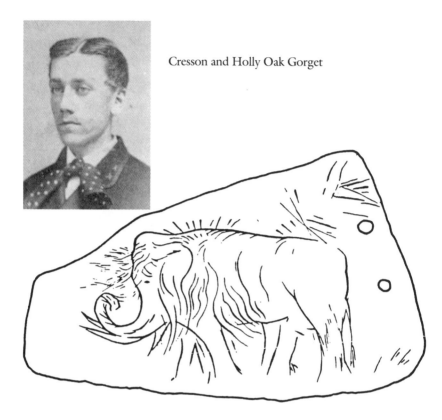

Cresson and Holly Oak Gorget

February 5, 1890, with Frederic W. Putnam presiding, the topic turned, at the president's initiative, to "early man in America and [he] brought forward some new evidence of the contemporaneity of man with mastodon and mammoth. This evidence is a rude figure unquestionably representing a mammoth, scratched on a portion of a Busycon shell [a marine whelk] found under peat in Clairmont County, Delaware [near Holly Oak in the lower Delaware River valley]."[1]

The published record of the meeting includes a lengthy appended paragraph giving, in some detail, the background of the interesting find written by Hilborne T. Cresson. Imagine the only two drawings of mammoths in the whole United States coming to light in the Delaware Valley—first Mercer's Lenape Stone and now Cresson's Holly Oak Gorget. But wait a minute, that is really not the right order, for Cresson said he actually found the object in 1864 but only first revealed it to Putnam just a month before the Society meeting. What went on between 1864 and January 1890—twenty-six years? Well, I said there were some time lags.

The answer will provide us with the background of both the tardy Hilborne Cresson and some apparently related developments in archaeology. We must backtrack to that exciting period after the Darwinian revolution when the French particularly took the lead in "discovering the buried past." The place is the now-famous Dordogne region in southern France, where the odd couple of the French scholar Edouard Lartet teamed up with the English businessman/collector Henry Christy. French savvy and British pounds combined in a most advantageous way to begin the archaeological research in the Upper Paleolithic with startlingly positive results from the rock shelters and caves of that picturesque region.

Suites of tools and associated fauna were found in distinct contexts; then, in 1864, at the La Madeleine rock shelter an even more exciting find was made. On a fragment of mammoth tusk there was found a very clear engraving for a woolly mammoth providing convincing confirmation of man's contemporaneity with that extinct form. Note well the date of the discovery: *1864*. This important discovery was published in 1865, and the engraving soon became one of the most widely reproduced pieces of prehistoric art, ending up in every book on the subject and in popular texts such as E. B. Tylor's *Anthropology*.

What, then, of Hilborne T. Cresson (1848?–1894)? He was born Jones in New York City but took his wife's last name at the time of their marriage as there were no male heirs; the Cressons were a wealthy family of some prominence in Philadelphia. Cresson's personal life is not well known, but we do know that he grew up near Claymont, Delaware, in the Delaware River Valley. It was near here in 1864 at the age of sixteen that Cresson (then Jones) found in the company of M. Surault, his French tutor, the Holly Oak Gorget. This gorget, made of marine shell, was engraved with the stunning likeness of a mammoth.

Workmen had been digging peat for fertilizer and ran into the deposit, which included other prehistoric artifacts as well. On a walk, Cresson and his tutor came upon the excavations and recovered the artifacts. It turned out that the enigmatic Surault knew the soon-to-be famous Edouard Lartet and thus had an interest in archaeology; Surault and Cresson made a rather sketchy drawing of the location and find spot.

Attempts to obtain further data on Surault, or even to locate him in Delaware in the 1860s, have failed. Perhaps we need a better Missing Persons Bureau. The date of discovery and connections to Lartet are a wonderful coincidence because the mammoth drawing on the Holly Oak shell looks remarkably like the one from La Madeleine. Even Cresson, years later, when he came forward with the specimen, mentioned this strong similarity. Some recent commentators have referred to this as "a show of chutzpah."

In the years following the purported Holly Oak discovery, Cresson continued to make interesting discoveries of Early Man in the nearby area, including a rock shelter and some strange underwater pilings on Naaman's Creek. He kept all these findings to himself, making them public much later. For Cresson this hazy interim (1864–80) was filled with some happiness and foreign travel. He married Elizabeth Vaux Cresson in the early 1870s; the Cresson family had a summer place near Claymont, which explains how the two met. By 1875 they had two sons. About that time he, and presumably his family, went to France, where Cresson "pursued studies at the Ecole des Beaux Arts and Ecole d'Anthropologie."[2] He visited museums and saw archaeological sites and collections in France and Switzerland.

Did he see at first hand the famous La Madeleine carving? We do not know; nonetheless, all this exposure to European archaeology was to stand him in good stead back in America. He did return, again presumably with his family, in 1880. Cresson was back in the Philadelphia area and in his amateur archaeological research made use of local museums; in 1883 and 1884 he wrote some short journal articles on prehistoric Mexican musical instruments that he found in their collections.

Cresson then apparently entered more formally into the archaeological profession via Putnam and the Peabody Museum since in 1887 he is listed as a Field Assistant. As part of the Peabody staff, he first worked in his home area of Delaware, again digging at the Naaman's Creek site. At first, he thought it related to the Swiss Lake Dweller pile structures, but later he saw it as an aboriginal fish weir. Cresson then began to look in earnest for traces of Early Man and teamed up intellectually with George Frederick Wright, an even more stalwart proponent of Paleolithic man than his boss, Putnam.

His summer field seasons were obviously filled with work for the Peabody, including assisting in some excavations in Ohio at much later sites. Nonetheless, Cresson took on, at the age of forty, the pursuit of a medical degree, which he completed in the spring of 1891. This period was certainly a very busy time for him, and it was also the time he chose to bring forth the Holly Oak Gorget. All this time the gorget had apparently been languishing in the hands of either Surault or a Mrs. Spencer of New York City, also an unknown personality.

How was the find received after Putnam showed it off in Boston in 1890? Cresson certainly believed that Putnam and also Professor William H.

Dall at the Smithsonian thought that it was "a beautiful specimen of aboriginal American art" and said so.[3] But what *did* Putnam say? Not much, if the truth be known. Putnam never used the engraving of the mammoth as evidence for Early Man in any of his published works. As David J. Meltzer and others have pointed out, however, there is in the Peabody Museum Archives an undated sheet of cardboard with drawings and photos attached that shows the Holly Oak Gorget and the La Madeleine mammoth side by side.

Cresson must have been heartbroken by Putnam's lack of action. Surely this find should have made Putnam's day: it was certain proof of the contemporaneity of Early Man and fossil forms that he had searched for all those years. But all was not well for Cresson. Words of outright disbelief were soon to follow from sources close to home; but first personal tragedy would strike.

In 1891 Cresson was working in Ohio at the Hopewell site under the direction of Warren K. Moorehead, who was making collections at this important Moundbuilder site for the upcoming Chicago World's Fair. Putnam was in overall charge of this operation. On December 4, 1891, Cresson was fired from the site by Moorehead, charged with the theft of specimens. Nonetheless, Putnam apparently kept him on the Peabody rolls until July 1892.

Cresson, it seemed, landed on his feet, showing apparently little outward concern for his dismissal; he got funds to do work on Maya glyphs and spent nearly two years in Mesoamerica, publishing a few short papers on his research. Despite the distance, Cresson could not, I'm sure, have avoided hearing the critical and damning comments of some of his colleagues concerning the Holly Oak find. Brinton, by now a respected spokesman for the field, said in the journal *Science* in 1893 that he considered both the Lenape Stone and the Holly Oak Gorget to be recent. Also, it is reported, there was talk about the accuracy of Cresson's work at Claymont, where the gorget had been found; even Mercer spoke obliquely but very questioningly about this discovery in his publications.

Cresson returned to the United States early in 1894 and spent part of the year traveling up and down the East Coast. His life came to a tragic and abrupt end on September 6, 1894, when he "blew his brains out in a park in New York City." Apparently he had been having strange hallucinations—his suicide note said that "he was suspected of *counterfeiting,* and that Secret Service detectives were continually on his track" (emphasis added).[4] Upon his death, there were recriminations in the profession as to who had caused the tragedy. Let's face it, it was a self-inflicted wound. We can only guess at the real causes; no single individual or specific action was to blame.

By the turn of the century Cresson and the Holly Oak Gorget were almost forgotten, as was the Lenape Stone. They were not worth bothering with. The question of Early Man in America had not been solved—that would not happen until the Folsom, New Mexico, finds in 1926. Indeed, the Smithsonian Institution would even intensify the level of combat over the question of Early Man in America. Ales Hrdlicka of the National Museum, a strong spokesman against the great age position, dealt harshly during the pre-Folsom period with any purported early skeletal finds, but that is another story.

The Holly Oak Gorget may have been lost sight of for a while, but it came back very strong. The May 21, 1976, issue of *Science,* the same journal that had carried Brinton's early cry of fraud, had a larger-than-life-sized illustration of the mammoth from Delaware on its cover. A geologist, John C. Kraft, and an archaeologist, Ronald A. Thomas, were doing a study of paleoenvironment in Delaware and, coming upon references to this interesting artifact, tracked it down at the Smithsonian.

Some scientists there, who were unfortunately not too familiar with either Cresson or the pertinent archaeology, declared it legitimate, which pleased Kraft and Thomas greatly. Tests at the Smithsonian were said to prove that incising was of the same age as the making of the gorget "and near the time of origin of the shell." These "tests" were hardly conclusive; they consisted of merely putting the artifact under a microscope, at which time the technician managed to "crunch" the shell accidentally, causing some damage to it—so much for nondestructive examinations.

Although Kraft and Thomas do suggest five alternative explanations, including fraud, for the gorget's age and origin, there is little doubt where they stand: "Re-examination of old discoveries [the Holly Oak find] . . . has led to an exciting new association of early man with the wooly mammoth in America."[5] Perhaps Cresson should stand up and take a belated bow. Having made the cover of *Science,* the Holly Oak Gorget became famous all over again. It now even appears in an introductory text as an example of Paleo-Indian art.

But never underestimate the Smithsonian Institution; its scientists can do more than crunch shells. Another Smithsonian curator, William Sturtevant, and a Research Fellow there, David Meltzer, answered in *Science* (January 18, 1985) with a strong critique of the Kraft and Thomas article. In a somewhat earlier and much longer discussion entitled "The Holly Oak

Shell Game: An Historic Archaeological Fraud," Meltzer and Sturtevant carefully dissected and debunked Cresson's creation very thoroughly. The second major salvo from the con group, this time including James B. Griffin and Bruce D. Smith, both of the Smithsonian, as well as Meltzer and Sturtevant, appeared in *American Antiquity*. They termed it a "Mammoth Fraud." It should not surprise anyone that Kraft, Thomas, and now a new colleague, Jay F. Custer, refuse to accept this conclusion in their reply to the second *Science* consideration of dear old Holly Oak. Mercer couldn't stand to give up on the Lenape Stone either.

Should we be concerned that "scientists" cannot agree on what is or is not an obvious fake? We shouldn't. For reasons that probably relate to strong interests in the Delaware area—Kraft, Thomas, and Custer are employed there—they feel so strongly about the Holly Oak Gorget that they refuse to consider basic archaeological principles; they forget that Meltzer and Sturtevant studied the find so carefully that they can tell which drawing of the La Madeleine find Cresson probably copied.

Archaeological context is singularly important in judging these cases. Cresson did not provide much: a confused story of the discovery that he told differently each time. But then, when the chips were down, Cresson did give Putnam what he thought he would want and need. He did it twenty-four years late, but he had the gorget photographed "with the materials with which it was found." There are labels still with these artifacts at the Harvard Peabody Museum. These labels, in Cresson's hand, say the objects were found with the gorget. Kraft and Custer insist strongly that this is an association "created in museum drawers." They have every reason to be concerned because the materials Cresson said were found with the shell gorget do not date to the time of the woolly mammoth; to that fact *all* will agree.

Thus something is terribly wrong with the context Cresson provided or created. Occam's Razor slices right through this one—the Holly Oak Gorget, with its wonderful woolly mammoth, is not a genuine prehistoric artifact of any significant age. Indeed, the shell gorget itself, with no engraving on it, may well be from the very late Fort Ancient culture of Ohio. Cresson dug on one such site, and he was fired for stealing artifacts in Ohio. A radiocarbon date recently run on the shell gorget dates it to less than a thousand years ago, but still the Delaware group is not convinced. What will it take? Even Fell's 1988 Epigraphic Society Occasional Publications volume branded it a fake based on the carbon 14 finding!

Meltzer and Sturtevant say they have found no smoking gun pointing to Cresson, but that seems to be a poor choice of words. Cresson, by his own final act, may really have given us the answer himself.

There is a common link in these three cases—Walam Olum, Lenape Stone, and Holly Oak Gorget—and that is the dependency of the "true believers" on old ways of thinking, ones that are nearly a hundred years out-of-date, or to translate into modern jargon, "the retention of out-moded interpretative paradigms." The retention of the Walam Olum as a significant document in Native American history demands that one regard the Migration Myth of the Delaware as a testable hypothesis concerning their actual past. With our current control of the archaeological chronology, that is absurd. We also know that virtually every tribe in the Eastern United States has a myth purporting that they came from the West and crossed a big river. Is this really an ancient memory, not just twenty or thirty generations old but fifteen thousand years old, concerning the crossing of the Bering Strait land bridge? One might just as well expect *Homo sapiens* to have a primordial memory of a distant ancestor's cozy little cottage in Olduvai Gorge.

The continuing support of Holly Oak, and to a lesser extent the Lenape Stone, which Kraft and Thomas mention and do not discard, must depend to a large extent on how the questions about Early Man in America were phrased one hundred years ago and what evidence was scrutinized. If one looks at the artifacts that bear the engravings, not just the picture, one finds the shell and stone gorget definitively of formal types that are temporally anachronistic—thousands of years too young. One must also look at the whole picture; no one wants to stress what is on the back side of the Lenape Stone. All those pictographs, which include a stereotypical long-stemmed pipe or calumet, have no place in Paleo-Indian lifeways as we know them today. You can't just focus on the mini-drama of the marauding mammoth on the Lenape Stone, or not look at the much later artifacts that Cresson unknowingly gave as the "true" archaeological context for Holly Oak. Selective use of data is not *real* testing.

American scholars can take some comfort from the fact that the most famous archaeological fraud in the world, the Piltdown Forgery in England, lasted as long as it did for some of the very same reasons. The "artifacts" and fossils supposedly associated with the skull and jaw fragments were real laughers when they, the purported context of the finds, were finally scrutinized carefully. But that was not done until after the fluorine dating had shown that the skull and the jaw were temporally of very different ages. Context will get you every time!

The breathless search for the Earliest Americans continues to this day, and it has remained a combative struggle of earnest young adventurers each trying to outdo the other for the oldest bone or artifact. Careers have been made and destroyed by the sheer measure of personal involvement. Testing and veracity have remained essential elements of discovery and denouement, and so they should.

7
Catastrophism: Sunken Continents and All That Jazz

And the rain was upon the earth forty days and forty nights.
GENESIS 7:12

That great calamities have struck the earth is a known fact; in my own lifetime I have been witness to, even if usually by remote sensing, devastating hurricanes, engulfing tidal waves, tremendous volcanic eruptions, and atomic blasts. Such events, the last one excepted, also occurred in the past and therefore could, and obviously did, form the background for mythic portrayals of disasters of great magnitude. As pointed out earlier, popular myths usually have some basic truth behind them. Thus when we look at various eighteenth- and nineteenth-century explanations, whether they be in geology with catastrophism or in archaeology as with Atlantis and its destruction, it is against this strong pattern of belief that we must try to understand them.

Of course the Old Testament recorded one of the most famous of these major planetary disasters—the Noachian Flood that covered the world and destroyed all life on the globe save that preserved by Noah and his crowded Ark. The search for the remnants of the Ark is a compelling aspect of Fantastic Archaeology that unfortunately takes us out of our North American sphere unless one follows the 1830s view of Josiah Priest discussed earlier. But the Flood itself is, indeed, a major part of the belief system of Western civilization and thus has to be factored into most of our upcoming discussions of other catastrophes. That is, believing in the Biblical Flood sets the stage for accepting analogous events, no matter how farfetched, be they sinking continents or world-stopping collisions with meteors or comets.

One may well ask what other great disasters gripped nineteenth-century minds besides the worldwide diluvian catastrophe? Events that must have had a major impact on their view of the way the world operated included tremendous volcanic eruptions, such as those in Indonesia at Sumbawa in 1815 and Krakatoa in 1883 and Mount Pelée in Martinique in 1902; earthquakes of great magnitude as in 1755 in Lisbon, in 1783 in southern Calabria, and in 1897 in Assam; and great "sea waves," erroneously called tidal waves, that resulted from earthquakes. Of course, both earthquakes and volcanic eruptions were well known to classical scholars because both occur with great frequency in Italy and Greece: Vesuvius, Mt. Etna, and Stromboli are well-known active volcanoes. Even staid old Great Britain gets its share of earthquakes, more than a thousand having been recorded, only a few dozen of which have been destructive.

Another supposed source of possible catastrophe has been the heavens. Comets and meteors have been observed for thousands of years, and early written records of their appearances have been found archaeologically in both the Near East and the Far East. By the eighteenth century, with the development of Newtonian physics and better telescopes, the periodicity of some of the major comets was well established, as by Professor Edmond Halley of Oxford in 1703, when he predicted the return in 1759 of the comet that now bears his name. It returned on schedule, in 1835, and again in 1910. In its most recent cycle (1985–86) it received its most careful inspection; its "tail" was even invaded by an armored space vehicle. But there were plenty of other comets that were viewed and studied in the nineteenth century besides Halley's. One of their supposed precursors became a *deus ex machina* for Ignatius Donnelly in part of his Atlantis saga.

With this growing understanding of the earth and sky, there appeared by the middle of the nineteenth century a division of opinion as to rates and methods of geologic changes that had been observed that can, in a simplified manner, be characterized as the Catastrophists versus the Uniformitarians. Like all intellectual debates, it was much more complex than that and goes back to the eighteenth century and important figures such as George Buffon and Abraham G. Werner. The significant aspect of the debate was that one group looked on the most important geological mechanisms as similar to those currently perceived—erosion, uplift, glaciers, localized volcanism, and so on. The fossil record showed these changes to be of moderate rate, although extinctions were noted. This side was the "Uniformitarianism" popularly espoused by Charles Lyell, its best-known advocate, whose work had a strong influence on Darwin and the *Annus Mirabilis*.

On the other side were the Catastrophists, who viewed the fossil

Ignatius Donnelly

record as showing that there had been a series of sudden and violent upheavals and floods that had caused widespread extinctions within a limited time span, that of the Biblical chronology in many cases. William E. Buckland was a noted Catastrophist who explained many geological features as resulting from the Biblical Flood; by 1840 he had agreed that glaciers instead had been the active agent.

Lyell and his group ultimately won the intellectual battle, although nineteenth-century Uniformitarianism is much too rigid a concept to be useful today. Most contemporary geologists would agree that there were periods in the past when there was, for example, much more volcanism on a worldwide scale than there is now and that there have been major changes in continental positioning, a phenomenon that would have been termed "fantastic" by most nineteenth-century scholars. Even in this modern age the hypothesis of continental drift had a very difficult time gaining general support because it demanded such a startlingly new view of the way the world worked.

This little digression into geology may seem just that—another sidetrack—but it is hardly such. The use of catastrophic events in the past to help explain the prehistory of the world was a major factor in the nineteenth century. We have already seen Rafinesque use it frequently in his history of mankind, but its major archaeological proponent would hit the big time with it on the popular level that was to change Fantastic Archaeology forever. That best-selling author, who even dragged Prime Minister William E. Gladstone along on his mythical journey into the past, was Ignatius

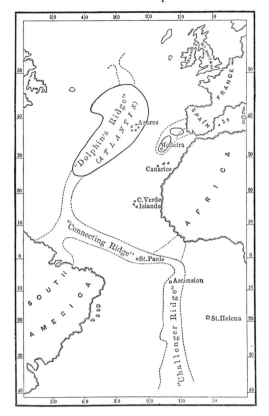

Atlantis in the Mid-Atlantic

Donnelly (1831–1901). His blockbuster duo, published in sequential years, 1882–83, was *Atlantis: The Antediluvian World* and *Ragnarok: The Age of Fire and Gravel*.

I cannot help but feel a special kinship with this remarkable man. My own copy of *Atlantis* was autographed by Donnelly in 1900, in the months just before he died, and is inscribed to an old friend of my grandmother. It is an eleventh edition! It went through many more; it was reset and republished in 1949 and is still in print. It has sold many tens of thousands of copies and remains a major source on Atlantis for a huge number of believers, including the numerous followers of Edgar Cayce, a twentieth-century psychic whom I will discuss later.

What caused the immense popularity of Donnelly's work in the middle of the Gilded Age? First, it is a well-written and convincing tale explaining the past in forthright manner and with just enough specific evidence to make it seem very plausible. Second, the author quickly, and without boring the reader, establishes that he has done his homework. When discussing a mid-Atlantic ridge as the actual site for Atlantis, Donnelly quietly cites a *Scientific American* article from 1877 with the supporting evidence of recent marine soundings. Third, he uses the comparative approach quite well in a multiplicity of fields: geology, physical anthropology, archaeology, linguistics, ethnology, and mythology. It is all pretty convincing.

What is his tale anyway? Quite correctly, Donnelly starts, as must all who discuss Atlantis, with Plato, and he does not stint. He gives great gobs of the original version. He is very Victorian in his scholarship; nothing is treated lightly or briefly—the volume runs to 480 pages and has a very good index. He discusses Plato's presentation of an island of Atlantis west of the Pillars of Hercules, which had a wonderful civilization but then sank beneath the sea, and tests some of the notions of possible destruction against contemporary geological phenomena. But let Donnelly speak for himself:

> Having demonstrated, as we think successfully, that there is no improbability in the statement of Plato that a large island, almost a continent, existed in the past in the Atlantic Ocean, nay, more, that it is a geological certainty that it did exist; and having further shown that it is not improbable but very possible that it may have sunk beneath the sea in the manner described by Plato. . . . An event, which in a few hours destroyed, amid horrible convulsions, an entire country, with its vast population—that population the ancestors of the great races of both continents, and they themselves the custodians of the civilization of their age—could not fail to impress with terrible force the minds of men, and to project its gloomy shadow over all human history. (Donnelly, 1882: 65)

What distinguishes Donnelly's discussion of Atlantis from many others is the logical presentation of the argument. The book opens with a list of thirteen propositions concerning Atlantis, and when he has discussed a topic such as "The Kings of Atlantis become the Gods of the Greeks," he lists the proofs of his proposition, in this case, seven in number. Few writers are as thorough in their presentation or as formal in their exposition of proofs. He uses the comparative method extensively in everything from myths to human complexions. His literary sources show a range of acquaintance from the classical scholars to Francis Bacon, and his archaeological sources range from Rafinesque and Squier and Davis to John W. Foster.

Ignatius Donnelly was born in Philadelphia on November 3, 1831, the son of a well-to-do Irish physician. He was educated in the public schools and graduated from Central High of that city in 1849. He studied law for three years in the office of Benjamin Harris Brewster, later Attorney General of the United States, and was admitted to the bar in 1852. Shortly thereafter he made a trip to the new territory of Minnesota to look at its potential. In 1855 he was married and emigrated to Minnesota early the next year. There, just south of St. Paul, he and some partners had purchased land to develop Nininger City, a would-be metropolis.

Construction began immediately, including a rambling mansion for Donnelly and his young bride, but the financial panic of 1857 wiped out this dream and left a ghost town when the railroad bypassed it. He turned to farming for a few years, but his prowess as a public speaker and his great energy led him to a political career, which saw him elected Lieutenant Governor at the age of twenty-eight. He then went on to serve three terms in Congress, 1863–69, supporting the Civil War and the Reconstruction policies of the Republican party. During this period in Washington he was said to have spent every free moment using the resources of the Congressional Library for personal research.

He failed to be reelected in 1870; the next decade was to be one of great change for Donnelly. He had always had liberal political leanings. Although he supported Reconstruction, he was deeply concerned for the general welfare of the inhabitants of the South. He had also tried to pass legislation to control the railroad land-grant system that had suffered so many abuses. Now, however, he left the Republican party and became editor of a weekly journal, the *Anti-Monopolist*. He was elected to the state legislature and in 1878 ran again for Congress as a Greenback-Democrat but lost. He was living in his rambling mansion, not far from Hastings, Minnesota, surrounded by a sizable library and his research notes from his Washington stint.

It was then in 1878–79 that he took up the Atlantis cause; one commentator has suggested that he was almost ready for the poorhouse because his attempts at farming were not very successful. Internal evidence suggests that he completed his *Atlantis* volume in 1880. Harper and Brothers brought it out in 1882 and soon had to add an extra shift at the printer's to keep up with demand, according to some sources.

While *Atlantis* went through edition after edition, Donnelly brought out his other volume of the same genre, *Ragnarok,* in 1883. The star of this tale was not a sunken continent but a fiery comet, Ragnarok, that smote the earth and was responsible for huge gravel deposits, which Donnelly felt had been attributed wrongly either to the Deluge or to the glaciers. Needless to say, he found much evidence besides the Drift deposits, especially in legends that recorded the comet's arrival among the myths and records of peoples around the world. He felt that the comet came twenty thousand years before the Biblical Deluge and thus about thirty thousand years ago.

As with *Atlantis,* Donnelly presented the data in a straightforward manner, though perhaps even with a bit more verve. He described the chaos after the arrival of the comet as follows:

> They go forth upon a wasted, an unknown land, covered with oceans of mud and stones; the very face of the country changed—lakes, rivers, hills, all swept away and lost. They wander, breathing a foul and sickening atmosphere, under the shadow of an awful darkness, a darkness palpable and visible, lighted only by electrical discharges from the abyss of clouds, with such roars of thunder as we, in this day of harmonious nature, can form no conception of. . . . The world is more desolate than the caves from which they escaped. The forests are gone; the fruit-trees are swept away; the beasts of the chase have perished; the domestic animals, gentle ministers to man, have disappeared; the cultivated fields are buried deep in drifts of mud and gravel; the people stagger in the darkness against each other . . . fear that shrinks before the whirling blasts, the rolling thunder, the shocks of blinding lightning; that knows not what moment the heavens may again open and rain fire and stones and dust upon them. (Donnelly, 1883: 227)

Those describing the aftermath of a nuclear holocaust might do well to take a few lessons from Ignatius Donnelly; he did have a way with words. Such prophecies of doom and destruction would continue in his writings until his dying day. *Ragnarok* was just another chapter in the catastrophic history of the world. Atlantis existed both before and after the arrival of the comet, only ultimately to slip away under the seas as civilizations rose to flower in the Old and New Worlds.

This second volume quite naturally focused more on geology than archaeology, although Donnelly did use Daniel Brinton on myths and John Foster for American archaeology. In his forays into European archaeology we even run into our old friend the La Madeleine mammoth. Perhaps Cresson was a closet Donnelly fan. Donnelly's imagination remained unrestrained in this field, too: he saw evidence in a Dordogne cave drawing of reins on reindeer and thus was convinced that they were domesticated. Some very deeply buried coins associated with clay layers in Illinois were enough data to allow him to state that a Pompeii was under the ground, of inconceivable antiquity—"a civilization was drowned and deluged out of sight under the immeasurable clay-flood of the comet."[1] Not surprisingly, *Ragnarok* was a publishing success too.

Primeval Storm from *Ragnarok*

To further his cause and sales, in these days before television morning and talk shows, Donnelly took the next best route. He went out to the lecture platform. He has been characterized as a portly man, good natured, smooth shaven in a day of beards, and well received by audiences.

Instead, he returned to writing and politics. Donnelly began to write his magnum opus, *The Great Cryptogram; or Francis Bacon's Cipher in the Shakespeare Plays,* and returned to Congress for a two-year term (1886–88). His eight-hundred-plus-page volume supporting the thesis that Bacon was the *real* author of the Bard's plays was published in 1888. It is an enormous piece of work.

Donnelly, writing in longhand with apparently no outside help, carried out his tireless analysis of a purported arithmetical cipher that was lurking in the Shakespeare Folios. The project is truly as amazing as it is foolish. It makes one cringe to think of the vast amount of time and energy spent on this fruitless task. The volume generated much interest, however, along with arguments with proponents of other worthy candidates for the mantle of the "real author" of the Shakespeare plays. Chicago was the scene of a vitriolic lawsuit on the topic in 1916, as aging newspaper clippings preserved in my copy of *The Great Cryptogram* indicate.

How do we evaluate Ignatius Donnelly today? First we must separate his impact from his scholarship. There is little question that he is the true father of the nineteenth-century Atlantis revival and the reason the myth has had such a long and verdant history; his work is surely the reason that the term can be used and reused in the popular press today with such quick recognition. Donnelly, a devoted Francis Bacon fan, built on Bacon's utopian use of Atlantis and was only one of a number of mid-nineteenth-century writers to tackle the subject. It was Donnelly, however, who hit the jackpot.

In assessing the quality of Donnelly's *Atlantis/Ragnarok* duo, I have been generous in my praise of his organizational skills. He presents the ideas in a logical way, although it is sometimes a bit difficult to run down exact sources and the like. I will focus mainly on the North American segments of his proposition because they are typical of his work and are most germane to this volume. I have said that Donnelly uses the comparative approach in many of his proofs; however, in *Atlantis* he selectively compares Choctaw and Shawnee Indians with Mediterranean physical types in a most superficial way.

Donnelly's archaeological comparisons of Natchezan pottery of the Mississippi Valley with that of the Swiss Lake Dwellers, the copper spearhead of Lake Superior with bronze hatchets also from Switzerland, and copper axes from Indiana with ones from Ireland are hopeless. They are all prime examples of the Radner and Radner grab-bag approach that is as easy as it is useless; it proves nothing. The artifacts are torn from their chronological and cultural contexts and shown side by side just because the forms are similar. Almost all copper axes worldwide have similar shapes, based on the simple and necessary relationship between form, function, and level of technology of manufacture. Actually it is even more interesting anthropologically if they do not resemble each other.

The same criticism can be made of the myths and legends that he details in both volumes. Donnelly found stories of floods and catastrophes around the world, but as Sir James Frazer, the well-known scholar of *The Golden Bough,* indicated that if many flood traditions were based on reminiscences of actual catastrophes, then there is no good reason for suggesting that such traditions are older than a few thousand years at most. Sprague de Camp, the current Atlantis student par excellence, who called Donnelly's book the "New Testament of Atlantism," also said, "Most of Donnelly's statements of fact, to tell the truth, either were wrong when he made them, or have been disproved by subsequent discoveries."[2]

I am not sure I would go that far, but then I have admitted my pro-Donnelly bias from the start. Actually I have only mentioned some of the

North American data; in a chapter entitled "The Colonies of the Mississippi Valley" he meets the Moundbuilder question head-on and finds significant proof of a connection to Atlantis, using mainly Foster and Squier as his sources. The Davenport Tablets had just been found, and Donnelly, although a bit hesitant, reproduced some of the glyphs in support of his Atlantis connection. His use of linguistic evidence was, indeed, one of the weakest links in his series of proofs and noteworthy for the sort of errors that de Camp stressed.

Whatever the facts, Ignatius Donnelly was believed by many. His career in both writing and politics did not end with his huge Shakespearean cipher volume. He would write four more books, including two novels, one of which was utopian fiction, *Caesar's Column,* and sold remarkably well (one million copies, so they say). Apparently his fictional vision of the future was as engaging and full of catastrophes as his views on the exciting past had been.

In politics during the 1890s, he made it into the big time as well. Donnelly helped found the Populist party, wrote the celebrated Omaha platform of 1892, and was twice nominated for the Vice-Presidency. His personal life was busy, too; he married a young woman of twenty-one, Marion Hansen, while he was in his late sixties. It is thanks to her that we possess a contemporary comment on his Atlantis volume with which I am in much accord: Charles Darwin wrote to Donnelly, "I have read the book with interest, though I must confess in a very skeptical spirit."

In the early minutes of 1901 he passed on at the age of seventy. He had had a long and busy life, with successes and failures enough in two careers for any one person. Fantastic Archaeology in America would never be the same again. Donnelly had managed to revive trans-Atlantic connections without significant religious or ethnic overtones, something akin to the Garcian tradition of old. Using Atlantis as the homeland for the civilizations on both sides of the Atlantic, which Plato had never envisioned, was Donnelly's contribution, as was his emphasis on Catastrophism.

With these two particular views, Donnelly would provide the basics for literally hundreds of *Atlantis/Ragnarok* sequels during the next century, whether the authors would identify their source or not. What Donnelly owed to some of his predecessors such as Rafinesque or even Joseph Smith is not so clear. One of his very strong supporters has characterized him as a "pioneer" who "took no 'leads' from other authors or authorities,"[3] but I find that view almost anti-intellectual, for one of Donnelly's real strengths was his broad knowledge of the contemporary literature. The synthesis was

Donnelly's; the views, whether in archaeology, geology, or mythology, were "of the period," wrapped in a very exciting package that caught a popular audience.

There were, indeed, numerous nineteenth-century figures who sought the limelight with their own views of Atlantis. One of these who used New World data in an innovative manner was Augustus LePlongeon. He carried out archaeological research in Yucatán in the 1870s and was notable for the real contribution made by his early photographs of the ruins. While in the area, however, he contacted Maya Indians and became confident that with their help he could read the hieroglyphics, which told of ancient ties to Atlantis and Egypt. LePlongeon then teamed up with Brasseur de Bourbourg to produce extraordinary Fantastic Archaeology for the Mesoamerican field, which was well described by Robert Wauchope in his excellent volume *Lost Tribes and Sunken Continents*.

Another of those who took up some of Donnelly's themes was one who could truly be termed an internationally known "character": Helena Petrovna Blavatsky (1831–91). Madame Blavatsky, or H.P.B. as she preferred to be called in her later years, was one of the founders of the Theosophical Society in 1875, and she had an impact on both England and America that is still felt, for although the Society is small today, it continues to publish H.P.B.'s works and commemorate her activities. I must confess that Blavatsky's connection with American archaeology is a very minor segment of her life, but her broad involvement with occult philosophy and psychic powers intersects with essential aspects of the study of pseudoscience and the popular acceptance of bizarre concepts and beliefs.

Her best-known writings, *Isis Unveiled* (1877) and *The Secret Doctrine* (1888), total something over thirty-seven hundred pages in length and with *The Key to Theosophy* (1889) form the basic literature of her philosophy and that of the society she headed until her death in 1891.

H.P.B.'s impact was broad. Her writings combined the materials from the religions of the world and the wisdom of the ancients, particularly that of India and Tibet, with occultism and psychic powers. Both Mohandas Gandhi and Jawaharlal Nehru were said to have learned from her teachings. Her Theosophical Society, in both New York and London, attracted a very mixed bag of celebrities from Thomas Edison and Abner Doubleday of baseball fame, to a devoted group of Irish writers including William Butler Yeats and the poet George Russell (AE). Annie Besant, an early feminist and political activist, became a convert, as did Arthur Conan Doyle, who was much involved in psychic phenomena. On the other hand, a more

Helena P. Blavatsky

outspoken Irishman, James Joyce, attacked her viciously in his famous work *Ulysses*.

Helena Petrovna was born in 1831 in Russia of noble lineage. As a child she was recognized as having extraordinary mental gifts; she also experienced what has been termed "spirit possession." She did not have a normal childhood, although it certainly cannot be linked directly to her difficult personality. Her mother died when she was ten, and her father was not around very much during her adolescence. Raised by her well-to-do maternal grandparents, she, at the age of seventeen, married Nikifor Blavatsky, a government official some twenty years her senior, and spent three months with him. The unhappy and unconsummated marriage ended when Helena ran off.

The years between her running off from Blavatsky (1849) and her arrival in New York City as an immigrant (1873) have been called the "Veiled Years" by one of her biographers. She traveled much, probably did get into Tibet in 1856, quite a feat, and even visited Canada, the United States, Mexico, and India. She did everything from working in a circus, to shopkeeping, to starting a short-lived Society of Spiritualists in Cairo. Then on the eve of her forty-second birthday she bought a steerage ticket from Le Havre for New York.

Arriving on July 5, 1873, Helena Petrovna Blavatsky found America what it was for so many Old World immigrants of that period, a land of great opportunity. At first, she had to scrape and scrimp for housing and even food, but she gained access both to a group of like-minded folk, the American Spiritualists, and to some willing supporters.

Her American stay (1873–78) was as successful as it was turbulent. She had a brief marriage with a much younger Russian refugee, legally bigamy because she was never divorced from Blavatsky, and she began a long-term relationship with Henry Steel Olcott, as much a Yankee as the name implies, who deserted his wife and two sons for H.P.B. Together they founded the Theosophical Society, so legend has it, but the facts are that it was mostly Olcott's show at the beginning. Also in this period H.P.B. wrote and published her first book, *Isis Unveiled*. Although first issued in the fall of 1877 in a run of only a thousand copies because the publisher had doubts, the book sold out in a week and quickly went into a second edition.

Despite some success in America, Blavatsky and Olcott went off to India in mid-December of 1878. There H.P.B. hoped to get in closer contact with the Indian or Tibetan mahatmas, her mythical "masters," who sent her messages. She and Olcott spent six years in India, which were a mixed blessing from the joy of founding a center in Adyar, which still exists today, to the usual cycles of financial crisis. They returned to Europe in 1884 to even greater woes. The psychic phenomena observed by the Theosophists were being studied by a newly founded Cambridge group calling itself the Society of Psychical Research. Charges of fraud were brought against Madame Blavatsky, some by former members of her organization in India, during the next three years. Henry Olcott tried but failed to defend H.P.B., much to her displeasure. He then returned to India, never to leave again.

Blavatsky continued to roam about Europe dodging accusations and finding, as always, a few faithful friends to support her. More important, she finally took up her much-delayed project of another major book, possibly in hope of deflecting the adverse criticism focused on her "little parlor tricks." Her book would be strictly theoretical. After all, she had always said that the philosophical side of Theosophy, not the psychic aspect, was the most important.

H.P.B. began to write *The Secret Doctrine* in a rather disjointed way, but soon a new idea developed. She decided to use the "Stanzas of Dzyan," taken from an ancient Tibetan manuscript and written in "Senzar," a language that she alone could translate, as the unifying theme. From the start she knew that some would say she had invented the book of Dzyan, but that did not matter. She wrote and wrote; only periods of deep depression or interesting visitors would interrupt her output. While on the Continent, she gathered a small coterie of devoted followers, especially three young well-to-do Britishers; they took matters in their own hands and moved H.P.B. back to London in 1887 and lodged her with sympathetic friends.

Her young friends, Archibald and Bertram Keightley and Edward Fawcett, had been helping with *The Secret Doctrine* before, and now they settled down to wrestle with the two-volume monster, retyping, checking references, and so on. They even did some of the writing or rewriting if the truth be told. Whatever the case may be, *The Secret Doctrine: The Synthesis of Science, Religion, and Philosophy* came out in the fall of 1888. As to its contents and purpose, one commentator has said, "It is an account of how the universe is created, where it came from and where it is going, what force fashioned it, and what it all means."[4]

In its scope, the topic reminds one of something Rafinesque would have liked to tackle. Fortunately, only volume 2 on anthropogenesis need concern us here; it is a chronicle of the evolution of man over millions of years, but we can skip the first two "Root Races" and begin about 18 million years ago. The cradle of Third Race is in the middle of the Pacific Ocean, the huge continent of Lemuria, which was destroyed by fire and then sunk beneath the seas.

Thanks to Marion Meade, one of Blavatsky's biographers, we have a synopsis of the next exciting events in H.P.B.'s drama:

> With the sinking of Lemuria, its successor rose in the Atlantic Ocean and became the dwelling place of the Fourth Race some eight hundred and fifty thousand years ago. This was the fabled Atlantis alluded to by Plato and other ancient writers and affirmed by Madame Blavatsky. . . . In psychic and technological respects, the Atlanteans were more highly developed than we; they invented airplanes and understood . . . super-electric forces. . . . [For a time] human beings were gigantic in stature, a fact that accounts for certain colossal forms of architecture such as Druid temples and the pyramids. Because the Atlanteans misused their knowledge, the race began to degenerate and portions of the continent gradually began to submerge. . . . [They] met their watery doom only 11,000 years ago. This final cataclysm was the basis for the deluge myth. (Meade, 1980: 415)

As if that wasn't enough for archaeologists to sink their teeth into, there are some other tasty morsels in *Isis Unveiled:*

The ruins which cover both Americas, and are found on many West Indian islands, are all attributed to the submerged Atlanteans. As well as the hierophants [interpreters of sacred mysteries], which in the days of Atlantis was almost connected with the new one by land, the magicians of the now submerged country had a net-work of subterranean passages running in all directions. In connexion with those mysterious catacombs we will now give a curious story told to us by a Peruvian, long since dead, as we [Blavatsky and friends] were traveling together in the interior of his country. There must be truth in it, as it was afterward confirmed to us by an Italian gentleman. . . . The informant of the Italian was an old priest, who had had the secret divulged to him, at confession, by a Peruvian Indian. We may add, moreover, that the priest was compelled to make the revelation, being at the time completely under the mesmeric influence of the traveler. (Blavatsky, 1877: 595)

The active mind of Helena Petrovna Blavatsky did make a lasting impact. The Theosophical Society, which she and Olcott founded over a century ago, still exists. I regularly get the newsletter of the Boston chapter and find that it has stayed up-to-date, offering a very broad mixture of martial arts and meditation, astrology and Tarot, ancient Egyptology and ideas from the *Secret Doctrine,* and a "medical clairvoyant nurse" doing health readings. So all is not forgotten.

H.P.B.'s writings stay in print despite the very stiff critical treatment they have gotten, being called "discarded rubbish" and "a large dish of hash" ever since they were first published. There is an appetite for such works that is not diminished by the words of higher authorities. Her recent biographer, Meade, had this closing thought on H.P.B.: "She used to say that even though her contemporaries did not appreciate her, she would be vindicated in the twentieth century when her teachings and her person would finally be understood. While that prophecy has not been totally fulfilled, there is no doubt that we can understand her better than did the Victorians. Perhaps a final assessment of her must wait until the twenty-first century."[5] Whatever the future of Theosophy, there is no question that the notion of sunken continents affecting the prehistory of the New World is my only excuse for including H.P.B., a charming charlatan, in this volume. Such ideas will remain a strong alternative view of the past for generations to come.

So far in this chapter I have by way of background tried to evoke some sense of the late nineteenth century: strange times indeed, with mysticism, anti-intellectualism, Spiritualism, and a crop of new cults and religions. It is hard to appreciate that past. But what of the 1980s? Half the nation was out jogging, the other half was watching their weight with some new miracle diet. We saw Moonies, Hare Krishnas, Creationists, and gurus vying for our souls and attacking scientific reasoning. Uri Geller apparently bent spoons by sheer force of his mind to everyone's delight, while others were looking skyward for landing craft from outer space and finding them. Yes, it is very different today.

In the early portion of the twentieth century, there were many who picked up the strands of Atlantis and Lemuria, followers of H.P.B. like Annie Besant and W. Scott-Elliot. The latter's reconstructions of times past included giant races on every side and awesome catastrophes at regular intervals, punctuating the rise of miraculous civilizations over a span of hundreds of thousands of years. But we must pick and choose from this rich panorama of fantasy so well described by Sprague de Camp in his classic *Lost Continents*.

My choice should come as no surprise: Colonel James Churchward (1850–1936), a Britisher, trained at Oxford and Sandhurst, and, so they say, a colonel in a regiment of Lancers in India. After India and a broken marriage, he came to the United States and worked for a while as a civil engineer, then entered the steel business in which his great financial successes were dashed by the forces of Big Steel, or so he said. Even his most supportive commentator indicated that Churchward had a reputation as an angler and a teller of tall tales. He also "had a thirty-third degree efficiency in the art of making enemies," according to the same authority.

By his own statement, his involvement with the "Land of Mu," his term for what others had called Lemuria, dated back to his India days (the 1870s, presumably), when he learned to translate "certain ancient Naacal tablets" which had been inscribed either in Burma or in Mu, the lost continent. These tablets were very, very old: probably over fifteen thousand years old. Of course, these fragile clay tablets were not in very good shape, and one of the ways that Churchward got the old high priest of the temple to show him these mysterious and very sacred objects was through his involvement in the restoration and careful storage of these treasures after they had worked out the translations. Of course, as is to be expected, no one since has ever seen or copied these Naacal tablets. So much for the chances of revisionist historical research.

It's the old "sacred tablets" gambit again. With the tablets come the unique translations by the maestro himself; after all, no one else but Madame Blavatsky could read the forgotten Senzar language, and Joseph Smith would have his special "interpreters" for the gold tablets. What did Churchward's tablets tell him, once they had been "deciphered and translated"?

The gist of them indubitably establishes to my own satisfaction that at one time the earth had an incalculably ancient civilization which was, in many respects, superior to our own, and far in advance of us in some important essentials that the modern world is just beginning to have cognizance of. These tablets, with other ancient records, bear witness to the amazing fact that the civilizations of India, Babylonia, Persia, Egypt, and Yucatan were but the dying embers of this great past civilization. (Churchward, 1926: v)

This quote is from the preface to Churchward's first book on the Land of Mu; after that it goes downhill. By that I mean that instead of the logical presentation that characterized Donnelly's book, we have a run-on narrative that mixes translations from the Naacal tablets with purported supporting documentation from Maya hieroglyphs, Easter Island tablets, and Tibetan sources. The book has no bibliography so that detailed checking of references is impossible, something that I, as a teenager, never noticed. It just flows along, not without some rather charming evocations of what Mu was really like:

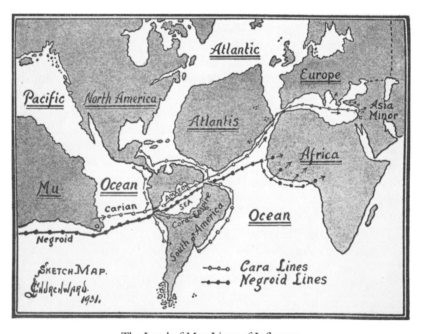

The Land of Mu: Lines of Influence

No mountains . . . stretched themselves through this earthly paradise to give an irregular, jagged, yet soft and graceful skyline. . . . Luxuriant vegetation covered the whole land with a soft, pleasing, restful mantle of green. . . . Over the cool rivers, gaudy winged butterflies hovered in the shade of the trees, rising and falling in fairy-like movements, as if better to view their painted beauty in nature's mirror. (Churchward, 1926: 23)

And who inhabited this lovely land? The dominant race was white, and exceedingly handsome people, although there were other races as well. They were great navigators who took their ships all over the world and spread their fine architecture and great monoliths along the way. Colonies were founded in all parts of the world, and the travelers were treated to POSH accommodations while afloat: "During cool evenings might be seen ships on pleasure bent, filled with gorgeously dressed, jewel-bedecked men and women. The long sweeps with which these ships were supplied gave a musical rhythm to the song and laughter of the merry passengers."[6]

But it was too good to last. There were warnings: along the south edge of the great Pacific continent a series of earthquakes and resulting waves from the ocean destroyed "many a fair city," but they were rebuilt. Generations later, however, the end came: earthquakes, huge cataclysmic waves, and volcanic eruptions wrought total destruction. The continent of Mu

The Destruction of Mu

sank beneath the Pacific, and its 64 million inhabitants died. "For nearly 13,000 years the destruction of this great civilization cast a heavy pall of darkness over the greater part of the earth. The pall is being lifted, but many spots remain covered by it."[7]

The few survivors on the tiny specks of land that remained above the immense sea were desperate. They regressed to lowest savagery and practiced the first cannibalism. Churchward shuddered to think of it: "One can readily image the loathing and repugnance that these cultured beings must have had for such food, and we may feel comforted in believing that many died before they could force themselves to partake of it."[8] The ebb and flow of culture is a wonderful thing.

Part and parcel of Churchward's notion of the centrality of Mu in the *whole* picture of "Man's Advent on Earth," as he put it, was that it was the Biblical Garden of Eden. As for theories of human evolution, Churchward makes short work of that "scientific" nonsense: "In their anxiety to sustain their monkey theories, scientists have tried to prove that man did not appear upon the face of the earth until the early Pleistocene Time [not far from their "crazy" current view today], but a pin-prick can dissipate this scientific bubble."[9] Churchward states that there are remains of man in Europe in gravels that date from the end of the Pliocene before the last "Magnetic Cataclysm"; likewise he indicates that William Niven in Mexico found a city that dates to before the Pleistocene. He felt that this evidence surely dispelled any chance that the scientists were right about their view of human origins.

Like so many books on Fantastic Archaeology, each page of Churchward's text could require a complete testing, and most of the evidence would prove to be either wrongly interpreted or false. I will look in detail only briefly at the work of William Niven in Mexico before turning to our proper subject, North America. Niven was a Scottish engineer who worked in Mexico in the late nineteenth century; he had an archaeological avocation that took him to some interesting sites in 1897; he shared some of his finds, such as ceramics and a dog skeleton, with Putnam at the Harvard Peabody Museum.

By 1910 Niven was focusing his archaeological work in the Valley of Mexico, where he made his most astounding finds. Here Niven came across layers of ancient ruins to the depth of thirty feet. In one stratigraphic cut, he found three concrete pavements representing three buried cities that had been overwhelmed by cataclysmic tidal waves; this site is now seven thousand feet *above* sea level. Niven felt that the lowest levels of the site might date back fifty thousand years.

Niven's Collection of Tablets

But that was not all, for in 1921 at another site in the Valley of Mexico, this time at a depth of only twelve feet, Niven "found" a veritable library of stone tablets, some twenty-six hundred in total. By the nature of the deposits in which they were found, he speculated that they were from twelve to fifty thousand years old. These pictographic tablets, about hand size on soft volcanic rock, were called a "mystery" by the noted Maya scholar Sylvanus Morley and by the other professional archaeologist whom Niven queried. That assessment makes sense because they are really unique and outrageous fakes. Whether Niven actually dug them up himself, after they had been planted, or whether these wondrous inscribed rocks were palmed off on him by wily "excavators" is not clear.

But the professionals' answer that the tablets were a mystery did not mean that all was lost. Through the kinship of Freemasonry, according to one commentator, Niven knew James Churchward, and he obviously held the key. Churchward examined the Mexican tablets and saw that the symbolic writing on them was easily translated because it had a direct relationship to the symbols on his Naacal tablets. Indeed, the Niven stones became for Churchward a major help in unraveling the tale of the Lost Continent. An entire chapter of his first book is devoted to the Niven discoveries and their archaeological implications, which confirm his earlier findings.

Niven Stones at Harvard

Mu and Prehistoric North America

Churchward agreed that Niven's inscribed tablets were probably more than thirty-five thousand years old. In his second book, *Children of Mu,* Churchward illustrated many more of the tablets and gave many translations.

Fortunately, I have been able to examine some of these remarkable documents at first hand because the Peabody's collections include nearly a thousand artifacts acquired from Niven between 1900 and the time of his death in 1937. The incised stones definitely do not have the patina of great age one would expect if the Niven-Churchward dates were valid; indeed, they look as if they were made yesterday, and I am afraid that is much closer to the truth than the thirty thousand or so years attributed to them. Since so much of what Niven did collect was genuine, these fresh stone tablets must have been provided to Niven by persons unknown. Whoever the makers were, they mass-produced the materials at a rate that is fantastic in its own right. No other inscribed tablets that resemble the Niven finds have ever been found in the New World. They are, indeed, unique.

When we turn to what Churchward referred to as the civilizations of North America, we find a similar mix of archaeological evidence to which extraordinary age is attributed. This mix includes genuine Southwestern Cliff Dweller material and many rock inscriptions. The latter are interpreted as messages from the survivors of Mu. Churchward states that many lines of evidence "prove that the Pueblo Indians originally came to America from Mu," probably about twelve thousand years ago. Indeed, their pathway from the Pacific was directly up the Colorado River into the Southwest proper, as shown on one of Churchward's rather quaint maps.

Churchward follows the Mu trail only as far east as Nebraska, where an amateur archaeologist, R. W. Gilder, like Niven, had purportedly found a civilization wiped out by ancient cataclysms. These Nebraska artifacts, which Churchward illustrates, are said to be from a Tertiary era civilization. Actually these finds, like those from the Pueblo area, are all well known to date from after A.D. 1000. Mercifully for the workers in the archaeology of the Mississippi Valley, like me, Churchward did not take his researches any further east; obviously he had run out of the high cultures that he would want to connect to the Motherland of Mu.

There is much more in Churchward, but enough is enough. I wince to think that I once swallowed all Churchward's nonsense as true archaeology. Except for the lyrical descriptions of ancient Mu, it is not as well written or as convincingly presented as Donnelly's Atlantis. Churchward's own hand-made illustrations do have a sort of "primitive" charm; perhaps he should be termed the "Grandma Moses" of Fantastic Archaeology. Overall, we would have to rate James Churchward as an important figure even though his translations are outrageous, his geology, in both mechanics and dating, is absurd, and his mishandling of archaeological data, as in the Valley of Mexico, is atrocious.

We cannot excuse any of that by saying, Well, it was long ago, and no one knew any better. That simply was not true; for example, Southwestern archaeology was well developed in the 1920s. But Churchward kept writing the same old stuff until 1933, with no notice of what was going on in important fields around him. As de Camp has written: "No fervent believer in Mu, it seems, will give up his belief for the sake of a few facts. Thus Churchward's pseudoscientific masterpieces have begotten progeny."[10] Yes, *The Lost Continent of Mu* does have "children"; one of them is this very book.

Of course, what de Camp had in mind was something rather different, and alas he is right about that too. Donnelly, Churchward, and their Atlantean cohorts have spawned what seems like a never-ending flood of modern-day adherents. The books on this one aspect of Fantastic Archaeology, Atlantis, alone exceed two thousand. They sell well and haven't let the side down as to the extraordinary claims they make. *Mu: Fact or Fiction* by Elizabeth G. Wilcox was published in 1963 and follows Churchward closely; its frontispiece is a supposed twenty-thousand-year-old bronze statue from Mu itself.

Charles Berlitz, who made quite a splash with the *Bermuda Triangle*, has recently published *Atlantis, the Eighth Continent*, which struggles to deal with the fact that no Atlantean artifacts have been identified or dated "to the satisfaction of the archaeological establishment." After rehashing all sorts of old "mysteries," including Colonel Percy Fawcett's lost cities in Brazil, Berlitz suggests that with increased ocean floor exploration "vestiges and eventually even artifacts of the legendary sunken lands" will be found. Indeed, he feels that such evidence may already have been found, but the Establishment is afraid to let the secret out.

Not so, according to the *Weekly World News*, which headlined its October 22, 1985, edition with "Atlantis Found in the North Atlantic." "More amazing than Titanic discovery, say experts." Perhaps the reason for silence in the rest of the U.S. press was that it was a Russian submarine on a deep-sea probe that made the startling discovery, and "they've got the evidence: a mind-boggling video showing the fabled lost city" in the depths several hundred miles east of the Azores. Donnelly was right in saying that such evidence "would be worth more to science" than any other possible archaeological find. Unfortunately, the Russians are typically not sharing this new-found archaeological treasure with Western scholars. Perhaps the videotape shows the discouraging revelation, as related by Jules Verne over a hundred years ago, that next to the inscription on the black basalt rock announcing "ATLANTIS," there is an additional bit of graffiti indicating that Captain Nemo and the *Nautilus* got there first.

Other recent visitations to Atlantis have been documented by American newspapers with little respect for its scientific significance; they put it on the comic page. "The Amazing Spider-Man" and one of his attractive girl friends made a trip to the western edge of the continent near the Bermuda Triangle. The underwater landscape depicted in the comic strip has an eerie resemblence to that figured on the endpapers of Berlitz's new book. Perhaps, "Krang, the Warlord of Atlantis," was right when he responded to the visitor's disbelief with "Fools! Most legends are truths not yet discovered." So we can only hope that Robert Ballard and his crew that was so successful with the *Titanic* will now turn their research, with a little more help from the National Geographic Society, to the search for Atlantis. We have waited long enough. Maybe scientists will see those fabled towers yet.

With an even more startling series of new developments, some other aspects of old ideas have recently received more substantial scientific support that should gladden the hearts of many Atlantean followers. The Catastrophism that is so central to the destruction of Atlantis and Mu has returned with a vengeance, and it has taken hold in areas that have long had a popular focus. Ragnarok is back. A comet hit the earth and the aftermath destroyed all the dinosaurs. That is pretty fantastic, yet a number of very credible scientists are proposing just such a scenario. Truth may sometimes be stranger than even Ignatius Donnelly's fiction.

Now on to the facts: there is plenty of evidence on earth, on the moon, and even on Mars, which we have gotten to know better recently with our deep probes, that large objects from outer space have hit the surfaces and have left major craters. On earth some huge craters have been identified near Bering Strait and, as was recently suggested, in the Everglades in Florida. These impacts cause dustlike particles to rise into the atmosphere and cause a blanketing that prevents solar energy absorption.

The "Nuclear Winter" hypothesis is based on analogies from the known effects of major volcanic eruptions in the recent past. Temperatures are substantially lowered for some months; the nuclear explosion model uses both dust and smoke caused by firestorms to create the temperature shield. In the dinosaur scenario, the temperature sensitivity of these animals is thought to have caused reproductive difficulties, but other extinctions at the same time are thought to have occurred as well.

Indeed, like all good hypotheses, why not expand it. If one mete- orically caused extinction is okay, why not have a whole series, about 26 million years apart, and bring in a dark Avenger star on a long orbit as the "bad actor" in this solar system drama. It has been done, or at least proposed, but not everyone has bought it. The chronological framework is so long, the data bits so scattered, that the reading of a cyclical patterning into both impact craters and correlated extinctions is stretching things a bit far, or so some scholars say. But it was a nice idea. Actually, some students of evolution like to see the pattern of externally caused extinctions as being more important in making fairly sudden changes in evolutionary develop- ment (punctuated equilibrium) than the model of slow and gradual change using survival of the fittest as the major mover, but that question is still being vociferously argued.

So science and argumentation progress. Now we even take the concept of Atlantis with us off the planet Earth—it is the name given to one of America's space shuttles. It remains, too, in our mythic projections as in the movie *Cocoon,* in which visitors return to Atlantis in the Caribbean for their old friends and provide eternal life to Floridian oldsters; *Cocoon II* was sure to follow, and it did.

Thus Atlantis serves us in many ways, as Sprague de Camp said in the conclusion of his study:

Atlantis provides mystery and romance for those who don't find ordinary history exciting enough, and can be turned to account to point to a moral lesson. . . . But most of all it strikes a responsive chord by its sense of the melancholy loss of a beautiful thing, a happy perfection once possessed by mankind. Thus it appeals to that hope that . . . there can exist a land of peace and plenty, of beauty and justice, where we, poor creatures that we are, could be happy. In this sense Atlantis . . . will always be with us. (de Camp, 1954: 277)

8
Archaeology and Religion: Where Angels Fear to Tread

On the west side of this hill, not far from the top, under a stone of considerable size, lay the plates, deposited in a stone box.
JOSEPH SMITH, 1830

A little more than one hundred years ago in 1884, Professor William James of Cambridge, Massachusetts, mused, "I sometimes find myself wondering whether there can be any popular religion raised on the ruins of the old Christianity without the presence of that element which in the past has presided over the origins of all religions, namely, a belief in new physical facts and possibilities."[1] Indeed, the nineteenth century had been a veritable treasure trove of "new physical facts and possibilities," which had accomplished just the result James had spoken of: the generation of new religions, including that practiced in the small stone Swedenborgian church, not a hundred yards from his home, which he attended.

Most Americans, I suspect, think of Christianity as a stable "old" religion, with Martin Luther as their landmark for important church schisms and reformations. That is, of course, hardly the case; during the nineteenth century new "evidence," either from revelations such as those of Emanuel Swedenborg and Mary Baker Eddy or from excavated sacred tablets as was the case with Joseph Smith, would provide the genesis of some important new sects within the Christian faith. Archaeology would play an important role as well during this period, providing both support for old beliefs with the archaeological documentation of peoples and places in the Old and New Testaments and new evidence for different interpretations of these old documents.

As one of my Near Eastern archaeological colleagues has emphasized to me, much of what went on during early nineteenth-century archaeology in his area made important contributions to understanding Ancient History as something more than the scant phrases available to scholars in the Bible. These discoveries included the Napoleon-Egyptian hieroglyphics-Champollion connection, the Layard and Nineveh excavations, and the Rawlinson-Bhistun-Babylonian puzzle solution. Thus other written histories were found and translated that did not necessarily dispute the biblical record but allowed the reader to see those sacred documents in a much broader perspective, both historically and culturally. There were other important actors on that Near Eastern stage whose heritage included myths, monsters, and even gods, which were part of the play as well. All these important archaeologically derived perceptions came to light long before Darwin and the *Annus Mirabilis.*

Even earlier there were individuals whose genius would be awakened by the rise of science in the eighteenth century; such a person was Emanuel Swedberg (1688–1772), born in Stockholm, Sweden, and better known as Swedenborg; the spelling of his name was changed by the title awarded him by the Swedish queen. Swedenborg was by all accounts a "polymath" of world-class proportions. He was raised in an academic family, his father being a professor of theology at Uppsala University and a bishop with nondogmatic leanings. It was a great place of learning; the innovative botanist Carolus Linnaeus (1707–78) had his residence in the old botanical garden of the University.

The young Swedenborg, trained at Uppsala, devoted himself initially to natural science and engineering. He was involved in successful national defense undertakings, hence his title, but most of his work was in mathematics (economics as well) and physical sciences (mining, paleontology, and physics). He was a very busy man between 1710 and 1740 making important contributions to physiological sciences, especially in studying the functions of the human central nervous system. This work would certainly have been of interest to William James.

It was in 1745 that Swedenborg said "heaven was opened to him." A few years later, he resigned his position with the Commission of Mines and spent the rest of his life interpreting the Holy Scriptures. By dreams and visions he was in direct contact with the Lord and through this connection he was given the "doctrines" of the New Church. He never attempted to preach or to found a new sect. He was satisfied to write and publish; his most important work was *Divine Love and Wisdom* (1763).

His voluminous works were ultimately translated into English, and followers in the 1780s, especially in England, where he died, began the Church of the New Jerusalem based on his philosophy and teachings. Early advocates were strongly antislavery, and lecturers in Philadelphia and Boston in 1784 spread the faith. Although the New Church was never large in numbers, its members around the world continue today the propagation of the faith based on Swedenborg's revelations.

That a scientist capable of pioneering work in a half dozen disciplines should turn to mysticism and spirit voices in middle age is, of course, the reason for our concern herein. Direct messages from the Lord are a far cry from mineralogical assays. Not only that, but others listened. Swedenborg's doctrine of infinite wisdom and divine love was not very controversial, and he did see connections and analogies between the natural and the spiritual worlds. It was the psychic source of his new information that is extraordinary. Yet by the 1880s many besides William James were willing to look for "a world of new phenomenal possibilities enveloping those of the present life." As I have discussed earlier, there was a strong and growing interest in Spiritualism at the time.

Mysticism and revelation were alive and well in the nineteenth century and would be a major factor in religious developments of that century. Good examples to prove the point are not hard to find. Mary Baker Eddy (1821–1910), the founder of the Church of Christ, Scientist, was a long-lived New Englander whose faith in self-applied cures using the Bible as an aid led her in 1870 to publish a short pamphlet on the subject. Her major work, *Science and Health with Key to the Scriptures,* came out in 1875. She started as the first practitioner, and she demonstrated her religion by healings in many cases. By 1892 the Mother Church was organized. Now Christian Science has spread around the world with a large membership.

Although most critical discussion of Christian Science focuses on the way healing is accomplished without the use of modern medical practices, the full doctrine emphasizes mental and spiritual harmony in all human needs. As for the sources of her religion, Eddy stated, "I won my way to absolute conclusions through *divine revelation,* reason and demonstration" (emphasis added).[2] This special combination of Yankee pragmatism and divine faith in healing with spiritual ties to the Bible has proven very effective; their broad educational influence through the calm and persuasive *Christian Science Monitor* newspaper is very laudable.

These examples of Swedenborgianism and Christian Science are, however, only introductory to the one new American religion that has a firm foundation in the archaeology of this period—Mormonism: the Church of Jesus Christ of Latter-Day Saints. None of these other new religions engendered such strong reactions as it did. The early history of the Mormon church, founded by Joseph Smith in upstate New York in 1830, is one of religious oppression and hate unrivaled in American history. Joseph Smith and his brother Hyrum were martyred for the cause in the streets of Carthage, Illinois, by a vigilante mob in 1844.

Earlier I spoke approvingly of the intellectual quest that took place in the Northwest Territory when the Ohio Valley was opened up. Men of scholarly interest were active during this period such as Atwater, Schoolcraft, Brackenridge, and Lapham. But it was a real frontier, and there was a frontier mentality that found some new ideas, even spiritual ones, unacceptable. Some commentators have suggested that the Mormon concept of plural marriage was the basic problem that caused outrage, but that was not espoused until just before Smith's death and not publicly recognized until after the move to Utah. Smith received a revelation at Nauvoo, Illinois, on the matter and did have more than one wife, as did some of the other Elders of the Church, but the major problems for the new Mormon church seem to have been economic and political as well as religious.

It is difficult to find unbiased commentary on the Church itself, but it is almost impossible to discover the same about the founder, Joseph Smith. He is made perfect by the church and vilified by the opposition. His critics, and he had them from the very beginning, paint him as a rascal, untrustworthy and brash, while the Church pictures him as almost shy, Bible-reading, and completely trustworthy. One of the most accessible books on Joseph Smith is that by Fawn Brodie, a former Church member and related to a member of the Church hierarchy. Her biography, *No Man Knows My History,* was not well received, even though it was very well researched; for it she was excommunicated.

The archaeological side of the picture was reviewed in a volume for a popular audience entitled *Moundbuilders of Ancient America* (1968), by Robert Silverberg, better known for his works in science fiction. Silverberg has done a more than credible job in researching the Moundbuilder myth and its connections to Joseph Smith. Another very useful volume is *Indian Origins and the Book of Mormon* (1986), by Dan Vogel, also a member of the Church.

Joseph Smith (1805–44) was born in Sharon, Vermont, son of Joseph and Lucy Smith. The family was of very humble means, living at that time with Mrs. Smith's parents on a small farm in rural Vermont. When Joseph was ten, the family moved to New York State, and he lived near Palmyra and later Manchester until he was twenty-one. It was here that he began, at about the age of fifteen, to have visions of visitations from God and his

Joseph Smith
Translating the Golden Plates

angels in response to prayers for religious guidance. The local citizenry was not impressed by his retelling of these miracles, or so he says. Others said he never mentioned them until long after he wrote his book, a typical standoff of opinions with no solution because no contemporary documentation exists on this subject.

At about this same time, the 1820s, there were many statements about another aspect of Joseph Smith's behavior, and these related to his involvement in "money-digging" and in his belief in and use of folk magic. There seems little doubt that Fawn Brodie's discussion of this topic in the chapter "Treasures in the Earth" will have to be accepted because some confirming evidence does exist. Brodie detailed Smith's strong involvement in treasure seeking and the use of a "seer stone," which he looked into for visions of the locations of the hidden monies. During 1825 Smith became involved with a gentleman named Josiah Stowell from Pennsylvania, where he took a contract to search in the mountains for a lost silver mine. Smith was unsuccessful in the treasure hunt, but while in that region he met Emma, who was to become his first wife.

Brodie also mentions Smith's use of a split hazel stick as an aid to finding treasures. Finally, she relates the thirdhand story (from Willard Chase to the elder Smith to young Joseph) that when the famous golden plates, the source for the Book of Mormon, were found, there was a toad guarding them, which changed into a man, who beat him. Who would believe all that? Verification, of a sort, recently came from a rather strange source: newly "found" Joseph Smith letters that the Mormon Church first accepted and then correctly branded as fakes.

First to appear was a letter from Joseph Smith to Josiah Stowell of Bainbridge, New York, written on June 18, 1825. It contains treasure-hunting information and says the treasure might be guarded by "a clever spirit." Smith also details the construction of the hazel stick divining rod. The letter closes with the statement, "I have almost decided to accept your offer," which we know he did do. The next discovery was an 1830 letter from Martin Harris, Joseph Smith's first supporter and to whom part of the Book of Mormon was dictated. The Harris letter says that Smith told him that a "white Salamander" was guarding the golden plates and it turned into an old spirit who struck Smith three times. This new evidence would be pretty amazing if true, but both letters turn out to be fraudulent. Veracity wins again.

The whole story of these "new" letters ultimately involves car bombings and murder. It has been recounted carefully in a book, *Salamander* (1988) by Linda Sillito and Allen Roberts. The documents, and there were many more than the two letters I have just mentioned, began to appear in 1978. The Church accepted them as genuine after careful scrutiny by authorities, including Charles Hamilton, the author of the definitive *Great Forgers and Famous Frauds* (1980).

But the story got much more complex; more documents were "found" (some of them genuine), and then there were some rather nasty turns: pipe-bomb murders in Salt Lake City. Finally, in 1986 a young Mormon named Mark Hofmann was brought to a preliminary trial hearing and plea bargaining took place. His guilty plea, including the two murders, was accepted on January 7, 1987. The full story of Mark Hofmann, a church member with great greed, cunning, and boldness, is quite a tale. Who says that this antiquarian business is tame?

Hofmann knew his Mormon history well. The two main letters actually did no more than make it easier to accept Brodie's and others' more human version of Joseph Smith's life and times in New York State during the 1820s. They were not blasphemous. Hofmann also went deeply in debt buying real documents to make his own creations easier to accept. Then, too, as has been true with other frauds, there seemed to be a will to believe—how else did such an amateur faker fool an expert like Hamilton?

I have run some 160 years ahead of the story here, so now we must return to north-central New York, Ontario County, in the western Finger Lakes region, about twenty-five miles southeast of Rochester, in the year 1827. It was here that the discovery and excavation of the gold plates from Hill Cumorah took place on September 21, 1827, near Manchester. The spot is now graced by a large stone monument, topped with a statue of the

Joseph Smith
Receives Gold Plates

Prophet Moroni. It was Moroni who appeared to Joseph Smith and told him of the plates and their location, although Joseph was not allowed to take them from the ground until he had met the angel at the spot repeatedly over a four-year period.

The golden plates were found buried in a stone box with a metal breastplate and two "interpreters," the Urim and the Thummim. These were stones with silver bows that Joseph looked into when he was translating the plates; they are sometimes referred to as "spectacles," and the method of using them is detailed in the Book of Mormon (Mosiah 8:13). The one who uses them for translating is called a seer, a title Joseph Smith took along with Prophet when he founded the Church in 1830. These "interpreters" sound very reminiscent of the seer stone that Joseph had used earlier in his money-digging activities. Smith's original seer stone is said to be in the Church's museum in Salt Lake City.

Once the plates had been recovered, Smith kept them well hidden, for he feared that they would be stolen. Apparently these concerns were well founded because we are told that such attempts were made. The plates, the exact number is not a matter of record, were kept well covered except when Smith was translating them. Even his good wife, Emma, never saw them directly; she only saw the package. Other witnesses, specifically those who helped transcribe the Book of Mormon from the plates, Martin Harris and Oliver Cowdery, and male members of the Whitmer and Smith families, eleven in all, gave testimony that they had seen the golden plates and actually "hefted" them. Once the translation had been completed, they were returned to the Angel Moroni for safekeeping.

I have carefully referred to these objects as "plates" instead of tablets because that is the only way they are ever referred to in the Mormon literature. Indeed, in reading the Book of Mormon, one is overwhelmed with "plates"; my indexed version contains over sixty references to them. There are three classes of record plates, plus the brass plates of Laban. Moroni's golden plates, those used by Joseph Smith, cover much of the history documented on all the other plates, although sometimes in abridged form. All in all, there is a tremendous focus on plates. Sacred tablets for divinely revealed information are part and parcel of many religions; witness the Ten Commandments. Moroni's plates were inscribed in what Joseph Smith termed "reformed" Egyptian characters.

To my knowledge, only one page of these inscriptions is extant, a copy made for Martin Harris, who was helping Smith with the translation and who was also financing the book's publication. A "new" *Anthon* transcription from the plates was among the fake documents that Hofmann produced; he obviously knew it would be of great interest to the Church. Harris showed the original copy to several scholars with disastrous results; one, Charles Anthon, a professor at Columbia University, later wrote that it was a linguistic hodgepodge. Some of the "Caractors" (sic) have a cursive and flowing style that might be either Demotic or Hieratic to this author's eye; others bear more resemblance to some of the Grave Creek inscriptions. Yet Harris was not turned off by the failure of scholars to accept the translation and continued to support the venture.

The translation and dictation took the better part of several years, although as usual even this is a matter of argument; the Church insists that Smith completed the 275,000-word manuscript that covers more than five hundred printed pages in approximately eighty days, though the calendar records and other events suggest otherwise. There is no question that Joseph Smith did develop a great facility for dictation; substantial segments are, indeed, lengthy direct quotations from the Old Testament. It was quite a feat, whether miraculous or not is for others to judge. The book's history covers the period from 2200 B.C. to A.D. 421. Unlike other "histories" such as the Walam Olum, this one has chronology under very strict control. Almost every page of my copy of the Book of Mormon contains a footnoted date.

It is the history of peoples who first lived in ancient Palestine and then came to America long before Columbus. There were three migrations: (1) the Jaredites about 2000 B.C., (2) the Prophet Lehi and his followers about 600 B.C., and (3) Mulek and his followers, also about 600 B.C. The Jaredites had a flourishing civilization with extensive agriculture and domestic animals, including horses, cows, and swine. One interesting addition is elephants, said to be especially useful to man (Ether 9:19). Though they had riches of gold, silver, and silk, the Jaredites fell into evil ways and were punished by a devastating famine. The end of the Jaredites takes place with a great battle at Hill Cumorah.

The next wave of emigrants to the New World, Lehi's group, came over about 600 B.C. but soon split into two factions, the Nephites and the Lamanites. These two factions became the Moundbuilders and the Indians; the Lamanites acquired a reddish skin color for their sins. Warfare ultimately broke out between the two groups: the civilized Nephites with great cities and forts and the fallen Lamanites, who nonetheless ultimately prevailed. Moroni, the last leader of the Nephites, prepared their history in their language, called "reformed Egyptian" (Mormon 9:32), and buried the plates in A.D. 421 at Hill Cumorah, scene of their last battle, as it was for the earlier Jaredites. This is but the briefest summary of a very complex history which has hundreds of participants and also several versions of the same events, since Moroni provided abridged versions of other histories.

What can modern scholars make of this document called the Book of Mormon put down on paper and ultimately published in 1830 by Joseph Smith? Church scholars believe that it is a revealed document which provides both a history of the past and a prophecy of the future. Others from very early on have tried to show that much of what passes for new history is either taken from the Old Testament or bears a strong similarity to current notions about the Moundbuilders and their ancient civilization. Smith, as a boy, was said to have been fascinated by stories of the Moundbuilders.

Others, as early as 1834, said that Smith plagiarized much either from a book entitled *View of the Hebrews; or, The Tribes of Israel in America,* published in 1823 by Ethan Smith, no relation, or from the unpublished manuscript of the Reverend Solomon Spaulding. The Ethan Smith volume contains some strong parallels to the Book of Mormon, including great battles of annihilation and the notion that the actual records would someday be found, but the evidence is hardly clear-cut.

Overall, one can say that the idea of relating the American Indians to the Lost Tribes of Israel was supported by many at this time. There is no question that the Book of Mormon states that the Lamanites were a

The Book of Mormon

remnant of the house of Israel, for it says so on the title page. Anyone who has read that volume will certainly feel the impact of the Old Testament in both word and deed. Whether the whole document came from the golden tablets found at Hill Cumorah via Joseph Smith using his "interpreters" (the Urim and the Thummim, two stones set in silver bows) to translate the "reformed Egyptian" is another matter. We have but a snatch of the document, not even an actual page but merely a list of characters, and it seems to be a jumble of symbols, to say the least.

What, then, of the history of America's past as related by Smith's document? By 1830 little progress had been made on unraveling the archaeology of the Ohio Valley; Smith was living at the upper end of that physiographic drainage basin, although most of the best mound groups were to the south and west of his home. Atwater had published his good maps of the sites and given us "Hindoos and Tartars" as the originators of them. More important for later developments in Mormon archaeology, John Stephens and Frederick Catherwood had not yet published their pioneering volume on the discovery of the Maya ruins in Yucatán, which brought these heretofore hidden cities to popular attention. Thus the drama of civilizations rising and falling in America was still being played out in the Ohio Valley, and Hill Cumorah was located in New York State, not too far from the Ohio mounds.

Today any educated person can rattle off the Maya, the Aztec, and the

Inca as the awesome cultures of the New World. Their stereotypes would include human sacrifice and towering temples in the jungle with exotic tombs and such. However, even by the late nineteenth century, it was clear that if one wanted remains of high civilizations such as those described in the Book of Mormon, one should *not* turn to the Ohio country.

Thus when archaeology was finally brought into the Mormon question, it was usually with regard to the high cultures of Mesoamerica and Peru. Today Mormon literature, including my copy of the Book of Mormon, is illustrated with color pictures of copper, bronze, and gold artifacts from Peru and with temples from Mexico, not Ohio Valley Moundbuilder relics. Christ is shown visiting the New World in the midst of a ceremonial plaza with a broken Maya stela on one side and what may be the great pyramid, El Castillo, from Chichén Itzá in the background. Indeed, some contemporary Mormon maps now show the migrations going directly to Central America; even Hill Cumorah is now being sought by some in Vera Cruz!

That is certainly a far cry from the locations Joseph Smith espoused, but one can expect formal religions to be flexible in their interpretations as new data that must be fitted into church doctrine come to hand. Another reason for this shift of locale is that as North American archaeology developed, it was increasingly difficult to suggest that the Ohio Valley sites of the Moundbuilders, the supposed forts of the Nephites, dated from about the time of Christ. Now, thanks to carbon 14, we know that is the case, but that knowledge came to us only after World War II, long after those interested in tying archaeology to the Book of Mormon had settled happily on the "high" cultures to the south in Mexico and beyond. Some of the surviving Nephites were said to have fled in that direction, anyway. You will recall that even Squier and Davis favored such a tie-in between the Ohio Valley and Mexico.

I have suggested earlier that dealing with revealed faith is a difficult subject, especially when feelings run high on both sides of the question. I hope I have been able to treat the matter of Joseph Smith and the golden plates from Hill Cumorah in a responsible fashion. I will admit that I am skeptical of the original discovery; the absence of the actual ancient documents makes detailed analysis impossible today.

We will turn next to related archaeological documents that soon came from the earth of the Midwest and have a bearing on this topic. We journey to Kinderhook, Illinois, in the westernmost part of central Illinois, not far from the Mississippi River. Here, in Pike County in 1843, we are still in

Joseph Smith country; Nauvoo, where Smith and his followers resided at that time, was a mere sixty miles to the north. A gentleman named Robert Wiley started digging in a ten-foot-high Indian mound on April 16, 1843. Rain, he said, drove him off; he returned on the twenty-third with a large group of citizens, including two Mormon elders. Under some rocks, remains were found, including charcoal, ash, and human bones, and a bundle consisting of six brass plates.

Of course, the plates were inscribed with hieroglyphs, as was discovered after they had been washed. They found their way into the hands of Joseph Smith at Nauvoo and ultimately into a private museum in St. Louis, from which they disappeared. The Church newspaper hailed the Kinderhook plates as further proof of the authenticity of the Book of Mormon for many years. Joseph Smith apparently translated the inscriptions soon after they were found, saying that the documents told about the person buried in the mound, who was a descendant of Ham via a pharaoh of Egypt. These readings by Smith were not revealed until 1859, long after Smith's murder, but the information does come from Church sources.

I have stressed the sources because much of what we know about the Kinderhook plates comes from very biased anti-Mormon sources (W. Wyl, *Mormon Portraits,* 1886; William A. Linn, *The Story of the Mormons,* 1901). But the truth will out: in June 1879 a Wilbur Fugate wrote in response to a query about the plates that he and Robert Wiley, the first digger, and Bridge Whitton, a blacksmith, had created a humbug. Fugate detailed the way the plates were made as a joke to fulfill a prophecy by Mormon Elder Orson Pratt that "truth is yet to spring from the earth." With this hoax, as with the Cardiff Giant, we seem to have the motives and methods well under control. The impact, for a time, was more significant but is now at rest. Not so with the next event.

Newark, Ohio, is on the northern edge of the distribution of the great cluster of mounds and elaborate earthworks that characterize what we now call Hopewellian culture, instead of Moundbuilder. In the Cherry Valley of the Licking River there is a truly amazing group of generally small mounds accompanied by miles of circular, octagonal, and parallel earthworks covering nearly two square miles. A portion of it is still preserved in an archaeological park and also in a golf course today. It was repeatedly mapped by the likes of Atwater and Squier and Davis and later by a local resident, David Wyrick.

In 1860 Newark was a town of five thousand and, although not on a major river, was on transportation lines, first the Ohio Canal and later the

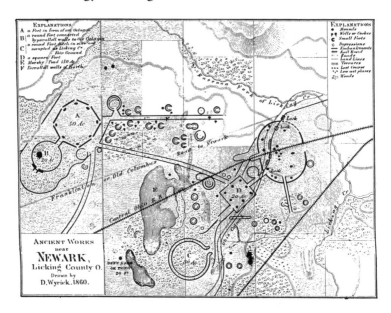

Ancient Works near Newark, Ohio

Central Ohio Railroad. The members of the Mormon Church on their western hegira stopped briefly in the northern part of the state at Kirtland, near Cleveland, until their bank failure and other problems that attended Joseph Smith in his early years forced them on to Missouri. Only then did they double back to Nauvoo on the Illinois side of the Mississippi River, where after a few successful years, with many immigrants flowing in from England as a result of very effective proselytizing by Brigham Young, Joseph Smith met his final destiny in the jail at Carthage, Illinois, in 1844.

Since the following decades were filled with strong debates about Mormonism and the ultimate sources of the Moundbuilders, the next events in Newark should not be too surprising. David Wyrick (d. 1864) was a sometime publisher until his paper failed and a good mathematics buff and county surveyor until crippling rheumatism forced him out of the job. Most important for us, Wyrick was an antiquarian. He came by this interest as a result of his surveying work, hence his careful map of the Newark works. He was also very committed to the Lost Tribes of Israel as the origin of the Moundbuilders.

On a summer day in late June 1860, Wyrick and his teenaged son were out puttering about in the Newark earthworks. The two were not digging in one of the numerous mounds but rather in the center of a circular depression on the northern edge of the site, an isolated spot. Indeed, Wyrick was in the habit of working alone.

Late in the hot afternoon of June 29, 1860, he hurried, despite his rheumatism, one supposes, into town, stopping at store after store proudly showing off his most recent find, which proved to his satisfaction that his Jewish theory of Moundbuilder origin was correct. The object, soon to be known as the Keystone or Newark Holy Stone, was a ground stone artifact about six inches long in the shape of a keystone and with an inscription in Hebrew incised on it.

By one of those coincidences that we are by now prepared for in Fantastic Archaeology, it just so happened that when David Wyrick went to his old friend and former teacher Israel Dille, he found him in the company of none other than Colonel Charles Whittlesey, West Point graduate, lawyer, geologist, and archaeologist. What a happy chance! They all hopped into a buggy and returned to the discovery spot, "where the earth they had thrown out was still fresh and moist."[3] The Keystone was found at a depth of only about a foot, and no other relics are mentioned as having been found with it. The dirt on the artifact, which still adhered to the stone, matched that in the excavation. Here was proof of context!

With Dille and Whittlesey as observers, once removed to be sure, the authenticity of the discovery was seemingly confirmed. The local citizens met in large numbers at the city hall on July 3 to see and hear about the remarkable discovery. A committee to study the local archaeological won-

The Keystone or Newark Holy Stone

der was set up; one member was Will Cunningham, a young insurance agent and something of an expert on Masonic symbolism. Cunningham was willing to suggest a tentative date of 431 B.C. for the object. Other members of the committee included an Episcopal rector and a local physician/antiquarian—a pretty good support team.

The inscription was the key, of course. Although a local Newark source said it was good Hebrew, the inscription was sent to Cincinnati, where more knowledgeable experts were called on for opinions. There was the usual carping about not having a good copy, but opinions were sharply divided with a majority feeling that the letters were of ancient style but others saying they were quite recent in form.

These generally favorable comments[4] were published in a local paper on July 10. The honeymoon did not last long—that very day the opposition newspaper cried "unmitigated hoax" and charged "some idle youth" with palming the stone off on the "too credulous" discoverer. Obviously following the opinion of Professor J. Cooper of Danville, Kentucky, the article stated that the inscription is in a "modern style [that] has spared the world the excitement of even [a] nine days' wonder." That just shows how wrong newspaper prophecy can be; the Newark Holy Stone is still with us 125 years later.

Typically, newspaper nay-saying did little to harm the case, and the locals in Cincinnati wanted to see the object for themselves. Events moved quickly in those days. Wyrick came down to Cincinnati on July 17 and had a very bad time of it. He was short of cash and could not afford the trip; he was told he would get some compensation for his trouble, but it would end up costing him all he had: $19. Besides, the results were even worse; the stone was called a hoax on every side. It was thought to be much too fresh and unstained to have lain for any length of time in the soil.

On July 27 even the *New York Times* got into the act with a letter signed "D," which branded the stone "Genus—bug, species—hum, recalling the celebrated Pickwick stone, belonging to the same category as the Gold Plates of the Mormon Bible." Wyrick was very upset and responded to his critics with an intemperate letter to the Cincinnati newspaper that had to be severely edited for publication. It does give a closer view of Wyrick's own feelings about the stone: "I am as anxious to know the true history of the stone as any one else." In response to rumors that it had been planted, he says that he had "a strong inclination that it might possibly be true—for I really had my fears from the time of discovery of such being the case—its having been deposited years ago, for a hoax."

Having publicly expressed so many doubts, some of them surely self-inflicted, David Wyrick was not prepared for the next attack. It too came out of the East and was signed D. Francis Bacon and published in *Harper's Weekly* on September 1, 1860. Possibly it was by the same "D" as in the *Times* letter; it was even more pungently written. The author was out "to crush and 'squelch' this serpent's eggs with a single tread." A recent commentator has called it "one of the most brutal diatribes imaginable." Certainly no other American hoax ever got such high-powered treatment, but Bacon attacked more than the stone and its inscription: Wyrick was portrayed as both the "contriver" and the receiver of monetary benefits; even Whittlesey's observations were impugned. Later in that same month one more nail in the coffin of authenticity would be driven by a Kentucky scholar and member of the American Oriental Society, who had photographs and tracings of the inscription; he was positive it was a hoax. When the object was shown at a society meeting, it was branded a "transparent fraud, or piece of pleasantry."

That was that for the Keystone, the first of the Newark Holy Stones, or so it would seem. But archaeology in Ohio in the summer of 1860 was not done with its surprises yet. About ten miles south of Newark on the border of Licking County was the site of the Great Stone Mound, once probably some fifty feet tall, not an unlikely estimate. By 1860 people were talking about where and how tall it *had* been since it had been destroyed for its stone fill decades before, in 1831–32. How big was it? It seems that over ten thousand wagonloads of fill, mainly stones, were carried off to make a dam. Earlier I discussed the magnitude of mechanical feats in the nineteenth century; this is one more disturbing example.

The site of the former great mound had been left pretty much alone since its major destruction, but some small earthen mounds had been left when the stone mantle was removed. In this peaceful summer of 1860, when the dogs of war would not be unleashed until the next spring, the local farmers apparently had nothing better to do in mid-July, with the crops laid by, than to dig in the nearby mounds. There had been enough noise in the local newspapers about Moundbuilders, purported inscriptions, and such to stir up some latent curiosity, or so it seemed.

On July 25, when all that controversy was breaking out in the local papers, David Wyrick traveled down to the Great Stone Mound to see what the local farmers had found in their little excavation there. A clay mound that had been covered by a stone slab mantle was revealed. At the center on top of a log platform was a wooden coffin, hollowed out of a log. In the

wooden burial container lay a skeleton; with or near it were copper bracelets.

This collection was what the farmers claimed to have found. It sounds
pretty fantastic. Well, not at all. Wyrick drew a cross-section of the mound
and a sketch of the coffin that was published at a much later date; they are
very believable. Many similar mounds have been excavated in Ohio since
1860, particularly from 1880 to 1920, and this complex of stone mantles,
central wooden tomb, and clay layers and platforms has been found over
and over. The log coffin is a bit out of character, but surprising preservation
could indeed occur in a mound of such magnitude. Size does mean something, and this huge mound was probably the burial spot of some very
important personages, hence the possibility of some very special treatments
such as a log casket. So I believe the story, so far. Wyrick removed the
wooden coffin; it was well preserved. The locals joked that this time Wyrick
had gotten an old water trough. What happened to the other artifacts is not
recorded. Wyrick took a curious visitor to see the site again in September,
and the drawings were made.

Then the situation got a bit more complex. For reasons that are not
entirely clear, except presumably the drive of natural curiosity, David Wyrick returned to the site on November 1 with a group of five men to make
further investigations. Perhaps they wanted to see if they could find another
sarcophagus. The group included Wyrick's cousin Jacob and a local dentist,
Dr. John Nicol. They puttered about in the ruins of the central chamber of
the mound, cutting through the bed of tough white clay with shovels. Then
Wyrick hit a stone in the clay that he had been cutting through like cheese.
After several more cuts he dropped his shovel, picked up the stone, and
exclaimed, "Here it is!" After jumping out of the hole in a single leap
(apparently his rheumetism was cured), he further exclaimed, "I've got it!"

"It" turned out to be the *second* Newark Holy Stone, also called the
Decalogue Stone because the Ten Commandments were written on it. It
was a nicely made small stone box containing a human image—Moses?—
surrounded by inscriptions. I have used David Wyrick's own description of
the discovery of the Decalogue Stone so his exclamations are not gratuitous
additions. Even Wyrick's most supportive advocate, Robert W. Alrutz of
Denison University, had to admit that "these outbursts make one wonder if
perhaps Wyrick had been prompted by someone (Nicol?) to expect to find
something unusual."[5] Dr. John Nicol had suggested that Wyrick test the
white clay. Was he the culprit? Three other artifacts were found in this same
location, a small stone bowl and two stone plumb bobs; the latter are
common Hopewellian artifacts.

Decalogue Stone (front and back views)

Although the Decalogue Stone was an interesting artifact visually, especially its long inscription, it got short shrift from the outside world. Even Nicol discredited the inscribed stone and the box. Two of Wyrick's friends, the Reverend McCarty and Israel Dille, brought the two Newark Holy Stones to the attention of the American Ethnological Society in New York. The recording secretary of that society, Theodore Dwight, seemed to handle the matter with fairness. He corresponded with Wyrick; through these letters we see the decline of Wyrick's finances. He offered to sell his precious discoveries for a mere $200. But not much was done, and the correspondence ended. Wyrick received $1,000 for sale of a piece of property in January 1862. The archival record stops, only to pick up again two years later on a tragic note: a notice in April 1864 of a forthcoming sheriff's sale of David Wyrick's property and then a short obituary telling of his death by his own hand. "He was a man of eccentric character and considerable attainment. . . . many persons regarded him as unsurpassed as a Surveyor. He had an investigating turn of mind and was a frequent correspondent of the Smithsonian Institute."[6] It also mentioned the Newark Holy Stones.

Unlike many of the other cases we have considered, this one has been carefully researched recently. In 1980 Robert W. Alrutz of Denison University, only a short distance from the find spot, wrote a lengthy review of the Newark Holy Stones, which he subtitled "The History of an Archaeological Tragedy." His review was thorough, and he made use of a large number of contemporary documents. This biologist, whom I met a few years ago, is a skillful scholar and a very dedicated biographer. His findings are for David Wyrick; he says: "the Newark Holy Stones shall remain enigmatic until new evidences are found or new techniques of evaluation are applied."[7]

There is no desire on my part to prosecute or persecute David Wyrick—that is not my intent; rather, I wish only to evaluate the archaeological evidence at hand, the ever-needed context and character of the artifacts, not of Wyrick. This case does not end quietly with an overdose of laudanum, "which he [Wyrick] had been in the habit of using." We must return to Colonel Charles Whittlesey, whom we last saw some years earlier on that exciting day of the discovery of the first Holy Stone. Whittlesey, surely one of the most distinguished figures in Ohio archaeology at this time, had been an early believer in the Newark finds, but he did not write anything of note on them, aside from some short newspaper articles, until much later.

In 1872, in a professional paper, Whittlesey described a series of archaeological frauds, including the Newark Holy Stones. He indicated that evidence was found after Wyrick's death which included suspicious materials among his personal effects such as a Hebrew Bible, engraving tools, and some black rock. These findings clearly indicated a hoax. Whittlesey was shocked; he took up the task of debunking frauds and wrote another important paper on the subject in 1879 in which he dealt with the Grave Creek Stone.

In his 1980 discussion of the Holy Stones, Alrutz tried to cast doubt on Whittlesey's discoveries and on Wyrick's direct involvement in the hoax. But Alrutz, a biologist, does not address the artifacts themselves. He is quite right that we cannot indict David Wyrick beyond a shadow of a doubt. There are a few, very few, loose ends, as there always will be more than a hundred years later.

But we can now address the Holy Stones themselves, and they fail every possible test. They still stand alone as the only inscriptions of their sort; the forms are not epigraphically correct for the time period. The artifacts are not like any Hopewellian forms that have ever been recovered. They are not part of larger contexts—if genuine Hebrew texts, why are they

Charles C. Whittlesey

not associated with other artifacts of Palestine at the time of Christ? Instead, these materials are placed in the context of the artifacts of North American Indians who built the sites at which the Holy Stones were found. Like all frauds, they had a purpose, whether to support David Wyrick's Lost Tribes hypothesis or to fool the local populace we will never know. They were not very successful outside of Licking County, Ohio, I'm afraid.

But what of the *other* Holy Stones? There are more? Yes, three more, all turning up in Ohio between 1865 and 1867 and all with a little Hebrew script on them. They are all so bad that I cannot even bear to present them. The reader will have to take it on faith that they are all egregious fakes, phonies, hoaxes, and frauds. I will present only two pieces of data: one inscribed stone was found *inside* a human skull; another was cherished by a doctor at a hospital for the insane. Indeed, a recent survey of old collection photos at the Peabody Museum that I made showed that almost every nineteenth-century Ohio collector had an "inscribed stone." Mercifully, few made it into the literature.

No, they do not prove that David Wyrick was right all along; what they do prove is that you can fool some of the people over and over again. There was a viable market for interesting artifacts in the golden age of American archaeology; Putnam's 1883 note in *Science* deals mainly with fakes of every kind being manufactured to fill that need—it is no more complex than that.

Further proof of that sentiment is to be found in a recent study of the Decalogue Stone by Barry Fell's Epigraphic Society. In this brief published revision of the textual reading from the inscription no mention at all is made of any question of the authenticity of the artifact; there is not a hint of a hoax. So take heart, David Wyrick. Perhaps your epitaph should be from Dylan Thomas:

> Do not go gentle into that good night,
> Old age should burn and rage at close of day;
> Rage, rage against the dying of the light.[8]

You have supporters yet.

Our next case is a very close neighbor to the one just completed both in time and in space. Variously known as the Michigan Relics or the Soper Frauds, they too have close ties to Joseph Smith and his saga of the early times in the Great Lakes area. The Mormon Church became an interested party to the investigation of these ingenuous artifacts that made their first appearance in central Michigan in 1890. The list of participants is right out of Central Casting: James O. Scotford, a sometime sign painter, who turns out to have even greater facility with a shovel; Daniel E. Soper, sometime Secretary of State of Michigan, later gratuitously called "Senator," collector and promoter of the Michigan Relics; and the Reverend James Savage, a Catholic priest, Dean of the Church of the Most Holy Trinity in Detroit, who had a great interest in the local archaeology and was a collector of artifacts.

It all started innocently enough, in October 1890, when James Scotford was out digging postholes for a fence in Montcalm County, Michigan, not far from Wyman. The farm was in the central part of the state, northeast of Grand Rapids. The fence line ran over a small hillock, and while digging there Scotford struck a hard object. He first found either a clay cup or a small earthen casket; the stories differ. The next spring other and more remarkable objects were discovered by excavations in some low mounds.

A "Syndicate" was formed in Stanton, the county seat, to continue these Michigan explorations and to form a collection. Photographs were taken of these wonderful objects and were sent to experts, including Putnam at Peabody (not found in our archives). Alfred Emerson of Lake Forest College near Chicago got some of these photos and came to Wyman to see the artifacts for himself at the end of June 1891. His conclusions, after

Daniel E. Soper

seeing this amazing collection of clay artifacts, which included as many as seventy-five small tablets, some disks, and several small caskets with "incumbent [sic] lions" on the lids, were strong and forthright: "The articles were bad enough in the photographs; an examination proved them to be humbugs of the first water. They were all of unbaked clay, and decorated with bogus hieroglyphics in which cuneiform characters appeared at intervals. These [hieroglyphics] were all stamped [on]. . . . On opening one casket we found that the lid had been dried on a machine-sawed board."[9]

Even after being so strongly denounced by Emerson, a group of these objects was brought in the fall of 1891 to the University of Michigan, where they were put in the hands of Francis W. Kelsey, a Classical archaeologist, for close examination. He found the inscriptions to be a jumble of ancient Oriental writing. The *unbaked* clay was indeed a problem; when tested at the museum at the university, the objects disintegrated readily in water. Thus they could not have been in the ground very long before they were dug up. To try to bring a stop to the deception, Kelsey put a story about the fakes in the local newspaper, and then he and Morris Jastrow of the University of Pennsylvania jointly published critical comments on the materials in the January 28, 1892, issue of the *Nation*.

That forthright debunking should have ended the matter, but it was only Phase I in this fantastic archaeological sequence. Cultural evolution is

Michigan Relics

not to be denied even to James Scotford, though it did take a little time, six years in fact. During the summer of 1898, a man of little means and suffering some travail appeared at the door of the University Museum in Ann Arbor loaded down with several wooden trunks. These contained some human bones and a miscellaneous collection of artifacts quite like those just described. Also included was a sizable seated figure holding a tablet.

According to a document left behind, these interesting artifacts had all been part of a traveling show hawked as being from "Deposits of Three Thousand Years Ago!" But our weary traveler, quite likely Scotford himself, had fallen on hard times and was now willing to sell these treasures, at first for $1,000 and later $100. The museum Curator told him they were all fakes and thus he was dealing in forgeries, a risky business at best. The result was that the whole collection was hurriedly deposited in the museum basement, pending the owner's return. These objects still rest in Ann Arbor.

The Phase II artifacts do show some progress; they are of improved workmanship, and the clay is baked hard. Also we note that some work on slate and metallurgy is just appearing—a few coins and bits of metal slag. Obviously this indicates a crucial time in cultural development. Continuity does exist in many categories; indeed, the selfsame stamps may have been used in the hieroglyphics, and the designs are nearly identical. A "Deluge" tablet takes off from a smaller version in Phase I; we have scenes with rain falling and then the Ark floating, and finally disembarkation. These haunting scenes will appear again in the climax stage of this art form in Phase III.

There are some clues to the origin of these fine artifacts included in the trunks so precipitously left in Ann Arbor. Besides the handbill quoted above and a few spare admission tickets, there is a document concerning the discovery of the "Winchester Casket," most of the contents of which seem to be in the current collection. Purportedly, the small clay box with cover was found on an altar in a bed of ashes and burnt bone that covered a series of thirteen skeletons. Some stone tools and two copper coins were found in the "casket." The document concludes with four signatures, all apparently in the same handwriting; one of the signers is William H. Scotford; the place is Winchester, Mecosta, Michigan. Mecosta is the county adjacent to the locale of the previous finds, but I have not yet located Winchester. Scotford is, of course, a familiar name. Thus ends Phase II with the artifacts safely out of circulation in the Ann Arbor museum basement.

As in all culture developmental sequences, Phase III is the classic period, the one in which technology reaches higher levels and the fruits of that technology are spread. Why should our saga of the Michigan Relics be any different? In the fall of 1908 the Copper Age began. Professor Kelsey gives us a firsthand description:

> From different and widely separated points have come reports that copper implements and tablets of unique character were being offered to collectors, and that the distributing center was Detroit. Some success in disposing of the specimens seems to have been met with; at any rate within a month I have visited a collector who had purchased not far from fifty. . . . The surface of these specimens had been corroded to give the appearance of age; but notwithstanding the difference in material, the designs are in part identical with those familiar from the previous forgeries. (Kelsey, 1908: 56)

The scenes on the copper tablets include the Deluge in four parts; the Tower of Babel, perhaps; a calendar; and the Ten Commandments. These identifications were *not* based on reading the texts on the tablets because no translations, thankfully, were available at the time. The content of each tablet is readily ascertained from the depictions on them; for example, the Commandments tablet is divided into ten blocks, each numbered by the well-known "dot method": one to ten dots tell the story. The graphics show a dependence on the straightedge and compass, and the inscriptions are punched into the metal, not engraved. They are quite hi-tech. The human figures are altogether another thing; one may compassionately term them childlike.

Kelsey was outraged at the wholesale spread of these fakes throughout the state and rushed into print early the next year (1908) with a well-documented article in the national anthropological journal, the *American Anthropologist*. He found clear evidence to connect James O. Scotford, then living in Detroit, with the sale of these bogus coppers. He thought no museum would be foolish enough to buy these obvious forgeries, but he did think that amateur collectors should be protected from such mistakes. His concern was well placed, as we shall see.

Two amateurs who took up the trail of finding these copper artifacts with perhaps the greatest assiduousness were the good Father James Savage, of Detroit's Church of the Most Holy Trinity, and Daniel E. Soper, the former Secretary of State. Their collections included some of the most important tablets, including the Deluge, all of which had been found very near Detroit.

Savage and Soper were deeply involved by November 1909 with these latest products of the Scotford "factory," when they were visited by a

James E. Talmage of Salt Lake City, Utah. Talmage had a Ph.D. in geology; his visit was part of an investigation he carried out for the Deseret Museum of that city. Talmage's interest had been sparked that summer by a clay tablet he had seen in an Ohio museum. It was a Michigan Relic, and he soon was in touch by mail with the unlikely duo of amateurs in Detroit.

It will perhaps be no surprise to anyone to learn, first, that Savage and Soper were soon to believe, if they did not already, that they were dealing with remains relevant to the descendants of the Lost Tribes of Israel and that some of the tablets documented the war between the prehistoric people and the Indians. Second, they learned that Dr. Talmage from Salt Lake City was in Detroit on a mission supported by the Mormons; *Deseret* is a Jaredite word used for the name of a putative Mormon state in the nineteenth century.

Talmage studied the collections of Savage and Soper with care, noting the "sign-manual" of the forger, as Kelsey had called it, on every artifact. This pseudocuneiform maker's mark is on every single Michigan Relic: talk about chutzpah—Scotford is the only faker in the archaeological field that I know of who dared so brazenly to identify his handicraft. Talmage further states in his report, not published until several years later, that if the objects in these collections were authentic, much of the history in the Book of Mormon would be confirmed by external evidence. In his report he does not mince words when making his conclusions. Before detailing his trials and tribulations in the little sand mounds near Detroit, Talmage states unequivocally that the relics are forgeries. Thus their confirmation of the Book of Mormon is not upheld and is false.

The secret was out, but it is very instructive to see how Talmage reached this conclusion; would that some of our other cases had been so adroitly tested! He had intended to open a few mounds on his own, scarcely hoping to find relics, but at least to study the structure of the mounds in which all the Phase III artifacts were found. His newly met mentors, Savage and Soper, agreed that that was a good idea and suggested that he hire James O. Scotford to be his digger. Talmage knew exactly who that was and demurred, but his host would allow him to make no other choice. Fully recognizing what was happening, he agreed.

Talmage made two field trips with Soper and Scotford and kept a journal of those little adventures. They took a streetcar out of town; Scotford had brought no digging instrument but borrowed a shovel from the "caretaker" of the property, which was termed Palmer Park. About a mile from the car stop, they came to a woodland with a "hummocky surface," where there were numerous small mounds, none more than about three feet high. Scotford selected a mound near one that had already been opened. A small and shallow excavation in the center was quickly made and bingo they had a copper ax with the usual maker's mark on it, as well as a few more axes.

I shan't detail the rest of these two very successful field expeditions except to give a tally of Scotford's luck: a large black slate tablet, well decorated; a small perforated slate pendant; the copper ax, already mentioned; a blade of slate with an elephant(?)-warrior confrontation that would make even Henry Mercer blush; and a large slate tablet—the prize of the lot, with the full Noachian drama in four acts on one side and a battle scene and a calendar on the other. Finally, there was found a small copper blade decorated with only the "tribal mark," as the devotees referred to Scotford's "trademark." It was quite a haul, but then a museum man from Utah does not come out to the site very often; it's the kind of digging luck one can only hope for.

Talmage was impressed with the way the objects were found; there were no obvious signs of previous excavations, and many of the artifacts were associated with charcoal layers. When they found the small slate pendant with a few drawings on it, Talmage was a bit taken aback by Scotford's statement concerning one of the designs: "This is like what was found on one of the plates from Mormon Hill, at Cumorah, New York."[10] How did he know that since the Book of Mormon does not provide such details? Although they did dig a few dry holes, generally they were able to get into a mound and out quickly. After a find was made, they rarely dug much further.

Leaving Detroit with his booty, Talmage traveled to New York and Washington to exhibit his six artifacts to museum people there. The artifacts were pronounced fakes by all. That information at hand, Talmage returned quietly to Detroit and went back to the site of his previous triumphs. With the aid of some newly hired diggers, he opened twenty-two mounds and did not find a single artifact. It was negative evidence, as he admitted, but "when cumulative [it] may become decisive." Not bad testing!

During his previous Detroit stop, Talmage studied the Savage and Soper collections in detail; he estimated that there were some two to three hundred artifacts. He examined the slate carvings and found with microscopic inspection that the lines were very fresh, comparable to those made experimentally. He also noted the tooth marks of a modern saw which had not been smoothed away on one of the tablets that he had observed being "found."

After a discussion by mail of this flagrant signature of modern workmanship with his Detroit correspondents, they demanded its return. Since Talmage had paid for the digger's time, he felt that he could keep it. Talmage found modern file marks on the battle-ax as well. He also had chemical analysis done on the copper and found it to be modern in origin, not made from the native ores as are genuine Indian artifacts. All in all, Talmage made an excellent review of the data, damning the characters of the inscriptions and the form of the art as well. There is not much else he could have done to prove his case except to get a confession from Scotford.

Now we know that Talmage actually got the next best thing. A recent article in the *Epigraphic Society Occasional Papers* (vol. 17, 1988) relates that study of the Talmage documents indicates he had contacted Scotford's stepdaughter. She fully implicated her stepfather in the fraud but asked that her statement not be made public until after her mother's death. Talmage kept his promise.

But while our gentleman from Salt Lake City was so confidently branding the finds as frauds, another worker from an adjacent vineyard published a very different report. This one was by Rudolph Etzenhouser, an official of the Reorganized Church of the Latter-Day Saints, a splinter group of Mormons that did not go west in the 1840s. This Mormon published in 1910 a brochure illustrating the Michigan Relics and stating that they were "pre-historic originals" whose inscriptions when translated would add an interesting chapter to the ancient history of this continent. He also provided a picture of Daniel Soper and said that to him "belongs the credit of having been for several years the moving spirit in the investigation of these prehistoric records."[11]

Kelsey kept up his attack on these frauds and found out that a Professor Charles Davis of the U.S. Geological Survey had stopped to see James Scotford at his home in Edmore before he moved to Detroit. Davis had heard of the wonderful discoveries but found Scotford not at home. His wife, however, showed him the relics that were at hand. She even brought out a volume of the encyclopedia to compare the drawings therein with those on the relics. They were remarkably similar. The editor of the journal in which Kelsey wrote told a pathetic story of a very old collector from Montcalm County, Michigan, near Scotford's home, whom he had visited. His demi-museum was crammed full of Michigan Relics for which he had paid a lot of money. Kelsey's concern for the amateur being ripped off was indeed real; frauds such as this one do have real victims.

The odd couple of Daniel Soper and Father Savage must now be discussed, as it is not for nothing that the Michigan Relics are also popularly often referred to as the Soper Frauds. There seems to be little question as to the Catholic Father's strong faith and commitment to the authenticity of the artifacts. In a 1911 article in the *American Antiquarian*, he broke a long silence by writing a strong defense of the relics. He came face to face, as it were, with the major debunker, Kelsey, who published a contrary view in the same issue. Father Savage wrote at length about the copper-using Indian cultures of Wisconsin and Michigan but said that their artifacts were not "chill hardened" and were easily distinguished from the copper objects Soper and he had found. In noting this difference, Savage was correct. He further stated that they had opened more than five hundred mounds in four counties. The trees growing on these mounds attested to their age. Surprisingly, despite a variety of other artifacts of clay, copper, and ground stone, there are no flint implements of any kind. Father Savage was sure that these were the remains of the descendants of the Lost Tribes, who were ultimately exterminated by the flint-using Indians.

Daniel Soper's story is a little more complex. When James Talmage from Utah first met Soper in Detroit, he indicated that he had heard "conflicting reports" about the man but in charity tried to believe the best he had heard. There is little question that Soper had a close personal relationship with James Scotford and those who dug with him. Thanks to some research into the Soper correspondence of the period, carried out in the 1950s by A. L. Spooner of Detroit, we are not dependent on hearsay for more information on Daniel E. Soper.

Soper was from Newaygo, Newaygo County, in west-central Michigan, about forty miles due west of James Scotford's locale. He ran a stationery store and later the county newspaper. He had a large collection of Indian artifacts from the area, many of which he had excavated himself. Apparently, his rise to state office was quick, and he did not serve out his term as Secretary of State, resigning and moving to Arizona following charges of fiscal misconduct. It is said that while in Arizona he "planted" some genuine Michigan Indian artifacts for the university people to find, but they were not fooled. These events apparently took place before 1900.

Soper then moved to San Francisco, where by his own account he first read in the newspaper about the Michigan Relics. Later, back in Michigan, Soper acquired some of these interesting artifacts, which he saw in a store window in Pontiac. By 1909 he was allied with Father Savage as joint collectors and supporters of the objects, as we know from Talmage's report. He was also joined by R. B. Orr, Director of the Provincial Museum in Toronto, who was fortunate enough to get some Michigan Relics for that institution. Most of the discoveries described above were made between October 1907 and 1912.

However, as late as October 1920, successful excavations were being carried out at some mounds at Halfway, near Detroit, and much of the same merry band was involved: Soper, Father Savage, R. B. Orr from Toronto, and his friend Major James. Two additions were A. L. Spooner, our informant, and his father, an old friend of Soper. No mention is made of James Scotford. By now perhaps his work was done; nevertheless, this group found two fine stone tablets and a pipe that was caught up in a tree root. This whole operation (1890–1920) must be one of the longest-running scams in prehistory.

Both Soper and Father Savage were long-lived. Soper died in his eighties shortly after 1922, and Father Savage passed away about 1927. The Soper collection might have gone to the University of Tennessee because he lived in Chattanooga in his later years; the Savage collection was donated to Notre Dame University. Both men retained their faith in the Michigan Relics to the end. Soper was vehement on the subject; he was always ready to face his critics. "I defy and challenge them," he wrote. He said he never sold artifacts; there is clear evidence that he bought them. In Soper's later years he took the title "Senator" and was known by many for his enthralling talks on prehistoric people. That Soper was deeply involved in the Michigan Relics operation for over twenty years is clear. He kept interest high in these amazing objects long after everyone else had laid them to rest. His motive was elusive, however; did he really believe, or was he just a slick charlatan?

I do not know for sure. What I do know is that as a current archaeological colleague from Ann Arbor has assured me, the Soper Frauds are like the miraculous Dragon Teeth of China: they keep turning up again and again in the darndest places. Some fine plates have recently surfaced at a Catholic monastery in south Louisiana, where I had a good look at them, maker's mark and all. I think I can trace them safely back to Michigan and Father Savage. James Scotford, wherever he is, indeed achieved a small touch of immortality. A recent book by a sweet old lady, Henriette Mertz, "proves" that his ever-present "trademark" is really a holy symbol, not yet deciphered.

There are remnant traces of some of these cases surviving even today: new translations of old hoaxes or new excavations in Middle America for the Mormon cause. Who could have guessed that the white salamander would reappear with the aid of Mark Hofmann, that Professor Alrutz

Black Slate from Louisiana

would carefully reinvestigate the Newark Holy Stones, or that Talmage's long-hidden notes on Scotford's daughter would finally come to light? It is a seemingly never-ending saga.

There is a post–World War II phenomenon that ties into this topic, and I will wind up with a very brief look at it. Creationism can hardly be seen as a new topic; after all, Biblical fundamentalism has strong nineteenth-century roots in America, and the 1925 Scopes trial in Tennessee is often seen as a landmark of sorts on this subject.

The Creationists had worked with both biology (evolution) and geology (chronology), the two most important aspects that had to be dealt with if an appropriate chronological alignment with the Biblical version was to be accepted. As early as the 1940s, archaeology came into the picture with the discovery of giant fossil footprints, possibly human, and their purported association with dinosaur footprints. This "evidence" made some Creationists hopeful that the theory of evolution could be destroyed in a single stroke.

But the real revival of Creationism did not begin until some thirty

Francis W. Kelsey

years ago under the leadership of Henry B. Morris from Texas. He was a civil engineer at Rice Institute, and he had coauthored a volume titled *The Genesis Flood* (1961), which took a very conservative position on the subject: it really was a six-day chronology of creation and included a worldwide flood that laid down most of the geological strata on earth. Its appeal was that it looked legitimate as a scientific contribution.

In 1963 the Creation Research Society was established as a place for like-minded scientists, and by the 1970s Morris had an Institute for Creation Research to carry out research and then train right-minded scholars. Both the society and the institute have met with considerable success, and they are turning out a variety of educational materials: books, pamphlets, and visual educational items to aid in the propagation of their beliefs.

The Creationists have continued to attack geological chronology, built, as they see it, on a misreading of the stratigraphic record and attributing much too much time to the fossil record. Their major archaeological emphasis has been on the man/dinosaur correlation and on attempts, so far futile, to locate Noah's Ark on Mount Ararat. Recently the dinosaur connection seems to be falling apart, and there have been strong actions from the American Anthropological Association and the AAAS, via the journal *Science,* to counter the flood of Creationist literature. We must hope that the truth will keep the public free from a regression into such religious conservatism and antiscientific prejudice.

Honestly, because of some current events in archaeology, the raison d'être for this volume, I am not as full of hope as that last sentence might indicate. As a result, I am most willing to throw in my lot with the opinion so forcefully presented by Francis Kelsey, who had watched with some disbelief by 1911 some twenty years of deep faith in the wild Michigan Relics. He said: "So long as human nature remains the same, it may be presumed that men [and women] will be ready to believe what they wish to believe, and that no hoax [or wild supposition] will be too preposterous to be without a following."[12] Amen, brother, amen.

9
Westward to Vinland:
The Vikings Are Coming

Though Scandinavians [Norse] may have reached the shores of
Labrador, the soil of the United States has not one vestige of their
presence.
GEORGE BANCROFT, 1840

When intrepid Viking seafarers finally made landfall on the North American continent, they certainly made history. Recovering information to
prove the time and place of that landfall has, however, been as challenging a
quest as any in New World archaeology. The tantalizing Norse sagas have
for nearly a century and a half been the siren songs leading dozens of
scholars and hundreds of faithful to believe that it was, indeed, the Vikings
who were the first Europeans to visit the New World, beating Christopher
Columbus by centuries. The sagas, first as oral narratives, then later, hundred of years later, transcribed as written medieval documents, told of the
westward voyages of these fearless North Atlantic explorers from Iceland to
Greenland and ultimately to Markland, Helgaland, and Vinland on the
North American continent.

Unlike the long-lived Atlantis myth and the Ten Lost Tribes of Israel
hypothesis, both of which started their explanatory careers as early as the
sixteenth century in the works of Acosta and Garcia, the Viking connection
is almost entirely a nineteenth-century discovery. Following the great bib-
liophile Justin Winsor in his old but still authoritative review of the topic,
however, there were a few casual references to Vikings in North America in
the previous century. But it was the work of Henry Wheaton, an American
who served as minister in Copenhagen, entitled *History of the Norsemen*
(1831), and even more especially that of the Dane Carl Christian Rafn (1795–
1864), whose volume *Antiquitates Americanae* appeared in 1837, that really
started the frantic and almost unending search for Viking remains.

This ceaseless search continues even though the noted historian

Carl C. Rafn

George Bancroft in 1834, after dismissing the sagas as not very good historical documents, said quite positively that "the intrepid mariners [Vikings] who colonized Greenland could easily have extended their voyage to Labrador; but no clear evidence establishes the natural probability that they accomplished the passage." Thus though opening the door to the possibility, Bancroft later (1840) stated categorically that "the soil of the *United States* has not one vestige of their presence" (emphasis added), and Winsor in 1889 added that that statement "is [as] true now as when first written."[1] The facts are that in the nearly one hundred years that have passed since Winsor's parenthetical addition those Viking vestiges in the United States have not been produced. Happily for all of us, the view from North America as a whole is nowhere near that gloomy.

The Vikings, one would have to say, were very logical visitors to the New World. Unlike the myth-shrouded Atlanteans or the more land-based Tribes of Israel, the Vikings' exploring and maritime feats are a well-researched matter of historic and archaeological record. The exciting documentation of Viking penetration even into the Middle East is known from the manuscript of an Arab, Ibn Fadlan, who was captured by Vikings in A.D. 922. His adventures served as the background for a recent novel by

Michael Crichton. Then, too, the facts of Viking settlements in Iceland and Greenland were well known and not simply matters of speculation. The sagas described the Viking voyages around A.D. 1000 in some detail, which could be related to documented personages such as Eric the Red and his son Leif Ericson.

Although events such as making landfalls were well enough described, it was the exact identification of these localities such as the long-sought "Vinland" that would be the difficult, if not impossible, task. Rafn's various publications, for example, included maps that put Vinland as far south as New Jersey, but the best guesses by 1850, including one by Samuel Haven, were that Vinland was in Narragansett Bay. Two pieces of hard evidence were frequently used to bolster that hypothesis: Dighton Rock on the Taunton River in Massachusetts and the Old Stone Tower in Newport, Rhode Island. Dighton Rock is a forty-ton boulder on the east bank of the river, eight miles north of Fall River in southeastern Massachusetts. The rock is covered with numerous incised markings, some possibly runic, and entered the documented archaeological record as early as 1680. The Newport Tower, in the center of present-day Newport, was known as early as 1677, and Rafn supported a Norse connection for it.

By the 1860s the stage was set for a rush to prove that Vikings had indeed come and left their marks on the venerable landscape of the United States. One measure of this Viking mania was that it was incorporated into the popular literature of the time. I refer to James Russell Lowell's *Biglow Papers*, which I obliquely mentioned when discussing Dickens and the *Pickwick Papers*. Lowell was a rather unlikely source for such a literary production. Best known as a serious poet and a member of the academic ranks, he was the author of the Eulogy for Jeffries Wyman I quoted earlier. During the Mexican War (1846–48), which he strongly opposed, however, he wrote a series of humorous letters and poems, at first anonymous, which presented his attitudes through several New England characters who used the dialect and mode of speech appropriate to their heritage.

He was a strong abolitionist, and, somewhat happily stunned by the success of his first series of *Biglow Papers*, he took up the pen again during the Civil War. It was in this second set of letters that the Reverend Homer Wilbur, M.A., his long-winded and pretentiously erudite parson, discusses at some length a discovery pertaining to the "ante-Columbian discovery of this continent by the Northmen." The letter was dated April 12, 1862. He had reported the discovery of this "relick" on the east bank of Bushy Brook in North Jaalam some months before. Jaalam was Lowell's Lake Wobegon.

He was not above such run-together names either, as evidenced by the given name of his character Mr. Swain: "Birdofredum."

The good Reverend Mr. Wilbur acknowledges the scholarship of Rafn and indicates that the most interesting runic inscriptions are those even the great Danish professor cannot read because they "accordingly offer peculiar temptations to enucleating sagacity." Wilbur had literary pretensions, and he lovingly larded his epistles with Latinate phrases. But he also provided us with the wonderful description of the activities of fantastic archaeologists that follows: "These last [the undecipherable rune stones] are naturally deemed the most valuable by intelligent antiquaries, and to this class the stone now in my possession fortunately belongs. Such give a picturesque variety to ancient events, because susceptible oftentimes of as many interpretations as there are individual archaeologists."[2] In good scholarly fashion Wilbur has had his treasure photographed and sent copies to many learned men. "I may hereafter communicate their different and (*me judice*) equally erroneous solutions." After trying many different ways to decipher the stone, the reverend fell back on a technique that is still widely used even today.

> After a cursory examination, merely sufficing for an approximative estimate of its length, I would write down a hypothetical inscription based upon antecedent probabilities, and then proceed to extract from the characters engraven on the stone a meaning as nearly as possible conformed to this *a priori* product of my own ingenuity. The result more than justified my hopes, inasmuch as the two inscriptions were made without any great violence to tally in all essential particulars. I then proceeded, not without some anxiety, to my second test, which was, to read the Runick letters diagonally, and again with the same success. (Lowell, 1900: 314–315)

His final test, requiring some labor, was to turn the stone upside down, and thank goodness, it still read perfectly. The inscription went as follows:

HERE
BJARNA GRIMOLFSSON
FIRST DRANK CLOUD-BROTHER
THROUGH CHILD-OF-LAND-AND-WATER

(Lowell, 1900: 315)

Wilbur indicates that this means that he drew smoke through a reed stem; thus it becomes the first written record of smoking tobacco. The *Bjarna* of the inscription is in fact "Bjarni Grimolfsson," a fictive early voyager known from *Erik's Saga,* who was purportedly lost at sea. Lowell has changed that a bit. Sadly, Wilbur tells us that a nearby clergyman has gratuitously deciphered the rock as a funeral slab of another Viking, which irks him considerably. He closes his letter on the happy note that the light has just struck the stone in another direction, and he is about to do yet another decipherment. Fortunately for archaeology, the parson died of an apoplectic fit on the afternoon of Christmas Day 1862 so the reading of the Jaalam Rune Stone is no longer being revised. But James Russell Lowell wrote more truth than spoof, as we will sadly see.

Not surprisingly, there was ethnic pride built into this "Vikings Discovered America" story, and the argument was fiercely debated, especially in New England, until after the turn of the century. Larger events, however, were shaping the next major Viking find, and it was not to be in New England. The flood of European immigrants from the 1830s on had radically altered the ethnic composition across America. As the railroads in the 1860s and 1870s completed the connections to the West Coast by the northern route, crowds of Scandinavians were sold boat passage to the East Coast with train tickets to the old Northwest Territory: Wisconsin, Minnesota, and Iowa. As wholesale lumbering pushed north in Minnesota, clearing the land as if with a giant scythe swung by Paul Bunyan, the Scandinavian farmers followed to plant the land as far north and west as the growing season and soil would allow.

Even in west-central Minnesota, called the Land of 10,000 Lakes, the edge-of-the-plains landscape was dotted with hundreds of lakes. We pick up the Viking story in Douglas County, Minnesota, in this lake-studded area only forty-five miles from the Dakota border and the true Plains.

The 1880s were years of development and growth for the Scandinavian population throughout the Upper Midwest, as the area is now called. The economic climb from hand labor, such as railroad work, to more skilled and more economically rewarding positions was being made by a number of these immigrants. First-generation Minnesotans now, they began to move into politics amd positions with more power. Just as in the East, however, the changes were slow. The old Anglo-Saxon stock, many of whom had gotten there just a generation or so earlier, were in control of lumber and milling enterprises that would make great family fortunes, which in turn would make it difficult for outsiders to get much chance to advance. Epithets like "Dumb Swede" would be current in the region for generations.

Thus one can understand very easily the interest and ethnic pride evidenced during the 1880s in the notions that Vikings had really made it to America long before anyone else, Native Americans excepted. The announcement of the World's Columbian Exposition in Chicago in 1892 to celebrate the four hundredth anniversary of the "Discovery of America" by Christopher Columbus was not met with great keenness by the Scandinavians of the Upper Midwest. Indeed, they were measurably angry, as the local papers demonstrated, and they set out to do something about it.

Private funds were raised, and when the fair opened a year late in 1893, there was a full-scale Viking ship riding the waves of Lake Michigan. Built on the pattern of a Viking ship excavated in Norway, this sturdy vessel had sailed across the North Atlantic, come down the St. Lawrence, and entered the Great Lakes. It was a great tribute to Viking maritime skills and is still on exhibit in Chicago. The Spanish did not make out so well; replicas of the *Niña, Pinta,* and *Santa Maria* just barely made it across and had to be towed part of the way. No question who won that sea battle.

With ethnic feelings still prickly, a crucial event took place on Olof Ohman's farm, near Kensington, Douglas County, Minnesota. In the fall of 1898 he was clearing a small knoll not far from his house. His son Edward was helping him remove some small trees, which were second growth because the land had been cleared earlier by the first settlers. As they grubbed out an aspen, they found a large, flat stone no more than six inches below the surface. It was clasped in the roots of this young tree, the size of which was later to be a point of contention. Edward brushed some of the dirt off the stone and noticed characters chiseled on it. After the stone was washed, Nils Flaten, a near neighbor, was called over for a look at the remarkable find and was shown the place of discovery.

The stone was then taken to the nearby town of Kensington and displayed in a shop window for all to see. Local citizens, including Sam Olsen and J. P. Hedberg, took an interest in the discovery. The newspapers in Minneapolis–St. Paul published stories on the Kensington Rune Stone, as it soon was called, once the strange characters had been recognized as being Scandinavian runes, a form of notation used in the Northland before the introduction of Latin and the Roman alphabet. The inscription was shown to several scholars, including a University of Minnesota professor named O. J. Breda, who gave a fairly complete translation with the exception of the date.

The stone told an exciting tale of Norsemen on an exploring expedition; the party was set upon by marauders (Indians?), and ten of the men were murdered. Both Breda and Professor George O. Curume from Evans-

Olof Ohman and Kensington Stone

ton, Illinois, declared the inscription fraudulent, citing incorrect runes and words of the wrong vintage. This debunking occurred in the early spring of 1899. At that time a group of local citizens, including Olsen and Hedberg, did some digging on the Ohman farm to see if they could turn up the burials of the slain Norsemen, but with no success. With the stone declared a fake, Olof Ohman took it back and used it as a stepping-stone, luckily placing it face down, in the position in which it had been found.

The Kensington Rune Stone might well still be there in the Ohmans' backyard had it not been for the arrival in the neighborhood in 1907 of Hjalmar Rued Holand. He was a young social historian bent on writing a thesis on the "History of the Norwegian Settlement of America." Holand was interviewing old settlers about their memories of the early days (1850s and 1860s) in that part of Minnesota but found that many of them wanted to talk more about the amazing rune stone that had been found nearby than about the hard work of pioneer farming. Holand's curiosity was piqued, and he went to see the stone. He was impressed, and Ohman soon gave him the stone. It would be the focus of Holand's life for the next fifty-five years.

At first, Hjalmar Holand was only an enthusiast, with little special knowledge but with a firm conviction that the Kensington Rune Stone deserved to be reconsidered. He published his first article on the subject in 1908; three books, dozens of papers, and surely scores of newspaper ac-

Hjalmar Holand

counts would come from Holand's commitment to the fabulous stone document. The stone in hand, not a bad feat as it is 36 x 15 x 5½ inches of dark graywacke and weighs about 230 pounds, Holand put his mark "H" on it and began to stir up local Minnesota interest.

The Minnesota Historical Society, operating out of its headquarters in St. Paul, set up a committee to look into the rune stone. The committee did a rather thorough job, checking on rumors about fakery and providing in its report one of the more impartial documents to be found on the subject. But there was one major failing; none of the five members of the committee was a specialist on the linguistic aspects of the rune stone, although all had some reasonable knowledge of the field, or so they said. The committee, on April 21, 1910, rendered a favorable opinion on the stone's authenticity, provided that a competent specialist on Scandinavian languages approved its conclusions. Professor Gisle Bothne of the University of Minnesota was asked to perform this special consultation. Bothne was Breda's successor at the university, and he came to a similar conclusion: "I do not consider the Kensington stone authentic."[3]

Bothne asked a young colleague, John A. Holvik, to assist the committee as well. That would start Holvik's lifelong association with the rune stone, and it would be Holand versus Holvik until death did them part.

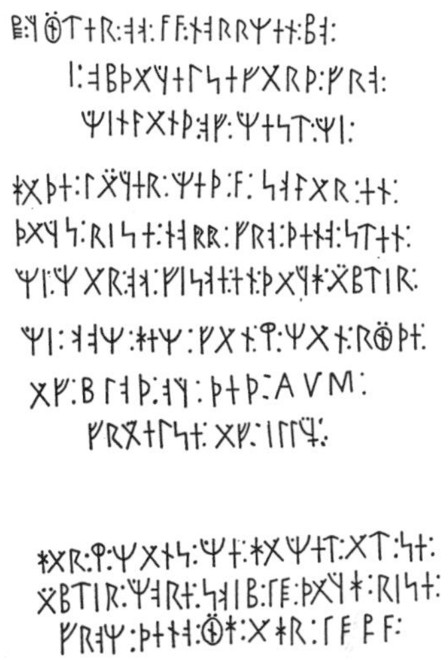

�ᚤᚭᛏᚤᚱ᛬ᚼᛁ᛬ ᚠᚠᛁᚼᚱᚱᚤᚼ᛬ᛒᚼ᛬
ᛁ᛬�ᛒᚤᛋᚤᛏᚵᛁᛏᚠᚴᚱᛈ᛬ᛈᚱᛁ᛬
ᚤᛁᛏᚠᚴᛏᛈᚤᛈ᛬ᚤᛁᚼᛏ᛬ᚤᛁ᛬

ᛁᚴᛈᛁ᛬ᛁᚷᚤᛁᚱ᛬ᚤᛏᛈ᛬ᚠ᛬ ᚼᛁᚠᚴᚱ᛬ᛁᛁ᛬
ᛒᚴᚤ ᚼ᛬ᚱᛁᚼᛏ᛬ᛁᚼᚱᚱ᛬ᚠᚱᛁ᛬ᛈᛏᚼ᛬ᚼᛏᛁ᛬
ᚤᛁ᛬ᚤ ᚴᚱᛁᛁ᛬ᚠᛁᚼᛏᛏᛁᛈᚴᚤᛁᛁᚴᛒᛏᛁᚱ᛬

ᚤᛁ᛬ᛁᛁᚤ᛬ᛁᛁᚤ᛬᛬ᛈᚴᛁᛈ᛬ᚤᚴᛏ᛬Rᚭᛈᛁ᛬
ᚴᛈ᛬ᛒᛁᛁᛈ᛬ᛁᚤ᛬᛬ᛈᛏᛈ᛬AVM᛬
ᚠRᚷᛏᛁᚼᛏ᛬ᚴᛈ᛬ᛁᛁᛏᚤ᛬

ᛁᚴᚱ᛬ᛈ᛬ᚤᚴᛏᚼ᛬ᚤᛈ᛬ᛁᚴᚤᛏ᛬ᚴᛏ᛬ᚼᛏ᛬
ᚴᛒᛏᛁᚱ᛬ᚤᛁᚱᛏ᛬ᚼᛁᛒ᛬ᛁᚠ᛬ᛈᚴᚤᛁᛁ᛬ᚱᛁᚼᛏ᛬
ᚠᚱᛁᚤ᛬ᛈᛏᛏᛁ᛬ᚭᛁ᛬ᚴᛁᚱ᛬ᛁᚠᛁᚠ᛬

Kensington Stone and Runic Text

Holvik made some important contributions to the Kensington Rune Stone controversy, but never, unfortunately, wrote his magnum opus on the subject. Bothne made one further suggestion: have the stone studied first-hand by Norwegian runologists. This would be the real test.

The commonly accepted translation of the Kensington Rune Stone is as follows:

> 8 Swedes and 22 Norwegians on exploration journey from Vinland westward. We had camp by 2 rocky islets one day's journey north from this stone. We were out and fished one day. After we came home found 10 men red with blood and dead. AVM save from evil. Have 10 men by the sea to look after our ships 14 days' journey from this island. Year 1362 (Wahlgren 1986: 102)

As with any minor historical investigation, one has to take one's data where one can get them. Much of what we know about the early study of the Kensington Rune Stone comes from the hand of Holand with the exception of the Minnesota Historical Society's report, a three-hundred-page tome. Some other little games were being played out at this same time; in 1910 Holand was trying to sell the Stone to the Historical Society for $5,000; he was also trying to get travel funds from the Society to take the stone abroad. He told the Society that once European scholars had authenticated it, it would be worth twice that price or more. Obviously, Holand never presented this aspect of the stone's history in his books.

However, Holand did make the trip to Europe with his beloved stone, and the Historical Society neither bought the stone nor paid for the trip. In later years Holand would make no mention of his 1911 sojourn among Scandinavian runologists and philologists, for it was from his viewpoint a disaster. We know this sad result from a brief and very obscure article that Holand himself wrote about the European visit. He found a situation that has a familiar nineteenth-century ring to it and declared: "There is in Europe a number of educators who tied down to their little round of duties have been led to believe, through unfortunate superstition, that all things American are tinged with humbug."[4] Yes, the Scandinavian experts all thought the Kensington stone a fraud, and the scorned suitor, Holand, found *their* opinions completely unacceptable: "not a single objection is valid."

To make things even harder for Holand to take, the Historical Society Committee's Report, published in 1915, contained a strong antistone article by George T. Flom, an eminent philologist at the University of Illinois. Despite all this, and the fact that the committee surely knew the results of the European trip as well, its final word was that, "after carefully considering all the opposing arguments, the Museum Committee of this Society, and Mr. Holand, owner of the stone, believe its inscription is a true historical record."[5]

But as with many academic final reports, the reverberations of its deeply buried conclusions were not heard round the world. After 1915, the stone made its weary way back to northern Minnesota. It languished apparently unloved in Alexandria, a fishing resort town, the largest one near Kensington. The stone's great advocate Holand settled in a small Wisconsin town, Ephraim, and there were nearly two decades of peace and quiet on the Kensington Rune Stone front. In 1932 Holand published a slim hardcover volume entitled *The Kensington Stone,* and things were never the same again. From then on, any discussion of Vikings in America would include Olof Ohman's great discovery.

Holand, with some research and imagination, added much luster to the Kensington story in his book. (1) He uncovered a possible source for the origin of the Viking voyage—an order by King Magnus Ericson in 1354 to Paul Knutson to go to Greenland and beyond to see that Christianity did not perish. (2) He traced a possible route for Knutson's party via Hudson Bay, the Nelson River, Lake Winnipeg, and finally the Red River and the Buffalo River into the Detroit lakes region north of Kensington. (3) Holand even located archaeological finds in the region, including "mooring holes," fire steels, and axes that may date to the period of the voyage. (4) Finally, Holand attacked the scholars who either found fault with the runic inscription or suggested that Ohman and some of his friends might have created a fraudulent rune stone. All this was done with the verve of one who knows that he is on the right side of the question; there is the appeal of the underdog fighting the academic nay-sayers and his apparent winning of every factual match. His book leaves no doubt as to that.

Thus by the late 1940s, Holand, who would continue to publish actively, had a very strong position in the eyes of the public. The Minneapolis papers and their letters-to-the-editor columns were heavily in favor of the authenticity of the Kensington Rune Stone. Then, in 1948, an even more dramatic event took place: in the jubilee year of its discovery, the rune stone went to Washington on loan to the Smithsonian Institution and was photographed in those near-sacred halls. There could be only one meaning to this ritual—the stone had been given authentication by the high muckamucks of the great red brick castle; at least, that is the way the press and the public viewed the act. This period was surely the high-water mark of the pro-rune-stone cause.

The truth was somewhat less exciting and less reassuring. The rune stone was actually brought to Washington to be studied by a group of Danish scholars, including William Thalbitzer, a student of Eskimo languages, who was interested in comparing it with a rune stone that had been found in Greenland. Thalbitzer, a professor from Copenhagen, felt that there was some reason to believe that "this peculiar inscription . . . may after all be genuine,"[6] but he did not completely endorse all Holand's theories.

Another of the Danish scholars, Johannes Brøndsted, said that archaeology could not speak to the genuineness of the inscription, and he called for new data and renewed linguistic study. He also asked, Who could have been the forger? The third scholar, a runologist named Sven Jansson, declared the stone a fraud and later wrote up his objections. The next year the stone was returned to Minnesota for participation in the state's centennial and ultimately went back up to Alexandria, where it now resides. Myths die slowly, however; many enthusiasts still think the stone lurks somewhere in the Smithsonian corridors, but my colleagues there say it just isn't so.

The next two decades, following 1950, would see an upswing of study and publication on the Kensington Rune Stone, with a strong shift away from the true believers. It did not start that way for S. N. Hagen, a professor at Franklin and Marshall College, who led off in 1950 with a well-documented journal article that defended many of Hjalmar Holand's views on the stone, although he wisely chose not to deal with any of the purported archaeological data. Hagen had done his homework, going to the find spot and even doing research at the Historical Society; he was able to justify to his satisfaction the language used in the text of the stone. He did make one new reading, substituting "sheds" for "skerries" (rocky islets) used by almost all other translators. The rest of the article was a detailed defense of the authenticity of the stone and the "alleged" culprit who might have forged the document. He concluded with a paean of praise for the Smithsonian, which is misplaced, deserving as that honored institution is, for he too thought that the rune stone would remain there forever under its watchful care. Not so, as we know.

But then the contra forces began a well-documented attack, using for the first time new and startling evidence that things were not as simple in sleepy old Kensington as some, including Holand and Hagen, had asked us to believe. The source for the new data was none other than our old acquaintance John A. Holvik, then a professor at Concordia College in Moorehead, Minnesota, in the western part of the state, not far from Alexandria. Holvik had thought the stone a fraud from 1910 and had been an adversary of Holand since then. Time did not change either man's views and Holvik provided a Danish runologist, Erik Moltke, with a copy of some materials he had uncovered in 1949 in the Minnesota Historical Society archives. Moltke was of the new young breed of scholars that Brønsted had called on to look over the Kensington Rune Stone one more time. Using the British journal *Antiquity* as his platform, Moltke published in 1951 a strongly worded denunciation of the stone with the major force of his argument drawn from Holvik's archival find.

What Holvik had found were documents pertaining to the earliest days of the discovery on the Ohman farm, specifically, a letter from J. P. Hedberg of Kensington to Swan J. Turnblad in Minneapolis, dated January 1, 1899. Hedberg had a broad spectrum of business activities, including real estate, loans, and furniture in Kensington, and it was to him that Olof Ohman had first turned following his discovery. Turnblad was the editor of a major Minneapolis newspaper. In the letter Hedberg describes the discovery briefly and suggests that perhaps Turnblad can find out what the inscription means. Hedberg says, "It appears to be old Greek letters." He encloses a copy of the inscription, possibly the one shown to Professor Breda for the stone's first translation.

This discovery would not seem very exciting unless one were John Holvik and had been studying the rune stone for nearly forty years. The *copy* of the inscription is done on an irregularly shaped (roughly rectangular) piece of brown paper. Lines have been drawn on the paper with a ruler to help keep the lines of runes straight. The inscription is "copied" in pencil. The paper looks old and has been mended; it is ruled in blue on the back. This still would not be unusual until one began to read the runes; then if one was as familiar with the document that was purportedly being copied as Professor Holvik was, something would appear to be very strange. It is not a "true" copy; there are "mistakes." Indeed, when the copy is carefully compared with the stone, at least a dozen differences are apparent. How could this be? Perhaps it is a "bad" copy—after all, they did not know what they were copying, maybe even old *Greek* letters, so you'd expect mistakes.

But then a patterning in the differences between the stone and the "copy" becomes evident: the word for *this* is spelled in runes *dene* on the copy twice, but both times it appears on the stone as *deno,* and the *e* and *o* runes are quite different. This is not the result of miscopying. There are also symmetrical changes in the use of the umlaut, which is hard to explain unless the person writing down the runes knew how the umlaut functions. Moltke's conclusion, and one with which I concur, since I have studied the original documents as well, is that what Ohman gave to Hedberg to send to to Minneapolis was not a *copy* of the stone, but a *first draft.*

Ohman perhaps had forgotten in the intervening years since the stone was buried, probably about six years before, that they had changed the text a little. But a little was too much, and then some early statements about difficulties in reading the inscription make more sense: one commentator in 1909 said, "At first there was considerable indecision [about authenticity], and this still more so because the first copies were somewhat *incorrect"* (emphasis added).[7] With this very positive suggestion that some of the finders might well have known quite a bit about runes and the like, it is time to scrutinize them as well.

Olof Ohman was a Swedish immigrant who came to Douglas County in 1879 and moved to his farm near Kensington in 1891. Often portrayed as a simple farmer, he really had a great interest in history and read broadly;

books known to have been in his personal library testify to this aspect of his personality. He had two close Swedish friends, Andrew Anderson and Sven Fogelblad, with whom he shared his intellectual interests, including mysticism. Anderson was a relative by marriage, and Fogelblad was the only one in the trio with a college degree.

Fogelblad (1829–97) was a graduate of the University of Uppsala, where he also got training in the ministry. He left the clerical profession after having some arguments over matters of faith, although he may have had some difficulties with alcohol as well. Fogelblad immigrated to the United States in 1870 and turned up in western Minnesota just about the time the Ohman family moved to the Kensington farm, around 1890. He was apparently down on his luck and was earning his keep by tutoring school-age children in their homes; they had a difficult time getting an education any other way. One home he stayed in was that of Olof Ohman. He was no fly-by-night intellectual; books from his own library show that he carried some scholarly volumes with him on his perambulations for more than thirty years.

This concern for the Ohman and Fogelblad libraries has just one point: were there volumes in their possession that could have served as sources for the runic inscription? The answer is yes, both for runes and for the history of the Swedish language. Ohman's library is better known, but a Fogelblad volume with his name on the flyleaf, inscribed "Stockholm. 1868," which contains a runic alphabet, is much less frequently cited. S. N. Hagen noted its presence in the Historical Society but says it is not significant to the question of origin of the runes. Having handled and copied the volume myself, I am somewhat mystified by this comment; all sixteen runes in that volume appear on the rune stone. There are others that do not, but then there are a number of Kensington "originals" which are unique to that inscription. Hagen tries to make the point that no one among the discoverers knew runes, a position held by Holand, but the facts are contrary to that opinion. Indeed, some knowledge of runes was a common part of nineteenth-century Swedish heritage, as Brigitta Wallace has pointed out in her thoughtful synthesis published in 1971.

What did other scholars do after Moltke's breakout in 1951? Two books, both strongly against the authenticity of the Kensington Rune Stone, were published a decade apart. The first, by Erik Wahlgren, was published in 1958, and the editor of *Antiquity* called it "masterful." Wahlgren's primary training was in Scandinavian philology, but he handled the historical aspects of the case with great success as well. He met Holand hand to hand as no other scholar had bothered to do and also established the credibility of Ohman as the forger, without coming right out and labeling him as such. Wahlgren remains today a major figure in all "Vikings in America" controversies, as his important and comprehensive 1982 paper and his 1986 Viking volume ably demonstrate.

The second book was by Theodore Blegen, a historian, and was published in 1968. Its publisher, the Minnesota Historical Society, thus had a late conversion to the negative position after its supportive 1915 Annual Report. There was, of course, evidence along the way that the Society was looking at both sides of the question, as shown during the 1950s by book notices of materials both pro and con. In publishing the volume, Blegen absolved the Society from incrimination. The book is a very strong piece of work, supported more than any other by detailed documentary research, as befits a historian. Blegen's research establishes the profiles of Ohman and Fogelblad as we have them today. Equally important, he discovered the long-misplaced field notebook of N. H. Winchell, a geologist and member of the Historical Society Committee, who traveled to the find spot in 1909–10 and interviewed many of the participants, including Ohman. Blegen tells much about those people and times that Holand did not provide. Thus a solid foundation to the con position had been laid.

With all this heavy ammunition coming from the contras, what were the pro-Kensingtonites to do? Their strong leader, Hjalmar Holand, died in 1963, but his torch had been passed in a rather strange direction: to a Scandinavian-American with a University of Chicago Ph.D. in physics and mathematics named Ole G. Landsverk. A specialty in atomic physics and radiation is not the intellectual background one expects in this debate. Although his first volume (1961) was traditional in approach, upholding Holand's views and thus seemingly in safe hands, the subsequent Landsverk volumes, coauthored with Alf Monge, a former U.S. Army cryptographer, went in a brand new direction. These works have shades of Ignatius Donnelly, for they espouse the new theory that behind the surface message of the runes there was another message buried in an elaborate cryptogram. Although his cofounder of "Runic Dated Cryptography," Monge, has now passed on, Landsverk continues on his own, even though two scholars, one Swedish and the other American, who specialize in cryptography have reviewed these new efforts with devastating criticism. Unfortunately, the disease seems to have spread even to some Phoenicians found in Brazil; but what else can be expected when one gets involved in Fantastic Archaeology?

Landsverk's new twists, which he has applied to runic inscriptions across the country, even in Oklahoma, have not diverted attention from the Kensington Rune Stone. In the 1970s the history establishment, represented by Samuel Eliot Morison of Harvard in his encyclopedic *European Discovery of America: The Northern Voyages,* gave the stone a very hard time. In the 1980s, however, a third linguist, after Thalbitzer and Hagen, came out in favor of the stone. He was Robert Hall, a professor emeritus at Cornell and a specialist in Italian, who wrote a small volume entitled *The Kensington Stone Is Genuine.* It is mainly a defense of Holand with a linguistic tolerance for divergences that prove to him that the stone is a genuine document.

Well, where are we in the clear light of the 1990s? Let's look at the archaeology first. New work has been done in the Arctic, and several recent summaries deal specifically with evidence of Norse contact. None of these data supports any voyages into Hudson Bay proper or down into Minnesota. Holand's numerous Norse mooring stones have turned out to be mid-nineteenth-century artifacts of quarrying and the like; such mooring devices are unknown in Norse seamanship, except for permanent anchorage. So too with the fire steels or strike-a-lights and the axes; none is of Norse attribution. Embarrassingly, the best-looking Norse "axes" are now known to be novelty tobacco plug-cutters from nineteenth-century country stores. There is not a veritable Norse artifact anywhere along the route to Kensington. Indeed, despite decades of archival search, there is still no documentary evidence that the Knutson party of 1354, touted by Holand, ever left base toward Vinland, or even that Knutson got to Greenland.

As for the stone itself, for ease of exposition I brushed over a few discrepancies along the way that may have some significance. For example, when *was* the artifact found? I have quoted from the standard text, the Committee report, and said it was November 8, 1898; however, an Ohman affidavit says it was in August. There are other questions about just who was there to see the stone wrenched from the tree roots. Another inconsistent figure is the diameter of the aspen tree with the flattened roots; is it four inches or ten inches? Thus is the tree seventy years old, as Holand would have us believe, or somewhere between ten and thirty years of age, as others have estimated. Maybe it does not matter, for with all this argument, Brigitta Wallace has interestingly suggested that perhaps the stone was found clasped in the roots as stated but was inscribed *after* its discovery. That is a difficult suggestion to evaluate.

Everyone but Holand has remarked on the freshness of the chisel marks; the inscription is not weathered at all. This characteristic was noted by the Committee's geologist, N. H. Winchell, a specialist on weathering. Indeed, the "H" that Holand put on the stone in 1907 now has a patina comparable to that on the inscription. Also noted is the fact that the chisel cuts are just one inch long, the blade size of common hardware chisels.

As to the inscription, without going into rune-by-rune analysis, one can say that a majority of linguistic opinion is, as Brigitta Wallace has pointed out, that the text is written in a special colloquial nineteenth-century "Scandinavian" that developed in Minnesota, where Swedes and Norwegians lived next to each other. The carver does seem to favor the Swedish aspect of the language; all those mentioned as suspects (Ohman, Anderson, and Fogelblad) were Swedish. The runes, as most runologists have stated, are not genuinely medieval and mix signs and accents in a unique manner. I have also shown that certain runic alphabets were available to Ohman and his friends and that some of these runes were indeed used on the stone. I have also dealt at length with the Hedberg-transmitted "copy" and the notion that the copy may, in fact, be a draft of the inscription.

But there is more. Recall the anti-Columbus feelings of the Scandinavians of the Upper Midwest in 1893 when the Chicago World's Fair was getting under way. The Viking ship, the replica of the archaeologically recovered Gokstad ship, at anchor in Lake Michigan was an object of great importance—a redemption of ethnic pride. It had a crew of thirty-two men when it arrived in Chicago. It sailed across the North Atlantic but was towed the last lap from Yonkers to Chicago. That trip took fourteen days. Do those numbers have significance? The Kensington stone says the Viking party had thirty members and that they had left their ships by the sea fourteen days' journey away. Perhaps the figures are coincidental. But what of the ten men murdered in 1362? Holvik once mentioned that in 1862, during the Indian wars that broke out during the Civil War, a group of Scandinavians at Norway Lake, not far from Kensington, came back from church and found ten of their number brutally killed by the Indians. Maybe it is more than just a coincidence, or am I reading too much into all this numerology, after the manner of Landsverk?

I and others, including Wahlgren and Wallace, feel that what was going on in Chicago was important to those involved with the rune stone. Ohman was a history buff and could have known of the Norway Lake Massacre. Perhaps it does all fit together. One thing is sure: the Kensington Rune Stone is not a genuine historical object.

How can I be so positive? Isn't it just a matter of bias on my part this time? Well, I admit to having been very sure that the funny old rock was spurious for more than thirty years, but perhaps a deathbed confession can be accepted as final proof. In 1973 a British television producer, working on a BBC show called "The Riddle of the Runestone," taped a statement of Frank Walter Cran, who now lies in a country churchyard near Kensington. His father was apparently a close friend of Ohman. The younger Cran reported shortly before he died that his father and Olof Ohman had carved the rune stone as a joke to fool the educated ones: it was to be "the biggest haha . . . in their life." When he was dying, Cran's father urged his son to see Ohman's son John, who was also at death's door, to confirm the story, which he did. I am not as convinced as Glyn Daniel was in his *Antiquity* editorial. It all sounds too pat—a ready-made scenario, with everyone gasping their last with the rune stone on their lips. Whatever the credibility of the Cran tape, I still vote no on the Kensington Rune Stone; but there are other cases to consider in the quest for Vikings in America.

From the very beginning, New England had been a hotbed of Norse connections. It was always much easier to consider Cape Cod or Martha's Vineyard as a veritable Viking landfall than western Minnesota. Thus it should be no surprise that we turn now to putative Norsemen in the Boston area, especially the broad Charles River estuary, on the north shore of which lies Cambridge. Eben Norton Horsford (1818–93) came to that city in 1847 as Rumford Professor of Science. He was born in upper New York State not far from the area where Joseph Smith had his religious experiences. Horsford's father was a missionary to the Seneca Indians, and the young Horsford grew up with a great deal of interest in local history and Indian matters. He was of a strong scientific bent and after graduating from Rensselaer Polytechnic Institute, he received valuable training in analytical chemistry in Germany under the noted Professor Justus von Liebig.

It was following that European experience that Horsford came to Harvard, where he helped to found the Lawrence Scientific School. For sixteen years he was a university professor, but then he resigned that post to take up the presidency of the Rumford Chemical Works in Providence, Rhode Island, a company he founded to take advantage of his useful chemical discoveries, the most successful of which was the invention of baking powder. Financial success came in abundance, and Horsford became a well-known member of the Cambridge intelligentsia, serving the nation by trying to develop marching rations for Union soldiers and aiding Wellesley College with significant additions to its endowment.

Eben N. Horsford

His palatial residence on Brattle Street made Horsford a neighbor of Henry Longfellow, and it was here in 1870 that he entertained as a house guest the Norwegian violinist Ole Bull (1810–80), to whom he credited his interest in Northmen. Bull was a charismatic musician of modest talent but great popular fame. He was also a Leif Ericson fan and suggested that a statue to the Norse hero be erected in Boston.

Horsford and other Cantabrigians such as James Russell Lowell and President Charles Eliot of Harvard supported the notion. The Leif Ericson statue was, however, much delayed and discouraged by the rather stubborn Massachusetts Historical Society, which, though not firmly against the idea of a Norse presence in the area, felt that acceptable evidence was not at hand to prove it. In this attitude the Society was correct. Nonetheless, Horsford proudly gave an address at the eventual unveiling of the large statue that still stands on Commonwealth Avenue with Leif looking westward from the prow of his ship toward the headwaters of the Charles. Few passersby know or care what it means.

Horsford had turned to historical matters in his later years, with a special interest in finding the fabled "Norumbega," the lost city of New England, shown enigmatically on some early maps. His first foray into this field favored a French origin for the site, but for the five years from 1888 until his death in 1893 his solution, expounded in six publications, would be solidly Norse, even to the locating of Leif Ericson's house in Vinland on the banks of the Charles not many blocks from his own home.

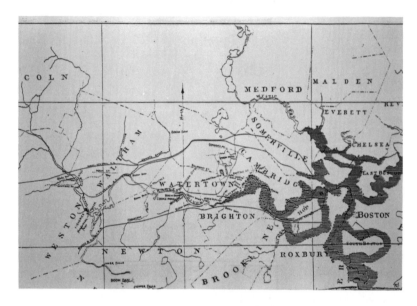

Horsford's "Vinland" on the Charles River

His vision of the Viking presence in the Charles Basin was not modest; Horsford felt there might have been as many as ten thousand residents at one time, busily exporting oak burls for the manufacture of much sought-after wooden drinking vessels and the like. His maps show the area dotted with sites; the long-sought Norumbega is on a high point overlooking the junction of Stoney Brook and the Charles, in Weston, just a few miles from where I am now writing this volume.

How could a professor with excellent scientific credentials go so wrong? How wrong was he? Harvard's Justin Winsor said, "The most incautious linguistic inferences and the most uncritical cartographic perversions are presented by Eben Norton Horsford," and "We can see in Horsford's *Discovery of America by Northmen* to what a fanciful extent a confident enthusiasm can carry it."[8] Even the ladies joined the supporting act; Mrs. Ole Bull wrote supportingly of New England Vikings after her husband's death, as did Horsford's daughter Cornelia, culminating in her 1899 volume *Vinland and Its Ruins*.

Horsford's "confident enthusiasm" is no better demonstrated than by his own description of how he found Norumbega after a literature and cartographic search: "When I had eliminated every doubt of the locality that I could find, I drove with a friend through a region I had never visited, of a topography of which I knew nothing, nine miles away, directly to the remains of the fort."[9] What he found was a few scattered rocks; now, thanks to his munificence and imagination there is a romantic stone tower perched in a small park overlooking the Charles. Horsford had found Norumbega: a six-foot-high bronze plaque on the tower declares that fact.

His confidence had told him that he would find the site, and he did. But Horsford did know the scientific method, of course. Let's follow his logic: "I had predicted the finding of Fort Norumbega at a particular spot. I went to the spot and found it. No test of the genuineness of scientific deduction is regarded as superior to this." He continues: "To test the guess or the hypothesis by the touchstone of physical fact, sequence, mutual relation, harmony of all parts with each, and the utter absence of an element of opposing evidence, is what the scientific method requires." Not badly put, but the sad case is that there really were no Norse artifacts or structures, those touchstones of physical facts that archaeology requires for proof. There was a total absence of evidence, confirming or opposing, other than the fact that it looked like a logical spot for a site, which it does.

Horsford did have some archaeological fieldwork carried out at the purported location of Leif Ericson's house, near Gerry's Landing in Cambridge, now near the Mount Auburn Hospital. The excavation was quickly done—three small test holes were dug, and parts of a stone foundation were discovered. Although not well reported, there was nothing here to relate this putative stone structure to the Norse by way of artifactual evidence or to date them in any archaeological manner—except, of course, some modern, non-Norse trash from the "upper levels." (There were no lower levels). This "late" material had nothing to do with Leif or "his" house as far as Horsford was concerned. Leif's house had been found: it was in the right place; what else could it be? Following her father's views and techniques exactly, Cornelia Horsford found Thorfinn's house as well. So again, as another of his critics (Julius E. Olson) wrote, "On points where there is occasion for deep shadings of doubt Mr. Horsford is dogmatic, and . . . his acquaintance with the literature of the subject is superficial."[10] These two structures were undoubtedly of the Colonial period.

Interestingly from the viewpoint of the intellectual history of Vikings in America, Horsford's lavishly published contention for Vinland in the Charles River Basin is a hypothesis that has not been taken up by many of the more recent enthusiasts. Even Horsford was a bit pressed to explain the disappearance of his ten thousand Norsemen, and then, too, the physical proof was pitifully thin; what he would have given for a well-written rune

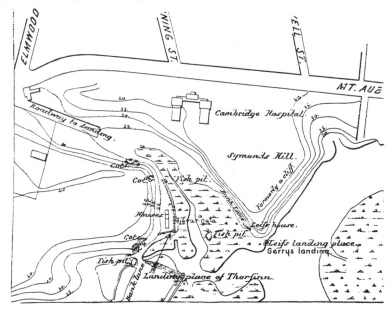

Horsford's "Norse Ruins in Cambridge"

stone! But that was not to appear for a long while, and then in Maine in the 1970s. If one wants real Norse artifacts, one must go north to Canada.

Port Arthur, Ontario, on the northwestern shore of Lake Superior, not far from the northeastern tip of Minnesota, is where this part of our search for Vikings begins. Here in the 1930s James Edward Dodd, a Canadian National Railway worker and part-time mining prospector, turned up with an impressive hoard of iron artifacts, including a broken sword, an ax head, and a rather curious object, first thought to be a shield handle but later identified as a rattle from horse trappings. There is no question that these are genuine objects of Viking age dating from between A.D. 900 and 1000. The problem, as in so many of our cases, is where they were actually found: the context. What evidence do we have? There are the usual handful of conflicting affidavits and the Johnny-come-lately testimony by the finder's adopted son. So what else is new?

James Edward Dodd said that he had found the artifacts while prospecting for gold on his "middle claim" some 125 miles north of Port Arthur, southwest of a small town, Beardmore, east of Lake Nipigon. He was dynamiting a trench through a possible ore deposit and discovered these ancient relics. This event took place apparently in the spring of 1931, although testimony varies. According to Dodd, he threw the artifacts care-

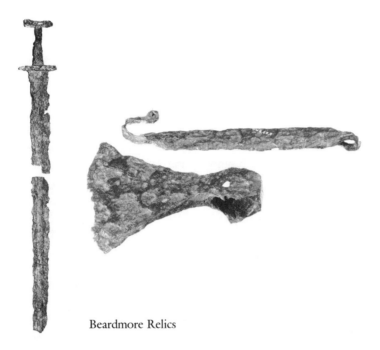

Beardmore Relics

lessly to one side, not recognizing what they were. He purportedly did not even bring them back to his house in Port Arthur until 1933. So much for the discovery part of the story.

It was not until 1936 that these iron objects were brought to the attention of the Royal Ontario Museum in Toronto, where they were to find a happy home, ultimately being purchased for $500 and embraced as genuine by the then curator of archaeology C. T. Currelly. The museum appropriately visited the find spot with Dodd, and the staffers were rewarded with a few scraps of iron, nothing more. The Norse artifacts were put on prominent exhibit at the museum and were said to come from a "burial on a portage on the route from Hudson Bay to Lake Superior." Here was more evidence that Vikings did roam the interior of the continent, perhaps even on the way to Kensington, although the dating of the artifacts at around A.D. 1000 would make Leif Ericson's party more reasonable than that of Paul Knutson in the 1360s.

As early as 1941 the authenticity of this discovery was questioned in responsible journals, but the Royal Ontario Museum's backing of the exciting Norse connection saw to it that the Beardmore Relics soon became a firm part of Canadian history and were so recorded in standard schoolbooks. As early as 1938 statements were published in local newspapers that suggested that instead of coming from a rocky deposit in Beardmore, these Norse artifacts were discovered in the basement of a house in which Dodd was living in Port Arthur. This house was owned by J. M. Hansen; Hansen said he had received the Norse relics as security on a small loan, confirmed by bank records, to one of his employees, Jens Bloch. Bloch's father was an artist in Norway with an interest in heraldry and a collector of armor. The elder Bloch had died in 1917. The discoveries in the basement were described by a witness, Eli Raggotte, and dutifully sworn to; within two months Raggotte had retracted that statement. Hansen too was under pressure in 1938 to change his story because the Norwegian community in Port Arthur was thinking of its own Viking monument. When Hansen was shown the much cleaned and curatorially treated specimens at the museum, he said that there must be *two* sets of Norse relics, one from Beardmore and the other from his basement!

Years later—not another deathbed scene, thank goodness—we do, however, get strong confirmation of the "relics in the basement" version of the Beardmore finds. In the fall of 1956, Walter Dodd, the "finder's" foster son, who had "witnessed" the discovery in 1930 or 1931 (even he could not be sure of the date) and had given a confirming statement in 1939 of his father's tale, now recanted. He said that as a youngster, aged twelve or thirteen, he had seen his foster father take the artifacts that had been found in the basement and plant them on his claim and then recover them sometime later. He further said that he had felt guilt about the untrue affidavit that he had been "forced" to sign. His foster mother, James Dodd's widow, however, said that the recanting was done out of spite and revenge on the part of their foster son.

There was one more sworn statement engendered by the call for new information on the Beardmore case by the museum in 1956, this time from a 1930s Beardmore inhabitant, Carey M. Brooks, who had dug on the "middle claim" for James Dodd. He said that Dodd had told him of the basement find of Norse relics but later said they came from the Beardmore claim. When Brooks questioned Dodd about this, he had answered, "Oh well, they have been found at Beardmore now."[11] Brooks also stated that he himself had dug the trench where the relics were purported to have been found and that he had seen no sign of the rust marks that Dodd then claimed as the precise location of the find.

Today the Beardmore Norse relics reside in the storeroom of the Royal Ontario Museum, "in limbo" as the museum's curator now puts it. On the whole, scholars interested in the subject are unanimous: James Dodd's artifacts are indeed Norse and of very respectable age, but they seem surely to have made their Atlantic crossing to Canada in Jens Bloch's footlocker rather than in the hands of a Viking seafarer.

We will turn now to a couple of "old chestnuts" in the Viking story, without which no discussion would be complete. I mentioned them briefly much earlier, since they have been on the quest for Norsemen's agenda since the 1700s: Dighton Rock and the Newport Tower.

Dighton Rock has something of the quality of litmus paper for testing the tides of current archaeological interpretations. The subject, a forty-ton boulder, once bathed by the tidal rise and fall of the Taunton River, now resides in a state of Massachusetts museum close to the original site. It has been drawn, photographed, and even videotaped endlessly since 1680, when John Danforth first drew a portion of the inscriptions. The carvings on its relatively smooth westward-facing surface now more closely resemble the tangled mess of signs on a graffiti-covered side of a New York subway train than a clear message from the past.

Inscriptions are devilishly hard to date, and Dighton Rock is a prime example. Even discounting nineteenth- and twentieth-century vandalism, it was a complex mass of petroglyphic symbols from the very start. And from early on scholars and statesmen tried to make some sense out of it. A contemporary scholar has now listed over twenty theories of authorship, many of which fall neatly into our category of Fantastic Archaeology, such as a prince from Atlantis, the Lost Tribes, Egyptians, Chinese, and, of course, Prince Madoc about A.D. 1170, to name just a few.

In the beginning the Puritans did very well in ascribing the authorship of the markings on Dighton Rock to the American Indians. Cotton Mather published the Danforth drawing in 1690 and in a sermon said that the "strange characters" were very old. In the next century a large number of drawings of the Rock were made, the first in 1730 by Professor Isaac Greenwood of Harvard; the next in 1767 by Ezra Stiles, then a minister in Newport and later president of Yale, with a documented interest in antiquities, as it was to him that a copy of the Marietta mounds was sent some years later. Professor Stephen Sewall of Harvard made a life-sized copy on a white sheet on September 13, 1768.

In 1788 Professor James Winthrop filled the marks on the Rock with printer's ink and took an actual impression of the petroglyphs. It was probably this version that was seen by President George Washington in 1789 when he visited Harvard. He was shown a representation of the

Dighton Rock inscription, and he commented that this "writing" resembled some made by the Indians that he had observed "in the younger part of his life" in the wilderness of Virginia. So far, so good; the pictographs reflected the Native American heritage.

That calm situation would not last long. A French scholar, Antoine Court de Gebelin, in 1781 seized on Stephen Sewall's drawing of the Rock and incorporated it as a piece of evidence into a larger scheme of Phoenician voyages throughout the Old World. He interpreted the Rock as documenting Phoenicians coming into friendly contact with the New World natives some three thousand years ago. Indeed, he saw the scenes as detailing events in the past, present, and future. Unfortunately, by 1783 Ezra Stiles saw Phoenicians in Narragansett Bay as well.

So much for reasonable interpretations of the Dighton petroglyphs. Other fantastic views were on the way, and it was not long before the Vikings made their appearance, thanks to Carl Rafn. The Danish scholar took a deep interest in the Rock and obtained from the Rhode Island Historical Society a set of carefully done drawings made in 1834. He published these in his *Antiquitates Americanae* in 1837 along with another plate showing seven different versions (1680 to 1812) of inscriptions on the rock. Whatever its value, Dighton Rock stands as the most frequently documented artifact in American archaeology.

Rafn, of course, came up with a completely new interpretation, hence the inclusion of the Rock in this chapter. He and his Icelandic assistant, Finn Magnusen, read a message there from the Vikings: "Thorfinn and his 151 companions took possession of this land."[12] Only part of this was "read" from runes—the number was in roman letters. The reference to Thorfinn is presumably to Karlsefni, one of the best-known figures in the sagas that relate to the Vinland voyages around A.D. 1000.

In 1860, at the suggestion of Ole Bull, the indefatigable Viking fan, the rock and some surrounding land were purchased by Niels Arnzen of Fall River, who then deeded the lot to the Royal Society of Northern Antiquaries of Copenhagen, presumably in a tribute to Rafn. The Danes did not keep it long, returning it to American ownership in 1889 as a gift to a Taunton historical society. This action might be seen as a statement by the Danes disavowing a belief in a Viking connection, but I am not sure. Dighton Rock did become for some at least, including Rasmus B. Anderson in 1874, an important part of the evidence for documenting the Vikings on the East Coast. Interestingly, neither Horsford nor Holand used the famous Rock in this manner.

But there was to be yet another turning in the interpretation of this venerable American palimpsest which would reflect strongly on the changing ethnicity of the Taunton River region. Edmund B. Delabarre was a distinguished psychologist at Brown University, and early in this century he had a summer home near Dighton Rock. By 1914 he had become fascinated by the carvings on it and began an exhaustive study of the Rock's history.

In 1918 Delabarre thought he clearly saw the date "1511" on the stone in arabic numerals, and he was soon able to tie this date to Portuguese maritime exploits, specifically, the voyage of Miguel Corte-Real in 1502, which could have taken them to this area. With the aid of flashlight photography Delabarre discerned some further messages and markings from these Portuguese explorers whom he felt had settled nearby, well before the arrival of the Pilgrims. In 1928 he published this interpretation in a large and impressive volume. The Taunton region has a substantial Portuguese population, and more recently there have been a few modifications and additions to this last major "reading" of Dighton Rock.

The Rock itself is now properly protected inside a museum structure, and it remains today a very significant document of American archaeology, however it is interpreted. I believe that it is the first American archaeological artifact to be captured by photographic means. Henry Rowe Schoolcraft, whom we encountered some pages ago with reference to the Grave

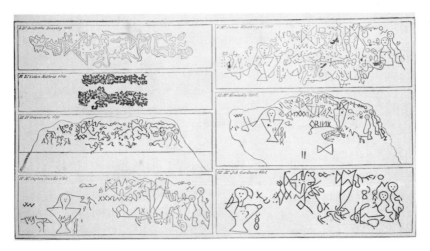

Rafn's Dighton Rock Images

Creek Stone, had as his major artist for his monumental six-volumne work a young West Pointer named Seth Eastman. His busy army career took him from Minnesota to Texas and finally to the Seminole Wars in Florida.

Eastman, a talented artist, carefully documented Indian life on the frontier while on these military travels between 1829 and 1849. Though much of his work for Schoolcraft was studio-done on artifacts and the like, he did travel to New England, where he drew both the Dighton Rock and the Newport Tower. These drawings are all fine and good, but Eastman made archaeological history in 1853 when he sat atop Dighton Rock in shirt-sleeves and a silk vest, with the inscription "enhanced" by chalk, and had a daguerreotype image made of the scene. What a way to be immortalized!

Schoolcraft used Eastman's drawing of the Rock in his 1854 work. Although he once wavered a bit on the origin of the inscription, as Haven was happy to point out a few years later, Schoolcraft ultimately came out for an American Indian source, as do most scholars today. There are unfortunately no associated artifacts to help settle this matter, but I would now tend to agree with Justin Winsor's 1889 statement, "that it is the work of the Indian of historic times seems now to be the opinion common to the best trained archaeologists,"[13] although just how recently the Indians carved it is quite impossible to say. The archaeological lesson the Rock does teach is that of perception: "In every object there is inexhaustible meaning,

Seth Eastman on Dighton Rock (daguerreotype)

the eye sees in it what the eye brings means of seeing" (from Thomas Carlyle).[14]

Not too far to the south, in Newport, Rhode Island, stands an interesting stone circular structure that likewise owes its first Viking attribution to Carl Rafn and his 1837 publication. Before that date this stone shell of a building, about twenty-four feet tall, which was generally known as the Old Stone Mill of Governor Benedict Arnold, had been thought to date to the 1670s. Rafn, who had obtained information from the Newport area concerning Dighton Rock, did not learn of the existence of the Tower until his first book went to press, but in succeeding editions he added this stone structure to the evidence for a Norse presence in the area. Other nineteenth-century Norse advocates such as Rasmus B. Anderson took up this bit of data too, but by Winsor's time (1889) most authorities accepted the colonial hypothesis. The arguments for a much earlier construction depended primarily on architectural details; few doubted that it served as a windmill in colonial times after the destruction by storm of the regularly used structure.

The major revival of the Norse origin of the stone tower can be credited directly to a volume, *Newport Tower*, written by Philip Ainsworth Means and published in 1942. Means was a gentleman archaeologist whose major contributions had previously been in the Peruvian area. A careful reading of his Newport Tower volume suggests that he should have stuck to the South American field.

The book, a 340-page tome and heavily illustrated, attempts to deal with both sides of the Norse-Arnold argument but fails to do so adequately because of Means's pro-Norse bias. Though well researched and with a lengthy bibliography, it lashes out at the Arnold/colonial theory continually, even as it thoroughly documents in about 100 pages the more than one-hundred-year controversy since Rafn started the argument.

Although Means admits that the pro-Norse direction of his research has bothered some of his academic colleagues, who helped him nonetheless, there are some telling signs in noting whose wisdom he really trusts. Hjalmar Holand and the Kensington Rune Stone are warmly embraced as genuine without question; those who criticize Holand are said to do it wrongly and in an ungentlemanly fashion. He also is a strong follower of Edmund Delabarre and his 1511 Portuguese interpretation of Dighton Rock. Means apparently does not need that evidence to strengthen his Norse hypothesis. Means tentatively dates the Tower's construction to about A.D. 1120 but is prepared to add a hundred or so years, making the

Philip A. Means and Newport Tower

Norse church building only a little more than one hundred years old when the Knutson party, supported by Holand and the Kensington Rune Stone, stopped by to receive a blessing in Newport.

The one saving grace in the Means volume is to be found on page 298. There Means, who was after all an archaeologist, makes a special plea for scientific excavations. This suggestion is made only after a lengthy comparative section on architecture that afforded him ample excuse to tour Europe in search of appropriate structures.

Means says that he had been urged to propose a dig by many correspondents. Although private funds for excavation were offered, the Park Commission of Newport "*flatly* refused to entertain the idea of any 'dig' whatsoever." There was fear that damage to the Tower would result. Means went on to suggest that the Excavators' Club at Harvard, made up of a group of graduate students in archaeology, would be an excellent choice to carry out the proposed work in Newport. He guessed the possible results as follows: 50 percent chance that nothing would be found, 35 percent chance that there would be Norse material (A.D. 1121–1400), 10 percent chance that Arnold and seventeenth-century construction would be confirmed, and 5 percent chance that it would date to A.D. 1492–1580, confirming the Portuguese hypothesis.

This is one case that does have a happy archaeological ending, even if it proved that Philip Means was not a very good gambler. After World War II the Newport Tower was taken up as a problem by the Peabody Museum at Harvard and a committee was formed to pick a proper excavator. William S. Godfrey, Jr., a Harvard graduate student, was selected and accepted by the powers that be in Newport. He was all Means could have asked for and more—a gentleman and a young scholar, who just happened to be a lineal descendent of Governor Arnold. That combination was hard to beat; how could the Newport brass say no to someone who wanted to dig on his own ancestral lands?

The results of Godfrey's excavations in 1948–49 were hardly what Means had predicted: the ten-to-one shot paid off. The right archaeological materials were there, not in great quantities but enough to prove that it was, indeed, a seventeenth-century building. Colonial artifacts of this early period were taken from under the main pillars and in other contexts that proved the period of construction was recent Anglo, not Norse of the 1100s or Portuguese of the 1500s. There was no additional ambulatory structure surrounding the tower, as Means had postulated for his Norse church.

The artifacts were humble fragments but surely of colonial origin: clay pipe fragments, gun flints, datable pottery, glass, and nails. There were no direct messages from Governor Arnold as Means had suggested in jest, but the hard-won archaeological evidence tells us two things. First, the Tower was built in about 1650, and second, as such it is "one of the oldest buildings still standing in continental North America," as Brigitta Wallace reminds us.[15]

So post a big X on the winning side for dirt archaeology and scratch some hopes for Norse and Portuguese presence. As we approach the present in our Quest for Vikings in America, we continue to get typically mixed data. A rune stone has turned up in Heavener, Oklahoma, for example. The Viking sailing directions, not recorded in the sagas, must have been as follows: turn right at Key West (watch out for sunburn), take another right at the first really big river (that's the Mississippi), then proceed about 300 miles north to the second river on your left (that's the Arkansas; the Red is red, you know); after about 150 miles, when you just cross into Oklahoma, take a left and head south on the Poteau River (the locals can help here) and go to the Poteau Mountains. There is a great little resort there and it is far from all the hustle and bustle of the East Coast.

At this point, and I have visited the site, you are now halfway up the side of one of the Poteau Mountains in Oklahoma. You now come upon a very pleasant little building tucked in a wooded glen sheltering a large rock with a short line of runes. If the Kensington Rune Stone inscription looked fresh, this one on the Heavener stone was done the day before yesterday, but then, too, it is very cryptic. It reads GAOMEDAT, not a recognizable word, unless you reverse a rune. Here Landsverk has been helpful because he can, as usual, read a cryptogram in it to give us a date of 11 November, 1012 A.D. What we don't know is what those Vikings were doing in Oklahoma. But if that seems off course, how about the newspaper account that a wreck of a Viking ship was sighted by an adventuresome couple in the California desert, only to be destroyed by an earthquake before it could be photographed. Well, I told you it was going to be fantastic.

A lot closer to home, in many respects, was the discovery of some rune stones in Maine in 1971. I wonder if the ghost of James Russell Lowell is listening. Walter J. Elliot was hunting artifacts at Popham Beach on the coast south of Bath, Maine, near the outlet to Spirit Pond, when he came upon these fine relics, as he relates the tale. Elliot's three rune stones included a map of the locality, a unique find on any known rune stones. Later a small fourth stone or amulet with a few runes on it was found.

At first, there were problems of identification and then ownership because the land on which Elliot found these rune stones had just become a state park. Ultimately, after a little money ($4,500) had changed hands, the rune stones came to the state museum and thence to some knowledgeable sources. Landsverk pronounced them genuine and full of cryptograms; Einar Haugen, a specialist in Old Norse at Harvard, found them to be rather peculiar frauds. Members of the New England Antiquities Research Association managed to produce a translation without, according to some critics, knowing any Scandinavian—quite a feat in itself.

The Peabody Museum, which I directed at that time, did some work for the state on certain objects excavated near the find spot. Most of these turned out to be historic materials, possibly related to early seventeenth-century settlement there; nothing of Viking age was found. Both the academic specialists, Haugen and Erik Wahlgren, found the runic materials to have close resemblances to the Kensington runes. Indeed, they went so far as to say that the Spirit Pond runemaster must have had a copy of Holand's book at hand as these new messages were being written. The inscriptions seem to want to tie these visiting Norsemen into the earlier voyages because the dates, using the same unique numerical system found at Kensington, indicate a date of A.D. 1010 and 1011, the approximate time of Karlsefni's visit to Vinland.

Spirit Pond Rune Stone

Although not of the quality of the Kensington Rune Stone, the Spirit Pond Rune Stones have spawned their own literature in the 1970s, somewhat removed from the normal path of journals and scientific reports. Calvin Trillin, a regular contributor to the *New Yorker* magazine, did one of his "U.S. Journal" accounts on the runes and later went so far as to produce a light piece of fiction entitled *Runestruck* that was given hardcover treatment. I found it somewhat wanting, but it featured one of the most foulmouthed young men I have ever met in fiction or real life, in archaeology or in Maine. As a modern version of Lowell's *Biglow Papers* it was not a great success, at least in my view.

The Spirit Pond Rune Stones, revealed as crude forgeries, had some elegant company at this time, for Yale's highly touted Vinland map had made its glossy appearance on October 11, 1965, and attracted many adherents. Here was direct cartographic proof of the Viking voyages that the sagas had needed. But less than a decade later, in 1974, thanks to finegrained scholarship and small-particle analysis of the ink, the Vinland map was shot down as a recent fake in London at a meeting of the Royal Geographical Society held in, of all places, its lecture hall in Kensington. How fitting. More recent research has even pinpointed the forger—a

Yugoslavian professor, Father Jelic, who produced it in the 1920s. So the Yale Vinland map no longer hangs in the balance, as Wahlgren has noted.

But we can finish our Viking quest on several high notes, one even from Maine, where in the late 1970s a genuine Norse coin of about A.D. 1070 was recognized at the Goddard site on the coast near the mouth of Penobscot Bay. The site has a prehistoric Indian occupation dating to about that time period. The coin, which was excavated quite a bit earlier by amateur diggers but misidentified as of English origin, seems to have likely been obtained in trade from Indians farther to the north. The coin had been perforated for use as a pendant. Further excavations at the site in 1979 did not provide any more Norse material but did reaffirm the trade hypothesis for the transport of what has been called the Maine Penny. It is not very big and not very beautiful, but it is Norse and it was found in these United States. It might have started its southward trip in Newfoundland or Nova Scotia, but we will never know for sure.

I have kept the best for last. The more-than-hundred-year Quest for Vikings in North America was finally successful when Helge Ingstad discovered the site of L'Anse aux Meadows in 1960. After a long and careful search it was located, just where one would expect it to be, on the northern tip of Newfoundland. It is more than just a few scrappy artifacts or a lonely rune stone. Excavations have been carried out there twice, between 1961 and 1968 and between 1973 and 1976.

The site, now partially restored by Parks Canada, consists of eight sod-walled structures, and literally hundreds of artifacts have been recovered from the lovely location poised above a shallow bay. It has a very rich environment, and it even provided bog iron that was smelted on site by these Iron Age Vikings. Some distinctive artifacts include a ring-headed bronze pin and a soapstone spindle whorl. Many iron nails were found near the doorways, suggesting wooden doors on the sod huts. A substantial suite of carbon 14 dates places the occupation close to A.D. 1000. The comparisons to the long-known structures in western Greenland are, not surprisingly, very close, as are the artifacts.

So I would insist that archaeology does work, if you are patient enough. All through the nineteenth century even the worst of the conservative curmudgeons did not deny the existence of the Vinland of the sagas; what they demanded was proof positive of its existence in the New World. Certainly it was likely to be in the Newfoundland–Nova Scotia–Maine area, and it was not going to have fine Gothic churches or huge megalithic monuments. Erik Wahlgren, in his most recent book, has bet on Vinland on

Passamaquoddy Bay near the Maine border. These are tough sites to find and are very difficult to excavate well.

I agree wholeheartedly with Brigitta Wallace when she says: "More [Viking] sites will be discovered in the future. . . . What we can expect to uncover are the nearly demolished remains of humble turf house complexes and simple everyday household articles. . . . Although neither elaborate nor spectacular they will clearly demonstrate man's quest for new horizons."[16] The Vikings were here!

10

Across the Sea They Came, Each with a Different Cause

I am more concerned in opening new channels of inquiry than in
trying to provide pat answers.
HAROLD S. GLADWIN, 1957

It was a warm August morning in 1924 as the touring car slowly made its way in an easterly direction across Arizona on a dusty dirt road. The itinerary was from Cameron on the Navaho Indian Reservation to Orabi among the Hopi. Although some of the passengers were newcomers to the American Southwest and its ancient past, one, a forty-year-old Harvard-trained scholar named Alfred Vincent Kidder, was at that time one of the leading figures in the field of Southwestern archaeology. That very year he had published his soon-to-be classic *Introduction to the Study of Southwestern Archaeology*, and he was acting as guide to the touring party that included his cousin North Duane and wife Ethel.

As the group passed a rather unprepossessing low mound near the side of the road, Kidder said: "There's a ruin." Characteristically, one of the party demurred: "I don't believe it; you've got to show me." So they stopped the car and tramped through the low undergrowth. Sure enough, the mound was covered with broken pottery fragments, "sherds" to the archaeologist, and Kidder was proven correct in his identification. The nay-sayer was a forty-one-year-old former stockbroker named Harold Sterling Gladwin, and that event was to change the pathway of his life. He said later: "By the time we had made a collection my future course was set."[1] Gladwin would, indeed, spend the rest of his very long life (he died in his hundredth year) as an archaeologist, and his new friend Kidder would help him get started in a proper manner.

It was another one of those "odd couples"; almost of an age, they both were well-educated gentlemen, and they would both spend many decades

A. V. Kidder in the 1920s

of their lives ferreting out the secrets of the past. Their dedication to this study of archaeology would be shared with their wives and some of their children—it was no passing fancy. But Kidder was a trained archaeologist with years of schooling, fieldwork, and scientific publication already behind him when he first met Gladwin.

Born in New York City, Gladwin took most of his schooling in England following his parents' divorce. After college (1901) he returned to the United States and was at loose ends for a few years. He even spent some time in the West on a cattle ranch before he began his business career in earnest; from 1908 to 1922 he had a seat on the New York Stock Exchange. Although very successful in his business career, he ultimately became disenchanted with his life in New York and pulled up stakes and moved to the West Coast. It was from there that he ran into Kidder.

Harold Gladwin had a creative and restless mind. He wanted to know things directly, not accept what others said about them; hence his need to be shown the proof of Kidder's simple statement about the ruin. His mind churned with questions, and there was a bit of the agnostic in him: "Question authority," the cry of the 1960s, was Gladwin's theme song in the 1920s and 1930s. But he did know he had to have help. He turned to trained professionals for that aid when he founded Gila Pueblo, his research institute, in 1927. The shape of that research structure was very original and revealing.

Gladwin says that it was in 1926, on another trip with Kidder and his wife to a Rio Grande pueblo, that he was struck with the thought that it would be wonderful to see Southwestern archaeological materials exhibited in their own surroundings rather than in the marble halls of stodgy museums. Gladwin had already followed up his newfound archaeological interest and was amassing a collection of artifacts at the Southwest Museum in Los Angeles, where he had been made an Honorary Curator. Indeed, he had been charging about the Southwest, digging with a crew at Casa Grande south of Phoenix, then buying a large collection of pottery that had been excavated in eastern Arizona, near St. Johns. While in that area he passed through the old mining town of Globe in Gila County, Arizona, and near there found a nice old lady digging an ancient Pueblo ruin with a pickax and a small coal shovel.

Finding that Mrs. Healy's health was failing and that she had hoped to find someone who appreciated her ruin, Gladwin quickly struck a deal and bought the twenty-acre property. He soon put together a dig crew, mainly of Pima Indians he recruited from the southern part of the state, and began excavation of Gila Pueblo, as he was to call his residence and research center. As the archaeological structure was excavated, the rooms were turned into living quarters and places to display the artifacts so that he realized his dream of having things shown in their archaeological context, even his own life.

For nearly twenty-five years, until 1950, Gladwin's Gila Pueblo would be a major research center for Southwestern archaeology. The results of its research would be published in thirty-nine volumes of its Medallion Papers, and Southwestern archaeology would never be the same again. Gladwin's own archaeological surveys would involve almost ten thousand prehistoric sites. The recognition of two new major cultural units, Hohokam and Mogollon, would come directly from Gila Pueblo research, as did the discovery of the then-earliest-known cultural manifestation: Cochise. It was all an extraordinary accomplishment for an Eastern amateur.

How did Gladwin do it? It was, as with many such discoveries, a combination of perception, good fortune, and the right personnel. Com-

Harold S. Gladwin and Gila Pueblo

bine that with a driving passion to know, an appropriate amount of funding, and perseverance, and it becomes easy. Gladwin had the passion, the money, and the time. He hired some fine workers and challenged them to go out and do their best, while keeping right at their elbows all the time with questions and new ideas, some half-cocked. Nevertheless, the questions had to be answered, and that wasn't a bad thing.

He also took a new and more comprehensive view of his problem area; he looked at the whole of the greater Southwest as his field of inquiry. He covered a wall at Gila Pueblo with a map from the Mississippi to the Pacific and from Utah to northern Chihuahua; he sent workers to Texas and into the southern Arizona desert, far from the sacred homelands of the Pueblos on the Colorado Plateau and their mysterious cliff dwellings, where most archaeological interest had been focused for over fifty years. Gila Pueblo was not locked into the academic year and could dig in the desert in the winter, instead of being tied to the usual summer field season of the university digs.

His methodology was simple and direct and, as usual, started with personal discoveries. While digging in southern Arizona at Casa Grande, Gladwin found black-on-white "pueblo" pottery mixed in with the standard indigenous Red-on-Buff pottery. When he dug at Globe in the north, he found only black-on-white pottery very much like that he had seen in the south. Obviously, the alien people at Casa Grande had come from the north and brought their characteristic pottery. Distributions and migrations were to be his focal points.

Thus he set forth straightforward methodology for a gigantic survey with sherd collections and site locations as the prime data base. He was particularly concerned with the history of the Red-on-Buff pottery of the southern desert area; Kidder had briefly mentioned it in his *Introduction,* but it was Gladwin and his workers who plotted its distribution and published their results. Then in the early 1930s Gila Pueblo began work at the large site of Snaketown, south of Phoenix; the excavations there would turn the simple Red-on-Buff pottery complex into the Hohokam, the great irrigation-based culture with strong ties to Mexico to the south.

Of course, Gladwin did not work alone during this period; he married Winifred MacCurdy, who went with him into the field and coauthored many Medallion Papers with him. His professional staff included Emil W. Haury, who was trained both at the University of Arizona and at Harvard, where he ultimately got a Ph.D., and Edward B. (Ted) Sayles, who was an experienced excavator. Many others ultimately contributed to the Gila Pueblo publications, which often had a multidisciplinary aspect. His stepdaughter Nora, for example, did thin-section and radiographic studies of pottery. So it was Haury, Sayles, and the Gladwins who put together the landmark *Excavations at Snaketown* monograph, published in 1937.

But Gladwin's broad-based skepticism and restless spirit did not make for easy interactions even with his own staff. He soon worked out his own revisions of the chronology at Snaketown that they had agreed on earlier. Then he took on another Southwestern sacred cow: dendrochronology, the tree-ring dating method invented by A. E. Douglass, a professor of astronomy at the University of Arizona. This very accurate dating technique had revolutionized Southwestern archaeology beginning in the late 1920s. Gladwin insisted that it was being done incorrectly, and he set about putting things to right with some new methods and his own readings of the dates. During the 1940s he wrote a number of volumes of a corrective nature on the tree-ring subject. None of these Gladwinian revisions has stood the test of time.

The postwar period was a time of change for Gila Pueblo. Its staff was

(By request)

Hooton and Gladwin in the "Doghouse"

depleted; Haury had gone to work for the University of Arizona after getting his doctorate. Gladwin turned to more whimsical matters, and it is here that we turn from the "right stuff" to the fantastic. He was only in his sixties, but the camaraderie of the dusty roads, of the tents pitched at the dig sites, and of the round-the-campfire arguments over potsherds was gone. Gladwin had had a continuing tie to the Establishment via Kidder, who was on the board of the Gila Pueblo, and through Kidder, one suspects, a friendship with Professor Earnest Hooton of Harvard. Thus in 1947, when Gladwin wrote his rather far-out *Men Out of Asia*, there was a preface by Hooton and a cartoon showing Gladwin and Hooton in the academic doghouse. Hooton did have a wry sense of humor and enjoyed being "out of step" with his colleagues, especially in his later years.

I have always regarded *Men Out of Asia* as a sort of "hyper-diffusionist" spoof. Why else would Gladwin get Campbell Grant, a skillful cartoonist, to do his illustrations? Why else would he have his "friend" Kidder caricatured in the volume as Dr. Phuddy Duddy, the hidebound isolationist? It was the fundamental struggle between the amateur and the Establishment, but done with a strong dose of humor, and Gladwin verbalized his own reservations in the Introduction:

> We are going to offer an explanation that will be a radical departure from those in current circulation . . . this tale will need a great deal of patching and strengthening before it will carry much weight. . . . I am more concerned in opening new channels of inquiry than in trying to provide pat answers . . . no harm will be done if when a new idea is launched it is regarded with due reserve, but also without prejudice. (Gladwin, 1947: xiv–xv)

But there were other reservations; there may have been some personal harm done because Kidder seems to have been quite hurt by this rather strong treatment. Gladwin's doghouse-mate, Hooton, also had reservations: "I, myself, do not agree with all Gladwin's theories and conclusions hereinafter set forth. In fact, I am profoundly skeptical of some of them, for example, the Nearchus fantasy. I doubt that America was peopled by successive waves of different pure races."[2]

What, then, were the major points of Gladwin's book? First, it was an attack on the widely held hypothesis of New World independent invention. Gladwin felt that the suggestion of independent invention of cultural traits seemingly shared by residents of both the Old and the New Worlds was a terribly overworked hypothesis. Gladwin favored instead the diffusion of these items, preferably by migrations of populations. He specifically notes five such migrations from Asia to the New World. Second, he was prepared to argue about the accepted chronology for New World prehistory at both ends of the time scale.

On the early end of the chronology, he saw a veritable conspiracy not to take into account the discovery in 1926 at Folsom, New Mexico, of positive evidence of late Pleistocene hunters of now-extinct bison. A cartoon shows Dr. Phuddy Duddy (alias A. V. Kidder) sitting on top of a safety valve holding down a late-arrival position. Though amusing, it is grossly unfair to Kidder, who was one of a small group of scholars called in to authenticate the Folsom finds, which he enthusiastically did. Gladwin surely knew that; besides, the position he attributes to the Establishment with regard to Early Man was grossly out-of-date for the profession as a whole by 1947, as any reference to the standard literature of the day shows.

On the other end of the time scale, the questioning was a bit more pertinent but just as wrongheaded. Gladwin held that the origins of the high civilizations of Middle and South America, the Maya and the Inca for example, were much more recent than had "heretofore been supposed"— so recent, in fact, as to be tied to "upheavals" taking place in the Old World about the time of Christ. This period was the platform for his Alexander's fleet hypothesis, which I will describe in a moment.

Gladwin was, however, reacting to a real archaeological problem, and that was that New World archaeologists working on these high cultures intermittently since the 1840s had for all too long focused mainly on the great crumbled ruins and their exotic sculpture and architecture. It was an archaeology of lost cities and treasure-laden tombs, not of lowly potsherds and mounds covered with mere stone-lined traces of room walls. Thus the

Kidder on Safety Valve
of Late Arrival

very basic question of where and when these civilizations had arisen was not a question of the first order of magnitude until the 1930s. Certainly there had been plenty of speculation on this topic earlier, much of it quite as fantastic as that pertaining to the Moundbuilders, but there were no hard data.

In the 1920s Herbert J. Spinden, a Maya specialist, had suggested that the higher cultures had come from an Archaic base culture; George Vaillant, a graduate student whom Gladwin knew, had then worked on the question in the 1930s. Even Kidder, who by then was heading the Carnegie-sponsored Division of History working in the Maya field, was to lead excavations at Uaxactún in the late 1930s that would give some of the first good "ground truth" to the formative phases of Maya civilization. But Gladwin was right, even in the 1940s, in holding that the definitive and well-dated material needed to settle this important question was not obvious.

But as usual, he overstated the case, as any good debater is wont to do. In fact, his chapter 18, entitled "What to Believe," is a stylized response by Dr. Phuddy Duddy, who, of course, predictably says all the outrageous things that Gladwin needs his "straw man" to say. One should note, however, that this chapter does not use genuine quotes from the current literature but is drawn instead from Gladwin's slightly out-of-date memory file—an easy way to win an argument!

The truth is that the Establishment was, indeed, just as concerned about the origins of the New World civilizations by the 1940s as was Gladwin, and within a decade the long-sought answers would begin to be found in the ground. Those discoveries coupled with the advent in the early 1950s of carbon 14 dating would complete the revolution, and all the cultures of the New World would soon have a respectable heritage going back thousands of years before the time of Christ. Thus the real gap between the Folsom "big game hunters" of ten thousand years ago and the pottery-making, village-living agriculturalists of about the time of Christ would finally and successfully be filled.

But Gladwin's gap-filler in *Men Out of Asia* was no less than the remnants of Alexander's fleet, leaving its Persian port in 323 B.C. after Alexander's death, and heading intrepidly eastward until running into the New World. I wish I were joking, for then we would have been spared some rather bizarre recent developments in Fantastic Archaeology, but no, that's just what Gladwin suggested.

The fleet of Nearchus made its way slowly out of the Indian Ocean, through Indonesia, and out across the broad Pacific. Gladwin mixed a little culture with a lot of sketchy biological anthropology to prove this travel route. The cultural cargo on board the heavily laden ships included astronomy, hieroglyphics, calendars, pyramid architecture, and metallurgy—the things any good civilization needed. The fleet picked its way happily through the Polynesian Islands and made several landfalls along the coast of South America, the northernmost point being in Ecuador, where the unloading of all those wonderful traits of high civilization could begin.

Now, *part* of this tale is not bizarre; the Polynesian voyagers who did settle the vastness of the Pacific, most likely in the first centuries of the Christian era, were remarkable seafarers. Their successful colonization of this huge area is a feat comparable to our twentieth-century voyages into outer space, but the sticking point of Gladwin's scenario is, of course, the total lack of the Greek influences suggested by their origin in Alexander's fleet, as outlined by Gladwin. That notion was preposterous, as Hooton pointed out then; today it is nothing but absurd.

But what about contacts between Polynesia and South America, a topic that Thor Heyerdahl would tackle only a few years later in *Kon Tiki*? There is rather definitive evidence that the sweet potato, a New World plant, appeared in Polynesia with a name that has ties to South American Indian languages. Gladwin specifically mentions this case, and rightly so. Heyerdahl made use of this fact as well, but to prove the contrary hypothesis that American Indians settled Polynesia. Gladwin uses the sweet potato to prove trans-Pacific contact, and with that alone I am in agreement. It is much more likely that the Polynesians with their proven maritime prowess

Loading Nearchus's
Fleet for New
World

once went to South America and returned with the sweet potato than that some essentially landlocked Andean cultures, with only minimal coastal fish harvesting to their credit, were the founders of a dynasty on Easter Island, as Heyerdahl would suggest in his later work, *Aku-Aku*.

However, enough of southern adventurers. Gladwin has his voyagers affect North America as well. He takes the Arawaks of the Caribbean, gives them a Polynesian origin, and then pushes them from the Gulf of Mexico up the Mississippi Valley, where they become the Moundbuilders. Until rereading this volume recently, I had mercifully forgotten how bad that chapter really was. It reads like something that only Rafinesque could love or believe.

Gladwin was so out-of-date archaeologically that he had trouble separating the Hopewellian burial-mound-builders of Illinois and Ohio from the Mississippian temple-mound-builders of Cahokia and further south. Indeed, the text is such a mishmash of cultural traits and time periods that it boggles the mind. Gladwin says that all Moundbuilders are not alike and then under the burial practices section calmly proceeds to mix Hopewellian cremations with Late Archaic flexed burials and Mississippian extended burials. It all adds up to confused thinking and bad data, I'm afraid.

Apparently, all that is clear is that the Arawak from South America helped found the high cultures of the Southeastern United States and that the earthen pyramids of that area also owe much to those in Mexico. To help show that latter connection between the Southeast and Mexico, Gladwin trots out the old and discarded (even in 1947) hypothesis of a "Q" complex to account for some of these resemblances, which included some pottery traits as well. It was a hypothesis put forward by Samuel K. Lothrop and Vaillant in the early 1930s; indeed, it is the only piece of standard archaeology cited and quoted in extenso in the whole volume, which lacks a bibliography, although some sources can be run down in the index. Better chronological control soon showed that though ceramic resemblances did occur, they were temporally so far out of line that, unfortunately for Gladwin's view, explanations other than direct diffusion had to be used.

One other explanatory device besides migration/diffusion that Gladwin made great use of was a strong positive correlation between biology and culture. Racism is perhaps too strong a term, but there is little doubt that in Gladwin's view, the bearers of certain culture traits invariably had a very specific biological configuration; the two went hand in hand. Chapter headings have score sheets listing the contributions by Australoids, Mongoloids, Eskimo, and others, and Campbell Grant's illustrations often portray the actors in Gladwin's busy drama of migrations in a stereotypical fashion that is very embarrassing today in light of increased sensitivity to both racial and gender concerns. In fact, Gladwin is at his weakest when discussing biological anthropology; he repeats such old "saws" as seeing characteristic Neanderthal traits among modern populations and has Grant draw a cartoon Neanderthal facing a beetle-browed Professor Hooton.

Why should a spoof cause so much concern? The volume was popular and went into a paperback edition. As I mentioned much earlier, I once used the volume as an example of poor archaeological thinking in some of my Sophomore Tutorials, but I know of little academic use or notice of it in the 1950s. Like similar volumes, however, it will come back to haunt us years later with new adherents who believe every word as the gospel truth, despite the terribly outdated arguments presented therein. Gladwin concludes *Men Out of Asia* with a pessimistic view, to say the least, of the chances that anything would change in the Establishment:

> All the lights in the House of the High Priests of American Anthropology are out; all the doors and windows are shut and securely fastened (they do not sleep with their windows open for fear that a new idea might fly in); we have rung the bell of reason, we have banged on the door with Logic, we have thrown the gravel of Evidence against their windows; but the only sign of life in the house is an occasional snore of Dogma. (Gladwin, 1947: 361)

A few years later Gladwin closed down Gila Pueblo and in 1950 permanently moved to Santa Barbara, California, where he had had a home

House of High Priests of American Anthropology

for a long time. The vast data collections, sherds, vessels, maps, and so on were given to the Arizona State Museum, which was directed by his old digger Emil Haury, with Ted Sayles from Gila Pueblo also as a staff member. That institution and the University of Arizona, Establishment though they were, would make major contributions to Southwestern archaeology through research, field schools, and graduates. Thus Gila Pueblo and its rich research materials continued to contribute to the field as they had in the good old golden days of the 1930s. The residence, Gila Pueblo itself, became very appropriately a National Park Service headquarters. Gladwin was very satisfied with that outcome, but he was not done with archaeology. Unlike many figures in the field who always planned to write a magnum opus summing up their years of work but usually failed to do so, Gladwin was again given the time, opportunity, and funds to do just that.

In 1957, at the age of seventy-four, Harold Sterling Gladwin produced a handsome, privately published, 380-page volume entitled *A History of the Ancient Southwest*. It was, in his words, "merely one man's attempt to fit the pieces of the puzzle together." It was very personal, written mostly in the first-personal plural, indicating his wife's significant contribution. There are vivid descriptive paragraphs telling of the excitement of the research at

Gila Pueblo: the reader follows his lines of thinking as new evidence appears and watches decision making take place as further fieldwork is indicated and undertaken. It is a remarkable document. For its time, it is also unique in the breadth of its compass; the period/chapter maps, although less than continental in scope, do try to chronicle the developments in the whole area, with no geographic bias. Although a summary, there are many details, with ceramic designs reconstructed on vessels, and even individual sherd drawings and photographs included where special points are made.

Gladwin uses his own chronology and his own terminology: chapters begin with an italicized narrative that tells a one- or two-hundred-year story of, for example, the interaction in A.D. 800 of the Basket Makers with the Reds, of the Farmers with small bands of Reds, and of the Mongollon with their Hohokam neighbors to the south. The map is covered with arrows as restless peoples and ideas move about the area in a splendidly complex interplay of data drawn from potsherds and excavations. Gladwin has personified the players in the drama, however, and there is an immediacy of statement that would make one think that the author had at his command many documents instead of meager bits of pottery. There is no question that ceramics play an important role in the interpretations of all South-western archaeologists, but perhaps Gladwin tries to make sherds and design analysis carry too much weight.

Also there is no question that Gladwin overemphasizes population movements. Migration, no doubt, played a part in the ancient history of the Southwest as it did in all prehistory, but Gladwin, as in his previous volume, makes it a prime mover almost every stop on the way. Culture change and the diffusion of ideas or even trade would often be a more economical explanation. One such major migration is that of the Athabas-cans, the ancestors of the Navaho and the Apache. As these nomadic peoples move south from Canada to the eastern fringes of the Southwest, they become in Gladwin's terms "The Enemy at the Gates" at A.D. 1000.

The Athabascans also become for Gladwin the archetypical "Bad Actors," the guys in the black hats, who ultimately drove the Pueblos out of their Chaco Canyon and Mesa Verde strongholds. Gladwin was not the only one to give the Athabascans this role. Indeed, the aggressions of the "Nomad Raiders" were first suggested by John Wesley Powell in the 1860s as an explanation for the construction of the cliff dwellings; Powell knew at first hand what sort of justice the nomadic peoples of the Southwest had to offer. A small group of dissident men left his first Colorado River descent to go overland; these deserters were murdered by a band of Paiutes.

But more important, Gladwin's dependence on the challenge of the Athabascan tribes for this well-known population displacement was based on his strong rejection of the conventional drought hypothesis, which was based on a reading of the tree rings. As early as 1929 evidence for a severe drought in the Colorado Plateau area was noted by workers such as A. E. Douglass. This supposedly catastrophic drought lasted from A.D. 1276 to 1299, and Mesa Verde's abandonment by the Pueblos was tied directly to that event. Gladwin would have none of it.

He lists six objections to the theory and uses his own revision of tree-ring interpretation as a major part of his dissatisfaction with the conventional view; he calls it "the uncritical acceptance of an unsubstantiated theory." Modern views of this crucial depopulation theory for the northern Southwest are less founded in a single cause: the Athabascans are out; they arrive much too late to drive the Pueblos out; and problems with rainfall are back in.

In his "Summing Up," Gladwin returns in spirit to his earlier financial career as a bond broker and gives his readers the "alibi" used by bankers that "nothing is guaranteed" regarding the many new ideas set forth in the volume, only that they are "based on information which we believe to be reliable."[3]

With an inspired prescience, he also gives us some earnest advice that proves ever useful in the hard job of debunking Fantastic Archaeology, including that from his own hand:

> It is always fairly easy for an imaginative individual to coin theories which may be difficult for more serious-minded specialists to disprove. You may think it is all perfect nonsense—as I do—but you would find it hard to prove that the fabled continent of Atlantis was not the cradle of native American civilizations; that American Indians were not one of the lost tribes of Israel. (Gladwin, 1957: 346)

I would have to say it takes one to know one; I realize that the task *is* hard, as you, my readers, are only too aware, but I still do not think it impossible. How else, then, can we go on to Harold Gladwin's last book?

His long last years were just as "uncomplacent" as Gladwin had hoped they would be in the last line of his magnum opus. But life is often not what one expects; he would live on and on, continuing to work for another full quarter of a century until 1983. Surely Gladwin could never have guessed that he would remain in quite good health of mind and spirit. One senses from his writings a steadily growing dissatisfaction with the Establishment, certainly nothing new, but surely fed by a lack of positive response by the professionals to his Southwestern summary volume, a tour de force in some ways but flawed in others.

Some say he was embittered by professional attacks on him, but published ones at least were very rare. He did continue his comparative studies to carry forward his theories, which fit well into what I have termed hyper-diffusion hypotheses. Over the years he filled notebooks with his findings, and there is a volume called *Men Out of the Past* dated 1975 in his last *Who's Who* listing, though I have never been able to locate the publication. During this period Gladwin did make some new friends. If not in the conventional "groves of academe," at least they were soul mates in the area of hyper-diffusion. In 1975 the Epigraphic Society, founded by Professor Barry Fell, honored Harold Gladwin in his ninety-first year. Both Fell, the founder, and an admiring colleague, George Carter, wrote warm letters of praise for Gladwin's steadfast support of the migration hypotheses as detailed in *Men Out of Asia*. For them it was no spoof; indeed, both embraced many of the fanciful theories espoused in that unusual volume.

Gladwin's last book was published in 1979, number 40 in the distinguished Medallion Papers series that Gila Pueblo's work had made so well known. The title was *Mogollon and Hohokam, A.D. 600–1100,* the two great prehistoric cultures of the Southwest that Gladwin and his staff had breathed life into, but what a travesty it is! These two interesting Native American cultures, whose prehistoric heritage in Arizona Gladwin had helped to unravel, are said in this unhappy parody of an archaeological monograph to derive from Libya in North Africa. The Hohokam are said to come from eastern Libya with connections to Egypt, while the Mogollon are said to relate to western Libyan tribes but also to have strong connections to Caddoan peoples and their neighbors in the Lower Mississippi Valley. I wonder if he had forgotten about the Arawaks; perhaps it is significant that he does not cite *Men Out of Asia*, although he does again use Vaillant's 1932 report.

Gladwin's connections to his new diffusionist friends are amply revealed in his citations, which contain many regular contributors to the Epigraphic Society publications. In an exceptional tribute to the past, he mentions the "contrary opinions" of Emil Haury's 1976 monograph on Snaketown so he is not completely out of touch, but all in all it is a very sad presentation. For example, there is a long and rambling section about the Libyans in the front of the volume that is not tied to any of the rest of his argumentation. It should be noted that nothing much of his *Men Out of Asia* theorizing got into the 1957 *History of the Ancient Southwest,* except that the "Reds" who came up from Mexico were also tied to the Caddoans far to the east in Texas. At least back then Gladwin was able to keep his trans-Pacific voyagers in check, but no more, only this time it was trans-Atlantic North Africans instead. I shall investigate the cause for that change later.

Thus today Harold Sterling Gladwin (1883–1983) must stand as the epitome of the subject of this chapter. He was a troubling spirit—either an erratic genius or a crank scientist—there is no other logical alternative, except to say he was probably both. This problem stands out clearly if we view his entire lifetime of nearly 100 years when making this assessment.

He too was the prototypical hyper-diffusionist, also the subject matter of this segment of my study of Fantastic Archaeology. In this résumé of Gladwin's life in archaeology, I trust that the telling reasons for his selection are obvious: the sadly disquieting range from important discoveries proven by careful excavation to wild transoceanic connections that are not subject to archaeological proof. The verdict is yours.

Now that we have finally managed to leave the East, we might as well stay out West. We have grown accustomed to the sparsely covered landscape, the red-on-buff potsherds among the cactus, and even some of the archaeologists, but not I hope to the next archaeological event: the discovery of a Roman-Jewish colony near Tucson, Arizona, dating to A.D. 700.

How did Gladwin miss this one? It is a good question, for our story begins in 1924, soon after World War I and the very year Gladwin first picked up a sherd. The Tucson Artifacts story burned brightly for half a dozen years and then quietly faded into oblivion. One of the architects of its rebirth was a history professor from Wake Forest University in North Carolina with the improbable name of Cyclone Covey. It was Covey's publication in 1975 of *Calalus: A Roman Jewish Colony in America from the Time of Charlemagne Through Alfred the Great* that gave this case more than local coverage; the Arizonans had all heard it before.

Covey, an Oklahoman (hence his first name) was educated at Stanford University in California, where he also received his Ph.D. in history. Most of his earlier works dealt with subjects in American history such as Roger Williams, "the gentle radical," and the travels of the Spanish explorer Cabeza de Vaca. After getting his doctoral degree in 1949, Covey taught in Massachusetts and Oklahoma, going to Wake Forest in 1968. He does not relate exactly what led to his study of the Tucson Artifacts, but by 1970 he was directly in touch with Thomas W. Bent (1896–1972), one of the main figures involved with the finds. Covey had planned to carry out excavations at the site in 1972, but legal complications prevented the Wake Forest–

sponsored dig. Following Bent's death that year, Covey decided to publish what he had learned of the strange artifacts.

Strange indeed, for they were some thirty-one lead objects: crosses, swords, and religious/ceremonial paraphernalia, most of which had lengthy Latin and Hebrew inscriptions engraved on them, with pictures of temples, angels, leaders' portraits, and even, if our eyes are to be credited, a "di-plodocus" dinosaur. The name "Calalus" is given to the "Terra Incognita" and dates from A.D. 790 to 900 are given in roman numerals preceded by A.D. And that was all there was—no sherds, no bits of broken glass, no skeletons, no hearths or houses—just hundreds of pounds of lead objects taken from deposits several feet below a tough caliche surface over a period of six years from a desolate spot some seven miles north of Tucson.

It is strange and hard to believe unless hyper-diffusion is your game and you can casually bring some Romans across the Atlantic and then overland to Arizona. The overland mileage to Tucson is two thousand miles from the most direct port on the Atlantic Coast and a thousand miles from the nearest port on the Gulf Coast. Now I know that Sun Belt real estate is pretty attractive today and can imagine the rock-bottom prices in A.D. 700, but it does seem like a long way to go for a suntan, and there was no air conditioning then. I hate myself for making fun of a serious case, but these hyper-diffusionists, and we must certainly class Professor Covey as one, seem to take the question of why these early adventurers made this trip and how they did it as an irrelevant query. Those topics are hardly mentioned; the focus is on the artifacts at hand, not the context, and certainly not the motives and methods of the travelers.

But we must get these objects out of the ground and on to the table for discussion before we can continue our dissection of the case. For that we have to go back to 1924 and the then small city of Tucson, in southern Arizona, not more than sixty-five miles north of the Mexican border. Founded by the Spanish in 1776 on a spot already occupied by the local Indians, Tucson lay in a section of Arizona that became part of the United States in 1856, and it was the territorial capital from 1867 to 1877.

The railroad arrived in 1880, spurring its growth, and the University of Arizona was founded there in 1891. The university, which also included the State Museum housing archaeology and natural history, grew from a few hundred students in 1909 to more than fifteen hundred in 1924. The city too grew rapidly in the post–World War I period, doubling in size from thirteen thousand to over twenty-six thousand by 1925.

Among the newcomers to Tucson in the early 1920s were two war

Cyclone Covey with Tucson Cross

veterans, Charles E. Manier and Thomas W. Bent, and they soon met at some veterans' organization get-togethers. The events a few years later in September 1924 at the site near the Nine Mile Waterhole would make Manier and Bent lifelong comrades in arms, but on quite another battlefield. It started peacefully enough, so it seemed; Manier and his family had been out for a jaunt in the countryside, and as they drove closer to town they stopped to inspect a deserted limekiln, one of many of the adobe-brick structures in that area which had been constructed in the nineteenth century to make commercial use of the limestone boulders common in the Tucson Mountain area north of the city. These abandoned kilns were local landmarks in a generally uninhabited and scrub-covered landscape.

As the small party—Manier, his wife, daughter, and elderly father—surveyed the desiccated landscape, Charles Manier saw a portion of a strange object protruding from the side wall of the pathway they were using. He tapped on it and it gave a dull metallic ring. It was no easy task to investigate the find further because it was solidly embedded in the local caliche, which was to be the major point of controversy concerning these finds from the very first day, as it remains today. Manier got a small army pick and a shovel from the car, standard equipment for Southwestern drivers of the period, and proceeded to extract a very heavy lead cross from the grasp of the caliche. Caliche is a hard soil cemented by calcium carbonate, often called desert cement and common throughout the southwestern United States. One unknown quantity concerning caliche is the time required for its formation, a crucial matter in this case.

The metal cross was crudely cast and weighed some sixty-two pounds—no tiny Grave Creek Stone, this first Tucson Artifact. After being lugged home and washed, it turned out to be a much more complex find than expected; it was, in fact, two crosses riveted together with a layer of wax preserving the opposing surfaces, which bore inscriptions in a language that was soon determined to be Latin. "Calalus, the unknown land," was there on this first find as translated by Professor Frank H. Fowler of the university.

It was an impressive discovery that was taken promptly by Manier to the State Museum, where the archaeologist Karl Ruppert studied it. Ruppert, who was to have a successful career as a Middle American specialist for the Carnegie Institution, was obviously impressed because he went to the site with the Maniers the next day and was rewarded with the discovery of a seven-pound piece of caliche with some inscriptions, including an A.D. 800 date. Ruppert was to continue working with the discoverers until leaving for the field early the next year.

It was shortly thereafter, in November 1924, that Manier brought his friend Thomas Bent into the picture. Bent was very interested in the first two finds; the two men formed a legal partnership and quickly added to their archaeological collection with yet another compound lead cross discovered only three days later. These crosses bore dates of 790 and 900. This new discovery obviously sold Thomas Bent on the project. Discovering that the land was not owned, Bent immediately set up residence in a tent and a corrugated metal garage and proceeded to "homestead" the property. By Bent's own statement, he felt there was money to be made in this operation; this view is emphasized by the formal partnership document and the quick action to establish ownership of the land and, therefore, the materials found on it.

Manier and Bent's prospecting went well during that surprising fall in Tucson. More crosses were found, including a crude one that looked like a "first try," according to Bent. How, indeed, do we know all the details of these amazing archaeological discoveries? We owe much of the information to the persistent and often patient work of Thomas Bent, for he wrote a well-documented manuscript some 350 pages in length entitled "The Tucson Artifacts."

Although it has not been formally published, photocopies are available from the Arizona State Museum, and the Bent manuscript (1964) has been a major source for all students of these finds, including Professor Covey and me. There are one or two drawbacks to the document: first, the writing of it was not commenced until nearly forty years after the major events took place, and second, although Bent tried to present a balanced view of the basic questions, his final summary is a point-by-point establishment of the validity of the finds. He concludes the manuscript by stating that his primary objective was to provide "an answer to the critics of the past, the present, and the future." I suppose that is only fair, and we do owe him a debt of gratitude for providing access to a large number of very obscure sources, since much of the controversy was covered in the local newspapers. But Bent's work, like Covey's own volume, lacks a critical evaluation of much of the archaeological evidence.

The Tucson Artifacts case is in many ways the most voluminous that I will discuss in this volume; there are more than thirty objects, each with its own find spot; the discoveries occurred over a period of some five years with dozens of individuals caught up in the observation of excavations and many more commenting on the discoveries during the six-year period (1924–30) in which most of the argumentation over the meaning of the artifacts took place. One is almost tempted to add up the numbers of people and opinions and divide by the crypto-numerical sum that must be hidden in the dates on the tablet to get the answer. But I will pursue truth in a more formal manner, albeit in somewhat outline form.

We have already met two of the major characters, Manier and Bent, on the pro side of the debate. From the rising opposition comes Professor Frank Fowler, the translator from the university, and a young archaeology graduate student at the university, who was associated with Gladwin, none other than Emil W. Haury, already on the Establishment side. The pro side is strengthened by Laura Coleman Ostrander, a recent Tucson immigrant and a high school teacher of history, who took on the historical background research, and Clifton J. Sarle, a geologist and former university faculty member. Ostrander and Sarle presented the Tucson Artifacts to both the press and the academic profession. The most significant figure, however, is Dean Byron Cummings, a major administrator at the university and Director of the Arizona State Museum, who was also the leading archaeologist at the university at this time. Cummings was a swing figure in the controversy; first a fervent believer in the artifacts' age and veracity, he ultimately in 1930 wrote finis on the project for the Museum by repudiating their authenticity.

Cummings was not the only local Establishment figure to support the amazing discoveries besides Sarle; Andrew E. Douglass, the trail-blazing astronomer, whose work with tree rings would in a few years be called dendrochronology and revolutionize archaeological dating, was also a firm believer. Cummings was away doing archaeological fieldwork in Mexico during the fall of 1924 and into the spring of 1925. Douglass would write him the amazing news of the discovery of the Tucson Artifacts; Douglass admitted to being very skeptical about the finds at first but then was convinced of their authenticity after actually seeing some being excavated. He wrote up the field notes of that particular discovery. Seeing is believing! Douglass would later quietly withdraw from this position, although there is no single document in his archives that says so unequivocally. At one point Douglass went so far as to contact the National Geographic Society to enlist its support for the project.

Certainly the opinion of Douglass must have had a strong influence on Cummings and his attitude toward the finds. Cummings, upon his return to Tucson, was treated in September 1925 to the experience of seeing a sword blade exhumed after it had been discovered by a digger. Almost immediately he stated his belief in the finds. Indeed, this same scenario was repeated over and over for various visiting dignitaries. The diggers, hired Mexican laborers, would run into something as they cut into the bank with their picks, digging would stop, and "authorities" would be asked to come out to the dig to give their approval of the validity of the excavated artifact.

One such famous participant was Cummings's nephew Neil Merton Judd of the Smithsonian Institution and the famous excavator of the great ruin Pueblo Bonita in Chaco Canyon, New Mexico. A well-trained archaeologist, he too "helped excavate" several artifacts and even took off his coat to do the actual digging himself. Judd's visit to the site also preceded that of Cummings and must have strongly influenced the latter because Judd had received his initial field training in archaeology from Cummings. Judd believed that the artifacts were genuine and in place when he found them, but with an important difference. He said they were of no great age, "not prehistoric," dating them to after the coming of the Spanish clerics into the Tucson area. Interestingly, years later when Judd wrote Cummings's obituary for several scientific publications, there was no mention of the Tucson Artifacts affair. Nor were these Tucson events noted in Judd's 1968 mini-autobiography, which discusses many other events and sites from this era connected with Dean Cummings, as Judd always referred to his uncle.

The selling of the Tucson Artifacts to the profession and the press began in December 1925. Cummings was the crucial participant then. He went to the American Association for the Advancement of Science meetings in Kansas City with ten of the artifacts in hand and later toured eastern museums and universities for further consultations. The *New York Times* broke the story on a national level on December 13, 1925, with a lead on the front page: "Puzzling Relics Dug Up in Arizona Stir Scientist."

Opinion was divided geographically: the Tucson quotes were from all the believers, the Eastern Establishment were the nay-sayers, some even using those unpleasant terms *fake, hoax,* or *fraud.* Judd continued to dismiss fraud and clung to the more modern date. Bradford Dean, Curator of Arms and Armour at the Metropolitan Museum of Art (the artifacts included were swords and the like), cried fraud on formal grounds, while others dissected the Latin inscriptions and winced at everything from the spelling to the grammar and vocabulary. Special concern was shown for the use of *Anno Domini* at this early date; most authorities suggested that the

Two Tucson Artifacts

usage was anachronistic. Another source consulted by the *Times* was William Channing Wyman, a collector of copper artifacts; Wyman made the interesting suggestion that there was a similarity in style between the Tucson Artifacts and the Michigan Relics and suggested that perhaps Scotford's handiwork had spread to the Southwest. Indeed, there was a bit of similarity in the very simplistic representations of the Roman figures on the Tucson Artifacts.

Cummings's tour with the artifacts was no pleasure trip. The professionals at the universities and museums were not impressed and told him so, but Cummings did not sway in his opinion yet. Early in 1926 there was in Tucson what Bent has called the "Boosters Meeting" at the university, at which Cummings spoke very positively about the finds. But the tide was turning even in Tucson; Professor Fowler, who did the first translations and had verified the excavations along with others, had grown suspicious enough of the inscriptions to do a little research and ultimately found that the phrases on the artifacts were from well-known classical authors such as Horace, Cicero, and Virgil. A little more research into the Latin textbooks available in the Tucson area contained phrases identical to those on the lead artifacts. Quite a coincidence! Simple analyses of the lead and of the wax (between the crosses) seemed to confirm a very recent date.

Next, there was the local newspaper story about a young Mexican boy named Timotéo Odohui, who supposedly had lived near the site and was a sculptor. Some suggested that the family, involved in the limekiln work in the 1880s, had come from an educated background in Mexico and that the son was capable of producing the lead artifacts. Bent called Odohui the "Phantom Sculptor," and he seems to have been right. Journalists were typically grabbing at straws for new leads in this case, although Haury said that at the time Odohui seemed more reasonable than the Romans.

Dean Cummings realized early on that the veracity of the archaeological situation could be tested by having the university carry out its own excavations at the site, but that option was a long time coming. Finally, in January 1928, some two years after the initial discovery, such excavations began. The contract with Bent and Manier was not a simple one: the university would have control over the excavation, but Ostrander and Sarle would also participate in the research. Finally, and this was surely part of the reason for the long delay, the university would pay Bent and Manier $16,000 for all the artifacts so far found and those that might be discovered in the excavations. Bent, responding to charges of price gouging, indicated that he and Manier had incurred costs that would make their real gain only about $3,000 each. There was one little escape clause for the university: this sum would be paid only if the artifacts were determined to be authentic, and Cummings was to be the judge of that.

The much-heralded dig got under way, and some artifacts, mostly fragments of small spearheads, were found. The work was under the direction of John Hand, one of Cummings's fieldworkers from the Mexican expedition, assisted by Charlie Conrad. Emil Haury was in Tucson at the museum at this time and went out to the excavations only when sent there by Cummings. Twice Haury went to the site to remove specimens that had been encountered by the diggers, and both times the objects bore fresh scratches that penetrated the lead patina. Haury took great care in removing the second specimen, fearing that he had caused the scratches on the first one accidentally. Both were scratched, however. Haury was convinced that he could see where a hole, longer than needed, had been made to accept the "planting" of the second artifact fragment. He remains convinced to this day that these specific artifacts had been "planted," although he does not make similar charges against the earlier finds.

However, at least one of the very first finds, the one viewed by Douglass, was also noted as having fresh-looking scratches on it. Indeed, there was a variation in the nature of the soils surrounding the artifacts; some were encased in hard caliche, others were found in much less compact soils, according to Bent's own documentation.

Rather precipitously the university excavations were closed down after not even two months' work. The cause for this action is not well explained in the data available to me. Certainly Bent and his cohorts were not given any specific reason for the cessation of the project. Cummings was very busy at this time, having been recently named acting President of the university on top of his other responsibilities. One can only guess that strong arguments against the validity of the finds were being made to him by his student Emil Haury. Certainly the reasons ultimately given in the final report for no longer backing the authenticity of the artifacts are remarkably close to those held by Haury.

Again for unknown causes, the final report did not see the light of day, or, better still, did not land in the newspaper editor's lap until nearly two years after the dig closed down. When the report was written (it is undated) and by whom is also not clear. Though Cummings signed it, there is some use of "we" referring to observations that are known to have been made by Haury. Another important source seems to have been used as well, especially with regard to the nature of the Latin inscriptions, and that is a 157-

page report by George M. B. Hawley, called "Facts and Artifacts," which dealt extensively with the purported textbook sources. The final report attributes all its critical remarks in this area to Professor Fowler, but Hawley had done some yeoman work on the topic too.

I hope I may be forgiven for drawing yet one more character into this complex case, but George Hawley does make a brief yet important appearance at a very crucial time, just when the university excavations were going on in January 1928. Interestingly, Hawley is the one person not mentioned by Bent in his otherwise comprehensive coverage of the case. It is true that Hawley's manuscript did not surface until 1956, but Covey indicates that Bent both knew its contents and was infuriated by some of the remarks. Indeed, Hawley's may have been one of the unnamed works which Bent mentioned as casting aspersions on those associated with the discovery and which made Bent decide to write up his side of the story.

Covey has, however, given quite a bit of space to Hawley, who came to Tucson from Rochester, New York, and seems to have stayed only for that winter season. A brash and outspoken lawyer, George Hawley took out after the supposed ancient artifacts with a vengeance. For example, he carefully documented many of the Latin phrases, word for word, as they appeared in the textbooks pointed to by Fowler. Even Covey had to admit that they "accumulated into a damaging case." By checking the dates of publication of the sources, he "proved" that the inscriptions were cut between 1914 and 1925.

But Hawley went even further; he felt he knew who two of the perpetrators were: Ostrander and Sarle. He thought they had even put their initials on the inscriptions, like James Scotford's mark. Some of Hawley's work was too much anger with too little data, but nevertheless if Cummings saw the report, it could very well have helped tip the scales against the Tucson Artifacts. Unfortunately, that hypothesis can not be verified because all Cummings's papers burned in a house fire before his death.

Needless to say, Bent and Manier were devastated by Cummings's about-face. They had lost a staunch ally and $16,000 to boot. We know how Thomas Bent took the change of position from his own document. He refused to believe that Cummings had really turned against the artifacts; he continued to quote over and over Cummings's earlier published support of their authenticity. An alternative to complete disbelief in the artifacts is proposed by Bent's allegation that Cummings had lost an academic struggle at the university and was forced by "the powers" to repudiate the finds and save the dollars as well. Bent was convinced until his dying day that Cummings had never ceased to believe in the Tucson Artifacts. The *Tucson Star* once editorialized: "Wherever the relics are placed in history, their worth cannot be depreciated by hasty decisions."

And there the matter rested until Cyclone Covey took up the banner in 1968, nearly forty years later. His book *Calalus* does Bent's cause some service, although the volume, published by a small vanity press with Wake Forest support, leaves much to be desired. The organization of the book is confusing to say the least; chapter 1 deals first with Roman seafaring and then turns to details of finds of various purported Roman artifacts in America without telling the reader the whys and wherefores of these topics. None of these data are used later to strengthen the plausibility of the Tucson finds, although one presumes that is why they were presented in the first place. Next we have "Synagogues of Rome" and then "Reference Points of Gregory and Charlemagne."

On page 31 of Covey's *Calalus,* the innocent reader first learns of some amazing discoveries of Roman objects in Tucson. For the next ninety-two pages Covey presents the case for the Tucson Artifacts, demonstrating that he has done some of his homework, although the amateur quality of the photos of the artifacts detracts from what would be a real service to put the whole collection in the published record. By his own statements it is clear that his purpose is to support the Bent position; indeed, he considered the publication of the volume a personal debt that he had to fulfill after Bent's death. There is only a modest presentation of contrary evidence and little or no attempt to provide a historical framework to explain the reason for this remarkable implantation of a Jewish Roman community in the American Southwest at A.D. 700 or any other time.

Covey's inattention to detail allows the volume to slip off into a new subject after page 122. He chases the chimera of lost cities in the Southwest, using first Spanish and then Apache sources. When Covey got to Tuzigoot, a Pueblo ruin in the Verde Valley, I could barely follow him. Although I have visited the site and region, the bleached-out photos and the confused descriptions left me gasping, but then we were off to some new marvels, "tall, artificially-deformed-headed mound tribes" that might have been met by the eighth-century migrants, our Arizona-bound friends heading for Calalus.

An inscription on clay from Big Bend Park on the lower Rio Grande pops up next. It makes the Grave Creek Stone look pretty shabby; there are some eighty-five characters, including three alphabets and even a Mayan number nine. Mercifully, this tablet has now disintegrated and disappeared, but I am sure there are plenty of translations already. Covey sees in the inscription ties to a Hebrew tablet written in Greek found in Roman Britain. Finally, we come to the Los Lunas inscription in New Mexico, which has been read by some as Hebrew with a bit of Phoenician and Greek thrown in. Covey closes his volume by musing that if the Calalus colonists did happen to stop by on the way to Tucson to see the Los Lunas rock, they probably could not have read it anyway. They would have looked at it and marveled, so he suggests, "Well, there are mysteries in the world, aren't there?"

But I have let Professor Covey carry us a long way off the subject; that's what happens with hyper-diffusion. Now let's get some closure on the Tucson Artifacts, the proposed colony of Calalus notwithstanding. The artifacts themselves give us pause: lead swords, crosses, and the like. Though the Romans did use lead, they never made any artifacts that resemble these so they are unique forms. There are no associated artifacts of other types to verify the Roman connection such as distinctive potsherds. The Latin in the inscriptions is poorly done; some are not sentences but just words thrown together. When there are decent Latin phrases, we can find the obvious sources in modern textbooks.

What of other kinds of testing? The lead was quantitatively analyzed in a simple manner in 1925; years later Bent asked Professor William C. Root whether it seemed to be Roman lead. Root, a good scientist at Bowdoin College in Maine and a specialist on archaeological metals from the New World, was not impressed by the artifacts and said so. The results of his spectroscopic analysis of the lead were similar to those done in the 1920s, but he had to admit that he could not compare it to Roman lead because he did not have that knowledge. The nay-sayers in Tucson and elsewhere had long insisted that the lead was either common plumber's lead or a variety used for casting printing type, both available in the Tucson area.

The data in the published assays indicate that the alloy is not appropriate for typesetting because it is not hard enough, but it also would make a very poor sword. I have discussed the lead with two local metallurgical experts, one of whom works with Roman lead, and they are very skeptical of both great antiquity and a Roman connection. New types of analyses are now available just for lead that make this area of research on the Tucson Artifacts of great interest. These tests should be done to solve some of the lingering questions once and for all.

Even without this new testing, the only real question left is how the unknown hoaxer (and I do not have any suspects) planted the artifacts so successfully in the caliche and left so little evidence of the intrusion. That geological aspect is the only worrisome part of this case that remains today. Of course, one also has to wonder how and why Cyclone Covey became so convinced of the validity of these very strange finds which stretch one's imagination to the limits of credibility. Once he was embarked on this pathway of belief, Covey's willingness to take in new wonders and add them imaginatively to the Roman voyagers' scenario was unfettered. He has thus happily joined the ranks of Fantastic Archaeologists whose works he cites uncritically alongside the more responsible ones.

That is not to say, however, that he has joined an undistinguished group of university-based members of that "band of brothers" whom we term "crank scientists" or even "rogue professors." They occur in every scientific profession from astronomy to zoology. Herein we have met Professor Horsford and his Vikings, and we will soon meet Professor Fell and his inscriptions. For now, I will give just a quick nod to a couple more that have also made hyper-diffusion their specialty.

Leo Wiener (1862–1939) was a Professor of Slavic Languages and Literature at Harvard for more than thirty years. Born in Bialystok, Russian Poland, he was educated in Europe before emigrating to America in 1882. He seemed to have a natural facility with languages, and although he had no formal training in linguistics, he taught European languages at several institutions before coming to Harvard as an Instructor in Slavic in 1896. The rest of his academic life was spent in Cambridge.

Wiener was prodigiously active; for example, he translated the complete works of Tolstoy (twenty-four volumes) "with amazing speed, yet with remarkable felicity and accuracy." But he did not focus solely on Slavic studies; he worked in Yiddish and German as well. To all his research he brought "iron industry and penetrating observation"; he was not impressed with "establishment" or old school theories. "He was a self-made and a self-taught man with the strong points and shortcomings of his genus." Personally he was an arresting figure, a famous character whose "lively temperament, genius and eccentricities lent color" to Harvard Yard.[4]

His radical turn to New World scholarship took place in the early 1920s, when he was working on *Comparative Grammar of American [Indian] Languages.* In studying these languages he discovered rather to his surprise that "Negroes have had a far greater influence upon American [Indian] civilization than has heretofore been suspected."[5] With characteristic speed, he tore into the subject and produced a three-volume work entitled *Africa and the Discovery of America* published in 1920–22. These are not light pieces of froth but very well-researched works with hundreds of sources, illustrations, and quotations. His thesis was that Negro traders (I use his terminology) were in continued contact with the New World from about the twelfth century. The Negro civilization that came to the Americas at that time had been strongly influenced by Arabic and Hindu ideas, especially in religion.

The historical and archaeological evidence that Wiener used to buttress these novel notions was wide-ranging and one would have to take as much space as in the original to refute them in detail. He spent much time and energy tearing apart the documentation for Columbus's voyages, for example. But more pertinent to our topic, there is a hundred-page discussion of tobacco and smoking pipes, both of which he tried to prove are of African origin, contrary to conventional wisdom. To accomplish this reversal of the standard hypothesis, he had to show that all pipes that are known archaeologically in North America date from rather late times. He could do that only by opting for an exceedingly shortened time scale, even considering the poor chronology that North American archaeology suffered from in the 1920s. On the European side, the twisting of data was even worse. Typical colonial clay pipes of the seventeenth century such as appear in dozens of period paintings were said to be proof of Roman use of tobacco because of a mixed deposit discovered in Italy.

It was in the comparative cultural approach that Wiener's "evidence" was most flagrantly mishandled. He discussed and illustrated a number of perfectly legitimate late prehistoric sculptures from the Southeastern United States which showed human figures with either headdresses or hair arrangements, it is hard to tell which, that featured buns or knobs. The faces of some of these figures also showed markings that might be tattooing. Wiener views these faces as having an African cast. The hair and facial treatments were duplicated by West Africans in the twentieth century, and he had the photos to prove it. What further proof of direct connections between the two areas was needed? Of course, we can now date these sculptures to about A.D. 1300, and we know that what he saw as African physical features are nothing of the kind.

Through connections that remain obscure, Wiener had received the encouragement and then the financial support of the wealthy dilettante John B. Stetson for his earlier work, as he acknowledges in one of the forewords to his three-volume work. Never one to slack, as soon as he had finished that work, he was off to show the substantial connections between

Africa and Mesoamerica. In 1926 he completed a very handsome volume entitled simply *Maya and Mexican Origins*. The gold-brushed edges of the pages, the lavish color plates of drawings from the Mayan Codices, and the Yale University Press imprint gave the work a solid academic look, all thanks to the strong support of Stetson; "rare generosity," Wiener called it.

The major hypothesis contained in the lavish volume can be set forth in the author's own words:

> The major part of the religious concepts of the Mandingos [a West African tribe], hence of the Mayas and Mexicans, arises from linguistic speculations bequeathed by the Arabs in their astrology and astronomy, as derived from a Hindu source, hence it is now possible to maintain that the American [Indian] civilizations were derived from Africa after the ninth century [A.D.], since it is only in the ninth and tenth centuries that the Hindu study of the sky became the preoccupation of the Arabs. (Wiener, 1926: xxvii)

All this is very straightforward and matter of fact with no questions and no ifs, ands, or buts—the connections are there, and Wiener sets them forth for all to see.

One judges, however, that there had been some "slight" critical questioning of some of his earlier speculations: why else would these rather heated words from Wiener appear in his foreword to the new publication: "Unquestionably, the archaeological dogs will continue to bay at the moon and will pursue the same vociferous methods as in the past, in order to suppress the truth with noise where reason fails, forgetful that the truth, wherever it be, will shine forth without such vocal emphasis."[6] Indeed, one wonders what was said by what archaeologists other than that their truth was different from Wiener's; he strongly characterizes these attacks as "the vilest private and public aspersions of the author." Following Wiener's own dictum, one must say that the truth about the purported African connections to the Maya and other American groups has shone through today in a manner that would still not please him.

Wiener's last years were not happy; "death came as a surcease on December 12, 1939." His son Norbert Wiener, a child prodigy and then MIT professor, was later to use linguistic talents of his own to coin the term *cybernetics* for his systems theory of information control. One sees unhappily in both Gladwin and the elder Wiener early intellectual triumphs that grew dim in their later years.

Lest it be thought that Wiener did his work in vain, however, let me add a footnote and indicate that some other scholars have picked up his fallen banner of African connections to the New World: Ivan Van Sertima and Alexander von Wuthenau. Van Sertima is a professor at Rutgers with a background in anthropology; by his own statement he was strongly influenced by Wiener's writings and then by those of von Wuthenau, an art historian from Mexico. Von Wuthenau saw strong evidence of African influence in the pre-Columbian art of Mexico, especially in the portrayal of Blacks in the giant heads at La Venta. Van Sertima agrees and goes further to suggest that there has been a conspiracy of silence regarding these remarkable stone heads uncovered in 1940 by Matthew Stirling of the Smithsonian. Because these digs were sponsored by the National Geographic Society, which has done its best over and over to bring these extraordinary sculptures to public attention, I find this argument hard to follow. If, however, what Van Sertima means is that they were not identified as proof of Wiener's hypothesis, then he is correct.

Another part of the Wiener thesis that Van Sertima continues to uphold deals with the African connections to be seen in both the smoking pipes and the hair knots shown on some of the sculptured pipes. It is one thing to allow Wiener some leeway on the chronology of North American archaeology in 1920; however, some fifty-five years later, in 1977, when Van Sertima wrote his volume, one must critically acknowledge that his failure to use the new archaeological data now available to all is unfortunate. He repeats Wiener's hypothesis almost word for word.

Both Van Sertima and von Wuthenau continue today to champion this hyper-diffusion explanation of trans-Atlantic connections and the impact of African culture on American Indian cultures in the pre-Columbian period. Unfortunately, this explanation clouds the extraordinarily exciting picture of very early New World developments toward civilization that researchers have been carefully excavating over the last few decades. They have finally found the data necessary for the foundations of the early formative stages of Native American cultures going back thousands of years—the very data that Harold Gladwin had scolded Dr. Phuddy Duddy for saying must be there but had not yet been discovered.

To close this chapter we must take a mercifully quick glance at yet one more hyper-diffusion hypothesis. If it were not enough to posit a Hindu-Arab–West African–American linkage, there is now the ultimate answer to the origin of the American Indians, a question that I discussed much earlier in a nineteenth-century context. Joseph B. Mahan, Jr., an anthropologist and graduate of the University of North Carolina, confidently suggests that "they actually were Indians," as he has entitled one of his research papers.

What Mahan means is that he believes that many of the Indian tribes of the Southeast such as the Creeks, Cherokees, and Shawnees are direct descendants of the originators of the great Indus Valley civilization exemplified by famous sites of Mohenjodaro and Harappa. This interesting civilization, covering a thousand-mile stretch of the Indus Valley in what is today Pakistan, reached its height about 2500 B.C. and then went into a decline around 1500 B.C. That much is known and generally accepted.

While Mahan was doing fieldwork in Pakistan, he was impressed by similarities that he saw between the Indus culture and that of the Southeastern Indians, which he had studied for a long time. Specifically, he noticed an identity in ceramic designs, axes, and sculptures. He also compared the costumes of nineteenth-century American Indians with those of known peoples of India—turbans, earrings, silver headbands, and other jewelry. Other ties were seen in religious philosophy and ceremonies and even in tribal names. Therefore, there is a direct connection between the two cultures, and the mystery of what happened to the Indus Civilization is solved; they all moved to the American Southeast.

Mahan says that there is plenty of hard evidence in America for such contact that has been uncovered since colonial times, but "this material was consistently discredited by American scholars who held, almost without exception, that all the American cultures before the time of Columbus developed on this continent completely independent of any influences—or migrations—from the ancient civilizations of the Eastern Hemisphere."[7]

Mahan feels that situation is changing and I agree: why else did I write this book? He suggests that in the last twenty years "an increasing number of serious scholars have drawn attention to the importance of this material"—that is, the evidence for trans-Atlantic connections. I will turn to those data in the next chapter. This segment ends, therefore, not with hyper-diffusion and crank scientists put to rest, but alive and well and (forgive the pun) cranking out more of the same old stuff. All that is needed to "prove" positive connections across either the broad Pacific or the stormy Atlantic are some rather simple artifact similarities and some "sounds-like" linguistic ties.

Mahan's Indus Valley hypothesis is a type case of what Radner and Radner called the grab-bag approach to pseudoscience proof; any similarity will do—don't worry about chronology or in-depth linguistic analysis. According to Mahan, the six names of the Yuchi tribe in Oklahoma sound like the names of Dravidian-speaking tribes of India, hence "these names provide positive identification of those once in contact—indeed were once the same people." Little does it matter that thousands of years and thousands of miles separate the two groups. It still is a tough choice: is Mahan an erratic genius or a crank scientist?

Broad seas were crossed in prehistoric times; of that there is no doubt. The Pacific Ocean and the Polynesian prehistoric migrations thereon are the best example of that fact in the world. It can be done, and it was done. But the hyper-diffusion cases just reviewed show the other side of the making and testing of hypotheses. It involves data encountered and then weakly constructed cases erected to prove that the migrations that seem to be required may have happened. Proof is often very thin: one kind of data (lead artifacts); or some sound-alike words; no sherds, or campfires, or burials; indeed, no rounded cultural context. Contrast that situation with the data on the New Zealand Maori settlements or the first inhabitants of the Hawaiian Islands. So I say yes to data-laden transoceanic migrations such as those; no to skimpy hyper-diffusionistic and mythic Roman Jewish settlements in Tucson. Not a hard choice.

11
Some Tales the Rude Monuments Tell

QUESTION: Why are these archaeologists . . . ? It seems as if they are
determined not to accept your beliefs.
FELL: I don't know why. It is a peculiar characteristic of archaeologists.

BARRY FELL, 1977

"The Celts are coming, the Celts are coming." That is not the happy cry of
New England sports fans as they welcome their perennially successful team
of basketball wizards back on to the worn parquet of Boston Garden. No,
what I am referring to is the even older tradition of looking across the ocean
for trans-Atlantic voyagers other than the Vikings. The northern Europeans called the Celts are a mysterious group even in their place of origin,
and much speculation surrounds their purported homeland and the time of
their transcontinental migrations.

They are seen by most prehistorians as invaders of the British Isles by
Early Iron Age times; the Celts therefore represent the distant ancestors of
the Scots, Welsh, Cornish, and Irish, all of whom spoke variants of a Celtic
language. With this well-established penchant for travel, it is not surprising
that even the well-known English chronicler of early voyages Richard
Hakluyt accepted and in 1589 published a manuscript relating to a possible
foray to the Americas by the Welsh Prince Madoc, a seafaring refugee from
civil war in Wales circa A.D. 1170.

As any student of American history knows, the Celtic migration has
continued almost unabated since those early times, or so it would seem. In
truth, if we turn to the New England states, where many of the historic
Celtic immigrants did indeed settle, we find an environment that is very
similar to the island homelands of these Welsh, Scots, and Irish. Indeed, the
comfortable congruity of the countryside is to be expected now that our
geological knowledge has been advanced by the theory of plate techtonics

and continental drift, which shows that Europe and North America were once quite close together but now are drifting some few centimeters apart every century.

The rockbound coast of Maine and the stone-scattered fields of much of New England have provided opportunities for special kinds of man-made structures that are the focus of this chapter. When residents of other parts of the United States first encounter the Northeastern farmlands bordered with stone fences, they realize that when New Englanders speak of "farming rocks," they speak the truth. The outlanders may even halfway believe the locals when they speak of their "crop" of stones, because with strong frost action plowing it does provide a rich "harvest" each spring of more rocks. That these impediments to agriculture were regularly laid up in piles and were then converted into fences at a time when cattle were also a major part of the economy seems both necessary and efficient.

But they built things other than fences—house foundations, root cellars, and animal pens. In this pattern of using stone they were, in many cases, following established patterns of construction that had been developed in the British Isles from whence they came. And as if they did not have enough raw material at hand, they quarried the rocks as well: granites, slates, limestone, and the like—all very fine building materials. Deeply buried minerals such as copper and coal would be eagerly sought in the nineteenth century, and Celtic experts in these trades—Welsh and Cornish men especially—were recruited to work in the New World mines.

The point is that a body of knowledge and raw materials came together in New England that made stone architecture inevitable during Colonial times. A New England farmer, a hired hand, a couple of pry (prize) bars, a yoke of oxen, and a stone boat (a crude sled for moving rock) could work wonders on the landscape, and they did. Not surprisingly, many of the rude monuments to these Celts' handiwork still remain today. They are slightly enigmatic and susceptible to many new interpretations, especially if found in now-deserted farmlands from which the wooden structures that once accompanied them have rotted and disappeared.

I have mentioned the Welsh and the supposed twelfth-century voyage of Prince Madoc, but even earlier, so that myths tell us, there was an Irish monk named Brendan, called the Navigator. The patron saint of County Kerry, he gave his name to Brandon Mountain on the lovely Dingle penin-sula, which stretches out to the fabled Blasket Islands, the westernmost point on the continent. St. Brendan's exploits, which were set down in Latin during the tenth century in a work termed the *Navigato,* involve a trans-Atlantic voyage that purportedly took place around A.D. 520–40. Such a trip has recently been given some credibility by the British scholar Geoffrey Ashe and a similar trans-Atlantic crossing in the 1970s by Tim Severin in a hide-covered boat manned by a stalwart crew of modern-day adventurers. Like the *Kon-Tiki* raft trip of Thor Heyerdahl, the successful crossing merely indicates that the voyage is possible; it does not establish the fact that the event occurred. For that proof other dry-land data are needed, and that search so far has not been too successful. The continual lack of ground-truth archaeological data has plagued most of the hyper-diffusionists' claims that I will consider herein.

But one must credit and continue to test the hypothesis that the Norsemen may not have had it all to themselves when it comes to beating old Christopher Columbus to the New World. Some fifty years ago a new partisan of such early Celtic adventures appeared on the scene, William B. Goodwin of Hartford, Connecticut. He was a well-to-do retired insurance man, who had dabbled in matters archaeological and historical for some time, beginning with an investigation in the mounds of Ohio when he was a resident there. While vacationing in the Caribbean, he took a critical interest in various aspects of Columbus's voyages.

Goodwin turned to the Viking question in the late 1920s and published a book entitled *The Truth About Leif Ericson and the Greenland Voyages to New England*. The title gives us an insight into his manner; not "New Data on Leif" or "Some Hypotheses about the Vikings"—just the truth as known to William Goodwin. His views were hardly sensational; he just said that the Norse sagas were dependable documents and that Vinland was in New England stretching from Maine to Cape Cod. There was nothing world-shaking about those "truths."

The Merrimack Valley north of Boston was to be the locale for Goodwin's most enduring foray into American archaeology. It was here on a bald hill of granitic schist, in southern New Hampshire, not far from the small village of North Salem, that Goodwin was first led in 1936 to some rather strange "caves" and stone constructions known locally as Pattee's Caves. Goodwin would quickly buy the site and dub it Stone Village; it would later bear other sobriquets including Mystery Hill and most recently the American Stonehenge. A fence was put around the site to protect it from vandals. It had been a popular picnicking area, but there also were many local and varied legends attached to it including being a robber's den, a stop on the Underground Railway, and the site of an illicit still.

Goodwin was not one to let grass grow under his feet. Although he

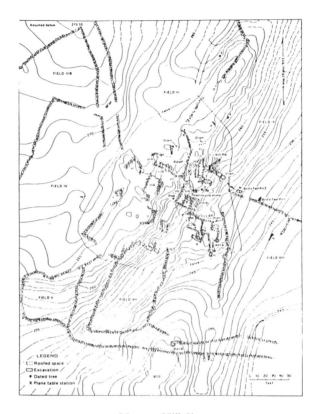

Mystery Hill Site

first thought the site might be Norse in origin, he soon turned to his ultimate explanation: it was the monastery of Irish monks who had fled Norse harassment in Iceland and arrived in the New World about A.D. 983. He never wavered from this opinion despite expert advice to the contrary. Goodwin was a robust and confident man from an old-stock Connecticut family; nearly seventy years old when he took up this adventure, he would grow very bitter about how the academic establishment treated his views on the archaeology of the North Salem site.

By a quirk of fate it happened that Harvard's Peabody Museum had, in the 1930s, been deeply involved in Irish anthropology with a multidisciplinary field project involving physical anthropology (Hooton), archaeology (Hencken), and social anthropology (Conrad Arensberg). Hugh O'Neil Hencken, the head of the archaeology portion, was an American who did his undergraduate work at Princeton but got his doctorate at Cambridge,

England, based on fieldwork in the British Isles. His fieldwork in Ireland combined talented Harvard graduate students as his assistants with local Irish scholars and out-of-work farmers to make very significant archaeological discoveries.

There was no one else in North America with such a fine background in northern European archaeology, and Goodwin counted himself lucky that Hencken was willing to look over the New Hampshire site. Goodwin wrote enthusiastically about his first meeting with this tall and very knowledgeable gentleman, who would spend his entire distinguished career at the Peabody. Other well-qualified scholars would also visit the site during this early period, including A. V. Kidder from Andover, whom we last met in the Southwest, and Hallam L. Movius from Harvard, who had dug with Hencken in Ireland.

What these archaeologists saw then did not impress them, at least not toward identifying the site as being pre-Columbian with an Irish flavor. One major question that will likely remain unanswered forever is what the site looked like before it was first scavenged for municipal building materials in the late nineteenth century and then "restored" by Goodwin's field man, Roscoe J. Whitney. The concern is, of course, how much of what one sees today, or even saw in 1938, was original and how much restoration. Unfortunately, the oft-published Whitney map of 1937–38 shows the site after it was cleaned up, with caves cleared, walls restored, and the "stone of sacrifice" raised on stone supports.

The statement is often made that Goodwin *excavated* the site, "assisted" by Whitney; that is simply not the case, as the record makes clear. Most of the work at the site was done in 1937, the year following the purchase by Goodwin, and it was done by Whitney, with only rare visits by Goodwin, who was summering elsewhere. I have hesitated to call what Whitney did archaeological fieldwork because Whitney had no training in that area of research, and most of the excavations were merely to remove debris from the structures. Some materials from these "digs" were saved and included only objects (artifacts) that were of the Colonial period. Some of these sherds have been saved, and I can verify that the period covered by these artifacts is about what Goodwin stated to Hencken: A.D. 1790 to 1850. The bricks, bits of iron, and a gun flint are more difficult to date; but there was nothing recovered in this early work to indicate occupation by Irish monks at a time around A.D. 1000, and that statement holds for other artifacts discovered in the more than fifty years that have now passed.

Despite these negative findings made by his own worker, Whitney,

Goodwin was deeply hurt by Hencken's report on his findings at the site that were published in the *New England Quarterly* in 1939 and in slightly revised form in the *Scientific American*. Hencken's report, although courteous to Goodwin's view, indicated that there was nothing in the architecture to suggest an Irish monastery and no artifacts of the proper sort or date to help support the case.

On the contrary, Hencken set out for the first time what can be called the Jonathan Pattee hypothesis in some detail. Pattee had owned the property from about 1825 on, and the house on the site burned in 1855. It was after this event that stone was removed from the site for construction purposes. Pattee lived on the site with his large family until his death in 1848, and Hencken was convinced that Pattee, termed an eccentric by the townspeople, was the builder of the rather amazing stone structures that Goodwin thought were of Irish origin.

At this time there were no direct dating means available, but there was one enigmatic piece of data that Hencken did not try to hide; it was the stump of a large white pine tree that was found close to one of the structures. Though it was too rotted to count the rings, it was of good size and substantial age, no doubt. Besides the problem of not being able to check the rings, there was no certain way to tell when the tree had been felled. So even if it were 162 years old, as has been estimated, one must guess its cutting date as well. On the basis of his own observations and a bit of digging around, Hencken suggested that the tree had started to grow before 1800, thus before Pattee's arrival at the site, indicating that Structure A might be somewhat older than the others but still not precolonial.

Hencken quite gently disagreed with some of Goodwin's historical research. Finally, by analogy with other stone structures known certainly to be of recent age (colonial and later), he showed the stone architecture of the Stone Village to be very comparable in scale and craftsmanship. There were some rather elaborate drains, but these were needed because rain falling on the bare rock crown of the hill had to be led away from the living areas. The "ruin" was not an Irish monastery.

Goodwin was not at all pleased; his early praise of Hencken had turned to invective. He saw Hencken's contrary view as typical of Harvard's arrogance—an unwillingness to accept the ideas put forth by those not members of the "club," Goodwin's own analogy. It was a club indeed, for Goodwin had another Harvard professor on his hit list: Samuel Eliot Morison, the historian, whom Goodwin called "the Young Columbus" for the research he had done on the Columbus voyages.

Earlier Goodwin had disagreed with some of Morison's views on Columbus, and now he felt that Hencken and Morison had ganged up on him, both to prevent publication of a paper on the North Salem site and to keep him from getting financial support for further research. It is quite hard to separate fact from paranoia, but it was true that Hencken and Morison were both friends and colleagues at Harvard, and they both differed with Goodwin on the interpretation of "his" site.

In 1945 Goodwin finally completed his four-hundred-page volume on the Irish monks and their New Hampshire site. Although the arrangement of the text is confusing, jumping from one topic to another, the book does contain some rather informative photos. Those relating to the North Salem site include some said to date to 1900, which are not too informative. Others, though not dated, are obviously of the site as it was being restored, and still others show the "cleaned-up" site. It is clear that major "rearrangements" have taken place such as the final resting place of the large "sacrificial stone," with its grooves said to be for draining off blood. Hencken suggested that its function might relate to the making of lye from ashes—how prosaic! Others have suggested it is part of a cider press.

Goodwin died in 1950, but he had done his best to spread his vision of the early Irish presence in New England. He befriended several newspapermen and writers who kept the North Salem site before the public in the late 1930s and 1940s; others would soon pick up the banner or the scent, depending on their persuasions. In 1952 Frederick J. Pohl, who was interested in Vikings on Cape Cod, wrote in his book *The Lost Discovery* that the site might be older than the coming of the Norsemen.

The only post-Hencken archaeology that has been done under the supervision of trained professionals was overseen by Junius Bird of the American Museum of Natural History. Bird's New World field experience had ranged from Tierra del Fuego and Peru to the eastern Arctic, including parts of Labrador. In 1945 he did some minor work at the site and turned in a report to Goodwin, who was characteristically critical of it because it did not fit his conclusions, and he said so. A decade later a group from Hanover calling themselves the Early Sites Foundation sponsored a professional dig at the site. It was carried out in 1955 by Gary Vescelius, a graduate student in archaeology at Yale, with whom I was acquainted. As a youth he had participated in the 1945 expedition, which was also under the overall direction of Junius Bird. A brief report of the results was quickly published in an archaeological bulletin; the conclusions were uniformly in favor of the Pattee hypothesis.[1]

Vescelius described taking apart one of the walls and finding inside of it in situ artifacts, all of which dated to the nineteenth century. The results were clear in this short note, but the detailed report with all the profiles and artifact counts would not be published for nearly twenty years, after Vescelius's premature death. Not that these more explicit results would have mattered; those convinced of the site's great age have put aside the fully reported evidence, despite its very clear message, just as they did Vescelius's condensed version. No historic materials dating to before the eighteenth century were found, nor anything of Irish or Norse affiliation.[2]

In 1957 the site was purchased by Robert Stone, who renamed it Mystery Hill, as it is now usually called. Stone turned it into a commercial venture with strong emphasis on its great age. Vescelius's excavations had shown that there was still archaeological evidence to be found at the site despite Whitney's restoration. With Stone's help and blessing, considerable work by amateurs has been carried out at Mystery Hill over the last twenty-five years. Nothing would do more for the site than the appearance of yet another Harvard professor, one who was very different from Hencken. He was a marine biologist, Barry Fell. There must be a Cantabrigian strain of the Fantastic Archaeology virus that brings so many into this discussion.

Howard Barraclough Fell (1917–) was born in Lewes, England, but grew up and was educated in New Zealand, where he got his undergraduate B.Sc. degree in 1938. He went to Edinburgh for his Ph.D. in 1941 and then did a stint as an officer in the British army, some say with training in cryptography. Following the war Fell returned to New Zealand, where he had a post at the University of Wellington. His field was marine biology with a specialty in echinoderms (sea urchins and starfish) about which he published extensively. He came to the United States in 1964 to take a post at Harvard's Museum of Comparative Zoology in marine biology and was given a tenured professorship the next year. He held that post and a curatorship in the museum until he took early retirement in 1977, at age sixty.

Fell studied Latin and Greek along the way, as well as some Celtic while at Edinburgh; in his later career he would use those parts of his education more than his biological knowledge. While in the British Isles Fell published a short article in *MAN,* the journal of the London Royal Anthropological Society, entitled "The Pictographic Art of the Ancient Maori of New Zealand" (1941). Much later (1977) he would refer to it as his first *epigraphic* paper; that is certainly not its content.

So much for background; "Barry" Fell, his preferred appellation,

Professor Barry Fell

would enter the field of New England archaeology from his Museum of Comparative Zoology post with a bang: he first visited Mystery Hill on June 14, 1975, and less than a month later would discover what no one else had seen there: inscriptions on the rocks of the various structures.

The inscribed messages were in two very different scripts: Iberian Punic and Celtic Ogam. This was the breakthrough Fell had been waiting for. "Within ten days we were seeing dozens of Ogam inscriptions."[3] By November of that same year, after a very busy summer of fieldwork, Fell finished his manuscript, and by mid-1976 his *America B.C.: Ancient Settlers in the New World* was published. Trans-Atlantic migrations from the Old World were said to have begun possibly as early as 3000 B.C. and to have continued unabated until 1400 A.D. A lead article based on the book appeared in the ever-popular *Reader's Digest,* and the book, published by Quadrangle/New York Times, went into four editions by 1977 and paperback as well. Shades of Ignatius Donnelly. New England archaeology, with his strong dose of hyper-diffusion, would never be the same again, unfortunately.

Fell's book, edited by a sometime ornithologist, never received any archaeological review before publication. One presumes that his academic status and accomplishments in another field were deemed credentials enough. But the volume did not suffer from the critical vacuum that has befallen many books in Fantastic Archaeology. This professional criticism, including a major review in the *New York Times* by Glyn Daniel, was not gentle.[4] Daniel, who was reviewing both Fell and Van Sertima, spoke of "a nadir in all this speculative nonsense" and asked, "Why do responsible and accredited professors write such ignorant nonsense?" He stated that both "books abound in factual and literal errors." The tone was very tough and was bound to generate screams of intellectual arrogance, which it did, but Daniel was correct. Fell's book was filled with factual errors; it was a rush-to-print job, and it was characterized by intellectual confusion and sloppy documentation.

How bad was it? A few examples must suffice, though every chapter is shot through with gaffs. Take his chronicling of the Mystery Hill site itself: "The large complex . . . became the property of a settler named Pattee . . . in 1823. In the following twenty-five years about 40 percent of the stone structures were destroyed or damaged severely by building contractors who visited the area to obtain stone for dams and bridges."[5] Not so; that was the very time that the site was occupied by Pattee; its destruction took place *after* the house burned in 1855.

In a later chapter entitled "The Libyans of Zuni," Fell attempted to prove that the Zuni Indians of New Mexico spoke a language that "should be reclassified as an American branch of the North African group." He further stated that one could characterize it as follows: "The Zuni tongue, with its apparently limited vocabulary (only some 1,200 words have been recorded) makes remarkably broad generalizations in the use of words."[6] I guess they would have to if that were true, but of course, it is not. There is not a single human language known on earth that has only twelve hundred words; Zuni actually has a documented vocabulary of many thousands of words, as a quick trip to any anthropological library will prove.

Fell has been critical of archaeologists who have disagreed with his numerous "readings" and translations; they know no linguistics and have not had the proper training in this area, he suggests. The usually unspoken counterpoint is "as I have had." Professor Fell is unfamiliar with the normal training of many American archaeologists, at least of my generation, when anthropology, a subdiscipline of which is archaeology, demanded that one receive exposure to all parts of the field.

I took basic courses in linguistics as a graduate student at Michigan and Yale and even worked with a native informant, a Potawatomi Indian, to produce a term paper in one of them. Many archaeologists have, indeed, studied linguistics, the broad study of the whole field of language. If some archaeologists are sometimes loath to speak with great authority on *all* language matters, it may be because we understand the complexities of doing a good translation. We would not be caught calling to task the nineteenth-century scholars as he has done: "The plain truth is that the devoted ethnologists [of the Bureau of American Ethnology] who collected the ancient literature of the Amerindians lacked the linguistic skills to realize what they were doing. [Frank] Russell, and apparently every other investigator, failed to recognize the Creation Chant as an ancient Semitic Hymn."[7]

What Fell means is that the Pima Indians of southern Arizona spoke a Punic language; no wonder that poor old Russell botched the translation. Professor Fell, who confidently works in at least a dozen American Indian languages (self-taught), manages the translation perfectly with a Semitic dictionary.

In some rather twisted logic, Fell sees a failure by anthropologists to recognize that many American Indian languages are heavily larded with wholesale borrowing from Mediterranean peoples, and says that this "does a grave injustice to the cultural tradition of the Amerindian peoples." Further, "the false notion that Amerindian tongues evolved as unique American phenomena has led to a classification of them that does not express their true affinities."[8] I can only suppose Fell means therefore that the only true happiness for the Amerindians is to realize that they too are a part of the great heritage of Western civilization like ourselves. The Native Americans must want to ask, "Why have the anthropologists wanted to keep us apart?" Why, indeed!

Some of Fell's linguistic derivations would be amusing if they were not so wrongheaded, and remember these are selected quotes, but back to the case of the Zuni:

> Again, a word that in Coptic has the sense *to prick*, in Zuni acquires the meaning to *copulate*, more or less as the ancient Anglo-Saxon used the verb *prician*, its modern use confined by convention to conversation between males. These features of Zuni speech suggest that it may have been derived from the limited and racy vocabulary in colloquial use on board Libyan naval vessels. (Fell, 1976: 177)

One will have to grant that this is a grand example of where "common sense" and what sounds like linguistic analysis lead one who has a trans-Atlantic hypothesis to serve. What has Anglo-Saxon usage got to do with Coptic, and just how and when did those ribald Libyan "navies" get to New Mexico? Don't tell me, I know: it must be Calalus.

These examples must almost suffice, although I cannot resist one more gross error-in-fact-filled paragraph that I just stumbled over. After "discovering" a Libyan word inscribed on a Peabody Museum pot, Fell became very interested in the prehistoric Mimbres culture of western New Mexico. Hence the following sentence: "During the 1930's excavations in New Mexico by a Harvard team and associated investigators, including Harold Gladwin, brought to light a previously unknown style of pottery now called the Mimbres ware, from the type locality of the find."[9]

How wrong is this? To start with, the Mimbres ceramic style had been known from 1910. A major publication on these lovely black-on-white figuratively painted vessels was written in 1914 by Jesse Walter Fewkes, with whom Fell has felt a kinship because they both shared employment by the Harvard Museum of Comparative Zoology. A. V. Kidder also wrote at some length about Mimbres pottery and its cultural meanings in his 1924 *Introduction to Southwestern Archaeology.* As for Harvard's Peabody Museum, it did conduct excavations at the Swarts Ruins under the direction of the Cosgroves, which produced a fine collection of Mimbres pottery including the one with the purported Libyan inscription. That dig was done in the 1920s, not the 1930s; the results were published in the 1930s; and of course, Harold Gladwin had nothing to do with the dig—I have checked the excavation report. Finally, the pottery and the culture is called Mimbres not because of the name of the type site, but for the Mimbres River Valley in which many of these sites are located. Picky, picky, picky; yes, I know, but hardly one of the facts in that sentence was correct.

Enough for the moment about Professor Fell. There are three new pieces of data from the site of Mystery Hill that must be dealt with. First, not very surprisingly, a few traces of prehistoric Indian occupation have turned up at the site, including materials found during the quite extensive excavations in 1955 by Gary Vescelius. These artifacts, some bits of pottery and a few stone artifacts, meager as they may be, are dated typologically to known pre-Columbian cultures as early as the time of Christ. They are not of European derivation.

The second set of new data came about as a result of the invention of carbon 14 dating, which brought absolute dating to archaeology. There are two things to remember about that sort of dating: (1) a single date means little—a series of dates is necessary, and (2) the *context* from which the date came must be known. Using one date from a questionable find spot is just as irresponsible as pretending there are no dates at all. There are some nine radiocarbon determinations from the site.

Professor Fell has detailed one in *America B.C.*; it is A.D. 1690 give or take ninety years. It comes from a tree root among the stone structures said, by some, to have been built by Pattee. Fell is overjoyed with the result. He feels that his view that the stone constructions are pre-Pattee is vindicated: "In 1975 the ruins are still considered by many to lack archaeological context, despite the radio-carbon dating," he asserts.[10] In addition to a slight misunderstanding of the usual meaning of "archaeological context," he has made three other archaeological errors: (1) the *one* date must be seen only as a first indicator, not the total solution; (2) he has not dealt with the exact location of the dated specimen; is it *under* the stone construction and, if so, in what relationship to the site's construction history?; and (3) he has neglected to deal with what the date means in real time. By this I mean that the plus or minus ninety years is not on the date merely for decoration.

What those numbers (± 90) relate to is the probability of the date being somewhere within that span of 180 years around A.D. 1690, thus between 1600 and 1780. If we up the probability to two chances out of ten, by going to a two-sigma range as is often done in archaeology, that is, double the 90 years to 180, we can say with a higher level of confidence that the date falls between 1510 and 1870. Therefore, what that one date really means is that Pattee's hand in constructing the ruins has not been ruled out by that one date if one considers the post-1850 part of the dating span.

There are, however, other radiocarbon dates from Mystery Hill, which apparently were not available to Fell in 1975. One of these dates, if accepted at face value, knocks the Irish and the Norse out of contention as builders of the site: it is 1045 B.C. ± 180. This date was derived from charcoal that was very deeply buried, more than three feet *below* the stone structures. I was shown the find spot in the test pit by the excavator. I have no reason to doubt the radiocarbon determination; the charcoal is probably three thousand years old. But what does this archaeological context suggest? Does it mean that the determination from the charcoal dates the stone construction far above it? Not at all. It does tell us that a piece of wood was burned long ago, by whom or what we cannot say, although either a forest fire or an American Indian are the best guesses.

That charcoal does not date the stone wall built over it, a long time after, as the stratigraphy in the test pit suggests. We cannot dissect all the other dates at this time; suffice it to say that they range all over the lot, with perhaps the edge going to those of Colonial period date. Thus carbon 14 has not solved all the questions at Mystery Hill, but that is not an unusual situation in archaeology. The question remains, What is being dated?

Professor Fell has brought us to the third set of data that must now be faced. On July 4, 1975, with a group of interested onlookers including George Carter of Texas A&M University, Barry Fell found the first inscriptions at Mystery Hill, and the unraveling of the mystery took yet another turn. A number of purported inscribed messages from the past have been discovered scattered among the some twenty stone structures at the site. For Fell these crude inscriptions are a surprisingly mixed bag: some in Punic by Phoenicians, others in Ogam by Celts, and even roman numerals by a Gaul. This nascent United Nations gathering is based primarily on interpretations of marks on the rocks, some of which one skeptical geologist insists are natural confirmations of the stone, not wrought by man at all.

Even if one were, for the sake of argument, to admit that there are inscriptions of some sort, written in Old World scripts, at Mystery Hill, a major archaeological question remains: where is the artifactual evidence for these trans-Atlantic wayfarers? Where is the ground truth? Did they not eat, did they not have tools, did they not bring a single item of material culture with them? Instead, we must posit a band of naked voyagers, with a mental culture only, living on high hopes and spiritual thoughts—no snug fires, no haunches of venison, not even a fillet of Merrimack shad and a dozen oysters to toast the spring solstice—a dismal prospect, indeed.

But we must also ask, How did we get to this strange state of archaeological absurdity? There are inscriptions in many European languages all over the Eastern United States and not a whit of archaeological culture to go with them, save stone structures that look surprisingly like root cellars and a scattering of coins of many dates and cultures. Not a single veritable site, like L'Anse aux Meadows, with hearths and houses, metal artifacts, and other positive signs of human occupation has been found after decades of searching.

To answer that question we must turn back to Harvard, where Fell had been teaching Marine Biology successfully since 1964. One of his courses would be turned into a handsome text: *Life, Space and Time: A Course in Environmental Biology,* published by Harper & Row in 1974. He also participated in Harvard's innovative Freshman Seminar program in which in a small-group atmosphere he introduced eager students to the biology of the Indian Ocean.

But that all changed in the fall of 1972, when instead of a marine biology subject he offered a Freshman Seminar "on Polynesian history, art and tradition with special reference to the New Zealand Maori." It sounded like regular anthropology; the dates assigned for the cultures in the Seminar blurb were conventional so even though the course was in Social Science instead of in Fell's regular Natural Science area, it was approved and taught.

Sober reflection now shows one hint of what was to come—a simple clause in the course description: the students would examine "stele inscriptions with Polynesian content in *Indonesia*" (emphasis added). It was conventional wisdom that Polynesian origins did, indeed, stretch back to Southeast Asia, but there were no written inscriptions known that related to their cultural heritage in that region; in fact, in the whole Pacific area, only the undeciphered Easter Island script indicated any attempt at early symbolic notation.

The Freshman Seminar plunged headlong into this topic although comment or protest from students was not recorded. Fell's strong commitment to some entirely new historical explanations for Pacific prehistory was first revealed publicly in a few last-minute notes slipped into his major text on marine biology just as it was going to press with Harper & Row in the fall of 1974.

A paragraph added to the Preface to what would be Fell's last book on marine biology (1975) tells of amazing archaeological discoveries in New Guinea caves, which provided inscriptions dating to November 19, 232 B.C., and told of "a Libyan Maori naval squadron sent out by Ptolemy III." The inscriptions date to "the eve of the Polynesians' epic voyage to America."[11] What a discovery!

This long trans-Pacific trip by six ships, as dangerous as it might seem at this early date, was not quite so difficult, Fell reassures us, because "the navigator, named Maui, employed star charts and sophisticated equipment, including two types of analog computers invented by the Libyan astronomer Eratosthenes." Professor Fell had made a heady start in his new field of rewriting culture history; what the editors at Harper & Row thought is not recorded. After all, it must have sounded like quite an exciting footnote by a solid Harvard professor.

Even in this late insertion, Fell cited a personal reference (Fell, 1974); this citation must be to Volume 1 of the publications of the Polynesian Epigraphic Society, quickly termed the Epigraphic Society because it soon broadened its scope to a worldwide perspective. The society was formed on July 4, 1974, at Professor Fell's home in Arlington, Massachusetts, exactly one year before his historic visit to Mystery Hill. He reported in his typewritten *Newsletter* that at that time more than a thousand stelae and tablets had been recognized that have inscriptions in Maori or Proto-

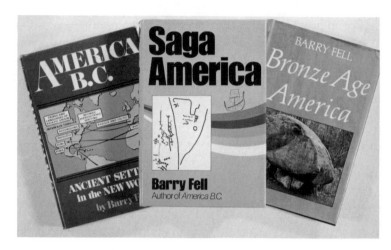

Fell's Books: 1976–82

Polynesian, with a direct tie to ancient Egyptian. Obviously a lot of work had been done before that Fourth of July, but I have been unable to run down two 1973 documents on Egypto-Polynesian alphabets and phonetics, which presumably grew out of Fell's Freshman Seminar project in 1972.

Fell's confidence in his newfound linguistic talents seemed to have developed quickly; he began to pour out brief articles, some twenty in the first *Newsletter* volume alone, at his home office. To begin with, all were from his own typewriter and mostly on the Polynesian subject. It is mind-boggling; sources were found, translations made, and the results and inter-pretations rushed into print.

And it continues at the same pace, even today; the 1988 edition (vol-ume 17) of *ESOP,* the *Epigraphic Society Occasional Publications,* is very impressive. It has a glossy full-color cover and 320 pages with 36 heavily illustrated contributions authored by dozens of society members. The Society has more than 800 members, 13 chapters and affiliates, and about 170 library subscribers around the world. It has come a long way from its modest Arlington, Massachusetts, beginnings; Fell has now moved the society headquarters to San Diego. Although more than ten years into retirement, he still proudly uses his Harvard affiliation on the masthead.

Fell has obviously filled some kind of void; his two hardcover books that followed *America, B.C.* were *Saga America* and *Bronze Age America,* and they have proven that point with their sales. His most recent publisher, Little, Brown, has written in the cover copy that these books have "established him as an important new voice in American history and archaeology." I will not argue that point, although these two newer volumes are no better put together than the first. One could excuse some of that by the great haste with which *America, B.C.* was rushed to press, but these new ones are equally lacking in archaeological review and just as full of unsubstantiated linguistic and archaeological speculation. Indeed, a quick review shows that in his three books, he has regularly used as "good" data at least seven of the finds that I have debunked in this volume, including Beardmore, Newport Tower, the Newark Holy Stones, Grave Creek Stone, Calalus, and especially the Davenport Tablets.

These new volumes continue to misuse American Indian data for Fell's own purposes. For example, although careful metallurgical studies clearly show that none of the copper artifacts made in North America is bronze, a copper-tin alloy, Fell continues to mislabel those North American artifacts as if that were not the case. Obviously, he wants the Old World connection, thus the title of his last book, *Bronze Age America*. He is thus forced to call a cold-hammered copper gorget from Ohio an ingot, a term applicable only to metal that was cast, a technique never achieved in North America.

He also revives, for reasons I cannot fathom, the notion that there was a race of pygmies in Tennessee in late prehistoric times. Indeed, Fell's picture adorns the back cover of his latest volume with calipers in hand and a pygmy (so-called) skull lying on his garden table; obviously, physical anthropology is just another arcane specialty he has brought to fruition in retirement.

Of course, with his pygmies in Tennessee, all the good professor has done is to revive John Haywood's early nineteenth-century "vagary" discussed much earlier. Typically, Fell does not deal with any of the academic scholars who have spent their entire careers on North American Indian skeletal studies. There are a number with whom he could discuss these Tennessee finds, but he chooses not to. He has found some Libyan inscriptions on some of the associated artifacts, and it is clear how those Establishment blokes could be expected to respond. It might seem that he leads a somewhat isolated life as a confirmed hyper-diffusionist.

But Fell does not have to feel completely outside the academic sphere, for since 1975 he has had strong support, with only a few minor caveats, from George F. Carter, Distinguished Professor of Geography emeritus, at Texas A&M University. It is to Professor Carter's contributions to Fantastic Archaeology that we now turn. Carter shares a number of things with Fell: they are both emeritus professors from good institutions (Carter was

Professor George F. Carter

at Johns Hopkins before going to Texas); they are both hyper-diffusionists of distinction; and Carter, for most of his career, questioned conventional views within his discipline, whereas Fell came to his anti-Establishment position in his fifties. Undeciphered inscriptions brought them together, along with Carter's long-held views of transoceanic connections, especially in plants and animals, which fitted in well with the data Fell was discovering around the globe. Although now partners in the "band of brothers" that takes great pleasure and pride in opposing conventional views of the past, Fell and Carter came together intellectually on very different trajectories.

Anthropology in California, especially at the University of California at Berkeley, had a different early history from that of the East Coast institutions. Starting later, the Department rose, at the turn of the century, primarily on the shoulders of Alfred L. Kroeber. He was a Columbia Ph.D., one of Franz Boas's early students, and came to California in 1900. In 1901 he received an appointment to the University of California at Berkeley, where he spent his entire career. When Phoebe Hearst started an anthropological museum at the university in 1901, there had been an Eastern infusion. She brought Frederic Ward Putnam out west, on a part-time basis, to start up the institution. Putnam got things going but soon returned to Cambridge, worn by age and ill health.

Kroeber carried the load very successfully. Some early archaeological work was carried out in one of the shell heaps in San Francisco Bay. In 1905,

Max Uhle, a peripatetic European, did the fieldwork, before he returned to South America and the Peruvian scene he knew so well.

But it was not in archaeology that Berkeley was to excel. After all, the East Coast was practically bereft of American Indians, but California had dozens of tribes, many with their languages, customs, and handicrafts still pretty well intact. It was to this rich anthropological resource that Kroeber turned. Putnam even sent one of his own students, Alfred Tozzer, later the distinguished Mayanist, out to work among the California Indians, learning the native languages and collecting their famous baskets for the museum. Archaeology, especially of the local sort, got very short shrift; Kroeber was to make a brief and important foray into the Southwestern field, and he also made a strong contribution working up the Peruvian materials that Uhle dug for the museum. But it was really the culture and languages of the California Indians that Kroeber of Berkeley was to make his own.

The result was that in the first quarter of this century California archaeology lagged far behind the developments in the Southwest and even in the East. Over the years there were a few workers at Berkeley and elsewhere who puttered about, finding the milling stones and shell ornaments of late prehistoric cultures, but little was done on earlier horizons. When the breakthrough on Early Man came via the Folsom discoveries on the High Plains, California was left high and dry; there did not seem to be any of those distinctive fluted points in the Golden West.

It was against this background of limited development in archaeology that a fifteen-year-old George Carter began to haunt the San Diego Museum of Man in 1927 and pester the Curator, Malcolm J. Rogers, in that baroque old structure left over from the Pan-American Exposition in 1915. Carter did not know how lucky he was, in more ways than one. There were few other field archaeologists working in California at that time; Rogers let Carter volunteer in the museum and later took him on a five-week field trip to San Nicolas Island during the summer of 1930 before Carter began studying at San Diego College. He transferred to Berkeley and got his B.A. in anthropology in 1934.

With jobs scarce in the Depression, Carter was lucky and happy to be offered a job by Rogers at his old stomping grounds at the San Diego Museum. For the next four years he was with Rogers doing a lot of fieldwork, both on the coast and in the deserts to the east.

Malcolm Rogers, a wealthy easterner who had been trained as a mining engineer and in the Marine Corps, came west after World War I and took up residence near San Diego as an orange grower. His avocational interest in archaeology drew him to the San Diego Museum; Rogers had natural talent for archaeology and proceeded carefully in the field. Not surprisingly, he was an Establishment man as to dating and the like; he believed what he read in the books and heard from the professors up at the University.

The inevitable clash between Rogers and Carter came over a fluted point that Carter found when they were out surface collecting in the Mohave Desert in 1937–38. Carter recognized it immediately as looking like a "Folsom" and said it was a major breakthrough that should be published immediately; Rogers dragged his feet and said that because he was in charge, he would publish it. We have only Carter's version of all this, including the split that followed. Rogers is correctly represented as thinking that human occupation in the area went back only four thousand years, whereas Carter says he was already thinking in terms of forty thousand years, based on geological evidence.

Rogers did publish this work in 1939; Carter's help in the fieldwork is not acknowledged. He classified the point and two others like it as "Folsomoid." He further very carefully states that these Mohave Desert Folsom-type points are all made of local materials and thus are not true Folsom "intrusives" from the East. Rogers further associated these points with those he had named Pinto, dating to after 800 B.C. It would be a generation or two before the whole Pinto Basin–Lake Mohave chronological sequence would be put to rights, if it is even there today. As for a forty-thousand-year position (Carter) and a less than 1000 B.C. niche (Rogers) for these fluted points, we now know that both are very wrong.

But to return to our narrative: well, split they did. George was "eased out of his job" at the Museum, perhaps by Rogers; but landed on his feet with a part-time teaching position at the local college. Friends there urged him to return to Berkeley to work with the geographer Carl Sauer, who had done some interesting work in broadly anthropological areas. Actually, Berkeley had about the only department in the country in which there were such close ties between anthropology and geography; it made for exciting interaction. Carter went north to the San Francisco Bay area in 1938 and took a Ph.D. in geography in 1941, with a lot of anthropology on the side. Kroeber was still a major figure at Berkeley, but there were, of course, many new people as well. Some of them, such as Robert Heizer, were doing California archaeology at long last.

When war came, Carter went to Washington and worked as an analyst at Strategic Services. In 1943 he joined the Department of Geology at Johns

Hopkins University, where he taught until he journeyed to Texas A&M. While at Johns Hopkins in Baltimore, Maryland, he continued to summer in his old hometown, San Diego. He was doing geological/archaeological fieldwork there and became even more certain that he was correct in the view that man had been in the Western Hemisphere for tens of thousands of years. During the 1950s, he published several articles espousing this point of view, as well as one (1956) that suggested the age of an archaeological deposit could be told from the color of the soil, and used examples from both coasts to demonstrate that theory. Archaeology, especially that of Early Man, would certainly be a lot easier if this easy dating method based on soil color alone were valid.

In 1957 he published a large volume entitled *Pleistocene Man in San Diego;* it was long on geological speculation and short on archaeology. The major site discussed in the book, Texas Street, was his linchpin of proof for his early dating, and the archaeological evidence there and at other sites was very critically dissected by the volume's academic reviewers. Some of the artifacts were seen as dating much later than Carter posited, and some were not thought to be artifacts at all. Carter's Early Man speculations were clearly not accepted by the Establishment, but it was ever thus.

From 1964 on, many of Carter's professional articles appear in the same unrefereed obscure journal, the *Anthropological Journal of Canada.* Despite its imposing title, it was a private organ edited and published by Carter's friend the late Tom Lee, who shared many anti-Establishment attitudes. Carter became, as he himself has written, a subject of jest: some of his early tools from Texas Street were said not to be artifacts but "cartifacts." That jeer must have been hard to take!

Carter published (1960–80) a series of short articles and papers that continued to hammer out the same litany of the Paleolithic in America and hyper-diffusion of other traits. Carter's views on Early Man went well beyond the arguments I have discussed as occurring between Putnam and Holmes; he felt that many tens of thousands of years were involved, just as in the Old World. I will not detail all his hyper-diffusionist arguments; rather I will just state that Carter relentlessly espouses long-distant contacts, often transoceanic, with only a modest amount of supporting evidence.

I will let him explain his method and theory himself:

> This is the hallmark of two very different minds. The difference man sticks to facts; he loves to measure and plot and weigh and calculate, and he

tends not to go one inch beyond his charts. The similarities man tends to look widely around him and to pick up tenuous bits of evidence, exclaiming with interest on how like this bit is to something that he has seen or read somewhere else. He tends to spin a web of connections. It is a spider's web to the difference man—insubstantial, unimpressive, unscientific. To the similarities man, it is symmetrical and beautiful and evidence of meaningful patterns, even if constructed of gossamer. There should be no doubt where I stand. I am a classic similarities man. (Carter, 1980: 317)

This exposition sets up some interesting contrasts, but I submit that most scholars manage to mix these two approaches, in differing proportions, no doubt, in the structuring of their research methodology. They find that the crucial skill is to be able to evaluate the data critically, both near at hand and far away. Web spinning may please spiders and their mates, but it is not of much help in the crucial testing of anthropological hypotheses.

I shall now focus on Carter's most recent (1980) major work, *Earlier Than You Think: A Personal View of Man in America* and a journal article on Barry Fell. When George Carter, a normally quite forthright person, calls something a "personal view," as he does in this volume, you can wager that it is a no-holds-barred discussion. The last chapter of the book reads much like a swan song but concludes with the view that his position that Early Man had been in America for one hundred thousand years is finally winning out.

Overall it is a rather contentious book, not surprisingly. He repeats much of the evidence for his case that he had presented before. But he specifically attacks some historical positions held by some of his mentors in a very unfair way. His emotions seem to have led him to rearrange or to misremember the facts.

The most egregious case is his treatment of Alfred Kroeber. Of course, Kroeber is a noted figure and thus subject to careful review. But I cannot help feeling that George Carter knows better, or perhaps best said, "he knew better." In the volume Carter winds up to take a crack at the Establishment and, from his viewpoint, at its outrageously conservative estimates for the antiquity of man in America, which he graphically presents (his fig. 2). In three different places (pp. 7, 285, and 316) he reiterates that the "Kroeberian school" (his term) "could insist in the 1930's that our hard evidence [for man in America] reached to only 2,000 years" (p. 316). On the top of page 7, however, we are told: "In the 1930's we were taught that the first immigrants entered America about 5,000 years ago." But at the middle of the page we find Kroeber "not opposed to a 10,000 year date," only to be told in the next sentence that in his most extreme position (the 1940 article) Kroeber had a preference for 2,000 years. This latter position Carter calls "so extreme as to defy comprehension."

Comprehension is what we need. What did Kroeber really say, and when did he say it? In the 1923 edition of *Anthropology* Kroeber says almost exactly the same thing twice within the space of three pages: "It [the American Indians] entered the New World perhaps 10,000 years ago" (p. 343) and "If the date of entry is set at 10,000 years ago, the elapsed period accounts very well" (p. 345). It is interesting to note that his figure 36 is from Spinden and represents the development of Native American culture. A note in the lower left corner indicates that Spinden thinks the "primary invasion from Asia" took place at "15,000–10,000 B.C." Kroeber makes no textual reference to this date but says his own undated chart (fig. 35) is quite comparable.

The second source is Kroeber's article in *The Maya and Their Neighbors* (1940). What did he really say in this well-known overview paper on New World archaeology that he wrote a dozen years after the publication of the Folsom finds? Kroeber first discussed these important new discoveries in the West, which he dated at more than ten thousand years ago, and possibly even fifteen thousand, as shown both in his text and on a chart. Kroeber then pointed out the important gap in our knowledge between the Fluted Point (Folsom) horizon and the later and well-dated culture histories of the American Southwest and Peru, both of which he knew at first hand.

These two sequences, each with about two thousand years of continuity, had been very well documented at this time; it is this two-thousand-year period which Carter has mistakenly referred to as the *total* sequence of cultures in this hemisphere. The gap that Kroeber pointed to between the Paleo-Indian materials and the later ceramic-using Neo-Indians remained a very significant challenge to American archaeology for almost two decades until carbon 14 dating of the Archaic cultures allowed them to be expanded and to fill the gap comfortably.

Contrary to Carter's view, Kroeber did not, in the post-Folsom discovery period, advocate a very short chronology for New World prehistory, nor did anyone else in the archaeological Establishment. J. Alden Mason wrote an article on this very topic more than twenty years ago (1966) reaffirming this view of the field's own history. I believe that it is extremely important to try to keep the intellectual history of the discipline as clear as possible without letting strong emotions from the past cloud the recounting of events.

With regard to history of the discipline, let's turn now to some more current events, as described in *Earlier Than You Think*. In espousing his thesis of very early finds of human occupation in the New World, Carter has put a major emphasis on some rather controversial dating of human skeletal materials from the California area. These dates, based on amino acid racemization, using protein from the bones, were first published in *Science* beginning in 1974. This dating was an experiment in a new technique by Jeffrey Bada, and they did very well by Carter's theory that these remains were much earlier than the old curmudgeons had been saying. They produced dates between twenty and seventy thousand years of age; Carter was deeply involved in this whole operation and a coauthor of the first article in *Science*. Needless to say, he was ecstatic over the results. He has described this situation in detail in *Earlier Than You Think* (pp. 54–59).

But negative voices were soon heard. For the racemization analysis to work correctly one had to be able to predict what temperatures the bones had been subjected to during their "lifetime" in their final resting place, a pretty difficult task for anyone to achieve. Certainly the archaeological contexts seemed to indicate much less age for the skeletal remains, something under ten thousand years for all the specimens dated. But Carter, in his *Earlier Than You Think,* and later Jeffrey Goodman used these early dates with gusto.

At the time I could not help wondering why *Science* magazine was giving so much space to such a controversial and ill-tested methodology that was producing such wild results. Much later, as the editor of that noted journal was stepping down after long and meritorious service, I read with interest that one of his scientific contributions was pioneering in the field of "racemization"; in fact, he had suggested in 1954 that it might be used as a dating method. No wonder the experimental work by Bada got such good and speedy press time in that authoritative journal.

Fortunately, there is a last chapter on those early dates that had disturbed much of the archaeology profession and pleased the extremists. Jeffrey Bada, in a very graceful and positive fashion, announced in December 1984 that he was retracting all the racemization dates on the human skeletal materials from North America. They had been subjected to other means of dating, including a special sort of carbon 14 testing (accelerator mass spectrometry), and *all* the bones were found to date to *less* than ten thousand years of age. Thus the specimens now fitted the archaeological contexts in which they had been found and the younger dates that had been archaeologically assigned to those contexts.

Bada did explain a bit about the "bad seed" that started him down this unfortunate side road; he had accepted apparently without question an early carbon 14 date on the Laguna Beach skeleton. It was dated at 17,150 ± 1,470 B.P. (before present). This dating had been done in California by Rainer Berger in 1969. At that time, it was one of the very earliest known dates for human occupation in America. Did no one urge caution? That one date had been factored into *all* his calculations as a constant. The Laguna skeleton was redated by accelerator mass spectrometry (AMS) at 5,100 ± 500 years B.P., or just a bit over 3000 B.C. Indeed, when Bada recalculated some of his racemization dates with this new constant, his results correlated well with the other carbon-14-derived dates. See what one carbon 14 date can do.

Now Carter did not have anything directly to do with the early dating of the Laguna skeletal material; however, it was at odds with all the other archaeological data, and Bada was apparently not warned about its very aberrant position by his coauthor. Why would he have been, when the date on Laguna fitted Carter's hypothesis so well? Indeed, when Carter published *Earlier Than You Think* in 1980, he acknowledged that questions about Bada's dates were being raised, but he said: "Actually I embroiled him [Bada] in the donnybrook over the antiquity of man in America, but he is a courageous fighter, and the facts are on his side, so there is no doubt that he will emerge triumphant."[12] As I have indicated, four years later Bada would withdraw all his dates for North American human skeletons, but not before we had had a decade of misinformation (1974–84). Who can say that Fantastic Archaeology doesn't matter?

Carter's book *Earlier Than You Think* is a paean of self-praise, as all autobiographical valedictories should be. All the sites prove his hypotheses, and contrary data or opinions are quickly brushed aside. This unwillingness to consider seriously both sides of the question also characterizes Carter's defense of his friend and Epigraphic Society colleague Barry Fell. This defense appears in an article by Carter entitled, appropriately, "Saga America: Going Over the Edge?" published in a small British journal called *Historical Diffusionism* (1981), the slant of which is obvious. Carter tries at first to be impartial in his review of Fell's position, but his commitment to diffusionism leads him both to expect writing in precontact America and to be pleased by its discovery.

Next Carter turns to one aspect of Fell's books that I did not raise earlier, which is the essentially racist attitude that is blatant throughout all of Fell's works. (This is not a view that I hold in isolation; why else the defense put forward below?) Various races are culturally stereotyped, often in a positive way; Celts are good at mining and metals so why not bring them over to help the Native Americans out with that phase of their culture? Indeed, Fell's view is clearly stated: by A.D. 1100 America was a melting pot, with some colonies of just trans-Atlantic European visitors, some mixed groups, and some pure Indian groups.[13] That sites for the first two groups are not archaeologically visible, to most archaeologists at least, seems to be of little consequence.

Carter, in this journal article, tackles the racist question head-on; he asks, Why should diffusionists be charged with such slander, since it is not true? "First, there is no American Indian race, but rather all of the major races of mankind were present in America. The fault, if there is one, is geographical and not racial."[14] That is a direct quote, not a paraphrase; what Carter is saying is that we are all in this matter together, so no one should have hard feelings. This view is not far removed from that of Gladwin in his *Men Out of Asia,* from which it may well be derived.

Carter goes on to say that all civilizations are mixtures of ideas, borrowed from their neighbors. He asks who could believe that "the American Indian Race (there is no such thing) reproduced virtually the whole cultural production of all the Old World Cultures and did it in a fraction of the time required in the Old World"? It sounds as if the Old World just lost the gold medals in the Olympic culture-building race, and Carter is having none of it. He continues: "To argue this is to invoke a super race. Should one care to use the inventionists tactic[,] one could now call the independent-inventionists Hitlerian-racists."[15]

How's that for an effective turnabout? I suggest that both Carter and Fell believe that the Native Americans could not have reached the cultural achievements the prehistoric records show without significant transoceanic diffusion to aid them in their efforts. Indeed, Carter concludes *Earlier Than You Think* by saying, "We have whole new chapters of cultural and racial additions to the American scene, roughly from the *Bronze Age* onward, to identify and to *separate* out from the races and *accomplishments* of the earlier Americans" (emphasis added).[16] I submit that is the kind of "stealing of their heritage" that Sharer and Ashmore had in mind in their warning about the results of pseudoarchaeology.

Of course, the facts are not as Carter has suggested. It is a matter of some interest that, for example, the rise toward a fully agricultural-based society in both hemispheres followed a long, slow trajectory and was not the Neolithic "revolution" once posited. But the timing of these developments in the Old and New Worlds is neither synchronous nor based on the same crops. The elapsed time for each development is fairly similar. We have been hard-pressed to know just when to start the stopwatch in both hemispheres, thus making this comparison and the awarding of the gold medal a bit dicey. Overall on this question, I would have to say that Carter has misspoken again.

In further defending Fell, Carter says he has had no luck in getting linguists to look at the data Fell has presented. Carter does not sense the meaning of this failure except as evidence of closed minds on the part of the Establishment. His discussion of the role that hoaxes and frauds may play in Fell's presentations is illuminating; Carter suggests that the Newark Holy Stones are probably fakes but will not say so for sure. He then allows as how "hoaxes and frauds tend to be self-solving"; I would be hard put to agree with that naive hope, based on the evidence I have presented to the contrary in this volume.

Carter is rather forthcoming on another aspect of Fell's work: "Fell clearly states that he alters letters at times to facilitate reading an inscription. . . . Too much reliance on poor copies and at times inadequate research into specific inscriptions has certainly occurred."[17] This statement is pretty straight talk from someone who has been listed for many years on the masthead of the Epigraphic Society publications. The rest of his review is much more positive and supportive of Fell. He concludes, "If Fell were only half right[,] we would have to rewrite world history. It seems to me that anyone viewing this subject from a broad perspective must see that he is far more than half right."[18]

In baseball, hitting .500 is exceptional, if not impossible; in scholarship it is not a passing grade, and I would figure Professor Fell's batting average at an anemic .100, to be on the generous side. How many of Fell's inscriptions in North America, which now must number in the thousands, are real messages from scribes writing in non–Native American languages (Eurasian scripts)? The real count, I fear, is few or none.

What is the real nature of these arguments by Barry Fell and George Carter in their confrontations with the Establishment positions of mainstream American archaeology? Do they have any analogs with the perceptions advanced in the previous chapters? Both Fell's and Carter's positions often involve hyper-diffusion and very special perceptions of their own data. Fell reads inscriptions that are virtually the sole indicators of frequent foreign visitors to these shores. Carter joins Fell in the search for the signs of transoceanic contacts in a range of evidence from plants and animals to widely diverse cultural traits. In these arguments one can see analogs to the Viking contacts that were sought for so long in the nineteenth century and later. The Establishment view was that such contacts were not impossible; indeed, they were even probable. But where was the objective evidence— the ground truth—for these claims? We can recall how long it took to find good data for that question.

The Fell inscriptions are everywhere, from Maine to California; the hard data range from Roman coins washed up on a beach in Massachusetts to a nautical map of the continent scratched on a slab of rock in Nevada, dated to A.D. 800. Carter has, over the years, followed chickens from China to Peru and cultural traits from blowguns to bolas. The main problem with all these data has been the finder's critical perception of them. Are these California Indian petroglyphs really Kufi Arabic writing? Are worldwide trait distribution studies the best pathways to unraveling the complex culture histories of this planet? There is nothing wrong with the questions—the only problem is the critical evaluation of the data.

So too with Carter's nearly lifelong insistence on very early occupations of the New World. In this hypothesis he has not been alone. Alan Bryan, the late William Irving, and others are stalwart members of that loyal opposition. They view the Establishment as inflexible in its views that there are no data before 10,000 B.C.—the Clovis hard-line position, most often credited to Vance Haynes and others, myself included. Here too there are analogs to the past: the Smithsonian duo of Holmes and Hrdlicka espousing the position of "nothing very old" versus Peabody's Putnam and others trying to say that the Indian occupation *was* old, and there are artifacts to prove it. As we saw in Chapter 6, that argument was not solved with a simple yes or no. So too today—Carter and others incorrectly characterize the Establishment position as antagonistic to any really early dates, while the opposition continues to say, Not so, just show us some good data: some real artifacts and some clearly associated dates.

That argument was hotly carried forward at the May 1989 World Summit Conference on the Peopling of the New World held in Orono, Maine. Almost all the above discussants were there in one room. The final results of the conference were differently perceived, as one would expect. It came down to a careful critical evaluation of the available evidence. The strong evidence at Monte Verde in coastal Chile for a pre-Clovis occupation (thirteen thousand years ago) was virtually unanimously accepted, even by the worst old curmudgeons. Other data and other sites were found wanting in credibility. It was ever thus.

The critical evaluations are *ad datum* (evidence), not *ad hominem* (the messenger); but those who cannot, or will not, accept the results of these evaluations will still eventually say, Why don't you like me and my evidence? A sad question and a hurtful misunderstanding of academic procedures. Ideas are the products of the human mind; hypotheses must be tested for validity and veracity and critically evaluated. If found wanting, the hypothesis is set aside, not the individual who has proposed it, unless veracity is questioned.

But some cannot bear the separation, and they often reside in the category of crank scientist. What, then, do we have here with Professor Fell and Carter, two accredited scholars whose current output is classic Fantastic Archaeology, with all its faults and foibles? Earlier I said I wasn't too happy with the term *crank scientist* although it is widely used; for Fell and Carter, as well as other members of traditional academia such as Eben Horsford, Leo Wiener, and Cyclone Covey, I feel another term is more appropriate.

I have coined the term *Rogue Professor,* as in "rogue" elephant. Rogue elephants look like other elephants, but they do not act like other elephants. Rogue professors have all the degrees and academic trappings of other professors; they even write and publish in the manner of other professors. Their papers and books have learned references and bibliographies and thus look the part, but they are not really what they seem.

These scholars have abandoned the appropriate standards of scholarly enterprise and can no longer make crucial judgments about the evidence. Thus they have the opportunity to "rogue" or defraud the public, like a rogue elephant loose in the library of knowledge. What a sad state of affairs in academe, where reasoned use of curiosity, testing, and veracity should be the norm; where data will be critically evaluated, and evidence will be sought from every side. You may well ask how dare *you* judge? I can only reply: if one forswears the admittedly heavy burden of making critical evaluations and speaking them, one must also, I believe, give up the painstaking pursuit of knowledge and the happy, but seemingly endless, pursuit of truth. I haven't.

12
Psychic Archaeology: Seeking Visions of the Past

Now . . . psychic archaeology has begun to move into the international research mainstream.
STEPHAN SCHWARTZ, 1978

Although it was only 8, the sun was already beating down fiercely on the hard-packed Delta clays, and my shirt was soaking wet. The dig crew sat carelessly and quiet, waiting. Waiting for me to decide. The site was large and important, but the test pits would be small and crucial. Still I hesitated, as a swarm of little sweat bees attacked my bare arms and time dragged on. Impatience grew in the eyes of my student assistants. Why couldn't I decide where to locate those test pits; we'd gone over that question endlessly the evening before.

Then I recalled waking that very morning, early at the time of false dawn, wringing wet, despite the drone of the window air conditioner; and I knew that I'd been through this scene before. I remembered going over to that slight rise on the western edge of the site, not far from the dilapidated tenant house, and finding a very special locality that seemed very promising. Yes, that's where we'd dig this morning; it really felt right at last. (Williams, Lake George Site, Excavation Log, July 10, 1959)

Decision making is a major part of leading any archaeological dig: it's pick a site, choose the students, hire the field crew, and then select the location for the actual excavations. But no, I've never made a decision such as that based on a dream; the above tale is based on literary license.

However, some archaeologists have done so; they call it psychic archaeology. Indeed, some call it "a movement to the furthermost frontiers of a new and revolutionary science." Psychic archaeology really got under way in America in the 1970s, and some of its practitioners are alive and well in the field today, getting supposedly important archaeological insights from their mediums and, on occasion, psychometrizing artifacts: holding specimens in their hands and getting "vibes" that are translated into pictures of the past.

Frederick Bligh Bond

Pretty fantastic; it all seems too far out, a hallucination and perversion of the can-do expedition-oriented Indiana Jones. Instead, you sit in your comfortable office and dowse maps for information on where to dig. It may sound amazing, but it really has been happening. As historians of this nascent field chronicle its birth, it all began in England during Edwardian times. This was the time when Sir Arthur Conan Doyle was about to slip into visions of fairies in the garden and the like. This time, however, it was an ascetic student of medieval architecture, Frederick Bligh Bond, who was investigating the ruins of Glastonbury Abbey in southwestern England. Bond worked in a respectable architectural office in nearby Bristol, but he had always been fascinated by ghosts and legends of King Arthur. The religious background of Glastonbury is strong; it has traditionally been called "the birthplace of English Christianity" and even possibly the burial place of the Holy Grail. Historically it was also tied into the Camelot legend and Arthur and Guinevere so there was much for archaeology to investigate when Bond began excavations there in 1909.

But the old question of "where to dig" was not as worrisome to Bond as to other archaeologists. He had special help, as he was to reveal much later. His medium, Captain John Allen Bartlett, put him in direct touch, via "automatic writing," with the monks and other earlier inhabitants of Glastonbury. When in doubt, Bond merely had to go into the past by way of his informants; in some cases they drew the layout of the ruined structure, and all he had to do was dig a bit to ground truth the message. How simple; talk about efficiency in archaeology—no more test pit here, test pit there. One needed only to follow the spirit suggestions and get it correct from the beginning. Indeed, that is how Bond told the story in his 1918 volume *Gate to Remembrance: A Psychological Study* in which he finally revealed his written communications with the past. These messages came sometimes in ragtag Latin but most often in slightly stilted English. Bond would place his fingers on the back of Bartlett's hand, which held a pencil, and ask questions. The answers would be written out on a piece of paper. It was strenuous work mentally, and they could keep at it for only an hour or two, but the results were well worth it.

According to most adherents of psychic archaeology, Frederick Bligh Bond's work at Glastonbury was not only the pioneering effort in the field but also some of the most conclusive work ever done. What did Bond really find other than the foundations of the cloisters and other very expectable structures around the central church building of the Abbey? He found five chapels that were attached to the main structure, the first of which was the Edgar Chapel, usually hailed as the most significant discovery of psychic archaeology. This addition behind the high altar was drawn and named by his ghostly informant and then excavated by Bond.

What an achievement? What nonsense! Culture is patterned behavior, and medieval cathedrals are some of the most patterned pieces of construction in our culture. "If you've seen one, you've seen them all," weary tourists will say as they rest their tired feet, sitting in yet another quiet cloister on a hard stone bench. I exaggerate, but cathedrals are exceptionally well patterned.

So why does psychic archaeology claim that Bond could not have found the Edgar Chapel without the medium's help? It truly passes understanding. We know that Bond was a well-trained architect with a specialty in ecclesiastical structures; all he had to do was turn to almost any nearby structure such as Salisbury Cathedral, less than fifty miles to the east, and see its Trinity Chapel behind the main altar and guess that Glastonbury would have one too. It would be a very likely and testable hypothesis, not something that one needs to go to ghostly writings for. In fact, it is even admitted by the most stalwart Bond supporters that such a chapel had been posited before Bond's work at Glastonbury. Much ado about nothing it seems to me.

Bond is credited at Glastonbury with several other "hits," as psychic confirmations are often called. One was another chapel, named Loretto, that he discovered after his book had revealed his use of psychic powers to aid his research and when he was being asked to stop his excavations. His psychic informants told him where to dig, and he did strike a foundation that he felt sure was the one he had been looking for. This chapel had been completely destroyed, except for the masonry footings, so he was not able to find the distinctive Italianate decor that gave the structure its name. But despite the lack of the specific physical evidence he needed for confirmation, he was sure he was correct in his identification.

His supporters agreed, but that is not how hypothesis testing is supposed to work. In many so-called tests of psychic phenomena, however, this is exactly what is called verification; if you hit you win, if you don't hit, you win because the failure to find data to affirm the hit does not mean it is not there but just that you haven't found it yet. With logic and rules like that, your batting average certainly improves.

Bond's other important discovery at Glastonbury was of a well-preserved burial along the south side of the nave as he was looking for the massive towers of the main structure. Although again his supporters said his last psychic "sitting" had told him "exactly where to look," he was apparently doing a little random trenching when he ran into this skeleton. This method of discovery sounds as if he was actually carrying out pretty normal field testing in searching for the foundations for these big towers; it is strange that he had to use that technique when he knew exactly where to look.

The newly found burial was not in a casket and had an additional human skull between its legs. What does this strange arrangement mean? Bond called up his "Watcher" and got a gory story with all the participants named and dated. Bond checked historical documents and found that the individuals were of a proper time period and that the person of the main burial was said to have been felled in a fight; sure enough, he has a broken forearm that could have been thus inflicted. But let's recall that the story of who was in the grave came after the excavation, not as a foretelling. Also there is not a shred of evidence in the ground that confirms the date of the burial or who the occupants in the ground were. Thus no actual confirmation of the archaeology is possible; the only proof is circular and substantiates Bond's story, not its relationship to the actual archaeological data.

Bond was prohibited from doing further work at Glastonbury after 1922. Even though in the 1930s he came forward with newly acquired information as to where to dig for the Holy Grail, he was not allowed to excavate. He continued to publish on the Abbey and on the documents he had obtained from the psychic past about the site. His cast of characters, mainly monks, was more than two dozen in number, and they were a communicative lot. There has been some attempt to suggest that the language they used in their messages was appropriate to the period from which they spoke, but on the contrary, it is not "church" Latin or anything special; indeed, it has a rather modern ring to it.

During the 1920s, things did not go well for Frederick Bond on a personal level either. He was then separated from his wife, with whom he had very difficult relations, and also from his daughter. To make things worse, his wife had accused him both of molesting the girl and of involving her in occult matters. At this time he made several long journeys to America.

After nearly a decade as an unhappy expatriate in America, Bond returned in 1935 to Britain and spent his last years in a nursing home in Wales, except for a few pilgrimages back to Glastonbury. He died in 1945. He may well have been happier visiting the past than suffering through his present.

During the post–World War I period, while Frederick Bond was involved with medieval times in Britain, there was a Polish psychic and clairvoyant in Warsaw who was biding his time before snatching the mantle of "Traveler into Prehistory." Stefan Ossowiecki was born in 1877 of well-placed Polish aristocrats living in Moscow. Schooled in Russian institutions, he learned early of his psychic powers. Although trained in engineering, he apprenticed himself to an elderly mystic, from whom he learned much. However, he lost his money and position during the Russian Revolution and ended up in Warsaw in the 1920s with only his paranormal powers and a few friends.

Ossowiecki went to work there as a chemical engineer but used his unusual gifts to help other people find lost objects or even to locate missing persons. He soon attracted the attention of those studying psychic phenomena in postwar Warsaw and quickly gained several noteworthy supporters. He was particularly adept at "reading" material in sealed envelopes, but it was not until 1937 that he became involved with archaeological subjects. His work was primarily in "psychometricizing" objects—that is, he would hold veritable artifacts in his hand and then, as one supporter has written, "the entire range of Paleolithic prehistory unfolded before his eyes in an endless panorama."[1] As adjuncts to his hour-long sessions, Ossowiecki would draw pictures of what he had "seen."

These parapsychological probings continued for some four years into

Stefan Ossowiecki

the period of Nazi conquest of Poland and provided, in the estimation of his followers, a totally new view of the long-forgotten past. Other commentators were not so enthralled, saying instead that he tended either to project the standard understanding of the subject at that time or to provide incorrect guesses about the past, including a rather precise description of a unicorn. His pictures of Paleolithic life and times are not great works of art, but again his supporters suggest that they do provide visual substantiation of archaeological data not known at the time of his readings. Most of these suggestions, however, stretch chance resemblances into verified hits.

Although he had a foreign passport, Ossowiecki remained in Poland during the occupation. Tragically, he and his Polish colleague, Professor Stanislow Pontiatowski, with whom he did his psychic work, were victims of Nazi death squads late in the war.

While all these psychic activities were going on in Europe, things were not completely quiet in America. Sleepy little Hopkinsville, Kentucky, in the western end of that state, not far from the junction of the Tennessee and Cumberland rivers, seems an unlikely spot to find a psychic after Glastonbury and Warsaw. But it was here from 1904 to 1910 that Edgar Cayce (pronounced Casey) first demonstrated his psychic powers. A quiet youth, he was said to take after his grandfather, Thomas Cayce, who had been a

Edgar Cayce with
his wife, Gertrude

famous water dowser. Edgar regularly went into a self-induced hypnotic trance or sleep when he sought to use his psychic powers. He did most of his early work in healing in conjunction with a Hopkinsville doctor. He later moved with his growing family to Alabama, thence to Texas, where one of his sons referred to his father's unsuccessful dowsing for oil to raise money to build a hospital as "the petroleum fiasco."

In the late 1920s Edgar Cayce moved his family to the sand hills of Virginia Beach, where he dreamed of establishing a curing hospital using his psychic readings. Although the hospital failed, Virginia Beach became, in 1932, Cayce's headquarters for the Association for Research and Enlightenment (ARE). Here today, following Cayce's death in 1945, are collected the thousands of readings that were produced by "the Sleeping Prophet," as he was later termed. In a period of forty-three years, the tall, bespectacled Cayce gave hundreds of readings, now compiled on nearly fifty thousand pages of transcripts. These documents were in response to questions put to him by the more than eight thousand individuals who sought his help; thus the messages were often rambling as to subject matter. Only after his death were they cataloged and better understood by his sons and other devoted followers.

Cayce's archaeological insights were mainly given to questioners as context for their previous lives, as he was a strong believer in reincarnation.

A great many of his subjects had ties to Atlantis during their earlier lives; in fact, the sunken continent is mentioned in more than 30 percent of Cayce's readings. Thus his documentation of that mysterious continent is especially rich, covering a period from before 50,000 B.C. to about 10,000 B.C., when Atlantis was finally and violently destroyed.

Cayce was said to have an extraordinary "Atlantis Channel"—*channeling* is a parapsychological term meaning a spirit connection. According to his information, Atlantis was a very advanced civilization having aircraft, radios, and very likely even laser beams, according to one of his son's interpretations. The survivors of the last destruction fled to France, Egypt, and the Yucatán via ships and even a few crude aircraft. Their technology had apparently suffered a decline, but they were still culturally superior to those among whom they settled. For example, Egyptian civilization got an important boost at this time from these Atlantean immigrants, according to most Cayce believers.

Some contemporary archaeologists, who have used psychics and who are happy followers of Edgar Cayce, such as Stephan Schwartz and Jeffrey Goodman, feel that there have been successful archaeological tests of some of the Cayce readings, especially in the Near East and Egypt. Cayce himself was content to make his readings and let others interpret them, saying simply that archaeological records to prove his statements had, indeed, already been found, but they had not been properly interpreted.

Although family members and followers insist that Cayce was not very well-read on archaeological topics, most of what he said about Atlantis, for example, sounded like reworked Donnelly or plagiarized Blavatsky. Interestingly, names like Churchward pop up in his readings and are duly recorded. Perhaps, like Joseph Smith and some other seers, Edgar Cayce's mind was not as unschooled as it might be convenient to believe. Needless to say, I feel that Edgar Cayce should have stayed with faith healing rather than muddying the waters of archaeology with messages brought by faint voices from Atlantis. Others, however, consider him the most famous psychic since Nostradamus.

In the post–World War II period, there was another special twist in archaeological techniques with the advent, especially in England, of the serious use of dowsing for buried prehistoric remains. The British had not been quiet on the psychic archaeological front in the 1920s and 1930s after Bond, thanks to the work of the redoubtable Alfred Watkins and others, with "ley lines" and "straight tracks" crisscrossing the quiet countryside from Stonehenge to Salisbury Cathedral and on, but that is another story for another book. What broke out in England, as led by a former army officer, a Scottish general named James Scott Elliot, was a rash of purported findings based on the conversion of water-dowsing techniques to archaeological prospecting.

They even did the map-dowsing trick over a simple piece of paper, where no special "powers," emanating from earth or artifact, could be reasonably brought in to explain how the dowser made his or her interesting discoveries. But it got better than that; one expert, Bill Lewis, found that by swinging a small pendulum in front of a huge moss-covered megalith, he could get responses to questions concerning not only the date of raising the great stone monument but also the sex ratio of the work crew employed on the project. No names, addresses, or phone numbers were provided, sorry to say.

With that feat, surely the gold medal or Guinness archaeological record for the farthest-out achievement in this dowsing tournament would go to the British, but don't sell the Yanks short. It seems that a young American female dowser, not a common calling for that sex, named Karen A. B. Hunt, sneaked in when no one was looking and did them all one better. According to her findings, when you are on the site you're investigating, you don't need any structural remains to dowse. What you dowse with your plain old forked stick is simply the *space* where the building *had* been, with the proviso that it had stood there for at least six months. If so, the atoms of space will have been permanently affected by its past presence and you dowse its former position. In fact, you can even locate the doors and windows of the once-standing structure.

Archaeologist Hunt has done much of her work in Missouri, on now-vacant farmsteads, but she recently exported her talents to Australia, where she was well paid to do a map of a now-destroyed nineteenth-century farm and successfully plotted the main house, outbuildings, and even fences and gates. The outcry from disgruntled and disillusioned Aussie journalists was something to hear. Apparently, they had no respect for taking an old British tradition to its illogical conclusion.

But all of this would be amusing and slightly irrelevant shop talk, if psychic archaeology had not gone further than a bit of rather harmless dowsing here and there. After all, Kenneth Roberts, the well-known author of many very popular historic novels such as *Arundel,* became, in his later years, a passionate believer in water dowsing. He wrote a book about Henry Gross, his favorite practitioner, and put up money to help the University Museum in Philadelphia find water at one of its Mayan archae-

J. Norman Emerson

ological digs via his dowser. The important excavations at Tikal were being stalled by a lack of drinking water for the diggers, and Gross tried the old map-dowsing bit. Unfortunately, drilling on the site at the spot indicated failed to produce the needed well.

However, a real academically based problem over the power of psychic archaeology to produce significant results broke into the scholarly profession in North America in 1973. At a scientific conference, J. Norman Emerson of the University of Toronto made the announcement that he was using information garnered from a psychic informant in his archaeological work. Emerson was anything but a Young Turk trying to jerk the chain of the Establishment; he was an elder statesman in his fifty-sixth year, who had been schooled in a conservative atmosphere in Canada, with a Ph.D. from the University of Chicago. He had focused his research career on the Iroquois of Ontario and had run a long series of summer field school digs that had trained a large number of students. Although hardly the "Father of Canadian Archaeology," the accolade bestowed on him by some of his more enthusiastic followers, he was a good journeyman archaeologist, who would be the least likely candidate for "rocking the boat."

Emerson turned to the psychic connection in archaeology on the basis of two unconnected events: his wife, Ann, had become interested in paranormal subjects during the 1960s and had joined an Edgar Cayce Study Group. Through this interest she had met the wife of George McMullen, a truck driver with psychic talents. The second event was the deteriorating health of Professor Emerson, which was due to a devastating illness that would ultimately claim his life. Mrs. Emerson brought the two men together, and George McMullen was able to make health-related recommendations via his psychic powers that seemed to help Professor Emerson. Not surprisingly, the effectiveness of these medical suggestions made a very favorable impression, and soon a previously skeptical Emerson and George McMullen were discussing archaeology and psychometry. Some of George's readings of the artifacts he was given to view astounded Emerson. He was soon getting, so he felt, heretofore unavailable data about the past from his new-found psychic source.

In the few short years left to him Emerson became a complete believer in the psychic path to archaeological knowledge. For an elder scholar in anthropology to go from a pragmatic scientist to a committed believer in the paranormal was not unique. Some years earlier, in 1952, John R. Swanton, a distinguished Harvard-trained Smithsonian anthropologist by then retired, wrote an open letter to his professional colleagues calling on them to join in the search for a new kind of truth via parapsychology. Swanton's letter was received by most of the profession with a slightly embarrassed silence. In 1953 Swanton privately published a small, well-reasoned and documented monograph discussing his results with parapsychology, but few scholars were aware of it. He died quietly five years later.

Emerson, by contrast, pursued his new faith in psychic phenomena assiduously, seeking new "contacts" and trying out their abilities to read the past from the artifacts alone. Some of his graduate students took up the cause and gave papers at meetings concerning this newfound way of getting at prehistory. Does all this mean that I should welcome J. Norman Emerson into the fellowship of Rogue professors? I am uncharacteristically hesitant to do so. There is little doubt that once on this path, Emerson threw away his former caution and his critically nagging questioning of "how do I know this to be correct." One must confess that there were very strong extenuating circumstances: he was terminally ill. How long he knew that to be true is unknown to me, but I suspect it was for much of the period under consideration, from 1973 until 1978, when he died.

Nonetheless, what Emerson was seen to accept and even encourage in psychic archaeology turned a trickle into almost a flood. Before the decade of the 1970s was up, three hardcover volumes by scholars with graduate training in archaeology would come out to try to take the field by storm. Psychic Archaeology was now a capitalized and presumably recognized subfield or discipline of archaeology. Jeffrey Goodman's 1977 volume was *Psychic Archaeology: Time Machine to the Past.* Stephan A. Schwartz produced *The Secret Vaults of Time: Psychic Archaeology and the Quest for Man's Beginnings* in 1978. The final volume of the trio was in 1979 by David E. Jones and called *Visions of Time: Experiments in Psychic Archaeology.*

The Goodman and Schwartz volumes were almost clones, describing the origin of the new discipline with startlingly similar characters, anecdotes, and critical viewpoints. Both authors had gone to the University of Arizona for some of their graduate training and may have met there, which may explain why the first chapters of both books deal with Frederick Bligh Bond. With that start, Ossowiecki and Edgar Cayce are sure to follow. If there was not a touch of copying somewhere along the way, at least we obviously have very good and irrefutable proof of psychic unity.

Jeffrey Goodman, who had hoped to study under Emerson, spiced up his volume with an early discussion of his remarkable work at the extraordinary Flagstaff, Arizona site. Here, at a site discovered by combining his own dreams with a psychic's readings, he found important "archaeological remains" very deeply buried and dating to much earlier periods than accepted by conservative Establishment archaeologists. Goodman throws down his gauntlet with a concluding chapter entitled "Put Your Shovel Where Your Mouth Is." Small wonder that some of my Southwestern colleagues did not try to rearrange the placement of that digging tool. Indeed, of the three authors under consideration Goodman has received the strongest critical reviews, some of which intimate that his published data and opinions are not honestly presented. Goodman's next volume (1978), *Earthquake Generation,* predicting seismic catastrophes, was seen as terribly one-sided and full of scare tactics even by a strong supporter of the use of psychic data who reviewed it.

Stephan Schwartz, in the second of these two review volumes, dealt with the problem of convincing the reader to his cause in a slightly less confrontational manner by suggesting that the switch to psychic answers in archaeology could be seen as part of a Kuhnian paradigm shift that may take a little getting used to. More than that, however, he concluded the volume with some detailed protocols for setting up research using psychics and testing the results. Would that some of his later work had carefully followed the methods of testing that he so conscientiously set forth in his first volume.

Jeffrey Goodman

David Jones's book was published by the Theosophical Society Press so we can clearly see that H.P.B. (Blavatsky) and her followers are still deeply involved in visionary subjects. Jones, unlike the first two authors, is a fully trained anthropologist, who had done credible and sensitive work as an ethnographer of the American Indians before turning his attention to the past. This book was not a history but rather a detailed report on his own experiments in psychic archaeology in which he had informants psycho-metrize artifacts. He published the full transcripts of these readings, some-thing not often done except by Cayce's research institution. One gets the feeling that Jones is somewhat amazed at the abilities of his informants, despite their lack of education, and he also tended to read more elaborate interpretations into the informants' responses than seemed to be there.

As with many other of the psychic "readings" I have discussed, these findings usually provide little new information or insights. One does come to wonder in Jones's case why he bothered. But Jones is, of course, the most serious and least sensationalist of the three. Interestingly, Schwartz and Jones were both members of a small group of psychically inclined anthro-pologists who were involved in a short-lived (1977–83) journal called the *Phoenix* published in Stanford, California, which also published Norman Emerson's writings.

One can ask what the professional archaeologists would do with this rash of pro-psychic archaeology literature. Would they give it the silent treatment as they did Swanton? Fortunately, the 1980s were different too, and the counterattacks, though not hardcover volumes, were at least very critical journal articles and book reviews. No longer would the profession sit back and ignore the presentation of unprovable hypotheses as archaeological fact. One textbook presentation titled "Psychic Archaeology???" starts with the aphorism by William Orton, "If you keep your mind open, people will throw a lot of garbage into it," but tries to remain restrained in its view of the validity of parapsychological phenomena in general. The author, archaeologist David Hurst Thomas, concludes that "the truest test of psychic archaeology is in the ground, not in the mind."[2] One wonders why he dropped this section from the second edition of this text: Beam me an answer, David.

There seems to have been a diminution of interest in this new field recently, although both Stephan Schwartz and Jeffrey Goodman have continued their activities. Schwartz, whose background included a research assistantship with U.S. Naval Operations, government speech writing, and free-lance journalism, now heads a nonprofit research foundation termed the Mobius Group, which specializes in using psychics in its research. Not surprisingly, he acknowledges significant influences from the work of Edgar Cayce and Norman Emerson; indeed, from the latter connection he even employed George McMullen as one of his team of archaeologically sensitive psychics.

In his most completely described research so far, Schwartz published in 1983 *The Alexandria Project,* a scientific venture touted on the book's cover as "a movement to the furthermost frontiers of a new, revolutionary science"—talk about the cutting edge, this is obviously it. The research planning began in 1978 with a focus on the time of Alexander the Great and the city he founded in Egypt, where he is also supposed to be buried. Schwartz's field group went to Alexandria in 1979 and included two psychics and some specialists in underwater archaeology, another of Schwartz's special interests. Although Schwartz has stated a strong concern for testing his psychic archaeology, this volume gives little proof of it; indeed, in his closing paragraphs he tries to forestall criticism by saying most of that will be "character innuendo" or sheer disbelief in psychic phenomena. He even admits errors in procedure, since corrected.

As to procedure, I would like to know what would have kept George McMullen from reading up on Alexandria before he accompanied Schwartz

Stephan A. Schwartz

to Egypt, a totally new area for him. George's psychic recreations of an ancient battle fought at Alexandria seem to me to be no more detailed than would be available in any easily accessible volume in the public library. I know that it would not be "cricket" for George to do a little background reading, but then who's checking on whom?

What were Schwartz's research results? He went to Alexandria to found out more about the period, to find the tomb of Alexander, and finally to lay to rest peacefully the "Conqueror of the Known World." There were exciting moments, plenty of psychic "hits" by Hella Hammid, his other psychic, and George, if you let *them* do the scoring. If you believe the "puffery" on the back cover, there was also "the actual finding of Alexander's bones." Unfortunately, the writer of that breathless prose had not read the book; even Schwartz admits that they do not know whether a sizable cache of bones kept by some monks in a wooden chest included those of Alexander. Besides, some Alexandrian scholars suggest that Alexander was probably cremated instead of mummified, as "seen" by George, so why search for bones?

If one looks critically at the fieldwork carried out by Schwartz's Mobius Group, one can say that some reasonable surveying and excavation did get done in the Alexandria locale, and some interesting finds both underwater and underground were made. But nothing very spectacular was found despite the hype of "daring project" or "dramatic discovery," and nothing really unexpected. So again, what important function did the psychics perform? It is more a sideshow act wrapped in glossy covers for popular consumption.

However unsatisfying this search for Alexander may have been, it does not leave one with the same distaste as do the recent activities of Jeffrey Goodman. Goodman, the creator of the psychic "time machine to the past" and our introduction to the Earthquake Generation, has taken on a new cause—rewriting the history of the American Indians, to whom he counts some genetic kinship. With two books, *American Genesis* and *The Genesis Mystery,* already out and a third promised, *The Origins of Mathematics and Science in Prehistoric America,* but still not available as far as I know, Goodman is carrying the message forward that all previous datings and descriptions of Native American history in the New World are rendered obsolete by his archaeological findings.

While Goodman was a graduate student in archaeology at the University of Arizona, he undertook in the 1970s the excavations near Flagstaff that I have mentioned briefly. At the site found using psychic clues, he dug a test pit almost thirty feet in depth. Although this excavation has not, to my knowledge, been formally written up, there are descriptions of some of the results scattered through Goodman's books. As best as I can reconstruct the finds, the most important discoveries include charcoal found at the fifteen-foot level and dated by carbon 14 at 25,000 years, some stone tools including a chopper and scrapers extending to a depth of twenty-eight feet and dated by geological "extensions" to perhaps 125,000 years, and finally, two engraved stones.

These two rocks are pretty special if we accept Goodman's conclusions. The "Flagstaff stone" is thought to be approximately one hundred thousand years old and possibly "one of the most important artifacts ever found in the whole world" says Goodman, citing in the last instance Alexander Marshack of Harvard's Peabody Museum.[3] This rock, actually a small piece of volcanic tufa no more than two and a half inches in length, has some faint lines "scratched" on it. According to Goodman, it is Paleo-Indian Art. How does it stand up to analysis? Marshack has said that he was badly misquoted by Goodman, and the date is arrived at by extreme extrapolation.

The second stone is even more bizarre. Termed the "Native First People stone" by Goodman, it was found in 1979 in Arizona. I am not certain whether it came from the Flagstaff site; the special report circulated by Goodman's followers does not make the provenance clear. Under a "weathering rind" there are glyphic markings that have been decoded. A "tephrachronologist" named Virginia Steen-McIntyre has dated the stone to possibly 250,000 B.C. Thus this inscribed record, which has been deciphered to have information on astronomical and calendrical subjects, is considered by some to be the oldest written document in the world. According to the same sources, it probably records Native American knowledge of mathematics, science, and astronomy at 70,000 B.C. Presumably this second stone will be the centerpiece of Goodman's forthcoming book.

The main thrust of Goodman's current views on Native American prehistory is that the New World was the center of both physical and cultural development. He suggests that we have the road signs all wrong on Bering Strait. The Garden of Eden, as far as modern man (*Homo sapiens*) is concerned, was in southern California, possibly as much as five hundred thousand years ago. By one hundred thousand years ago these modern human forms had radiated all over the world. The Bering Strait crossing was made well before thirty thousand years ago, but instead of ancestors of the American Indians coming into the New World, these prototypical American Indians were heading for France. They arrived there, footsore and tired, by about 30,000 B.C. Possibly they were soon revived with a little of the famous Dordogne cuisine for they took on the barbarian Neanderthals, whom they quickly displaced. Thus the Upper Paleolithic was in good *Homo sapiens* hands and France was saved for artists and culinary triumphs.

This scenario is the result of the steadfast work of the American Indians, who, according to a list compiled by Goodman, scored firsts in a staggering series of topics. They invented plant and animal domestication, freeze-dried food, pottery, the calendar, astronomy, physics, and medicine. Goodman calls these "gifts from the 'Before People'" and really does mean that he feels that American Indians have priority claims to all these inventions from a worldwide perspective. How preposterous! The spurious evidence used to prove these statements includes, for example, the purported association of a Pleistocene mammoth with pottery in Peru, a tale long ago shown to be completely false.

Of course, much of this view of the past holds water only if Goodman's very extended dating of many archaeological events in the New World is accepted. This extreme position for human occupation of the New World at a magnitude of more than one hundred thousand years is founded on two exceptionally shaky pedestals. First, there is the early dating of human skeletal remains based on amino acid racemization, the work of Jeffrey Bada, who has categorically retracted all these dates as a result of further testing.

The second pillar is a heterogeneous mélange of archaeological finds ranging from Old Crow in Alaska, now also drastically redated to less than two thousand years of age, to the very controversial finds at Calico Hills in California, which sadly caught the approving eye of Louis Leakey just before his death. Another supportive archaeological voice has been that of George Carter. Goodman goes so far as to use "Earlier Than You Think" as a chapter title in his second volume, *The Genesis Mystery*. This title is obviously appropriated from Carter, but with no specific reference to that author.

A review of this book by Goodman was written by John Cole for the major American archaeological journal, *American Antiquity,* and he pointed out that, like my rogue professor, this volume looks and sounds much like the real McCoy: "It mimics a scientific book very well."[4] But like most Fantastic Archaeology books, it fails to present both sides of the evidence, or worse than that, it often twists the data and interpretation of others to fit the author's hypotheses.

Thus appropriately as the last example that I have chosen to discuss, Goodman's work is quintessential Fantastic Archaeology; he attacks the Establishment and authority with gusto; Charles Darwin is one of his recent targets. He is interestingly selective in his references, only rarely citing fellow believers; but then Velikovsky never cited Donnelly either.

Goodman never really tests, whether it be psychic information or interpretations of stratigraphy. When someone gives him a contrary opinion, he sort of wishes it away. When we reach veracity in that triad I spoke of at the beginning of this volume, the record is not good. In some cases the word *error* might suffice, in others, where current scholars are misquoted or misrepresented, a stronger term seems warranted. Anything is used to win the argument, or so it appears.

The problem is larger than that, though, for the whole course and achievement of Native American prehistory are gravely distorted by Goodman; at times there are ludicrous exaggerations as in his extraordinary claims for priority of inventions. At other times there is an ingenuous appeal to external or outside intervention to solve important mysteries. Thus he commits an intellectual crime on the very people he seeks spiritually to uplift with his discoveries, the Native Americans. That is a strong statement, but I feel in complete accord with the authors of a recent text, Robert Sharer and Wendy Ashmore, in their wise comments that "archaeology has a responsibility to prevent pseudo-archaeologists from *robbing* humanity of the real achievements of past cultures."[5] I shall attempt to restore that theft with my final chapter.

Epilogue: North American Prehistory—The Real Fantasy

Without fantasy, science would have nothing to test.
KENNETH BOULDING, 1980

As we began this odyssey through the tangled maze of Fantastic Archaeology in North America, I discussed the differences between science and pseudoscience and the necessity for scientists to ask the question "what if," in other words, to dare to make hypotheses beyond those supported by the data at hand, the "fantasy" of Boulding quoted above.

The genre Science Fiction in its most common form is said by the dictionary to be "fiction based on prediction of future scientific possibilities" so it, by this definition, also leans on hypothesis and fantasy as any reader of this brand of fiction is well aware.

What has all this to do with Fantastic Archaeology? Quite a lot. We have seen many purveyors of pseudoscience take a bit of data, genuine or not, and spin fantastic hypotheses usually without too much concern for logic or testing. What is the real difference? Don't "real" archaeologists dig carefully in the sacred sands, wrench a few precious data bits from their contextual settings, and then build quite elaborate hypotheses for the enjoyment of themselves and their readers? What do professional archaeologists know for sure? Isn't all archaeology just a bunch of tenuous hypotheses strung together with a few solid facts?

Well, if you've come this far, you know some of the answers. Yes, archaeologists are, of necessity, always going to press with less data than they would like to have; they are always filling in gaps with analogies, sometimes with reasoned guesses; and they are often not sure of all the answers. Then they may see a new piece of evidence and change their views completely. This must be very confusing for the lay public; just as soon as they have learned a bit of archaeological dogma, the archaeologists change their minds and their hypotheses. Why they sound no more reliable than weak fiction writers, with modest academic credentials, producing romantic histories of the past.

"Real archaeologists," indeed: don't ask me to run to their defense, for I am about to venture forth into the real fantasy of American archaeology myself to visit the prehistory of North America as I presently perceive it. We will dip into the past, as with a net into a running stream, to catch a few shining moments as we can now recreate them. It is not an even-paced or consecutive narrative, nor can it ever be; we see archaeological glimpses of old events only through fortuitously opened windows, where chance and surviving artifacts combine to give us these rare vistas of the past that was.

*   *   *

We begin our fantasy as that wondrous event of discovery of the New World by *Homo sapiens* occurs, some ten, or twenty, or maybe even thirty thousand years ago. For help in this time travel I turn to another anthropologist, Chad Oliver, whose science fiction writings have the ring of truth; he has created exciting fantasies based on hard evidence. From his *Winds of Time* comes this compelling vignette as the survivors of a wrecked space vehicle from a distant world search for a safe haven to wait out the arrival of the space age on the planet Earth.

>   The coast curved toward the east, a tongue of land licked by a choppy sea. . . . There. One great continent stopped, and another began. Between them was a narrow band of shallow water—they could see the rocks on the ocean floor. It looked as though it were really one land mass and a playful giant had splashed a few buckets of water into a trough to cut them apart.
>   The water was perhaps sixty miles across, and was broken in the middle by some tiny forsaken islands. It was not a formidable barrier; there were undoubtedly times when a man could walk from one continent to the other on a bridge of ice.
>   The copter hummed over the water, and in doing so it moved from Siberia to Alaska over the Bering Strait, from the Old World to the New. . . .
>   "A funny feeling," Tsriga said looking down over Arvon's shoulder. "What?" asked Arvon, though he knew what the boy meant. Tsriga gestured vaguely. "All that down there. If Derryoc was right, this part of the world is practically uninhabited by human beings. Just think: millions of square miles that have never seen a man." "Yeah," said Nlesine. "We call them lucky miles." . . .
>   They saw animals in profusion now: lumbering elephants, a few wild horses, fantastic herds of big bison that blackened the plains for miles.
>   And they saw men, dark figures that hunted in packs like wolves, stalking the herds with spears at the ready. Once they flew over a camp at evening, a rude skin shelter, a woman patiently scraping at a hide with a stone tool, a child watching her solemnly.

Arvon stared at them, imprinting them forever on his mind. *You there!* he thought. *You tired hunter, hungry child, working woman! Do you know that you have conquered a world? Do you know that men like you will live and die for centuries, and then be replaced by men with guns from the other side of oceans you have yet to see? Do you know you have won a continent, and that one day it will be taken from you? Eat your meat, hunter, and laugh while you can! Tomorrow will be long, and a great night creeps from the depths of the sea. . . .*

The copter hummed through the skies, over the sea of grass. The plains continued into what would eventually be the eastern part of the state of Colorado. (Oliver, 1957: 133–37)

Although he wrote that passage more than thirty years ago, Chad Oliver has given us a glimpse of what the past was quite probably like. He set his story about fifteen thousand years ago, and recent archaeological research would not change that date very significantly for the Clovis Hunters of the High Plains, as we now call them. They are the first well-documented peoples of the New World dating to 10,000 B.C., or twelve thousand years ago (Table 1). Reasonable speculation and some few bits of data suggest even earlier arrivals, as much as twenty thousand years ago, but definitive proof still remains strangely elusive.

The Clovis culture has now been found over most of North America, in southern Canada and all of the forty-eight contiguous states. They are often referred to as Big Game Hunters, for some of their best-known sites are "kill sites" of the elephantlike mammoths and large now-extinct bison, but we are sure that they probably took a wide spectrum of animals in their hunting, not all of which were big. Gathering was undoubtedly important too.

Only recently have we gotten a scant view of Clovis ceremonial or sacred life. A series of very elaborate caches, six in number, have been discovered across the Rocky Mountain West. They contain huge chipped stone points as well as other wealth such as preforms of fluted points; these artifacts have been buried, probably with human remains. There is still much we do not know about this early culture.

One extraordinary thing, however, about Clovis culture is its rapid and rather uniform spread over much of the Northern Hemisphere. For example, very characteristic projectile points of high technological quality and some other specific special-function tools are virtually identical wherever found. This similarity of artifacts is true at the Lehner site, where several mammoths were killed, in the now arid desert near the Mexican border in southern Arizona and at the Bull Brook site on a sandy knoll east

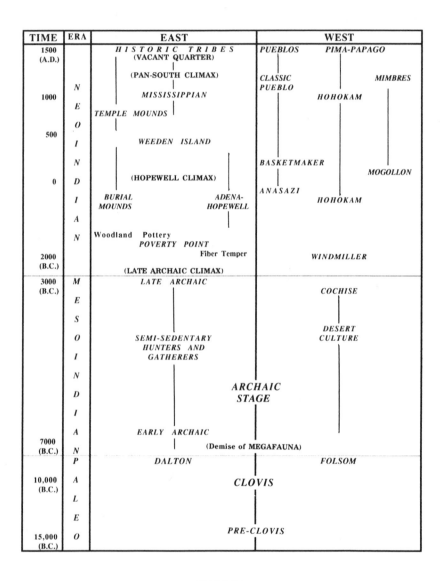

TIME	ERA	EAST	WEST
1500 (A.D.)		*H I S T O R I C T R I B E S* (VACANT QUARTER)	*PUEBLOS* *PIMA-PAPAGO*
	N	(PAN-SOUTH CLIMAX)	*CLASSIC PUEBLO* *MIMBRES*
1000	E	*MISSISSIPPIAN*	*HOHOKAM*
	O	*TEMPLE MOUNDS*	
500	I	*WEEDEN ISLAND*	
	N		*BASKETMAKER* *MOGOLLON*
0	D	(HOPEWELL CLIMAX)	*ANASAZI*
	I	BURIAL ADENA- MOUNDS HOPEWELL	*HOHOKAM*
	A		
	N	Woodland Pottery POVERTY POINT	
2000 (B.C.)		Fiber Temper	*WINDMILLER*
		(LATE ARCHAIC CLIMAX)	
3000 (B.C.)	M	*LATE ARCHAIC*	*COCHISE*
	E		
	S		*DESERT*
	O	*SEMI-SEDENTARY HUNTERS AND GATHERERS*	*CULTURE*
	I		
	N		*ARCHAIC STAGE*
	D		
	I		
	A	*EARLY ARCHAIC*	
7000 (B.C.)	N	(Demise of MEGAFAUNA)	
	P	*DALTON*	*FOLSOM*
10,000 (B.C.)	A	*CLOVIS*	
	L		
	E		
15,000 (B.C.)	O	*PRE-CLOVIS*	

TABLE 1

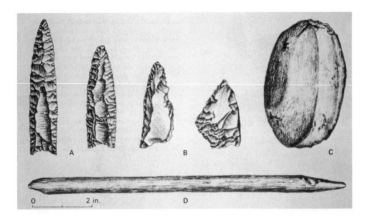

Clovis Artifacts

of Ipswich, Massachusetts, overlooking the broad and gently undulating coastal plain, now a salt marsh, and probably then populated with grazing mammoths and other large Pleistocene beasts.

I do not mean to suggest that one pleasant fall afternoon the Clovis hunters pulled up stakes in New England and struck out for the Sun Belt, but the striking similarity of artifact forms does make direct communication of some kind a very plausible notion. Our evidence for this connection is the strong formal similarities of artifact types found at the two distant sites; although made of raw materials native to their own locales, the virtual identity of shape and technology make any other conclusion difficult to accept.

If Massachusetts to Arizona seems a long haul, what about Bering Strait to Tierra del Fuego? The facts are that those "lucky miles" alluded to by Oliver's extraterrestrials which gave elbow room to the first arrivals were very quickly traversed, or so it seems. Native American groups, albeit apparently small in numbers, were spread throughout the Western hemisphere in perhaps less than a thousand years. Such a brief span of time when one considers the vastness of the territory and the difficulties of penetrating certain tremendously challenging regions, such as the narrow link between our major continents, which was not appreciably wider or less tropical than it is today. New data indicate that pre-Clovis occupation of South America, Chile to be precise, began more than thirteen thousand years ago. This long trek is a major testimony to the indomitable will of humankind, although it can be suggested that these ancient travelers probably did not know the magnitude of their own accomplishment.

Only a few other events strike me as similarly challenging as this conquest of the New World; they include the spread of the ancestors of the native Australians from Southeast Asia south into that great island-continent at what now seems certainly to have been about fifty thousand years ago and next the much more recent pioneering effort of the Malayo-Polynesians in their navigational triumph of conquering the vast Pacific beginning at about the start of the Christian era. Only our own recently star-crossed conquest of space can compare to these three epic human adventures, all of which began in eastern Asia. I might remind the reader that our present knowledge of these great events in the past is all based on diligently pursued archaeological research, surely reason enough to justify my concern for keeping the story of our archaeological past free of the taint of Fantastic Archaeology.

But to continue our narrative, the next window was actually our first view of these Paleo-Indian finds that settled once and for all the questions wrangled about so long by Putnam, Mercer, Holmes, and Hrdlicka. One summer a Black cowboy named McJunkin, riding the range on the High Plains at the foot of the Rockies, spotted some eroding animal bones in a gulley near Folsom, New Mexico, and reported them. Somewhat later, in the summer of 1926, a field party from the Denver Museum of Natural History began excavations at the site and during the next summer's dig (1927) found indisputable evidence of the coexistence of stone projectile points and extinct bison. The context was clear—the fluted point was found between the buffalo's ribs. This Folsom find was confirmed on site by a blue-ribbon panel of experts that included A. V. Kidder, Frank H. H. Roberts of the Smithsonian, and Barnum Brown of the American Museum of Natural History.

What Lartet and Christy did for French Paleolithic archaeology in five years with their digs in the Dordogne had taken the American archaeologists more than sixty years, but that is another story. With the Folsom finds in hand and quickly accepted, Paleo-Indian research burgeoned in America. Frank H. H. Roberts quickly followed up with confirming finds at Lindenmeier in southwest Colorado for the Smithsonian. Holmes lived long enough to see his beloved Smithsonian Institution come full circle and believe in these Early Man finds. The 1930s and 1940s saw successful careers founded on the pursuit of these remains, most of which were discovered in the West.

It would be only in the 1960s that eastern archaeologists would make breakthroughs of their own and show both strong concentrations of Clovis

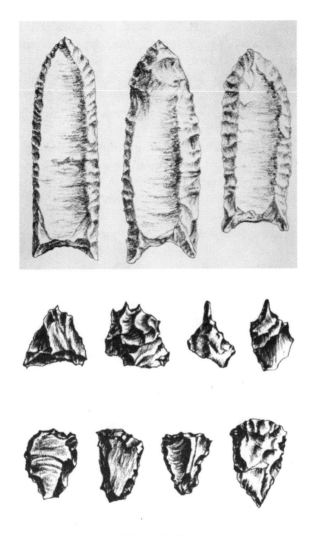

Folsom Artifacts

points in places such as southern Ohio and the development of slightly later cultures such as Dalton, circa 7000 B.C., that would have broad distributions over much of the eastern half of the country. The Dalton cultural assemblage shows a strong linkage to the earlier Clovis forms.

Strange anomalies persist even today; for example, there still is not a single well-documented association of artifacts with extinct fauna east of the Mississippi River. There are plenty of Pleistocene fossils and plenty of carbon 14 dates to show quite clearly that a number of cultures of that age, between twelve thousand and nine thousand years ago, when most of the megafauna became extinct, existed in the East. I repeat, we have only tiny peepholes on the past, and for excavators in the East that one special opportunity still eludes us at this moment.

While all these so-called Big Game Hunters were doing their own thing, others, in less obvious and less well-watered areas such as the Great Basin, were making their way in simpler but, in some aspects, just as effective lifeways. After all, as the diversity of cultures on this planet exemplifies, there are many ways to get your groceries, even if you don't have a choice of supermarkets and specialty gourmet shops.

There were pretty successful seaside or maritime adaptations, and even the fringes of Death Valley were not completely inhospitable, especially in the period of the late Pleistocene, when the great freshwater lakes filled by ice melt from the mountains were sites of shore-front habitations by many small bands of hunters and collectors. Some of these long-lasting desert cultures have persisted; surviving nineteenth-century descendants, such as the Paiute, show that cultural elaboration may not be the best route to cultural continuity—talk about survivors!

Sandals for the feet and caves for shelter, animal snares and grinding stones for wild seeds, woven containers such as bags and baskets, spears and sticks to throw at small game; these sparse items that make up a partial inventory of the Desert cultures, when combined with a detailed knowledge of the environment, were the survivors' handbook. Pretty remarkable, but then add the cold and inclement weather of the tip of South America and ask, How did the Yahgan and Ona last as well as they did? Indeed, looking only at New World examples, one must admit that the saga of the early spread of humankind, from the Arctic to the Strait of Magellan, to complete ultimate hemispheric adaptation, is a pretty remarkable achievement, when seen against the time perspective of over ten thousand years.

Do I need any other justification for my lifelong focus on New World cultures? The Western hemisphere has rightly been called a laboratory for

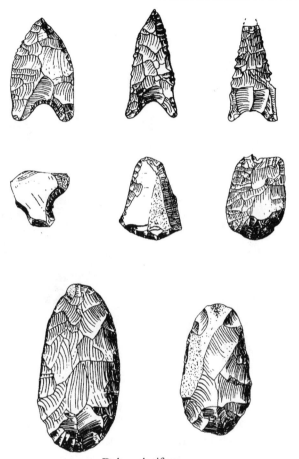

Dalton Artifacts

testing hypotheses not only of the rise of independent civilizations but for an understanding of the rich diversity of cultures through a long time span. At no time is that rich diversity better seen than during what is called the Archaic or Meso-Indian period in the Eastern United States. Here from 7000 to 2000 B.C. we get a view of a bountiful life of well-adapted hunters and gatherers, and fishers, too, that exploited the full range of the ecology, wherever they might be. One of our best "windows" is in the central Southeast, on the Tennessee River, where these Archaic peoples exploited both fresh-water resources such as fish and clams and terrestrial animals like the white-tailed deer and many small mammals.

The environment that was being exploited would be very familiar to us

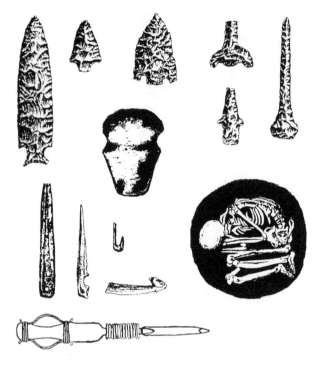

Southeastern Archaic Assemblage

today, since by about 7000 B.C. or shortly thereafter we entered the Holo-
cene or Recent Epoch in geological terms. The great beasts of the Late
Pleistocene were gone; no more would large herds of mammoths graze on
the western plains or mastodons trumpet and crash through the swampy
woodlands of the East. Gone too, interestingly enough, were horses and
camels, whose ancestral home was the New World. Both would return to
America through the agency of military forces—the Spanish conquistadors
brought back the horse, and in the nineteenth century the U.S. Army tried
an ill-fated corps of camels in the Southwestern deserts.

This era of American prehistory was thus played out in almost familiar
surroundings. True, some of the great Pleistocene lakes of the West, of
which the Great Salt Lake is the best-known survivor, still existed but in
diminishing scale. The major drainage systems would be in place. The sea
level, lowered more than three hundred feet at the maximum of the glacial
expansion, would continue to rise and probably also continue to cover and
thus hide from the archaeologist some important cultural evidence of

successful seaside dwellers. We have no good window on the past for those areas unless we are using a glass-bottomed boat or scuba gear. The latter has been used very successfully on some sites in Florida, where underwater exploration has given us glimpses of both artifacts and human skeletal remains right at this crucial time.

The plants, animals, and fishes are all "modern"—meaning that they or their close relatives are those species that we encounter today. Some distributions have changed, and we have had some extinctions, unfortunately, like the passenger pigeon and the Carolina parakeet. But by and large, the white-tailed deer, the raccoons and skunks, the wild turkeys and prairie chickens, even the frogs and snakes, were here.

The scope of knowledge which these Archaic peoples had of this environment, as we understand it both from archaeologically recovered remains and by analogy with contemporary groups whose lifeways we have studied, was truly amazing. Not a bird or beast was unknown; their knowledge of the plant kingdom was equally encyclopedic, whether it was edible food plants or medicinal herbs and potions. Even today modern drug manufacturers, and I mean proprietary drugs, not those used by local experimenters, have found many useful sources for new medicinal products based on ethnographically recognized substances.

I stress this aspect of Archaic life both because it was central to its success and longevity and because *hunters and gatherers* have become pejorative terms used by many generations of smug farmers and herdsmen to denigrate a way of life that really had a lot going for it. Sort of like prehistoric "Airstream" caravaners in their sleek silver mobile homes, they were always on the go, but with seasonal stops at favorite watering and eating places. They came together for yearly "roundups" and did those social activities that go so well with such large groupings: found mates, exchanged lies about their successful hunts and the size of the fish they had caught, and even bad-mouthed their crazy neighbors to the north and west.

As they sat around their campfires I am sure they said, "It doesn't get any better than this." Only they did not have any Miller, Old Milwaukee, or even Coors to make the evenings around the glowing embers seem just a bit better than they were. Unlike their neighbors to the south, none of the North American peoples seem to have had alcoholic beverages of any kind; they used tobacco in late prehistoric times, but whether they were making use of some of the potent hallucinogens and other mind-altering drugs that can be obtained from native plants is information that is just not archaeologically recoverable, at least not at this time.

Another stereotypical aspect of hunters and gatherers is that they led a very tough life, hunting all day for the menfolk and digging roots, collecting berries, and grinding seeds from dawn to dusk for the women and the small children. Not so, say studies of the last remaining descendants of this way of life that survive today, the Australian aborigines and the bushmen of the South African desert, who live in economically marginal lands. Their broad knowledge of the environment and their effective ways of "cropping" it allow them to have a fair amount of time on their hands.

Indeed, when one looks carefully at the archaeological record of the time of transition from hunting and gathering to agriculture, the so-called Neolithic Revolution, as V. Gordon Childe termed it, was no revolution at all, or at least not unless one is prepared to wait several thousands of years for victory after one has taken to the barricades. This same story is repeated in both the Old and New Worlds, although at different times. The implication from both sets of data is that farming, the food-getting method of choice for all right-minded Neoliths, was labor-intensive and not always as successful as the bright images on the seed packages or billboards would have one believe. Seed catalogs are great midwinter reading, but when that searing dry wind comes across the land and kills all the crops, the chilly fall becomes a trying time with empty granaries and sad-eyed children with distended stomachs. Was farming really worth this?

You see the old way was pretty good; there were many options. Such bad weather had come before, in the time of the elders; if one area or one plant was not bearing this season, they would move on; they were not tied to the land as farmers were, and there was always something new over the next rise. Besides, they knew all about storing and drying and thinking about the future long before these fancy farmers moved in with their gaudy pots, new gods, and maybe even beer.

So we can now return to our window in the American Midsouth, on the great rivers that drain the western slopes of the Appalachians, the Ohio, the Cumberland, and the Tennessee. Here, at about 5000 B.C. we find bands of Archaic hunters and gatherers, living a seminomadic life-style that is moving toward a sedentary mode. There is a central base camp to which they return at regular intervals; here we find evidence of repeated occupations and cemetery burials, often by the score. These interments, although simply done in the midden areas where they live, indicate concern for the individual. The burial offerings often seem to show some of the special activities of that person, whether a hunter, a craftsperson, or possibly a medicine man.

There is a wide spectrum of artifacts: crude tools for coarse food processing, finer tools for grinding and polishing, specialized hunting artifacts, and elaborate ground stone atlatl or throwing-stick weights made of specially selected raw materials imported from distant sources. There are elaborate bone tools, well preserved from the soil acids by the numerous shells that make up much of the midden heaps. These bone artifacts also run the gamut from functional awls to long pins bearing elaborately carved and incised designs.

One gets the impression that these were hardly ragged savages running through the woods in search of elusive game animals—they were instead efficient denizens of a land they knew extremely well. They picked and chose from a wide spectrum of plants and animals; in not too many millennia, by 2000 B.C., they would even get a few cultivated plants, gourds and squash from distant strangers far to the south in Mesoamerica, although some *cucurbita* may be of native North American origin. They had already been "playing" with native crops to the extent that the genetic structures of some had been modified so that the seeds were larger and the plants more productive; but they were apparently not tied to the locale by horticulture. They seemed to like these plants, but they were not yet ready to play full-time keepers. There are some analogies for such intermittent plant-man relationships among some known ethnographic groups.

But there are windows open on other areas too; on the New England coast some intrepid mariners went to sea in some sort of craft and caught the delightfully edible offshore prize the swordfish. The distinctive swordfish bills have been found in such numbers at a few Archaic sites that no other explanation seems possible—the only way to take swordfish is by harpoon in deep offshore areas, unless the fish have changed their habits markedly since then. So they must have had seaworthy boats, for which there is not a shred of archaeological data other than the swordfish. You see how slender our lines of evidence can be.

Far across the Great Plains, the inhabitants of the Desert West were putting up with a deteriorating situation. The lakes were almost all dried up, life was getting tougher, yet these Desert Archaic people survived; in the Southwest we call them the Cochise culture, named for the famous old Apache chief who was quite a survivor too. The root and seed collecting continued. Their band numbers were not large, but they knew this harsh land and it was theirs; the sites are scattered and small, the artifacts rather crude but sturdy, except when we luckily find a dry cave. Here we see the delicate and well-fashioned perishables: baskets and bags, strings and snares, clubs and spears. If we could only see into their minds as easily as we sometimes can see their material achievements.

In a much more salubrious situation, where else but that hedonistic spot, California, at about 2000 B.C. would we find a very different aspect of Archaic lifeways. On the banks of the Consumnes River, in central California, not far from Sacramento, the Windmiller culture has been discovered. Known from a number of sites perched on the natural levees of this meandering river, we see a culture that adapted well to this riverine environment.

Most of what we know of the Windmiller culture has come from burials, which are rich in artifacts that display a level of technology very similar to that known from the Southeast, thousands of miles away. Even some of the artifact forms are quite similar: long projectile points with a simple square base and well-crafted ground stone artifacts, not atlatl weights but showing comparable sophistication in technology. Their use is unknown: "charm stones" the archaeologists call them, which just means they don't know. Other remarkable similarities to typical Eastern Archaic artifacts include tubular pipes, worked quartz crystals, and various forms made from steatite (soapstone).

Since the soils are alluvial in this California delta area, stone is a rather rare commodity that must be imported. As a result, there are in the cultural inventory round objects which are hand-modeled from clay, possibly to serve as cooking "stones" for use in earth ovens. Pottery containers, however, are not known anywhere in western North America at this period.

Overall, the Windmiller culture demonstrates a complex level of interaction; lithic raw materials were imported and shells from the coastal region were being traded in and made into ornaments. Indeed, widespread trade in sea shells characterizes the entire West from Archaic times to the Historic. This elaborate Archaic culture served as a foundation for the later developments in the region lasting down to the historic tribes such as the Miwok.

At this same time, about four thousand years ago, the Late Archaic cultures of the Eastern United States were reaching a cultural peak or climax. From the cold Arctic reaches of northern Labrador to the shores of Georgia and Florida caressed by the Gulf Stream, and from the rocky coasts of Maine to the cypress swamps of northern Louisiana, these hunters and gatherers par excellence had established trade communications that cannot be denied. No longer will I speak of "some sort of connections"—the hard goods are there to prove that materials were moving distances that stagger

Windmiller Archaic: California

our conceptions of the archetypical isolated bands of wandering nomadic hunters.

For example, there is a special kind of stone, Ramah chert, known only from quarries in northern Labrador, which is found as chipped stone artifacts of spectacular quality at the Watertown Arsenal on the Charles River not far from where I now write. Specimens of this distinctive stone have been discovered even farther south; what was its value in the Washington, D.C., region after being carried that far at about 2000 B.C.? We can only guess.

Copper came from surface deposits and later from shallow mines in northwestern Michigan, on Isle Royal, and in northeastern Minnesota. It was traded as far south as northern Louisiana—it was cold hammered and beaten into beads and awls. Nearer to the source it became a mainstay of this Late Archaic culture that is called, not very originally, Old Copper.

"Old Copper" Archaic Assemblage

Found in Michigan, Wisconsin, and Minnesota, many of the artifacts are utilitarian spear and knife forms, as well as more ornamental items such as beads, pins, and rings. These copper items must have approached gold in terms of native wealth at this time period: there is a burial cache from southern Indiana that contained dozens of items, necklaces of beads and bracelets that must have been worth a king's ransom in their terms. It is these artifacts that Barry Fell mistakenly calls "Bronze."

Even in staid old New England gaudy objects were used in Late Archaic times: burial practices show an elaboration that was not at all Puritan in nature. Cremation burials contained beautiful slate "bayonets," showing off the banded colors of the raw material, found in the oval burial pits covered with pounds of powdered red ochre—hence the popular name Red Paint culture. Even in the distant offshore islands such as Newfoundland fine representations of these Maritime Archaic climax cultures were found in graves loaded with stone and bone artifacts. In Labrador large houses or contiguous dwellings as much as a hundred feet long have been found for this Late Archaic time period. These folk were beyond simple hovels.

Pottery, that sine qua non of high-status living the world around, seems to have been made first in North America in the coastal area of Georgia and north Florida. From the Savannah River south, rather crudely made ceramic vessels have been found to date before 2000 B.C., and archaeologically we can watch the technology and decoration improve through the next millennium. While the container revolution took place here, another innovation occurred both in New England and in the Southeast. Vessels were carved out of a soft rock, steatite, or soapstone as it is popularly called.

What the stimulus for this nearly synchronous development in containers was remains an open question. That even earlier pottery appears apparently for the first time in Colombia and Peru in South America about 3000 B.C. is a piece of data that cannot be easily tied to the events just discussed, although some have tried. As I have said before, there is no shame in saying we do not have the answer to that question at this time.

Saving the best for last and moving to the locality with which I am most familiar, we end our tour of the Late Archaic at still another enigmatic site: Poverty Point, Louisiana. Located on Bayou Macon about fifteen miles west of the Mississippi River, the site contains earthen monuments of a size and scale larger than any man-made structures at about 1000 B.C. in all of North America; indeed, they would not be exceeded in magnitude for more than two thousand years. They are fantastic, to say the least. The main earthen mound is 70 feet tall and contains more than 200,000 cubic yards of dirt; a second large mound to the north is over 50 feet tall, and there are semicircular earthen enclosures, concentric half-circles, the largest of which has a diameter of 3,960 feet, nearly three-quarters of a mile.

The quantity of artifacts and raw materials at the site beggars the imagination: there are thousands of stone tools and literally millions of baked clay balls, called Poverty Point objects, which likely served as cooking and baking stones, just as did the ones described above for California in the Windmiller culture. The lapidary technology was at a very high level; there are hundreds of stone beads and dozens of rarer emblematic forms, including tiny owls no more than half an inch tall yet perfect in every detail. The raw materials are a litany of imported goods, for example, lead ore (galena) and iron ore (hematite), used as ground stone ornaments, and copper too. Stone for chipped artifacts came from the Ohio Valley and a dozen other distant locations, and steatite from Georgia and Alabama was used for vessels, some with effigies carved on them. Because of the acidity of the soil only a few bone artifacts have been recovered, but those that have been found resemble forms of both Georgia and Tennessee.

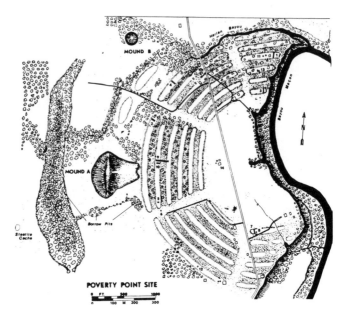

Poverty Point Site, Louisiana

I hope I have made my point—it is a remarkable site—but there are a few more interesting aspects. The first question is about how these people lived. We know little or nothing about their form of habitation; only a few postholes and hearths have been found, and only a very few aspects of their economic lifeway have been discovered at the great ceremonial center, which I have just described. Evidence from a small nearby site indicates a heavy dependence on the prolific riverine supplies of fish and other aquatic creatures. The second question, still unanswered, is why Poverty Point? What could have caused this location to be such a major node in this far-flung Late Archaic trade network? There are no local resources that make this a logical center. What was leaving Poverty Point and going out in exchange to the sources of these exotic trade materials? We can't just guess.

These archaeological questions must be answered in rather different ways. To find out more about Poverty Point lifeways, the humdrum matters such as housing and getting the groceries, standard archaeological data recovery techniques will have to be used. Excavations have gone on at the type site for many years, but many questions remain unanswered. It is a large site, and only a fraction of it has been explored. We can expect to answer that question with better recovery techniques, greater site coverage, and a bit of good luck. Perhaps other sites hold the key.

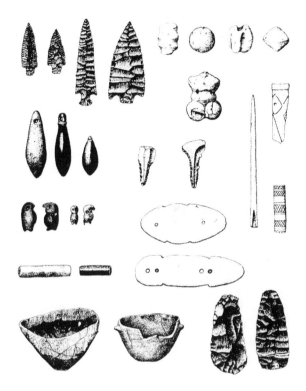

Poverty Point Assemblage

The other question, that of what was happening at Poverty Point to generate the trade position it obviously held, requires a rather different approach. If we were to generate a set of hypotheses, we would want to face the basic geographic question first. Is there something about its location that can help explain its success? Locational analysis is a new way of stating this simple question, and it is of little help here. We can, of course, hypothesize trade in perishable goods that have unfortunately all disappeared: feather robes or even an important but soluble commodity like salt. But lacking documents to spell out the nature of this ephemeral trade, we are just where we began. Some have suggested that "they" were selling old-fashioned religion—like some of the television-aided faith programs of today; again, unless there are specific icons, it will be impossible to prove.

So must we give up the search for an answer to this question, or resort to some of the fantasies that even this site has spawned, such as the interpretation that the clay balls, and there are millions of such fragments, are markers for trade and that there may even be a chance to "read" some of them. No, we can live a little longer with uncertainty and hope that by increasingly careful tracing of the trade networks something in those patterns of distribution will give us a clue as to what that was leaving Poverty Point in outgoing exchange. And yes, luck could play a part too; perhaps along the trade route, a small site, and perhaps not a very spectacular one at that, will by good fortune of preservation show us a trader's outfit, if not a signed bill of lading. Stranger things have happened; insight aided by a fortunate find has made the career of many an archaeologist.

But we must take up our journey through the past again; the time is getting late, and there are fantastic discoveries ahead. Of course, if one uses the concept of culture climaxes, as I have just done for the Late Archaic, then there must be periods of decline, or at the very least, times when the ordinary and the everyday hold forth. Such is the millennium or more before about 500 B.C., when the next climax situation begins to build.

In the eastern United States, this period goes by the stirring name Early Woodland, but an explanation of that dull term need not deter us further. Ceramics, which started in the southern part of the region, spread slowly north with the sorts of changes that are dear to the hearts of ceramophiles. Some of the pottery actually takes up both sides of the container revolution and combines clay with an admixture (*temper,* archaeologists call it) of steatite. If you can't lick them, join them, and so they did.

Lifeways were probably very little different, but the trade and communication networks that sparked the earlier climax were nearly nonexistent. Exotic materials were now what was over the next hill, and the elaborate ceremonialism tied to religion and the death practices either collapsed or took a nonpermanent form. The latter option is what makes archaeologists cringe. Look closely at a huge ceremonial gathering among ethnographic peoples in the recent past, then wave a devastating wand of destruction to all that rot and dampness and insects would destroy, and the lavish ceremonial feast becomes a dull bread-and-water fast—thus it is with archaeological evidence. Thank goodness for stone altars and the rare glimpses we get because of special conditions of preservation. Despite these negatives, the generations rolled by, and no one told the Woodlanders of the great triumphs of the past that saw the elaborate trade connections provide artisans with raw materials not even known at 700 B.C.—copper, for example, dropped out of use almost completely.

By 500 B.C. the use of conical earthen mounds as markers of important tombs began. The Adena people were the makers of the great Grave Creek

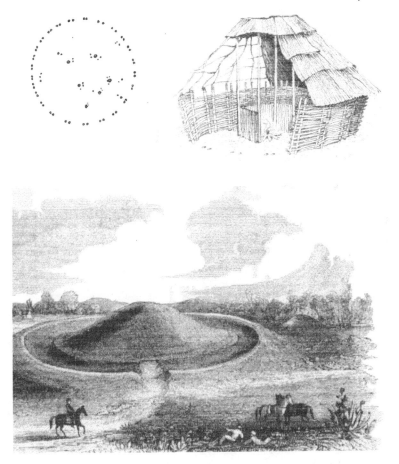

Adena House and Earthworks, Kentucky

Mound in West Virginia. The trade goods of copper and shell found within that mound, purportedly with the infamous stone, signal again the renewal of the far-off connections that tied these cultures into a network of exotic sources. By the time of Christ the second great climax was in place.

In both Ohio and Illinois the Hopewell culture represents the best-known members of this widespread cultural florescence. In Ohio the mounds and especially the geometric earthen embankments are classic expressions of the ceremonial activities of the exuberant Hopewell culture. An early twentieth-century estimate of the amount of earth piled up in these ceremonial structures is an awesome 30 million cubic yards, not a bad day's work by the basketful. These were the mounds and "forts" of the

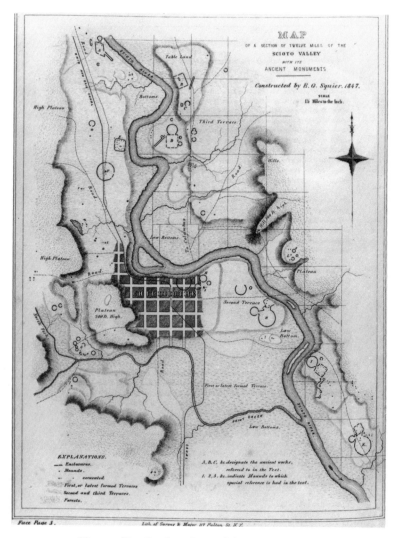

Hopewellian Earthworks on Scioto River, Ohio

Moundbuilders, as they were known to generations of early Ohio Valley residents, whose elaborate interpretations of the relics of this vanished civilization have been the subject of a previous chapter.

Although no "vanished civilization," the Hopewell culture is a very remarkable development that has many aspects worthy of our esteem, even though it lacked the writing system that most commentators require of true civilizations. Also, their system of government as we understand it now was not that of a state but at the most multiple chiefdoms. In art and craft technology they were highly developed, with sculpture in the round in stone, bone, and clay. Using copper, silver, and even some gold, they made extraordinarily complex artifacts in large numbers. They had a special penchant for rare raw materials, and their long-distance trade was to make that of their ancient Archaic ancestors seem small-time in comparison.

The copper and silver came from Michigan and Ontario, but they went even farther afield for other items. From Yellowstone Park in Wyoming came volcanic glass (obsidian) for ceremonial blades, and perhaps from the same area came the large teeth of the grizzly and black bear for special ceremonies. On their western treks, someone must have heard of a strange "rock" in Kansas, for they also collected and used meteoric iron from a meteor fall in central Kansas and from other meteor falls. Sheets of bright mica were fetched from North Carolina; it was then cut, engraved, and painted to be used as sewn-on decorations on elaborate ceremonial garments. Masks and headdresses represented animals such as wolves and deer, and on stone pipes delicate sculptures represented a whole panoply of animals and birds that were of special interest to them, possibly as clan totems. Again, the raw materials were from a variety of sources—chlorite from a cave in Indiana, freshwater pearls probably from the Tennessee and Ohio rivers, hematite and galena from mines in Missouri and northwestern Illinois. Their level of craftsmanship was outstanding.

Much of what we know about Hopewellian culture comes to us from the burials in the conical mounds which the early settlers found so intriguing, and these burial mounds remained in the forefront of interest for the archaeologists as well. Thus, as with Egyptian archaeology, we know more about death practices than we do about everyday life of the Hopewell people. Few houses have been excavated; for many of the elaborate earthwork structures we have to guess where the people may have lived. There were also, at a few sites, flat-topped platform mounds which contrast with the standard conical burial mounds; their exact functions are only now being investigated.

Hopewellian Assemblage

Recent work, especially in Ohio and Illinois, has helped add to our general knowledge of these more mundane aspects of Hopewell culture, but we are still not as clear about the basic economic foundation of this culture as we would like to be. For a time, it seemed obvious that such an elaborate way of life must have an intensive agricultural base with corn as a major crop, but the best evidence today suggests that that was not the case. Some feel that corn may have been grown only as a curiosity. Whatever the true situation, nothing can dim the achievements of these two-thousand-year-old craftspeople who had style enough to silver plate the mouthpieces of some of their ceremonial copper panpipes. Louis Armstrong would have approved, I'm sure.

But, then, "things fall apart; the center cannot hold," as Yeats once said, and the workaday "good gray" cultures took over once again. But before we continue our Eastern odyssey, we must turn briefly to the West, wherein the foundations for the important developments in the American

Hopewellian Pipes and Figurines

Southwest were being laid. There was no Late Archaic climax in the West, but shortly before the time of Christ influences from the important cultures of Mexico were being felt for the first time. Logically, these developments are first seen in southern Arizona in the Gila and Salt valleys near present-day Phoenix; here the stirrings of a great irrigation-based society we call the Hohokam are first noted.

Ceramics made a late arrival in this part of America, almost two thousand years after the fiber-tempered pottery of the Southeast, as Eastern specialists like me are not shy to remind our Western colleagues. The Hohokam owe much more than ceramics to Mexico; later their trade network would bring cast copper bells from there and exotic sea shells from the Pacific coast. The date of significant corn agriculture in the Southwest is now a hotly debated topic, but it surely was there at about the time of Christ.

In the northern part of the area, near the Four Corners region, where Utah, Colorado, Arizona, and New Mexico join, the wonderfully preserved remains of the Basketmaker culture are known from the caves and cliffs of this scenic country with its deep canyons, solitary mesas, and gaudy sunsets. These northern Basketmakers, who first lived in rock shelters and semisubterranean pithouses, were the ancestors of the modern Pueblos. In the south the Hohokam were probably the forerunners of the Pima and Papago tribes. Only in a few areas of this huge country, unfortunately, can we make such certain connections between the modern Native Americans and their ancestors. We will return later to their interesting history and its climax at about A.D. 1000.

Meanwhile, back in the rich Midwestern farmlands, the Woodland Indians were hunting, fishing, and apparently tending domesticated native seed-bearing plants in a horticultural fashion. Far to the south by around A.D. 500 we see activities in north Florida in a ceremonial vein that seem to represent the first beginnings of yet another moundbuilding emphasis that would ultimately spread over most of the eastern United States. These were not primarily burial mounds, although some were used as such; the important functional aspect was that they had a flattened top, upon which structures were built. These buildings on top of the earthen mounds would serve special functions: houses for chiefs and priests and "residences" for honored dead. The mounds were often set around a plaza or sacred area where ceremonial activities were held.

Indeed, this description sounds more than vaguely like something that the Maya or the Aztec would be familiar with. But we are still looking for the close tie-ins to Middle American cultures at this very time. Unlike the Southwest, there are no direct Mexican ties—similar notions, no doubt, but not a shred of physical evidence to prove the point. Ceremonial ideas from these innovative Weeden Island people of northern Florida certainly traveled west to the Lower Mississippi Valley, where, in Louisiana and Mississippi, the Coles Creek Indians were, by A.D. 700, deeply involved with constructing pyramidal earthen mounds arranged around ceremonial plazas.

Farther to the north, near the mouth of the Ohio River, similar ideas were catching on with regard to mounds and presumably some of the ceremonies that went with these earthen structures. By A.D. 1000 another climax would be building, which would again tie together, via lines of trade and communication, much of the eastern half of the country from the Ohio Valley to the Florida peninsula and from the North Carolina piedmont west to the edge of the Oklahoma plains.

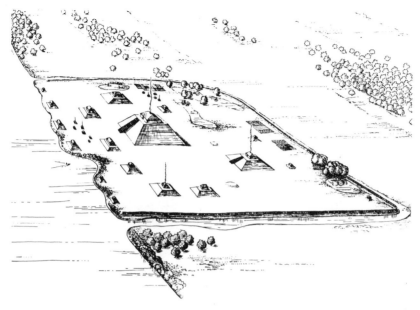

Lake George Site, Mississippi

This "Pan-Southern" tradition is often referred to as Mississippian, and once again, just as in Late Archaic and Hopewellian times, copper became a major ceremonial item that was passed from one center to another. In some cases the objects are of such idiosyncratic design that we are quite sure they were made by the same artist, although one copper repoussé human head is found at the Spiro site on the banks of the Arkansas River in Oklahoma and its mate is found at the Mount Royal site on the St. Johns River in northern Florida. This specific trade connection took place during the century from 1300 to 1400, when the Mississippian climax peak was about over.

What Poverty Point is to the Late Archaic, and what southern Ohio is to the Hopewell, the area in Illinois east of St. Louis, termed the American Bottom, is to the Mississippian climax. Here the largest site with the largest earthen mounds is found: it is Cahokia, and its huge main structure is called Monks Mound, named for some eighteenth-century Trappists who used the mound and noted by Henry Marie Brackenridge on his early visit to this impressive site.

The great mound is one hundred feet tall and contains about 22 million cubic feet of earth. As such it surely bears comparison with some of the largest man-made structures in the Western hemisphere. The site covers some six and one-half square miles and has more than one hundred mounds.

Although some have called it an urban center, Cahokia really lacks the density and scale of population normally required for true urbanism. Population estimates have, over the years, ranged from as high as fifty to sixty thousand to as low as ten thousand. Although such archaeological estimates are, perforce, very difficult to prove or disprove, a consensus in the range of ten thousand people seems reasonable at this time for Cahokia itself; the American Bottom as a whole would have had a much larger number.

Cahokia was definitely a ceremonial center, with very likely a sacred precinct surrounding the major mound group, enclosed by a palisade. There are well-recognized domestic remains, indicating fairly dense occupation in the city center, but these midden deposits and architectural remnants do not cover an area large enough to encompass occupation by thirty or forty thousand people. Recent work within the American Bottom but outside of Cahokia proper has given us the clearest view of the development and expansion of Mississippian culture through time. This work, under contract with the Illinois Department of Transportation, has by its scope and synthesis let us watch whole settlements grow and change in a truly remarkable fashion. The program, termed the I-270 Project, has given archaeology a wonderful new window on the past over a four-thousand-year time scale and is a model of Contract or Salvage Archaeology for which we can all be very grateful.

From the edges of the American Bottom, an alluvial valley of some 175 square miles, we see small villages and farmsteads grow and prosper, with minor mound centers as the focal point of their ceremonial life. There must have been times when much of the population of the whole area came together at Cahokia, but they did not live there permanently.

One other important factor must be taken into consideration when looking at these Mississippian farmers, who were the first intensive corn agriculturalists in the East: they could use only a small portion of the varied alluvial soils that characterize the American Bottom. Today, with drainage ditches, powerful tractors, and effective fertilizers, much of the total area is under cultivation, even the tougher clays; however, in the prehistoric past and even in the eighteenth and nineteenth centuries farming was much more restricted. The rich natural levee soils, sandy loams, were all put under cultivation by Indians and early Anglo settlers alike, but they represent less than a third of the total area. Such a difference in farming capabilities must be factored into our estimates of populations; such limitations show again why the area as it exists today is not a direct guide to the past.

But whatever restrictions their technology may have imposed, these Mississippian village farmers were extremely successful, and they plied their trade in all the rich alluvial bottomlands of the entire Southeastern United States. Again trade networks would be reactivated and in a more comprehensive manner than ever before. One spectacular tomb at Cahokia is an impressive testament to that. It contained at least seventy ceremonially interred individuals, some of whom were young maidens sacrificed at the death of an important leader. Along with the interments and thousands of shell beads were rich tributes from distant chiefs, including bundles (or quivers) of arrows, the variations in the stone projectile points telling the story of long-distance connections to Wisconsin and Oklahoma and places farther to the south. This tomb in Mound 72 at Cahokia is one of the rare views of the lavish Mississippian ceremonies that must have taken place regularly throughout the centuries between A.D. 1000 and 1300.

In contrast to Hopewell, we know quite a lot about the everyday life of these Mississippian folk. They lived in thatch-roofed houses often set in orderly rows in their moderately large villages, which ranged in size from one hundred occupants to minor centers that probably had populations of nearly a thousand. Although they were intensively farming corn, beans, squash, and tobacco, as well as native seeds, they continued to get almost half their groceries from hunting, fishing, and gathering. Some groups seemed to have overdone the corn diet to the extent of putting their health at hazard; this effect is especially obvious in the poor condition of their teeth. Most other Mississippians were in good condition, and populations grew throughout the southern part of the United States.

In each section of this area there were some very large ceremonial centers, but not quite of the scale of Cahokia. They were impressive sites nonetheless, with fifty-foot-high major mounds and a series of smaller mounds arranged around the main plaza. Each region had its own variant of Mississippian culture, but there was exchange in specialized forms such as the copper ritual artifacts already mentioned. Other special items such as engraved marine shells and fancy pottery were decorated with many motifs that were shared throughout the whole area. Whether every symbol meant the same thing to each separate group will never be known, lacking as we do any written documents, but communication was manifestly widespread.

Thanks to a special "window" we can even watch the spread of a group of Mississippians into a new territory, possibly because of the pressure to find additional farmlands. This event took place about A.D. 1275 in southeastern Missouri, from whence a band of Mississippians moved westward

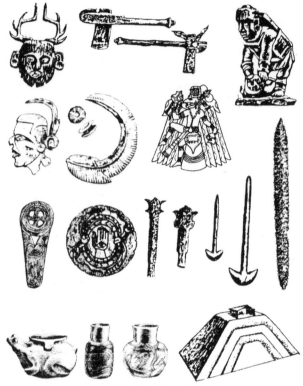

Mississippian Assemblage

into the edge of the Ozarks, perhaps led by a charismatic leader—this is partially fantasy, remember. They took up residence in a region with ridges of sandy soils; after building a major ceremonial center, they established more than half a dozen smaller villages, often set out as nearby pairs. Everything was neat and orderly; the villages were broken up into clan-delimited segments and surrounded by palisades.

Things seemed to be going quite well, but after about three generations (A.D. 1350), the maximum life span of our putative charismatic chief, it all collapsed. The villages were deserted and burned, but not from attacks—the villagers took most of their possessions with them, and no slain villagers were left in the ruins. They moved back toward the main section of the Mississippi Valley from whence they came and apparently were amalgamated with other displaced groups before A.D. 1400. No, we do not know all of this for sure; we are least certain of the casual aspects—why did they go over there in the first place, and why did they leave? But the rest of the tale is based on good archaeological evidence—the makings of a novel, perhaps.

By A.D. 1400, the times they are a-changing all over the East, but before we follow that saga to its end, we must return to the Southwest, where remarkably similar things had been happening. I do not wish to be misunderstood by my use of the word *similar*—what I am saying is that when we compare cultural complexity, scale of villages, and regional interactions we find similarities—no hundred-foot temple mounds in Arizona and no sacred underground ceremonial structures in Illinois, but interesting comparisons from an anthropological point of view.

In the southern Sonoran Desert the Hohokam had taken charge of the Gila and Salt rivers via a major network of irrigation canals and major sites like Snaketown, about twenty-five miles southeast of Phoenix, giving them both political and ceremonial control over a wide area. Their imports from Mexico now included the "ball game," played with rubber balls in a series of well-built courts that stretch all the way north to Flagstaff. Whether any ball players ever went from the bush leagues of Arizona to the majors in Mexico is not known, but such a switch on today's situation is amusing to contemplate. There were major sites with all the trappings of Mexican civilization not far south of the border such as the great site of Casas Grandes in Chihuahua, where stone-faced pyramids and small temples palely reflect the grandeur of ceremonialism far to the south in the Valley of Mexico.

At Snaketown, first excavated by Harold Gladwin and his Gila Pueblo group, there are some very low earthen platforms that just may be related conceptually to these Mexican mounds, but they do not have structures on them. Nevertheless, the Hohokam reached a high level of technical skills on their own. For example, they invented a resist/etching on marine shells using an acid made from a cactus, and their achievements in painted ceramics and stone sculpture are remarkable. To take this desperately arid environment and make it their own was a tremendous achievement; not until twentieth-century irrigation techniques were introduced was as much land again under cultivation. One recent popular magazine article on Hohokam archaeology praised their accomplishments but referred to their dwellings as hovels. In fact, their mud-plastered structures with slightly sunken floors were very satisfactory homes, and they had shady outdoor ramadas or porches for summertime living.

Hohokam culture seems to have reached a peak about A.D. 1000–1200, and then a slow decline set in. By the time of first contact by the Spanish, the innovative irrigation systems were no longer in use. A modest amount

Hohokam Assemblage

of dry farming is possible in some parts of the area; this was the way of life of the Pima and Papago, who used hunting and gathering as a necessary adjunct. The cause for the Hohokam decline is not well understood at this time, but we will return to that question after looking at everyone's favorite group, the Cliff-Dwelling Pueblos.

When we last looked in at these denizens of the Colorado Plateau about A.D. 500, their ancestors, the Basketmakers, were making out all right in this challenging region. Remember, Mesa Verde itself is at six to seven thousand feet, and most of the plateau is at more than six thousand feet. The artifactual remains of these early farmers, called the Basketmakers for their fine craft in woven containers, are truly remarkable: we have wonderfully preserved rabbit-fur robes, fragile ceremonial flutes decorated with bright feathers, and supple woven bags with two- and three-color designs. The climate gives us this fantastic insight into their otherwise perishable artifact inventory.

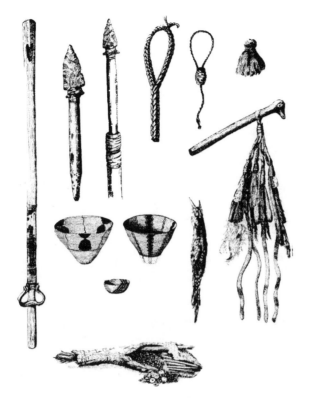

Basketmaker Artifacts

The forest cover that adds the Verde (green) to the Mesa sometimes makes one forget that it is also quite arid, but, of course, there is more rainfall in this high country than in the desert to the south. Dry farming is possible here, and there are usually enough frost-free days (about one hundred are required) to raise corn, beans, and squash, the familiar trio of domesticated plants grown in both the East and the West.

Ceramics came into the Basketmaker-Pueblo continuity at around A.D. 500, and soon the typical black-on-white painted pottery tradition was under way. This format remains one of the longest-lived ceramic traditions that is still extant in North America. Another stereotypical Pueblo trait is that of masonry contiguous-walled structures, and these began about A.D. 800. The first masonry dwellings are on the mesa tops; the movement into the cliffs did not take place until about 1200. Although impressive in extent, it was a short-lived phenomenon.

The international notoriety of the Cliff Dwellings is based on the

Classic Pueblo Assemblage

extraordinary preservation of the structures and is well justified. A modern visitor gets the feeling that the inhabitants moved out yesterday; one can see dried corn cobs and worn-out sandals lying about just where they were left hundreds of years ago. Archaeology does not get any more immediate than that.

So far, I have been talking about Pueblo culture history from the point of view of Mesa Verde, and quite naturally so, for that National Park is one of the best-known archaeological sites in America. But the really impressive early part of the Pueblo story was played out seventy-five miles to the south in northwestern New Mexico in the San Juan Basin at Chaco Canyon National Park. Here, beginning before A.D. 1000 and climaxing by A.D. 1150, was one of the most remarkable developments in American prehistory. They call it, understandably, the *Chaco Phenomenon*, for here in the now arid and treeless canyon grew to fruition a series of large masonry towns most of which line the eastern side of the canyon. The most famous is Pueblo Bonito, but remember it is only the largest and most completely excavated of the ten sites. They started as rather small pueblos but soon increased in size until Bonito and its Chaco Canyon neighbors probably had a population of more than six thousand, all of this development in the space of a few hundred years.

How can we be so sure of the chronology? Recall that this is the place that tree-ring dating was developed, and, despite a few necessary technical caveats, dendrochronology is the most accurate dating method in all of archaeology. Thus we can quite literally "see" the rooms and additional stories being added on to these masonry towns, whose wooden beams give us the great gift of dates. The wood itself is quite a tale: as I said, the region is now virtually treeless, but it was not always so. Timber use and increased aridity caused the situation that we experience today. Even at A.D. 1100, however, there were no large trees growing there of the sort needed for the construction of their largest ceremonial buildings called Great Kivas. These were huge underground rooms often requiring spans of over thirty-five feet. It has been estimated that almost two hundred thousand large beams were carried, not dragged, more than forty-five miles from the mountains to the west and south of Chaco.

Smaller trees, piñon particularly, were then available in the Canyon region; however, when one figures the number of rafters needed just for dwelling-sized structures and the amount of firewood required in this quite cool environment during the fall, winter, and spring, it is easy to understand the scarcity of wood. One must remember, too, that these trees were growing in a semiarid environment; thus this forest cover did not have the ability to regenerate quickly like the fast-growing Southeastern pine woods. With these conditions, one sees clearly the staggering amount of time and effort required for the extraordinary construction activities of the Chaco culture.

But the trek for trees is not the only unusual aspect of Chacoan communications. Thanks to aerial photographs, a series of "roads" has been traced out across the countryside. Since these people had no domestic animals or wheeled vehicles, perhaps the term *paths* would be more appropriate, but whatever we call them, they show long-distance connections tying together major centers far to the north (fifty miles) on the San Juan and Animas rivers, as well as many "outliers"—smaller Chacoan structures, some forty in number, that were part of the Chaco System.

As with some of the other cultural networks discussed before, we are sure they existed; we are less sure just how they functioned—what passed from center to outlier and so forth. We do know that a number of "exotics" are found in the Chacoan system: cast copper bells and macaws (Mexican parrots), raised presumably for their feathers, both imported from Mexico, as well as large quantities of turquoise, which was probably converted into finished products at Chaco after arrival.

But however well the network functioned for a while, and the signs are that it did operate successfully, for one reason or another the Chaco System failed. The big houses were deserted before A.D. 1200; refugees may have moved east and south. Was it a simple cause like drought or disease? It does not seem so. It may have been failure of the system—overextended lines of trade—or even some political or social unrest. We are not sure, but here, as in the East as well, the next few centuries would be dark and treacherous, even without the fearful aliens lurking beyond the horizons of the endless sea.

The Chaco collapse was not shared by their kin to the north, at least not right away. Recent excavations in the Yellow Jacket region a short distance to the northwest of Mesa Verde have added to the complexity of this important area. Here there are huge sites with more total rooms than in all the Cliff Dwellings on the Mesa. One author has suggested that Mesa Verde itself was just the ceremonial area for this very populous region: the pilgrimage area for sacred functions and other activities.

The thirteenth century was the moment of glory for the Mesa Verde region, glorious unless one wishes to dig a little deeper and inquire just why these people spent an inordinate amount of time, labor, and resources to build numerous and sometimes enormous stone structures, dwellings, and kivas—ceremonial rooms—in inaccessible cliff locations. There would seem to be some paranoia here—they built defensive positions to be sure, but who was the enemy?

Two things are clear. First, most of the structures that one now sees at Mesa Verde itself were completed in a span of less than ninety years. To get a sense of this crowded atmosphere, one can take a pair of binoculars and follow the cliff edges and see structure after structure crammed into impossible locations. Second, there is little direct evidence either here or elsewhere in the Southwest of much actual warfare. We know that as the century wound down, there was a drought (1276–99) and changes in rainfall patterns that may have affected crop yields just as markedly as actual decreased precipitation. So life was becoming uncertain; wood was becoming scarce, again as much from overuse as from drought.

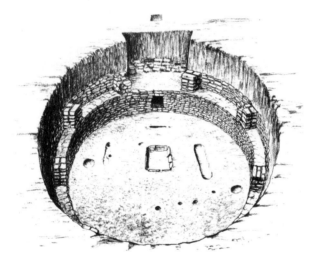

Cliff Dwelling and Pueblo Kiva

The times were perilous with drought and overcrowding. No wonder the people seemed to be afraid of their own shadows, as I feel was probably the case. At one time outside aggressors, such as the Navaho, were thought by archaeologists to have played a significant role in this saga, but now we know they were not even on the scene at the right time. We are left with one other possibility—that the "who" were other groups of Pueblos, their own kinsmen. They were being put in jeopardy by the winds of change in the atmosphere and in their intertribal relationships, which were fragilely dependent on these crucial factors of agricultural production and population size.

And change they did—the north was virtually abandoned, not in a week or a month but over a series of years. The inhabitants seem to have slipped away in small groups, leaving their silent masonry dwellings with open doors and windows staring out on empty canyons. Beautiful pottery vessels and half-filled looms were abandoned. Refugia were sought, found, and briefly occupied where more abundant rainfall and more elbow room made the old lifeways once more possible. But then problems arose again, and the move was on, always further south and often in an easterly direction to the great Rio Grande and its seemingly endless supply of water on a year-round basis. By the mid-1400s most of the Pueblo peoples were in the Rio Grande Valley, with only a few survivors in the west: the Hopi in northern Arizona and the Zuni and a few others in western New Mexico.

The Rio Grande was indeed great—it provided for group aggregation on a level never achieved before, even in the halcyon Chacoan days, and it was a place for survivors, as even contemporary history tells us. The last five hundred years have given the Puebloans time to build traditions in their new homeland. Of course, the Rio Grande Valley was not empty when they came so that today's residents are a mixture of the old inhabitants, Pueblos like themselves, and the newcomers from the north. There are legends of these migrations, and one day archaeologists cooperating with the various tribal groups may be able to sort out the exact history of each contemporary pueblo. That story and the unraveling of the Spanish contact period remain exciting challenges for the coming generation of Southwestern archaeologists, who are already beginning to tackle these problems.

We left the East just as we approached the crucial century for that area too—A.D. 1300 to 1400. Like the Pueblos of Chaco Canyon, the Mississippians at Cahokia were not able to sustain their great ceremonial center in the American Bottom, and a slow decline set in. Here it is less likely to have been related directly to sheer environmental factors. Drought does come to this area but hardly selectively enough to cause Cahokia to decline; the other centers in every direction remained strong and viable at this time. Again systemic matters may be the main casual factors: perhaps they lost control of their trade and interaction routes; perhaps their leaders no longer had the social or political or religious power necessary to continue to control such an extensive domain. "The center did not hold," and by 1350 Cahokia was no longer the great site it had been. The looming mounds still stood, but the temples were empty and the wooden palisades no longer maintained. Population had declined markedly at Center City.

Throughout the southeastern United States Mississippian culture was reaching a climax during the fourteenth century with large ceremonial sites like Spiro in eastern Oklahoma and Etowah in central Georgia exchanging many ritual artifacts and making spectacular interments in some of their earthen mounds. There was little hint of disaster. Manufactures in ceramics, copper, marine shell, and stone were of the highest quality in both art and technology. Populations were expanding and richly endowed cultural "cousins," mixtures of Mississippian and local modes, were being formed around the great central hearthland in the Mississippi Basin. But, as with the Southwest, the decline that started at Cahokia spread irresistibly through neighboring centers in southern Illinois at the mouth of the Ohio and up the Ohio to include the Tennessee and Cumberland rivers.

By A.D. 1450–1500, well before the Spanish explorers under De Soto's command arrived, no more were the grand ceremonial centers, in what I have termed the Vacant Quarter, the nexus of these thriving chiefdoms of the Mississippi Basin. These once grand monumental assemblages were empty. The well-kept earthen pyramids, formerly crowned with sacred temples, grew up in trees and weeds; the buildings atop them were either burned or had collapsed; the tall palisaded walls with numerous bastions surrounding the towns lay scattered and rotting on the ground. The birds and animals took back the broad plazas for their own, and the fertile fields were cane-covered and vine-entangled once again. There was now an echoing silence where throngs of sweating ball players, engaged in an early form of lacrosse, had once noisily been challenged in near life-and-death contests.

Elsewhere in the Southeast, however, things were very different— peaks of activity and population would be reached at the very time (A.D. 1540) of the Spaniards' arrival. It was not a period of decline; trade networks were still in place and would remain so for a century or more after that first Spanish contact. Population aggregations would swell on the

Mississippi just south of the Vacant Quarter and reach new heights, just as they did at this very same time in the Southwest on the Rio Grande. But the end was definitely in sight.

For a sensitive treatment of the coming peril I turn to another well-known science fiction writer, Ray Bradbury, who echoes some of the very thoughts with which Chad Oliver led off this chapter. Bradbury in *Perhaps We Are Going Away* takes us imaginatively to the Florida coast in the 1520s, where a pair of concerned watchers lurk by the sea.

> Far ahead, a single light burned on the shore.
> With the moon rising, the Old Man and the rabbit boy padded on the sands, heard strange voices in the sea, smelled wild burnings from the now suddenly close fire.
> They crawled on their bellies. They lay looking in at the light.
> And the more he looked, the colder Ho-Awi became, and he knew that all the Old Man had said was true.
> For drawn to this fire built of sticks and moss, which flickered brightly in the soft evening wind which was cooler now, at the heart of summer, were such creatures as he had never seen.
> These were men with faces like white-hot coals, with some eyes in their faces as blue as sky. All these men had glossy hair on their cheeks and chins, which grew to a point. One man stood with raised lightning in his hand and a great moon of sharp stuff on his head like the face of a fish. The others had bright round tinkling crusts of material cleaved to their chests which gonged slightly when they moved. As Ho-Awi watched, some men lifted the gonging bright things from their heads, unskinned the eye-blinding crab shells, the turtle casing from their chests, their arms, their legs, and tossed these discarded sheaths to the sand. Doing this, the creatures laughed, while out in the bay stood a black shape on the waters, a great dark canoe with things like torn clouds hung on poles over it. . . .
> This was the terrible weather. This was how the summer would end. This made the birds wheel south, shadowless, through a grieving land.
> No! Go back! cried the boy, to the empty sky, the birds unseen, the unshadowed air. Summer, stay!
> No use, said the Old One's single hand, moving by itself. Not you or me or our people can stay this weather. It is a season changed, come to live on the land for all time. (Bradbury, 1965: 71–74)

It surely would never be the same again. No matter the intent of those who would follow, the result would be the same for the Native Americans. Their lands would be taken, their peoples decimated, their religious beliefs smothered. There would be Massacre Cave, broken treaties, the Trail of Tears, Little Big Horn, and Wounded Knee, to name just a few points in that sad saga. And yet there are survivors, don't forget that!—but only a fraction of the millions who once owned this hemisphere, who had discovered it, tamed it, and raised great cultures here throughout thousands of years.

I have briefly laid out the bare outlines of the fantastic story of individual skills and collective greatness that is the archaeological past of North America as we now know it, a narrative history of the Native Americans of this continent. Therefore, forget Fantastic Archaeology—this is the real fantasy!

Acknowledgments

As with any protracted piece of research, one generates an indebtedness first to the other scholars who have dealt with the same problem before, and next to those closer at hand who have aided one in the difficult task of research, discovery, and learning about a multidimensional field of inquiry such as this one.

My first formal introduction to the subject that I have called Fantastic Archaeology was via Robert Wauchope's pioneering and scholarly volume *Lost Tribes and Sunken Continents* (1962), in which the finely crafted prose may still hide from some readers the breadth of special knowledge that he had attained. I have reread it several times during the past few years with increasing awareness of its thorough coverage, to which all subsequent scholars are indebted. I only wish that I could now discuss my current interests with this fine old friend and former Southeastern archaeological crony.

More recently, other significant volumes have taken up the topic with a broader scope and in a very meaningful way: Peter White's *The Past Is Human* (1974) and Charles Cazeau and Stewart Scott's *Exploring the Unknown: Great Mysteries Reexamined* (1979). My friend and former colleague Jerry Sabloff has contributed a *Scientific American* reader, *Archaeology: Myth and Reality* (1982), and William Steibing has made an important contribution with his well-documented *Ancient Astronauts, Cosmic Collisions and Other Popular Theories About Man's Past* (1984). I have used all of these as texts in my courses, and they have been intellectually stimulating and bibliographically contributing.

A relatively small group of like-minded colleagues in American anthropology have also been important voices on this difficult topic with their sound journal articles and trenchant book reviews on the subject: John Cole, Ken Feder, William Fitzhugh, Ives Goddard, Frank Hole, Marshall McKusick, William Rathje, Dean Snow, Dennis Stanford, and Gordon Willey. Kenneth Feder has also now contributed a text—*Frauds, Myths, and Mysteries: Science and Pseudoscience in Archaeology* (1990). I am deeply indebted to all of them as well.

If one were to pick one commentator who has led the whole archaeological profession toward an understanding of the significance of facing the challenge of Fantastic Archaeology, it would be Glyn Daniel. From his editorial desk at *Antiquity*, the British journal whose first editor, O.G.S. Crawford, set a precedent with his battle against the wild discoveries at Glozel in France, Glyn commented often and with strong words against "fringe or alternative archaeology." His interest in and support of this volume is most gratefully acknowledged; he urged me to write this book, even if I could not accept his suggested title, "Myth America." Another's pun is hard to adopt.

Glyn also wrote me favorably on an early version of part of this work; I can't describe how meaningful that support became when I had some difficulty finding a final resting place for the completed manuscript. My regret is therefore strong that he did not live to see either the final version of this manuscript or the printed volume. But I raise a posthumous toast in fine vintage wine, French to be sure, to the memory of that always helpful friend and staunch foe of illogical flights of archaeological fantasy: Glyn Daniel.

I definitely owe the start of this long process toward a serious study of this phenomenon to a suggestion made some years ago by my former colleague Geoffrey W. Conrad. He and I team-taught Introductory Archaeology at Harvard. In that course he regularly "performed" with me in a skit I had written for a one-lecture introduction to the subject of Fantastic Archaeology. One day over lunch in my lab he remarked on its obvious success with the undergraduates. Just as he made the further suggestion of a full course treatment for the subject, the phone rang as if on cue, and yet another nagging inquiry came in on a Fantastic topic. As I put down the phone, he said, "I told you so." This volume is but one result of his gentle push in a new direction for me. I hope that he can take some pride in this eventual outcome; I thank him for it.

As I began to get seriously involved in Fantastic Archaeology by generating an undergraduate course on the subject, I had the help and wise counsel of a number of Harvard graduate students both as summer assistants and as Teaching Fellows. John Hoopes began our foray into the tangled web of case studies, unlikely finds, and unusual personalities in the summer of 1982 with support from the Dean's Special Funds for course generation. Mike Geselowitz, Mike Toplyn, Steve Black, Grant Hall, Li Pai, Steve Pendery, Gloria Greis, Fred Hiebert, Mat Murray, Curt Sandberg, Rob Tykot, Ian Kuijt, and Ken Sasaki all have helped guide the course as

Teaching Fellows with useful suggestions, bibliographic additions, and tempered enthusiasm for a walk on the wilder side of archaeology. A number of Harvard undergraduates also aided in this research as Faculty Aides during the summers and regular term time; most memorable were Mark McKay and Nicole Rousmaniere, who served admirably in such positions, searching out obscure references and keeping some order in my research notebooks.

I am also, of course, indebted to the more than five hundred Harvard undergraduates and Extension students who have joined me in this inquiry into "Alternative Views of the Past" during the past years. Their interest, their questioning, and their accomplishments in their term papers have helped me immeasurably, especially in the area of bibliographic sources in a field in which pertinent data are often sequestered in some very strange nooks and crannies.

A number of my friends and colleagues read parts of this manuscript with care and offered helpful suggestions, many of which I have followed. I am grateful to all of them for their willingness to perform such an onerous act of unrewarded generosity: John S. Belmont, Jeffrey P. Brain, Ian W. Brown, Douglas E. Coulter, Stephen J. Gould, James B. Griffin, Vance Haynes, Jesse D. Jennings, T. R. Kidder, Richard Marius, Bruce D. Smith, Albert C. Spaulding, and Gordon R. Willey.

The final work of manuscript editing and more has fallen to those wonderful young people that a professor may seem to take for granted: Larry Magid was not an anthropology concentrator but a good critic and a very fair judge of the writer's intent, not to mention maker of indexes and lists of illustrations. Chris Fung, a graduate student in the department, proofed and commented wisely on a much cleaner version. Ayesha Owens and Jennifer Donaldson did the tedious work on text and illustrations under the gun of a summer deadline with great care and good cheer. Because of my faithful DEC computer on which I logged over four hundred hours I do not have to give special thanks to a weary but careful typist.

The conclusion of my five-year labor with this volume came finally with the encouraging interest of Acquisitions Editor Patricia Reynolds Smith of the University of Pennsylvania Press. What sweet relief to find Glyn's faith in me and the volume finally justified. I am also most grateful to the careful and helpful ultimate readings by Bruce D. Smith and James B. Stoltman at the end of the line.

The final translation of a manuscript into a printed volume has been accomplished with the help of copy editor Trudie Calvert and members of the University Press staff including Ruth Veleta. Here at Peabody, one last summer found helpful students and staff ready to attack the carcass of the "monster" manuscript with good will and a clear eye: staff assistant Roy R. Robson and students: William Griswold, Arnetta Girardeau, Bryan Geon, and Penny Drooker. The final touches in proofing and indexing were carefully applied here by Michelle Graham; at the Press there was excellent closing aid by Alison Anderson. My most appreciative thanks to all these helpful individuals.

I wish to acknowledge and show my appreciation for the strong and necessary support of my intellectual efforts for more than a decade by three very special friends who have made possible my research in many areas, this topic included, with concern and great understanding:

to Albert H. Gordon and the Gordon-Rousmaniere Fund, whose help has included a special subvention for the publication of this volume;

to Joan T. Cave and the Margaret C. Tozzer Fund, Harvard University, whose father certainly understood the problem addressed in this volume all too well; and

to Doris Z. Stone and the Zemurray Foundation, who knows very well the weight of authorship from long personal experience.

All of your generosity has been extraordinary. I only hope the outcome has been satisfactory.

Finally, to three of my mentors in the field of real archaeology, my gratitude for their special teaching of what has turned out to be very essential qualities for this research: Irving Rouse of Yale, who did not suggest "question authority" but rather taught one never to speak authoritatively on a subject without having read the original sources—thanks, Ben; James B. Griffin of Michigan, who never took anything for granted and spoke out strongly (but with some compassion) when he saw nonsense paraded as archaeological fact—thanks, Jimmy; and finally Philip Phillips of Harvard, who showed me where intellectual curiosity could lead and who has wisely counseled restraint in word and deeds after a very thorough consideration of all the facts in the case—thanks, Phil. I hope I have not disappointed any of you with this effort.

S. W.

Cambridge, Mass.
June 1990

Endnotes

INTRODUCTION
   1. Daniel 1979: 3.
   2. Sharer and Ashmore 1979: 545.
   3. Shaw 1906: 56.

CHAPTER 1: Byways of Fantastic Archaeology
   1. Boulding 1980: 832.
   2. Gardner 1957: 8.
   3. Evans 1946: 260.
   4. Pope Pius XII 1950: lvii.
   5. Evans 1946: 274.

CHAPTER 2: American Curiosity and the American Indian
   1. Imlay 1793: 282.
   2. Boorstin 1965: 362.
   3. Atwater 1820: 107.
   4. Atwater 1820: 195.
   5. Atwater 1820: 213.
   6. Atwater 1820: 240–41.
   7. Stanton 1960: 83.
   8. Haven 1856: 158.
   9. Haven 1856: 158.
   10. Haven 1856: 159.
   11. Haywood 1823: 112.
   12. Boewe 1982: 15.
   13. Munsell, as quoted in Boewe 1982: 16.
   14. Priest 1833: iv.
   15. Pidgeon 1858: 39.
   16. Pidgeon 1858: 112.
   17. Pidgeon 1858: 161.
   18. Pidgeon 1858: 177.
   19. Pidgeon 1858: 326.
   20. Lewis 1886: 69.

CHAPTER 3: The Golden Age
   1. Peabody 1868: 26.

CHAPTER 4: The American Humbug
   1. Cole 1955: 8.
   2. Schoolcraft 1845: 387.

3. Mallery 1886: 250.
4. Haven 1856: 134 note.
5. Read 1879: 139 note.
6. Read 1879: 140–41.
7. Read 1879: 148.
8. Fell 1976: 21.
9. MacDougall 1958: 125.
10. Farquharson 1877: 103.
11. Fell 1976: 268.

CHAPTER 5: The Walam Olum
1. Rafinesque 1836a: 319.
2. Pennell 1942: 31.
3. Rafinesque 1824: 23.
4. Rafinesque 1836b: 151.
5. Brinton 1885: 150.
6. Brinton 1885: 151.
7. Rafinesque 1824: 14.
8. Rafinesque 1838: 21.
9. Brinton 1885: 154, 155–58
10. Lilly 1954: 211, note 9.
11. Brinton 1885: 158.

CHAPTER 6: The Earliest Americans
1. Putnam 1890: 468.
2. Meltzer and Sturtevant 1983: 340.
3. Cresson 1890: 469.
4. *Philadelphia Inquirer,* Sept. 8, 1894.
5. Kraft and Thomas 1976: 761.

CHAPTER 7: Catastrophism: Sunken Continents
1. Donnelly 1883: 359.
2. De Camp 1954: 43.
3. Allen 1971: iv.
4. Meade 1980: 413.
5. Meade 1980: 9.
6. Churchward 1926: 27.
7. Churchward 1926: 30.
8. Churchward 1926: 33.
9. Churchward 1926: 43.
10. De Camp 1954: 50.

CHAPTER 8: Archaeology and Religion
1. James [1884], quoted in Brandon 1984: 77.
2. Eddy 1875: 109.
3. Whittlesey 1872: 3.

4. Alrutz 1980. I have relied heavily on his detailed account.

5. Alrutz 1980: 46.

6. *Newark Advocate,* April 15, 1864.

7. Alrutz 1980: 48.

8. Thomas 1971: 128.

9. Emerson, in Kelsey 1908: 50.

10. Talmage 1911: 12.

11. Etzenhouser 1910: 4.

12. Kelsey 1911: 28.

CHAPTER 9: Westward to Vinland

1. Winsor 1889: 93.

2. Lowell 1900: 313.

3. Minnesota Historical Society Museum Committee 1915: 268.

4. Holand 1911: 267–69.

5. Minnesota Historical Society Museum Committee 1915: 286.

6. Thalbitzer 1951: 38.

7. Gjessing 1909: 114.

8. Winsor 1889: 98.

9. Horsford 1889: 12.

10. Olson 1891: 6.

11. Tushingham 1966: 15.

12. Winsor 1889: 104.

13. Winsor 1889: 104.

14. Carlyle 1837, as quoted by Professor Francis M. Rogers of Harvard in Dighton Rock Museum pamphlet (1977).

15. Wallace 1971: 172.

16. Wallace 1971: 174.

CHAPTER 10: Across the Sea They Came

1. Haury and Reid 1985: 271–72.

2. Hooton, in Gladwin 1947: xi.

3. Gladwin 1957: 346.

4. "Harvard Memorial Minutes," 1940.

5. Wiener 1920: foreword.

6. Wiener 1926: xxvii.

7. Mahan 1977: 5.

CHAPTER 11: Tales the Rude Monuments Tell

1. Vescelius 1956: 13–14.

2. Vescelius 1982–83: 2–16, 28–42, 59–67.

3. Fell 1976: 91.

4. Daniel 1977: 8–12.

5. Fell 1976: 84.

6. Fell 1976: 177.

7. Fell 1976: 169.

8. Fell 1976: 171.
9. Fell 1976: 175.
10. Fell 1976: 90.
11. Fell, 1975: ix.
12. Carter 1980: 58.
13. Fell 1980: 386.
14. Carter 1981: 35.
15. Carter 1981: 36.
16. Carter 1980: 322–23.
17. Carter 1981: 37.
18. Carter 1981: 53.

CHAPTER 12: Psychic Archaeology
1. Goodman 1977: 36.
2. Thomas 1979: 287.
3. Goodman 1981: 214.
4. Cole 1985: 602.
5. Sharer and Ashmore 1979: 545.

Epigraphs and Extracts: Sources

Page 1: Priestley, J. B. *Delight* (New York: Harper & Bros., 1949): 52.

Page 5: Daniel, Glyn. *Cambridge and the Back-looking Curiosity: An Inaugural Lecture* (Cambridge: Cambridge University Press, 1976): 29.

Page 11: Daniel, Glyn. "Editorial." *Antiquity* 36, no. 142 (1962): 167.

Page 12: Daniel, Glyn. "Editorial." *Antiquity* 36, no. 142 (1962): 167.

Page 13: Eiseley, Loren. *Night Country* (New York: Scribners, 1971): 81.

Page 28: Jefferson, Thomas. *Notes on the State of Virginia* [1787], William Paden, ed. (New York: W. W. Norton, 1982): 100.

Page 38: Brackenridge, Henry M. Letter to Thomas Jefferson [1813]. *Transactions of the American Philosophical Society,* new series 1, no. 7 (1818): 158–59.

Page 61: Powell, John W. *12th Annual Report of the Bureau of Ethnology* (Washington, DC: Government Printing Office, 1894): xli.

Pages 61–62: Powell, John W. *12th Annual Report of the Bureau of Ethnology* (Washington, DC: Government Printing Office, 1894): xli.

Page 77: Barnum, P. T. *The Humbugs of the World* (New York, 1865): 20.

Page 98: Rafinesque, Constantine S. *Life of Travels* (Philadelphia, 1836a): 93.

Pages 109–10: Rafinesque, Constantine S. *The Ancient Monuments of North and South America,* 2d ed. (Philadelphia, 1838): 28.

Page 116: George Peabody. "Letter of Gift" [1866], in *First Annual Report of the Trustees of the Peabody Museum of Archaeology and Ethnology* (Cambridge, Massachusetts: Peabody Museum Press, 1868): 26.

Page 130: Old Testament, Genesis 7:12.

Page 134: Donnelly, Ignatius. *Atlantis: The Antediluvian World* (New York, 1882): 65.

Page 136: Donnelly, Ignatius. *Ragnarok: The Age of Fire and Gravel* (New York, 1883): 227.

Page 143: Meade, Marion. *Madame Blavatsky* (New York: G. P. Putnam's Sons, 1980): 415.

Page 144: Blavatsky, Helena. *Isis Unveiled* [1877] (Point Loma, California: Aryan Theosophical Press, 1919): 595.

Page 146: Churchward, James. *The Lost Continent of Mu* (London: Neville Spearman, 1926): v.

Page 147: Churchward, James. *The Lost Continent of Mu* (London: Neville Spearman, 1926): 23.

Page 155: de Camp, L. Sprague. *Lost Continents: The Atlantis Theme in History, Science and Literature* (New York: Dover Publications, 1954): 277.

Page 156: Smith, Joseph. Book of Mormon [1830] (Salt Lake City, Utah: The Church of Jesus Christ of Latter Day Saints, 1974): xiv.

Page 180: Kelsey, Francis W. "Some Archaeological Forgeries from Michigan." *American Anthropologist* 10, no. 1 (1908): 56.

Page 189: Bancroft, George. *United States,* vol. 3 (Boston: Little, Brown, 1840): 313.

Page 192: Lowell, James Russell [fictional Rev. Wilbur]. "Speech of Honorable Preserved Doe in Secret Caucus." From *The Biglow Papers,* Second Series, no. 5. In *The Writings of James Russell Lowell,* vol. 9 (Boston: Houghton Mifflin, 1900): 314–15.

Page 224: Gladwin, Harold. *History of the Ancient Southwest* (Portland, Maine: Bond Wheelwright, 1957): xiv.

Page 229: Gladwin, Harold. *Men Out of Asia* (New York: McGraw-Hill, 1947): xiv–xv.

Page 234: Gladwin, Harold. *Men Out of Asia* (New York: McGraw-Hill, 1947): 361.

Page 237: Gladwin, Harold. *History of the Ancient Southwest* (Portland, Maine: Bond Wheelwright, 1957): 346.

Page 253: Wiener, Leo. *Maya and Mexican Origins* (New Haven, Connecticut: Yale University Press, 1926): xxvii.

Page 257: Fell, Barry. "Ancient Vermont." *Proceedings of the Castleton Conference* [1977], Warren L. Cook, ed. (Rutland, Vermont: Academic Books, 1978): 95.

Page 267: Fell, Barry. *America B.C.: Ancient Settlers in the New World* (New York: Quadrangle/The New York Times Book Co., 1976): 177.

Pages 277–78: Carter, George. *Earlier Than You Think: A Personal View of Man in America* (College Station: Texas A&M University Press, 1980): 317.

Page 286: Schwartz, Stephan. *The Secret Vaults of Time* (New York: Grosset & Dunlap, 1978): 290.

Page 305: Boulding, Kenneth. "Science: Our Common Heritage." *Science* 207, no. 4433 (1980): 832.

Pages 306–7: Oliver, Chad. *The Winds of Time* (Garden City, New York: Doubleday, 1957): 133–37.

Page 344: Bradbury, Ray. "Perhaps We Are Going Away." In *The Machineries of Joy* (New York: Bantam Books, 1965): 71–74.

Selected and Annotated Bibliography

Because this volume is designed for the general reader, I have judged it reasonable to give good but not comprehensive coverage of the materials upon which the data and their interpretation rest. I have also tried to make sure that both sides of each question are adequately represented in this section.

INTRODUCTION: General Works on Fantastic Archaeology
I have set forth the background reading for the general topic of Fantastic Archaeology in my Acknowledgments section, with the works by Robert Wauchope (1962), Peter White (1976), Jeremy Sabloff (1982), Charles Cazeau and Stuart Scott (1979), and William Stiebing (1984) noted as particularly helpful. A more recent volume entitled *Cult Archaeology and Creationism* edited by Francis B. Harrold and Raymond A. Eve (1987) looks at a number of aspects of the topic and includes an article "Fantastic Archaeology, What Should We Do About It?" by this author, which has a current bibliography including journal articles on the subject. I have written a journal article as well (Williams 1988).

With regard to frauds in archaeology, a major subtopic of this volume: Robert Munro's *Archaeology and False Antiquities* (1905) is an early analysis of the problem. More recent works include Sonia Cole's *Counterfeit* (1955) and Adolf Reith's *Archaeological Fakes* (1970). There is some number of journal articles on this subject (Witthoft, 1960), but overall this is a somewhat neglected area of concern, with the strong exception of the Piltdown case.

CHAPTER 1: Byways of Fantastic Archaeology
I have found Kenneth Boulding's article "Science: Our Common Heritage" (1980) very instructive and valuable in the general area of scientific methodology. In the area of general pseudoscience I have found the short and amusing volume *Science and Unreason* by Daisie Radner and Michael Radner (1982) to be especially informative. It contains a guide to the pseudoscientific and a checklist of characteristic methods of befuddlement often found in that genre. There are, of course, many other sources on pseudoscience, ranging from "The Fine Art of Baloney" by Carl Sagan (1987) to the recent work of longtime skeptic Martin Gardner, *The New Age: Notes of a Fringe-Watcher* (1987). Gardner's earlier works are valuable too: *Fads and Fallacies in the Name of Science* (1957) and *Science: Good, Bad and Bogus* (1981).

The fascinating topic of problems with perception is well discussed by Gary Wells and Elizabeth F. Loftus, *Eyewitness Testimony: Psychological Perspectives* (1984). The question of veracity in science has been addressed at length by William Broad and Nicholas Wade in *Betrayers of the Truth* (1982), with special emphasis on recent cases in the biomedical field. Argumentation over the interpretation of paleoanthropological data is presented in an interesting manner by Roger Lewin in *Bones of Contention* (1987), which has some very strong implications for archaeology as well.

A good brief introduction to archaeological methods and practices can be found either in Wendy Ashmore and Robert Sharer's *Discovering Our Past: A Brief Introduction to Archaeology* (1988) or in Brian Fagan's *Archaeology: A Brief Introduction* (1983). I have used both in my course on Fantastic Archaeology and they are available in paperback.

The source for "The Tale of the Tub" is Bergen Evans's *The Natural History of Nonsense* (1946). In June 1979, Glyn Daniel delivered his presidential address to the Royal Anthropological Society in the presence of H. R. H. The Prince of Wales. Its title was "The Forgotten Milestones and Blind Alleys of the Past." I have stolen, in feeling only, a bit from that Housman quote that Glyn used for my chapter title.

CHAPTER 2: American Curiosity and the American Indian

The history of American archaeology is a rather new subject, but the best current summary is to be found in Gordon Willey and Jeremy Sabloff's *A History of American Archaeology* (1980); an older but still useful presentation is found in James Fitting's edited volume *The Development of North American Archaeology* (1973). Two even older works, which remain monuments to their authors' broad knowledge and excellent critical judgment, are Irving Hallowell's "The Beginnings of Anthropology in America" (1960) and Justin Winsor's *Critical and Narrative History of America* (1889), especially volume 1. I have used both as mainstays for sources and timely comment. Samuel Haven's groundbreaking *Archaeology of the United States* (1856) provides a clear view of mid-nineteenth-century attitudes and is, like Winsor's work, amazingly comprehensive.

John Jakle's *Images of the Ohio Valley* (1977) provides a broad economic and intellectual background of the area under consideration. I have made great use of Lee Huddleston's insightful review *Origins of the American Indians* (1967), which provides a critical interpretation of the intellectual background of thoughts about the American Indians. Caleb Atwater's "Descriptions of the Antiquities Discovered in the State of Ohio and Other Western States" (1820) was part of the first volume published by the American Antiquarian Society. Squier and Davis are well-known figures, as is their famous *Ancient Monuments of the Mississippi Valley* (1848); William Stanton's excellent volume *The Leopard's Spots* (1960) provides one with a very valuable view of Squier, especially his more aggressive and manipulative side.

The first volumes reviewed as being part of the Fantastic Archaeology genre are John Haywood's *Natural and Aboriginal History of Tennessee* (1823), Josiah Priest's *American Antiquities and Discoveries in the West* (1883), and William Pidgeon's *Traditions of De-Coo-Dah and Antiquarian Researches* (1858). For comments on Haywood see the 1959 reprinting with an Introduction by Mary U. Rothrock and archaeological notes by Madeline Kneberg. The topic of European coins in New World contexts has been recently addressed by Jeremiah Epstein in "Pre-Columbian Old World Coins in America: An Examination of the Evidence" (1980). For Priest see Winthrop Duncan's detailed study in the *Proceedings of the American Antiquarian Society* (1934).

It is interesting to note, as none seem to have, that Priest was a strong racist; his antiabolitionist volume, *Slavery, as it Relates to the Negro* (1845), retitled *Bible Defence of Slavery* (1852), is quite shocking, although I must confess I am not as familiar with that bibliography as I might be. Pidgeon took the rather standard view of the light-skinned Moundbuilder versus the red Indians; he also believed the mixture of the black and white races would cause the extinction of both.

Some valuable critical comment on nineteenth-century archaeology, especially on the Pidgeon volume, comes from a rather unlikely source, Robert Silverberg, better known for his science fiction works. However, Silverberg's *Moundbuilders of Ancient America* (1968) is a well-researched piece of historical work for the most part, showing weaknesses only in the area of current archaeological conceptions of Hopewell and Mississippian cultures.

Glyn Daniel's many excellent volumes on the history of archaeology, including *A Short History of Archaeology* (1981) and *A Hundred and Fifty Years of Archaeology* (1976) provide a comprehensive view of developments in the discipline, especially good on the Old World side. See also Geoffrey Bibby's engaging classic *Testimony of the Spade* (1956).

CHAPTER 3: The Golden Age

The post–Civil War period is mostly the story of the archaeological programs of the Smithsonian and the Harvard Peabody Museum. For the former see the Smithsonian Classics reprint of Cyrus Thomas's *Report on the Mound Explorations of the Bureau of Ethnology* ([1894] 1985), with Bruce Smith's new detailed Introduction. John Wesley Powell has been much written about; I find the biography by William C. Darrah, *Powell of the Colorado* (1951), one of the most helpful for insight into his archaeological interests, although a more detailed study of this aspect of this complex and significant figure is surely needed. Curtis Hinsley's recent *Savages and Scientists* (1984) focuses strongly on his administrative activities, not on his intellectual concern for the past.

Frederic Ward Putnam of Harvard, the other major participant, has not been as comprehensively written about. Ralph Dexter has written many short articles on Putnam: J. O. Brew's *Early Days of the Peabody Museum at Harvard University* (1966) and his Introduction to *One Hundred Years of Anthropology* (1968) are important sources, as is, of course, Gordon Willey and Jeremy Sabloff's *A History of American Archaeology* (1980).

John Wells Foster was the author of two pertinent volumes: *The Physical Geography of the Mississippi Valley* (1869) and the more archaeological *Pre-Historic Races of the United States* (1873). Silverberg (1968), among others, has commented critically on Foster. Clarence Bloomfield Moore was quite a different sort. His shelf of publications on Southeastern archaeology is a foundation block for the prehistory of the area. For a contemporary view on the skeletal remains of the Moundbuilders, see Stephen Jay Gould's *The Mismeasure of Man* (1981).

CHAPTER 4: The American Humbug

P. T. Barnum has been much written about; the best biography so far is that by Nell Harris, *Humbug: The Art of P. T. Barnum* (1973). I have mentioned Barnum's own book *The Humbugs of the World* (1865) in the text.

The first major problem case discussed is that of the Grave Creek Mound and its inscribed stone. In the ranks of believers we find the discoverer Abelard Tomlinson; he is joined (1845) and then deserted (1851–57) by Henry Rowe Schoolcraft; the most ardent current supporter is Barry Fell. Those calling it a fraud include John W. Foster, Charles Whittlesey, Matthew Canfield Read, and Cyrus Thomas. Read produced a significant test in his article "Inscribed Stone of Grave Creek Mound" (1879). Whittlesey's work "The Grave Creek Inscribed Stone" (1879) is especially significant for the on-site data it recorded. Among the recent doubters include Robert Silverberg.

The Cardiff Giant has been called the "greatest hoax of all time" by Curtis D. MacDougall in *Hoaxes* (1958). Other detailed discussions of this well-known find are in James Taylor Dunn's "The Cardiff Giant Hoax" (1948) and Barbara Franco's "The Cardiff Giant: A Hundred Year Old Hoax" (1969).

The Davenport Tablets were excavated by the Reverend Jacob Gass and accepted as genuine by him. Robert J. Farquharson and Charles Putnam (no relation to F. W.) of the Davenport Academy of Sciences were strong supporters of their authenticity. The most outspoken critic was Henry Henshaw of the Smithsonian. Frederic W. Putnam received the photos that illustrate the tablets in this volume from Farquharson and wrote to him on February 15 and 23, 1877, saying he thought they were frauds. Cyrus Thomas, of course, held the strong Smithsonian line against the tablets. McKusick, cited below, provides detailed documentation of these presentations.

Marshall McKusick's book *The Davenport Conspiracy* (1970) was the classic debunking of the tablets. A revised edition is entitled *The Davenport Conspiracy Revisited* (1990). Silverberg (1968) has given a thoughtful exposition of this institutional clash, though he sides with the debunkers. Barry Fell, in *America B.C.: Ancient Settlers in the New World* (1976), and others in his Epigraphic Society still maintain that the tablets are genuine and have offered translations of the inscriptions.

CHAPTER 5: The Walam Olum

Constantine Rafinesque has been written about often and with gusto, most frequently with regard to his botanical works. Unfortunately, no one has discussed at length his contributions to archaeology, which were considerable. He is a controversial character, as I have suggested in the text, but some individuals have committed long and diligent hours of research to try to give his work a fair evaluation. For major biographies, see Richard Ellsworth Call's *The Life and Writings of Rafinesque* (1895) and Thomas Jefferson Fitzpatrick's *Rafinesque: A Sketch of His Life with Bibliography* (1911)—this has been reprinted and edited by Charles Boewe. See also Francis W. Pennell's excellent "The Life and Writings of Rafinesque" (1942).

Elmer D. Merrill, of Harvard's Arnold Arboretum, dealt at length with Rafinesque's botanical materials in *Index Rafinesquianus: The Plant Names Published by C. S. Rafinesque and a Consideration of His Methods, Objectives, and Attainments* (1949). However, he has a sound and sensitive treatment of the man himself. It was a decade-long piece of research.

Charles Boewe (1988) has written at length in Rafinesque's favor, including upholding the existence and veracity of the painted sticks (Walam Olum). I am grateful to him for sharing many of his documents with me. Boewe's works, which include a revised and enlarged version of Fitzpatrick's biography of Rafinesque (1982), are impressive for the depth of research. He has researched archives, discovered lost manuscripts, and traced the linkages of intellectual ideas. Both Merrill and Boewe have tried in recent years to render justice to Rafinesque with some good effect—he was surely not mad in any clinical sense and his range of interest and knowledge was staggering. Still, I remain unconvinced of the authenticity of the Walam Olum's derivation from a set of original Native American painted sticks. I hope to return to a detailed study of Rafinesque's neglected but notable writings on archaeology at a later time.

E. G. Squier made good use of Rafinesque's data, which he borrowed from a Baltimore family: he published maps and other archaeological materials and part of the Walam Olum manuscripts. The latter was in an article called "Historical and Mythological Traditions of the Algonquins" (1849). He obviously felt that the manuscript was a valid record of Delaware mythology.

Daniel Garrison Brinton was an important figure in American anthropology as the volume by Regna Darnell, *Daniel Garrison Brinton: Fearless Critic of Philadelphia* (1988) clearly delineates. Brinton was pro the Walam Olum in his major work on the Lenape (Delaware), *The Lenape and Their Legends* (1885), and defended it, although he was critical of some other aspects of Rafinesque's work. In suggesting that Brinton may have been wrong in this view, Darnell cited John Witthoft's work "Brief Note" (1955), which declared that the Walam Olum was a fraud.

The major modern proponent of the Walam Olum was Eli Lilly, of whom a biography has been published by James H. Madison (1989). Lilly's faith in the veracity of the document was deeply held, as evidenced by his support of the detailed study of it: *Walam Olum or The Red Score* (1954). Most anthropologists today remain skeptical, but they probably have not seen Charles Boewe's challenging article "The Other Candidate for the Volney Prize: Constantine Samuel Rafinesque" (1988), which goes so far as to suggest that Rafinesque probably also had access to two other sets of somewhat similar pictographic records from the Ojibway and the Shawnee. This is a plethora of new data that I cannot now evaluate.

CHAPTER 6: The Earliest Americans

Henry Chapman Mercer wrote *The Lenape Stone; or, The Indian and the Mammoth* (1885) the same year that Brinton published his work on the Lenape. Brinton would soon brand both Mercer's mammoth and that of Cresson as frauds. Mercer's find, for some reason, would never get the attention and mention that Cresson's did, although Mercer's was well published and Cresson's was not. In light of my later disagreements with George Carter, it might be useful to note that his paper "That Elephant from Bucks Co., Penn." (1966) also finds the Lenape Stone to be a fraud. Mercer's other major work in North American archaeology was a little-known 178-page volume entitled *Researches Upon the Antiquity of Man in the Delaware Valley and the Eastern United States* (1897). The volume contains the important site reports on his excavation at the Argillite Quarry and at the village site at Lower Black's Eddy. For an up-to-date study of the topic, see David J. Meltzer's article "The Antiquity of Man and Development of American Archaeology" (1983).

Hilbourne T. Cresson and the Holly Oak Gorget made a brief splash in the late nineteenth century, but then the gorget received scant attention by archaeologists. A discussion of the find and its finder appeared in C. A. Weslager's *Delaware's Buried Past* (1944). Weslager's *Delaware Indians: A History* (1972) contains positive support for the Walam Olum and for both the Lenape Stone and the Holly Oak Gorget. The latter volume also indicates that Weslager was well acquainted with a Delaware geologist named John C. Kraft.

The recent rehabilitation of Cresson and the gorget began with the publication by the same John C. Kraft and Ronald A. Thomas of "Early Man at Holly Oak, Delaware" (1976). Their first footnote was to Weslager's *Delaware's Buried Past*. Some time later a reply would be published by David J. Meltzer and William C. Sturtevant in the Letters column of *Science* (1985), which branded it an obvious fraud. The response was immediate with a letter by John C. Kraft and Jay F. Custer published in the same issue of *Science*. The opposition has now produced two well-documented, and to my mind, definitive treatments of the gorget: David Meltzer and William C. Sturtevant's "The Holly Oak Shell Game: An Historic Archaeological Fraud" (1983) and James B. Griffin, David J. Meltzer, Bruce D. Smith, and William C. Sturtevant's "A Mammoth Fraud in Science" (1988).

CHAPTER 7: Catastrophism: Sunken Continents
There is a detailed discussion of Catastrophism in geology in Stephen Jay Gould's recent and searching review of the nineteenth century in the field: *Time's Arrow/ Time's Cycle: Myth and Metaphor in the Discovery of Geological Time* (1987). The larger question of Catastrophism in astronomy has been reviewed by Clark R. Chapman and David Morrison in *Cosmic Catastrophism* (1989).

The major story in Catastrophism in archaeology is Atlantis, and the one sure source on that subject is Sprague de Camp's classic volume *Lost Continents: The Atlantis Theme in History, Science and Literature* (1954). This book is a tour de force that is unequaled in the entire area of Fantastic Archaeology, for the author's broad knowledge of the subject is such that here, for once, one can see the effect of these fantastic ideas on literature and art and drama—a coverage that no one has ever equaled or even striven to attain. For example, I have collections of cartoons and novels on the subject but neither the time nor the wisdom to put them into their social, cultural, and historical context. That is surely the work of yet another student of the genre as well versed as de Camp.

If Sprague de Camp is the intellectual historian, then Ignatius Donnelly is the modern father of Atlantis and Catastrophism with *Atlantis: The Antediluvian World* (1882) and *Ragnarok: The Age of Fire and Gravel* (1883). As a quick look at de Camp's volume will surely indicate, Donnelly was not the last, just the most effective purveyor of the old Atlantis myth. But Donnelly still has many followers today, and the redoubtable Edgar Cayce, via his son, continues to speak to modern audiences on the topic (1968). The most recent but surely not the last Atlantis book that has come to hand from that source is an edited volume from his family research foundation, Edgar Evans Cayce, Gale Cayce Schwartzer, and Douglas C. Richard's *Mysteries of Atlantis Revisited* (1988).

The most successful recent spinoffs from Donnelly's Atlantis are in a Caribbean setting: these range from Marvel Comic's *Spiderman* to Robert Ferro and

M. Grumley, *Atlantis; The Autobiography of a Search* (1970), to Charles Berlitz's *Atlantis the 8th Continent* (1984). The Bahamas and their pleasant reefs have been turned into "pavement" and "columns" of lost Atlantis. Geologists have little difficulty showing that the rock formations are not man-made, but to no avail.

Helena Blavatsky and the Theosophists are something of a digression, but Atlantis was part of her message. Her major publications were *Isis Unveiled: A Master-Key to the Mysteries of Ancient and Modern Science and Theology* (1877) and *The Secret Doctrine: The Synthesis of Science, Religion, and Philosophy* (1888). The Theosophical Society keeps her books in print, and the volume *The Key to Theosophy* (1889) is still a good introduction to the subject. Her most recent biography is that by Marion Meade, *Madame Blavatsky* (1980). Edmund Garrett's *Isis Very Much Unveiled* (1894) is a well-documented contemporary debunking of Theosophy.

James Churchward's classic *The Lost Continent of Mu* (1926) was followed by *Children of Mu* (1931). Wauchope has a good commentary on these, as does de Camp, of course. There is some supportive commentary on Churchward to be found in the rather erratic reporting of Peter Tompkins in *Mysteries of the Mexican Pyramids* (1976). Churchward's aid in written documents (the Valley of Mexico tablets) came from William Niven, who remains poorly known. Most of what we have comes from Churchward, although Niven did write some straightforward archaeological articles much earlier. Tompkins and Wauchope discuss him too. There is a rather remarkable Mu volume by Elizabeth G. Wilcox, *Mu: Fact or Fiction* (1963), and the most recent addition to the genre is David Hatcher Childress's *Lost Cities of Ancient Lemuria and the Pacific* (1988).

CHAPTER 8: Archaeology and Religion

The pervasive nature of nineteenth-century spiritualism is well developed by Ruth Brandon in *The Spiritualists* (1984). The bibliography on Joseph Smith and Mormonism beggars description. As I mentioned in the text, feelings ran high from the very beginning (1830s) and continue today, as our final segment on the Salamander Papers tells us. Any student must start with the Book of Mormon; to do otherwise would be to study Christianity without reading the Bible. Smith's life is covered by many works both pro and con. I realize that with my positive reference to Fawn Brodie's *No Man Knows My History: The Life of Joseph Smith* (1954) that I have provided some readers with a "tilt" of skepticism that may be hard to overcome.

I have covered a number of other volumes, including the two on the Kinderhook Plates that are good representatives of strong anti-Mormon books: W. Wyl's *Mormon Portraits: or The Truth about Mormon Leaders from 1830–1886* (1886) and William A. Linn's *The Story of the Mormons—From the Date of Their Origin to the Year 1901* (1901). A more interesting and recent one is *Indian Origins and the Book of Mormon* by Dan Vogel (1986), which is again written by a member of the church. It is a very well-documented book from a college senior, and it puts Joseph Smith in an accurate 1830s perspective. The Book of Mormon, Vogel concludes, is thus seen as a production strongly influenced by the times, including the Myth of the Moundbuilder. I have found Silverberg's treatment of this aspect of the subject valuable too.

Salamander: The Story of the Mormon Forgery Murders is the title of a recent book by Linda Sillito and Allen Roberts (1988). The title is a code name for one of the most fascinating recent frauds (by Mark Hofmann) to come down the pike, as I have briefly described in the text. Forgery authorities included Charles Hamilton, the author of the definitive *Great Forgers and Famous Frauds* (1980).

The Newark Holy Stones found by David Wyrick are related to the notion of the Lost Tribes of Israel, an important part of Mormon historiography. The best descriptions of the finds are in Robert N. Alrutz's recent mini-monograph, "The Newark Holy Stones: The History of an Archaeological Tragedy" (1980). This treatment is very sympathetic and supportive, but uncritical. A new translation by Ernest Bloom and Jon Polansky of these materials of Wyrick has appeared in the *Epigraphic Society Occasional Publications* (1980).

Charles Whittlesey, one of the near eyewitnesses to the discovery, provides data in his article "Archaeological Frauds: Inscriptions Attributed to the Mound-builders—Three Remarkable Forgeries" (1872), which makes Wyrick's fraud a practical certainty. In a later paper, "Archaeological Frauds," he debunks Grave Creek and other finds (1876), and eventually returns to the Wyrick case (1881).

The Michigan Relics, or Soper Frauds as they are often called, were first strongly debunked by Francis W. Kelsey and Morris Jastrow in the *Nation* in 1892. Some years later, Kelsey went directly to the professionals in his article "Some Archaeological Forgeries from Michigan," in *American Anthropologist* (1908). He found that twice was not enough for Thomas Scotford, and he had to write still another critical article, "A Persistent Forgery" (1911). As noted in the text, Mormon interests are involved; James E. Talmadge carefully debunks them in "The Michigan Relics: A Story of Forgery and Deception" (1911), and they are strongly supported by Ralph Etzenhouser, a member of the Reorganized Mormon Church of Missouri, in *Engravings of Prehistoric Specimens from Michigan USA* (1910).

More recently A. L. Spooner gave a detailed account of the last gasp of the Scotford drama in a talk titled "Michigan's Controversial Finds," at a meeting in Detroit on April 18, 1953; I have a copy of that speech provided by friends in Ann Arbor. New interpretations of the Scotford artifacts continue to appear. A rather detailed recent volume by Henriette Mertz entitled *The Mystic Symbol* (1986) focuses on what is generally assumed by most other students, including this author, to be Scotford's own "maker's mark." Obviously Kelsey still has work to do.

CHAPTER 9: Westward to Vinland

The Vikings in North America also have a large bibliography. Three excellent introductions to those sources are to be found in chronological order: Justin Winsor's *Critical and Narrative History of America* (1889), chapter 2, "Pre-Columbian Exploration"; Samuel Eliot Morison's *The European Discovery of America: The Northern Voyages* (1971); and Brigitta L. Wallace's "Some Points of Controversy" (1971). All three have made this chapter much easier to write.

It all began with Henry Wheaton's *History of the Norsemen* (1831) and Carl C. Rafn, *Antiquitatae Americana* (1834). In the 1860s James Russell Lowell would add comic relief with his *Biglow Papers,* to be found in *The Writings of James Russell Lowell* (1900). The most recent comprehensive volume is Erik Wahlgren's *The Vikings and America* (1986), which is far and away the best work done on the subject to date.

Other critical reviews of the Viking problem are to be found in journal articles by Dean Snow, "Martians and Vikings, Madoc and Runes" (1981), and by Marshall McKusick and Erik Wahlgren, "Vikings in America: Fact and Fiction" (1980). Glyn Daniel put together a program for British television called "Myth America" (1985), which had a strong segment on Vikings and included this author, Erik Wahlgren, and Brian Fagan in the cast. It has been shown frequently on educational television in subsequent years.

The Kensington Rune Stone itself boasts a shelf of books; the three best known are Hjalmar Holand, *The Kensington Stone* (1932); Erik Wahlgren's *The Kensington Stone: A Mystery Solved* (1950); Theodore C. Blegen's *The Kensington Rune Stone: New Light on an Old Riddle* (1968). Holand was, of course, the major proponent, with Wahlgren and Blegen on the con side. Wahlgren's 1986 volume contains a fine update on this old faithful fraud. See also O. G. Landsverk's *Runic Records of the Norsemen in America* (1974) and also his earlier work with Alf Monge, *Norse Medieval Cryptography in Runic Carvings* (1967), for supposed cryptograms in this and many other American rune stones. For basic information on the topic of runes see *Runes* (1987) by R. I. Page.

Eben N. Horsford wrote voluminously on this subject for a decade. His most comprehensive volume is probably *The Landfall of Leif Erickson* (1882). A good response to Winsor is found in Horsford's *The Problem of the Northmen* (1889). After his death his daughter Cornelia wrote *Vinland and Its Ruins* (1899), which does provide evidence of some excavations. See also the joint volume in 1893 containing Horsford's *Leif's House in Vinland* and Cornelia's *Graves of the Northmen*, which briefly discuss their excavations (1893). The more critical appraisal of Horsford comes from Winsor (cited above) and from Julius E. Olson in a slim volume that, remarkably, Horsford himself put privately in print (1891); but he did include a "Reply." A recent and quite sympathetic short note on Horsford by a Harvard graduate student, Richard R. John, Jr., has appeared in the *Harvard Magazine* (1988).

The Beardmore finds in Canada are best reported by A. D. Tushingham in *The Beardmore Relics* (1966) and by Edmund S. Carpenter in "Frauds in Ontario Archaeology" (1961).

Both the Dighton Rock and the Newport Tower have such lengthy bibliographies that I can only suggest Winsor, Morison, and Wallace for the path into that literature. Major volumes include Edmund D. Delabarre's comprehensive *Dighton Rock: A Study of the Written Rocks of New England* (1928) and Philip Ainsworth Means's *Newport Tower* (1942). William S. Godfrey's doctoral dissertation (1951) was not published; instead there are only his articles "Newport Puzzle" (1949) and "Vikings in America: Theories and Evidence" (1955).

On more recent finds, Gloria Farley has been the major supporter of the Heavener rune stone. See her "The Oklahoma Runestones Are Authentic" (1973). Einar Haugen has written an excellent critical review of the Spirit Pond Rune Stones in *Visible Language* (1974). Then there is Calvin Trillin's by-product and spoof: *Runestruck* (1977).

William W. Fitzhugh's edited volume *Cultures in Contact: The European Impact on Native Cultural Institutions in Eastern North America AD 1000–1800* (1985) has carefully reviewed the evidence for early connections to North America with mainly negative results. The best-grounded archaeological evidence for Norse landings in North America is to be found in Anne Stine Ingstad's *The Discovery of Norse Settlement in America: Excavations at L'Anse Meadows, Newfoundland 1961–68* (1977).

CHAPTER 10: Across the Sea They Came
Several recent reviews of the life and times of Harold S. Gladwin have come from Arizona: the obituary by Emil W. Haury and T. Jefferson Reid (1985) and a historical review of Gila Pueblo by Emil W. Haury (1989). An earlier appreciation is to be found in "In Honor of Harold S. Gladwin," by Barry Fell and George Carter (1975). Gladwin himself provides some important personal insights in his *History of the Ancient Southwest* (1957). Gladwin's most significant other publications as far as this discussion is concerned are *Men Out of Asia* (1947) and his last work, "Mogollon and Hohokam AD 600–1000" (1979).

Little has been published on the Tucson Artifacts until recently, with the work by Cyclone Covey, *Calalus: A Roman Jewish Colony in America from the Time of Charlemagne Through Alfred the Great* (1975); there is also a brief note by E. B. "Ted" Sayles, "Lead Crosses," in *Fantasies of Gold* (1968). For the earlier period I have depended on materials from the archives of the Arizona State Museum and the Library of the University of Arizona, Special Collections. I am grateful for the help of staff members at both of those institutions for their help. The major document is that by Thomas Bent, which both Professor Covey and I used. I have also made use of the biography of Andrew E. Douglass by George E. Webb (1983), who helped me to find Douglass's own materials on file at the library. Emil W. Haury has provided me in a personal communication his own recollections of that period.

In the area of hyper-diffusion and trans-Atlantic connections, we turn to Leo Wiener, whose books *Africa and the Discovery of America* (1920) and *Maya and Mexican Origins* (1926) would later be taken up by Ivan Van Sertima in *They Came Before Columbus: The African Presence in Ancient America* (1976) and by Alexander von Wuthenau in *Unexpected Faces in Ancient America* (1975). The most recent proponent of this view is Michael Bradley in his *The Black Discovery of America* (1981). Typically, Bradley cites none of the above authors. Joseph B. Mahan has recently published a volume on his own ideas concerning ties across the Atlantic, which include the Indus civilization. His volume is *The Secret: America in World History Before Columbus* (1983). Earlier he wrote a short article, "They Actually WERE Indians" (1977), in which he first set forth the Indus civilization connection.

CHAPTER 11: Tales the Rude Monuments Tell
As I have mentioned in several of these segments, there is a large literature on some of these topics, often in ephemeral publications. With regard to Megalithic monuments in New England there is a comprehensive and helpful volume edited by Renee Kra, "New England Megaliths: Fact and Fancy" (1981). It includes a bibliography by David A. Poirier which covers several other topics, including Dighton Rock.

With regard to Mystery Hill (now also known as the American Stonehenge) there is a specific source: *The Mystery Hill Source Book* (1979), edited by Richard V. Humphrey. The basic volume on Mystery Hill remains that by William B. Goodwin, *The Ruins of Great Ireland in New England* (1946); the early skeptical works are those by Hugh Hencken, "The Irish Monastery at North Salem, N.H." (1939), and "What Are Pattee's Caves?" (1940).

The important excavations of Junius Bird (1982) and Gary S. Vescelius (1982–83) have been carefully published by the New England Antiquities Research Association (NEARA), and edited and commented on by Richard V. Humphrey. The Bird report includes a commentary by Goodwin. These site reports, including section drawings of the excavations and a catalog of finds, are *must* reading for anyone purporting to explain or date the site. The Cazeau and Scott text (1979: chapter 2) gives lengthy treatment to the debunking of the site.

Barry Fell has been the most widely heard recent supporter of Mystery Hill and many other Megalithic structures in New England. His books are, in chronological order: *America B.C.: Ancient Studies in the New World* (1976); *Saga America* (1980); and *Bronze Age America* (1982). His publication series, *Epigraphic Society Occasional Papers,* has been running since 1974 under several titles but now is an annual volume of more than 300 pages. As a result, Fell adds a great many articles to his bibliography each year, which I will not try to enumerate. I must cite, however, the March 1983 articles in *Wonderful West Virginia,* reporting on discovery of a long Ogam inscription; in it Professor Fell gives the clearest and most detailed exposition of his own methods of translation. I have made some use of documents available at Harvard concerning Fell's research, although I have been unable to track down the archival cache at the Widener Library that Fell so helpfully cites in his first book (1976: 306).

Fell's work has been critically reviewed by a number of North American archaeologists, including William Fitzhugh, Fred Hole, Marshall McKusick, Kenneth Feder, and John Cole. His linguistic efforts have been the particular focus of the work of Ives Goddard of the Smithsonian (see Kra 1981 for bibliographic details of the contra-Fell statements). His own Epigraphic Society member George Carter reviewed *Saga America* with the subtitle query "Going Over the Edge?" in the journal *Historical Diffusionism* (1981). It was a substantially supportive comment, despite the challenging subtitle. A close-up view of Fell in an early meeting with his critics and in a short press conference is to be had in "Ancient Vermont," *Proceedings of the Castleton Conference,* edited by Warren L. Cook (1978). The most recent volume on American epigraphy has been published by James P. Whittall, Jr.: *Myth Makers: Epigraphic Illusion in America* (1990). It is a volume full of critical evaluation and strong dissent concerning some of Professor Fell's decipherments. Finally, see the article "Linguistic Sleuth" by Laura Shefler (1990), which describes linguist Sally Thomason's work questioning Fell's translations on linguistic grounds.

For a view from the other side, I recommend the lengthy compendium by Norman Totten: "Archaeology and Epigraphy: Confrontation in America" (1981). It deals in detail with many of Fell's critics, including most of those listed in the preceding paragraph, and this author as well. My course on Fantastic Archaeology at Harvard has been critiqued by George Carter in the same journal (1987).

George Carter has a large number of publications; I have focused mainly on the archaeological ones, leaving the ones that are mainly botanical to specialists in that field, such as E. D. Merrill and Paul C. Mangelsdorf. Carter's major publications in archaeology are *Pleistocene Man at San Diego* (1957) and *Earlier Than You Think: A Personal View of Man in America* (1980). The former was given a rather severe review in *American Antiquity* (1958) by Frederick Johnson and John P. Miller. I have not been able to track down a review of the latter. With regard to the Folsom finds in the Mohave Desert, see Malcolm Rogers's "Early Lithic Industries of the Lower Colorado River and Adjacent Desert Areas" (1939). I have particularly stressed one aspect of Carter's view of Kroeber and other contemporary American archaeologists, and that is that Carter insists that the entire Establishment believed in a very short chronology before the Folsom discovery in 1926. See especially A. L. Kroeber's *Anthropology* (1923) and his article "Conclusions: The Present Status of Americanistic Problems" (1940). I am indebted to David Meltzer for pointing out the 1966 article by J. Alden Mason, "Pre-Folsom Estimates of the Age of Man in America (with comment by Cotter)."

With regard to the question of amino acid racemization the following references will give access to the major articles on the subject as they relate to Early Man in North America: Jeffrey L. Bada, R. A. Schroeder, and George F. Carter, "New Evidence for the Antiquity of Man in North America Deduced from Aspartic Acid Racemization" (1974); Jeffrey Bada et al., "Accelerator Mass Spectrometry Radiocarbon Ages of Amino Acid Extracts from California Paleo Indian Skeletons" (1984); R. E. Taylor et al., "Major Revisions in the Pleistocene Age Assignments for North American Human Skeletons . . ." (1985); Jeffrey L. Bada, "Aspartic Acid Racemization Dates of California Paleoindian Skeletons" (1985); and Jeffrey Bada, "Paleoanthropological Applications of Amino Acid Racemization Dating of Fossil Bones and Teeth" (1987).

Recent evidence on the hyper-diffusionist views that Carter and others have expounded concerning the peopling of the New World does not hold up under careful scrutiny. I am thinking here both of the various linguistic studies of Merrett Ruhlen and Joseph Greenberg and the studies in genetics by Christy G. Turner II and Stephen L. Zegura. For good popular presentations by these authors on these topics, see the recent articles in *Natural History* magazine's series "The First Americans," published from November 1986 to July 1988. Both the linguistic and bioanthropological study show three migrations at most: one early migration and two rather recent ones, with Athabascans and Eskimos as the latecomers. The recently reviewed evidence suggests that there was no great onslaught of a multiplicity of racial types over the millennia on the New World as Gladwin, Fell, Carter, and others would hypothesize.

CHAPTER 12: Psychic Archaeology
Although the field of psychic archaeology has been a "named" segment of the discipline for a short time, there is already a substantial literature on the subject. Two books have set out the background of psychic archaeology in a laudatory manner: Jeffrey Goodman's *Psychic Archaeology: Time Machine to the Past* (1977) and Stephan Schwartz's *The Secret Vaults of Time* (1978). Critical review has come quickly, as well, with some journal articles taking the new field to task; namely, Kenneth Feder's "Psychic Archaeology: The Anatomy of Irrationalist Prehistoric Studies" (1980), and two by Marshall McKusick: "Psychic Archaeology: Theory,

Method, and Mythology" (1982) and "Psychic Archaeology from Atlantis to Oz" (1984).

Frederick Bligh Bond, the "pioneer" in the field, wrote several books, starting with his groundbreaking *The Gate to Remembrance: A Psychological Study* (1918). I have depended primarily on works of Goodman and Schwartz for my discussion of Ossowiecki. See Schwartz's bibliography for pertinent references.

Edgar Cayce, like Helena Blavatsky, has an ongoing and sustaining organization. For Cayce it is the Association for Research and Enlightenment (ARE) in Virginia Beach, Virginia. Headed by Cayce's children, the ARE has kept his work in the public eye, and publications abound. The most useful biographical information can be found in Jess Stearn's two books: *Edgar Cayce: The Sleeping Prophet* (1967) and *A Prophet in His Own Country: The Story of the Young Edgar Cayce* (1974). I have discussed a recent work on Atlantis in the Chapter 7 segment. His son Edgar Evans Cayce has written or coauthored with his brother Hugh a number of volumes, such as *Atlantis—Fact or Fiction* (1962), *Edgar Cayce on Atlantis* (1968), and with Hugh, *The Outer Limits of Edgar Cayce's Power* (1971). Goodman is especially impressed with the value of Cayce's work.

Jeffrey Goodman seems to be one of the more active members of this field. His *American Genesis* (1981) has become widely known, and critical comment abounds. The Smithsonian's Dennis Stanford wrote "Who's on First?" (1981) and pulled no punches. One of his former mentors at Arizona, William Rathje, who was not depicted as very sympathetic by Goodman in his book, has become a forthright critic of the fantastic field: "The Ancient Astronaut Myth" (1977). Goodman has made a number of speaking tours around the country. Although I have tried, I have not been able personally to see his *The Genesis Mystery: A Startling New Theory of Outside Intervention in the Development of Modern Man* (1983). John Cole has reviewed it very critically in *American Antiquity* (1985).

Norman Emerson wrote a number of journal articles in the years after his "conversion" to the subdiscipline which he termed Intuitive Archaeology. They included "Intuitive Archaeology: A Psychic Approach" (1974); "Intuitive Archaeology: Egypt and Iran" (1976); "Intuitive Archaeology" (1977); and "Intuitive Archaeology: A Pragmatic Story" (1979).

David Jones has made only one major foray into this area and it was quite restrained. He has provided good data on the nature of his inquiry in *Visions of Time: Experiments in Psychic Archaeology* (1974). Stephan Schwartz, following his start in the field with his history thereof, has provided an upscale approach to the field. His much-touted *The Alexandria Project* (1983) is disappointing; it promises more than it can deliver. For example, in his history volume he set forth rather careful protocols for his work in this "difficult" field; these methods were not clearly followed in the research on the Alexandria project.

EPILOGUE: North American Prehistory

Although I have made a strong pitch for the colorful and interesting story that North American archaeology has to tell, I must now admit that there are rather few exciting books on this theme that have been written for the layperson. C. W. Ceram, the gifted German writer, who gave us the best-selling *Gods, Graves, and Scholars*

(1967), struck out with his attempt to capture this market. *The First American—A Story of American Archaeology* (1971) was not a great success. There are some large-format, picture-book volumes that are useful for giving the reader a good sense of what the hard goods of North American archaeology really look like. These include Dean Snow's *The Archaeology of North America* (1976) and the exhibition catalog of *Ancient Art of the American Woodland Indians* from the Detroit Institute of Arts (1985), done by David Brose, James Brown, and David Penney.

By far the most balanced continental coverage is found in the textbook *The Archaeology of North America* by Jesse D. Jennings, (3d edition, 1989). I have borrowed heavily from that valuable volume for my illustrations in this chapter. If one is looking for more detail, I would recommend the volume edited by Jennings, *Ancient North Americans* (1983), which has chapters by experts on the various areas.

On the general topic of the First Americans, I recommend Brian Fagan's recent volume *The Great Journey: The Peopling of Ancient America* (1987); for an interesting New England Clovis site, see Richard M. Gramly's "The Vail Site: A Paleo-Indian Encampment in Maine" (1982). There is a fine volume on the southern Plains, *Ancient Texans: Rock Art and Lifeways Along the Lower Pecos,* by Harry J. Shafer (1986).

There are some good specialized volumes on an area basis. For the Southwest, see Linda Cordell's *Prehistory of the Southwest* (1984) and David Grant Noble's *New Light on Chaco Canyon* (1984). On the Southeastern United States there is a handful, including Jefferson Chapman's *Tellico Archaeology [Tennessee]: 12,000 Years of Native American History* (1985); John Walthall's *Prehistoric Indians of the Southeast: Archaeology of Alabama and the Middle South* (1980); Charles Bareis and James Porter, *American Bottoms [Cahokia] Archaeology* (1984); for an interesting survey of Eastern earthworks, an update on Squier and Davis, William Morgan's *Prehistoric Architecture in the Eastern United States* (1980). For the West Coast there is Michael J. Moratto's *California Archaeology* (1984); Ruth Kirk with Richard Daugherty, *Exploring Washington Archaeology* (1978); and for the Northwest Coast there is Knut R. Fladmark's *British Columbia Prehistory* (1986).

Finally, I have borrowed segments from the works of two authors whose other works I like as well. Chad Oliver is a working anthropologist at the University of Texas, Austin, who just happens to be a fine writer of science fiction as well. *The Winds of Time* (1957) is an interesting story, from which I have excerpted my beginning. There are anthropological characters in it who remind me of some old colleagues. For other stories of his with an anthropological bent, see *Shadows in the Sun* (1954), *Another Kind* (1955), *The Shores of Another Sea* (1984a), and *Unearthly Neighbors* (1984b).

Ray Bradbury, whose short story "Perhaps We Are Going Away" (from *The Machineries of Joy* [1965]) helps me finish this volume, is too well known to need much comment. I can only say that I guess one reason that I like his work, especially *Dandelion Wine* (1957), is that I share with Bradbury a Midwestern childhood and I even had a friend named John Huff. I do not know from whence Bradbury got the cast for his Indian story, unlike his better-known *Martian Chronicles,* but they too are veritable Native American characters. Thanks to both authors for their permission to use their fine words.

General Bibliography

Allen, Paul M.
  1971 Introduction to Donnelly [1883]. *The Destruction of Atlantis/Ragnarok: The Age of Fire and Gravel*. Reprint. Blauvelt, New York: Multimedia Publishing.
Alrutz, Robert N.
  1980 "The Newark Holy Stones: The History of an Archaeological Tragedy." *Denison Journal of Scientific Laboratories* 57: 1–72.
Ames, Michael M., and Marjorie M. Halpin, eds.
  1980 *Manlike Monsters on Trial: Early Records & Modern Evidence*. Vancouver: University of British Columbia Press.
Ashe, Geoffrey, ed.
  1971 *The Quest For America*. New York: Praeger Publishers.
Ashmore, Wendy, and Robert Sharer
  1988 *Discovering Our Past: A Brief Introduction to Archaeology*. Mountain View, California: Mayfield Publishing.
Atwater, Caleb
  1820 "Descriptions of the Antiquities Discovered in the State of Ohio and Other Western States." *Transactions and Collections of the American Antiquarian Society*, vol. 1. Worcester, Massachusetts.
Bada, Jeffrey L.
  1985 "Aspartic Acid Racemization Dates of California Paleoindian Skeletons." *American Antiquity* 50, no. 3: 645–47.
  1987 "Paleoanthropological Applications of Amino Acid Racemization Dating of Fossil Bones and Teeth." *Anthropologischer Anzeiger* 45, no. 1: 1–8.
Bada, Jeffrey, R. Gillespie, A. J. Gowlett, and R.E.M. Hodges
  1984 "Accelerator Mass Spectrometry Radiocarbon Ages of Amino Acid Extracts from California Paleo Indian Skeletons." *Nature* 312: 442–44.
Bada, Jeffrey L., R. A. Schroeder, and George F. Carter
  1974 "New Evidence for the Antiquity of Man in North America Deduced from Aspartic Acid Racemization." *Science* 184: 791–93.
Bancroft, George
  1840 *United States*, vol. 3. Boston.
Bareis, Charles, and James Porter
  1984 *American Bottoms Archaeology*. Urbana: University of Illinois Press.
Barnum, P. T.
  1865 *The Humbugs of the World*. New York.
Bent, Thomas
  1964 "The Tucson Artifacts." Unpublished manuscript.

Berlitz, Charles
    1984   *Atlantis the 8th Continent.* New York: G. P. Putnam's Sons.

Bibby, Geoffrey
    1956   *Testimony of the Spade.* New York: Alfred A. Knopf.

Bird, Junius
    1982   "Trips to Sites Near Raymond and North Salem, New Hampshire." *NEARA Journal* 16, no. 4: 101–12. With Reply by William Goodwin and Editorial Comments by Richard V. Humphrey.

Blavatsky, Helena
    1877   *Isis Unveiled: A Master-Key to the Mysteries of Ancient and Modern Science and Theology.* Point Loma, California: Aryan Theosophical Press, 1919.

    1888   *The Secret Doctrine: The Synthesis of Science, Religion, and Philosophy.* Point Loma, California.

    1889   *The Key to Theosophy.* London.

Blegen, Theodore C.
    1968   *The Kensington Rune Stone: New Light on an Old Riddle.* St. Paul, Minnesota: St. Paul Historical Society.

Bloom, Ernest, and Jon Polansky
    1980   "Translation of the 'Decalogue Tablet' Ohio." *Epigraphic Society Occasional Publications,* 8, part 1: 15–20.

Boewe, Charles
    1988   "The Other Candidate for the Volney Prize: Constantine Samuel Rafinesque." In John Leopold, ed., *Volney Essay Prize II.* Dordrecht, Germany: D. Reidel.

Boewe, Charles, ed.
    1982   Thomas Jefferson Fitzpatrick. *Rafinesque: A Sketch of His Life with Bibliography* [1911]. Reprint. Weston, Massachusetts: M & S Press.

Bond, Frederick Bligh
    1918   *The Gate to Remembrance: A Psychological Study.* New York: Basil Blackwell.

Book of Mormon
    1974   Salt Lake City, Utah: The Church of Jesus Christ of Latter Day Saints.

Boorstin, Daniel J.
    1965   *The Americans: The National Experience.* New York: Random House.

Boulding, Kenneth
    1980   "Science: Our Common Heritage." *Science* 207, no. 4433: 831–36.

Brackenridge, Henry M.
    1818   Letter to Thomas Jefferson. *Transactions of the American Philosophical Society,* new series 1, no. 7: 158–59.

Bradbury, Ray
    1957   *Dandelion Wine.* Garden City, New York: Doubleday.

    1965   *The Machineries of Joy.* New York: Bantam Books.

Bradley, Michael
    1981   *The Black Discovery of America.* Toronto: Personal Library.

Brandon, Ruth
    1984   *The Spiritualists: The Passion for the Occult in the Nineteenth and Twentieth Centuries.* Buffalo, New York: Prometheus Books.

Brew, J. O.
    1966   *Early Days of the Peabody Museum at Harvard University.* Cambridge, Massachusetts: Peabody Museum.
    1968   "Introduction." *One Hundred Years of Anthropology.* Cambridge, Massachusetts: Harvard University Press.

Brinton, Daniel Garrison
    1885   *The Lenape and Their Legends: With the Complete Text and Symbols of the Walam Olum.* Philadelphia.

Broad, William, and Nicholas Wade
    1982   *Betrayers of the Truth.* New York: Simon and Schuster.

Brodie, Fawn
    1954   *No Man Knows My History: The Life of Joseph Smith.* New York: Alfred A. Knopf.

Brose, David, James Brown, and David Penney
    1985   *Ancient Art of the American Woodland Indians.* Detroit: Detroit Institute of Arts.

Call, Richard Ellsworth
    1895   *The Life and Writings of Rafinesque.* Louisville, Kentucky.

Carlyle, Thomas
    1837   *The French Revolution: A History.* London.

Carpenter, Edmund S.
    1961   "Frauds in Ontario Archaeology." *Pennsylvania Archaeologist* 31, no. 2: 113–18.

Carter, George
    1957   *Pleistocene Man at San Diego.* Baltimore: Johns Hopkins University Press.
    1966   "That Elephant from Bucks Co., Penn." *Anthropological Journal of Canada* 4, no. 3: 2–6.
    1980   *Earlier Than You Think: A Personal View of Man in America.* College Station, Texas: Texas A&M University Press.
    1981   *"Saga America:* Going Over the Edge?" *Historical Diffusionism* 31: 31–58.
    1987   "Fantastic Archaeology at Harvard." *Epigraphic Society Occasional Publications* 16: 280–85.

Cayce, Edgar Evans
    1962   *Atlantis—Fact or Fiction.* Virginia Beach, Virginia: Association for Research and Enlightenment.
    1968   *Edgar Cayce on Atlantis.* New York: Paperback Library/Coronet Communications.

Cayce, Edgar Evans, and Hugh Cayce
    1971   *The Outer Limits of Edgar Cayce's Power.* New York: Harper & Row.

Cayce, Edgar Evans, Gale Cayce Schwartzer, and Douglas C. Richard
    1988   *Mysteries of Atlantis Revisited.* San Francisco: Harper & Row.

Cazeau, Charles, and Stuart Scott
    1979   *Exploring the Unknown: Great Mysteries Reexamined.* New York: Plenum.
Ceram. C. W.
    1967   *Gods, Graves, and Scholars.* New York: Alfred A. Knopf.
    1971   *The First American—A Story of American Archaeology.* New York: Harcourt Brace Jovanovich.
Chapman, Clark R., and David Morrison
    1989   *Cosmic Catastrophism.* New York: Plenum.
Chapman, Jefferson
    1985   *Tellico Archaeology: 12,000 Years of Native American History.* Knoxville: University of Tennessee Press.
Childress, David Hatcher
    1988   *Lost Cities of Ancient Lemuria and the Pacific.* Stelle, Illinois: Adventurer-Unlimited Press.
Churchward, James
    1926   *The Lost Continent of Mu.* London: Neville Spearman.
    1931   *Children of Mu.* Binghamton, New York: Vail: Ballou Press.
Cole, John
    1985   "Review of *The Genesis Mystery: A Startling New Theory of Outside Intervention in the Development of Modern Man.*" *American Antiquity* 50, no. 3: 692–93.
Cole, Sonia
    1955   *Counterfeit.* London: John Murray.
Cook, Warren L., ed.
    1978   *Ancient Vermont: Proceedings of the Castleton Conference.* Rutland, Vermont: Academic Books.
Cordell, Linda
    1984   *Prehistory of the Southwest.* Orlando, Florida: Academic Press.
Covey, Cyclone
    1975   *Calalus: A Roman Jewish Colony in America from the Time of Charlemagne Through Alfred the Great.* New York: Vantage Press.
Cran, Frank Walter
    1973   *Riddle of the Runestone.* British Broadcasting Corporation.
Cresson, Hilbourne
    1890   "Remarks." In Putnam 1890: 467–69.
Daniel, Glyn
    1962   "Editorial." *Antiquity* 36, no. 142: 167.
    1976a   *A Hundred and Fifty Years of Archaeology.* Cambridge, Massachusetts: Harvard University Press.
    1976b   *Cambridge and the Back-looking Curiosity: An Inaugural Lecture.* Cambridge: Cambridge University Press.
    1977   "Review of *America BC* and *They Came Before Columbus.*" *New York Times Book Review,* March 13: 8–12.
    1979   "The Forgotten Milestones and Blind Alleys of the Past." *Royal Anthropological Society Newsletter,* no. 3: 3–6.

1981   *A Short History of Archaeology.* New York: Thames & Hudson.

1985   "Myth America." Video format: Anglia Productions.

Darnell, Regna

1988   *Daniel Garrison Brinton: Fearless Critic of Philadelphia.* Publications in Anthropology, no. 3. Philadelphia: Department of Anthropology, University of Pennsylvania.

Darrah, William C.

1951   *Powell of the Colorado.* Princeton, New Jersey: Princeton University Press.

de Camp, Sprague

1954   *Lost Continents: The Atlantis Theme in History, Science and Literature.* New York: Dover Publications.

Delabarre, Edmund D.

1916   *Early Interest in Dighton Rock.* Cambridge, Massachusetts: John Wilson & Son.

1928   *Dighton Rock: A Study of the Written Rocks of New England.* New York: Walter Neale.

Donnelly, Ignatius

1882   *Atlantis: The Antediluvian World.* New York.

1883   *Ragnarok: The Age of Fire and Gravel.* New York.

Duncan, Winthrop

1934   "Josiah Priest." *Proceedings of the American Antiquarian Society* 4: 45–102.

Dunn, James Taylor

1948   "The Cardiff Giant Hoax." *New York History* 29, no. 3: 367–77.

Eddy, Mary Baker

1875   *Science & Health with Key to the Scriptures.* Boston: Trustees Under the Will of Mary Baker G. Eddy.

Eiseley, Loren

1971   *Night Country.* New York: J. P. Scribner's Sons.

Emerson, Norman

1974   "Intuitive Archaeology: A Psychic Approach." *New Horizons* 1, no. 3: 14–18.

1976   "Intuitive Archaeology: Egypt and Iran." *ARE Journal* XI, no. 2: 55–65.

1977   "Intuitive Archaeology." In Joseph K. Long, ed., *Extrasensory Ecology.* Metuchen, New Jersey: Scarecrow Press.

1979   "Intuitive Archaeology: A Pragmatic Story." *Phoenix* 3, no. 2: 5–15.

Epstein, Jeremiah

1980   "Pre-Columbian Old World Coins in America: An Examination of the Evidence." *Current Anthropology* 21, no. 1: 1–20.

Etzenhouser, Ralph

1910   *Engravings of Prehistoric Specimens from Michigan USA.* Detroit: John Bornman & Son.

Evans, Bergen

1946   *The Natural History of Nonsense.* New York: Alfred A. Knopf.

Fagan, Brian
  1983 *Archaeology: A Brief Introduction.* Boston: Little, Brown.
  1987 *The Great Journey: The Peopling of Ancient America.* New York: Thames & Hudson.
Farley, Gloria
  1973 "The Oklahoma Runestones Are Authentic." *Popular Archaeology* 2, no. 1: 5–15.
Farquharson, Robert J.
  1877 "Account of the Discovery of Inscribed Tablets by Reverend J. Gass." *Proceedings of the Davenport Academy of Natural Sciences* 2: 103–16.
Feder, Kenneth
  1980 "Psychic Archaeology: The Anatomy of Irrationalist Prehistoric Studies." *Skeptical Inquirer* 4, no. 4: 32–43.
  1990 *Frauds, Myths, and Mysteries: Science and Pseudoscience in Archaeology.* Mountain View, California: Mayfield Publishing.
Fell, Barry
  1975 *Introduction to Marine Biology.* New York: Harper & Row.
  1976 *America B.C.: Ancient Settlers in the New World.* New York: Quadrangle/The New York Times Book Co.
  1980 *Saga America.* New York: Time Books.
  1982 *Bronze Age America.* Boston: Little, Brown.
  1983 "Wyoming County & Horse Creek Petroglyphs." *Wonderful West Virginia,* March.
Fell, Barry, and George Carter
  1975 "In Honor of Harold S. Gladwin." *Epigraphic Society Occasional Papers* 2, no. 25.
Ferro, Robert, and M. Grumley
  1970 *Atlantis: The Autobiography of a Search.* New York: Bell Publications.
Fitting, James, ed.
  1973 *The Development of North American Archaeology.* Garden City, New York: Anchor Books.
Fitzhugh, William W., ed.
  1985 *Cultures in Contact: The European Impact on Native Cultural Institutions in Eastern North America AD 1000–1800.* Washington, D.C.: Smithsonian Institution Press.
Fitzpatrick, Thomas Jefferson
  1911 *Rafinesque: A Sketch of His Life with Bibliography.* Des Moines, Iowa: The Historical Department of Iowa.
Fladmark, Knut R.
  1986 *British Columbia Prehistory.* Ottawa: National Museum of Canada.
Foster, John Wells
  1869 *The Physical Geography of the Mississippi Valley.* Chicago.
  1873 *Pre-Historic Races of the United States.* Chicago.
Franco, Barbara
  1969 "The Cardiff Giant: A Hundred Year Old Hoax." *New York History* 50: 420–40.

Gardner, Martin
1957 *Fads and Fallacies in the Name of Science.* New York: Dover Publications.
1981 *Science: Good, Bad and Bogus.* Buffalo, New York: Prometheus Books.
1987 *The New Age: Notes of a Fringe-Watcher.* Buffalo, New York: Prometheus Books.

Garrett, Edmund
1894 *Isis Very Much Unveiled: The Story of the Great Mahatma Hoax.* London: Westminster Gazette.

Gjessing, Helge
1909 "Runestenen fra Kensington." Translated by Elias J. Lien. *Symra* 5: 113–26.

Gladwin, Harold S.
1947 *Men Out of Asia.* New York: McGraw-Hill.
1957 *History of the Ancient Southwest.* Portland, Maine: Bond Wheelwright.
1979 "Mogollon and Hohokam AD 600–1000." *Medallion Papers* 40. Santa Barbara, California: privately published.

Godfrey, William S.
1949 "Newport Puzzle." *Archaeology* 2, no. 3: 146–49.
1951 *Digging a Tower and Laying a Ghost.* Harvard University Ph.D. thesis.
1955 "Vikings in America: Theories and Evidence." *American Anthropologist* 57, no. 1: 35–43.

Goodman, Jeffrey
1977 *Psychic Archaeology: Time Machine to the Past.* New York: Berkley Publishing Co.
1981 *American Genesis:* New York: Summit Books.
1983 *The Genesis Mystery: A Startling New Theory of Outside Intervention in the Development of Modern Man.* New York: Times Books.

Goodwin, William B.
1946 *The Ruins of Great Ireland in New England.* Boston: Meador.

Gould, Stephen Jay
1981 *The Mismeasure of Man.* New York: W. W. Norton.
1987 *Time's Arrow/Time's Cycle: Myth and Metaphor in the Discovery of Geological Time.* Cambridge, Massachusetts: Harvard University Press.

Gramly, Richard M.
1982 "The Vail Site: A Paleo-Indian Encampment in Maine." *Bulletin of the Buffalo Society of Natural Science* 3.

Griffin, James B., David Meltzer, Bruce Smith, and William Sturtevant
1988 "A Mammoth Fraud in Science." *American Antiquity* 53, no. 3: 578–82.

Hagen, S. N.
1950 "The Kensington Runic Inscription." *Speculum* 25, no. 3: 321–56.

Hallowell, Irving
1960 "The Beginnings of Anthropology in America." In F. de Laguna, ed., *Selected Papers from American Anthropologists.* Washington, D.C.: American Anthropological Association: 1–90.

Hamilton, Charles
    1980   *Great Forgers and Famous Frauds*. New York: Crown Publishers.
Harris, Neil
    1973   *Humbug: The Art of P. T. Barnum*. Boston: Little, Brown.
Harrold, Francis B., and Raymond A. Eve, eds.
    1987   *Cult Archaeology and Creationism*. Iowa City: University of Iowa Press.
"Harvard Memorial Minutes"
    1940   *Harvard University Gazette:* 124.
Haugen, Einar
    1974   "The Runestones of Spirit Pond, Maine." *Visible Language* 8, no. 1: 33–
          64.
Haury, Emil W.
    1989   "Gila Pueblo Archaeological Foundation: A History & Some Personal
          Notes." *Kiva* 54, no. 1: 1–77.
Haury, Emil W., and T. Jefferson Reid
    1985   "Harold Sterling Gladwin, 1883–1983." *Kiva* 50, no. 4: 271–80.
Haven, Samuel
    1856   *Archaeology of the United States or Sketches, Historical and Biographical, of*
          the Progress of Information and Opinion Respecting Vestiges of Antiquity in
          the United States. Washington, D.C.: Smithsonian Institution.
Haywood, John
    1823   *Natural and Aboriginal History of Tennessee*. Nashville, Tennessee.
Hencken, Hugh
    1939   "The Irish Monastery at North Salem, N.H." *New England Quarterly*
          12, no. 3: 429–42.
    1940   "What Are Pattee's Caves?" *Scientific American* 163: 258–59.
Hinsley, Curtis
    1984   *Savages and Scientists*. Washington, D.C.: Smithsonian Institution
          Press.
Holand, Hjalmar
    1911   "The Kensington Rune Stone Abroad." *Records of the Past* 10, no. 5:
          267–69.
    1932   *The Kensington Stone*. Ephraim, Wisconsin: privately published.
Horsford, Cornelia
    1899   *Vinland and Its Ruins*. New York.
Horsford, Eben N.
    1882   *The Landfall of Leif Erickson*. Boston.
    1889   *The Problem of the Northmen*. Cambridge, Massachusetts.
    1890   *The Discovery of the Ancient City of Norumbega*. Boston.
Horsford, Eben N., and Cornelia Horsford
    1893   *Leif's House in Vinland* and *Graves of the Northmen*. Boston.
Huddleston, Lee
    1967   *Origins of the American Indians*. Austin: University of Texas Press.
Humphrey, Richard V., ed.
    1979   *The Mystery Hill Source Book*. Salem, New Hampshire: Teaparty Books.

Imlay, Gilbert
  1793 *A Topographical Description of the Western Territory of North America.*
        London.
Ingstad, Anne Stine
  1977 *The Discovery of Norse Settlement in America: Excavations at L'Anse
        Meadows, Newfoundland 1961–68.* Oslo: Universitetsforlaget.
Jakle, John
  1977 *Images of the Ohio Valley.* New York: Oxford University Press.
Jefferson, Thomas
  1982 *Notes on the State of Virginia* [1787]. William Paden, ed. New York:
        W. W. Norton.
Jennings, Jesse D.
  1989 *The Prehistory of North America.* 3d edition. Mountain View, Califor-
        nia: Mayfield Publishing.
Jennings, Jesse D., ed.
  1983 *Ancient North Americans.* San Francisco: W. H. Freeman.
John, Richard R., Jr.
  1988 "Eben Horsford: Vita." *Harvard Magazine* 91, no. 1: 44.
Johnson, Frederick, and John P. Miller
  1958 "Review of *Pleistocene Man at San Diego.*" *American Antiquity* 24, no.
        2: 206–10.
Jones, David
  1974 *Visions of Time: Experiments in Psychic Archaeology.* Wheaton, Illinois:
        Theosophical Publications.
Kelsey, Francis W.
  1908 "Some Archaeological Forgeries from Michigan." *American Anthropol-
        ogist* 10, no. 1: 48–59.
  1911 "A Persistent Forgery." *American Anthropologist* 33, no. 1: 26–31.
Kelsey, Francis W., and Morris Jastrow
  1892 [Accounts of the Michigan Forgeries] *Nation,* January 28. As cited in
        Kelsey 1908.
Kirk, Ruth, and Richard Daugherty
  1978 *Exploring Washington Archaeology.* Seattle: University of Washington
        Press.
Kra, Renee, ed.
  1981 "New England Megaliths: Fact and Fancy." *Bulletin of Archaeological
        Society of Connecticut* 4.
Kraft, John C., and Jay F. Custer
  1985 "Letters." *Science* 227, no. 4684: 242–44.
Kraft, John C., and Ronald A. Thomas
  1976 "Early Man at Holly Oak, Delaware." *Science* 192, no. 4241: 756–61.
Kroeber, A. L.
  1923 *Anthropology.* New York: Harcourt Brace.
  1940 "Conclusions: The Present Status of Americanistic Problems." In
        Clarence L. Hay, et al., eds., *The Maya and Their Neighbors.* New York:
        Dell Publications: 460–87.

Landsverk, O. G.
    1974 *Runic Records of the Norsemen in America.* New York: Erik Friis.
Landsverk, O. G., and Alf Monge
    1967 *Norse Medieval Cryptography in Runic Carvings.* Glendale, California: Norseman Press.
Lewin, Roger
    1987 *Bones of Contention.* New York: Simon & Schuster.
Lewis, T. H.
    1886 "The 'Monumental Tortoise' Mounds of De-Coo-Dah." In *American Journal of Archaeology & the History of the Fine Arts,* vol. 2: 65–69.
Lilly, Eli
    1954 *Walam Olum or The Red Score.* Indianapolis: Indiana Historical Society.
Linn, William A.
    1901 *The Story of the Mormons—From the Date of Their Origin to the Year 1901.* New York: Macmillan.
Lowell, James Russell
    1900 "Speech of Honourable Preserved Doe in Secret Caucus." From *The Biglow Papers,* Second Series, no. 5. In *The Writings of James Russell Lowell,* vol. 9. Boston: Houghton Mifflin.
MacDougall, Curtis D.
    1958 *Hoaxes.* New York: Dover Publications.
McKusick, Marshall
    1970 *The Davenport Conspiracy.* Iowa City: University of Iowa Press.
    1982 "Psychic Archaeology: Theory, Method, and Mythology." *Journal of Field Archaeology* 9: 99–118.
    1984 "Psychic Archaeology from Atlantis to Oz." *Archaeology* 37, no. 5: 48–52.
    1990 *The Davenport Conspiracy Revisited.* Ames: Iowa State University Press.
McKusick, Marshall, and Erik Wahlgren
    1980 "Vikings in America: Fact and Fiction." *Early Man* 2, no. 4: 7–11.
Madison, James H.
    1989 *Eli Lilly: A Life, 1885–1977.* Indianapolis: Indiana Historical Society.
Mahan, Joseph B.
    1977 "They Actually WERE Indians." *Oklahoma Today,* Autumn: 2–6.
    1983 *The Secret: America in World History Before Columbus.* Columbus, Georgia: Institute for the Study of American Cultures.
Mallery, Garrick
    1886 "Pictographs of the North American Indians." *Fourth Annual Report of the Bureau of Ethnology.* Washington, D.C.
Marvel Comics
    1985 *The Amazing Spider Man.* February 7.
Mason, J. Alden
    1966 "Pre-Folsom Estimates of the Age of Man in America (with comment by Cotter)." *American Anthropologist* 68, no. 1: 193–98.

Meade, Marion
    1980   *Madame Blavatsky.* New York: G. P. Putnam's Sons.
Means, Philip Ainsworth
    1942   *Newport Tower.* New York: Henry Holt.
Meltzer, David J.
    1983   "The Antiquity of Man and Development of American Archaeology."
            Advances in Archaeological Method and Theory 6: 1–51.
Meltzer, David J., and William C. Sturtevant
    1983   "The Holly Oak Shell Game: An Historic Archaeological Fraud." In
            Robert C. Dunnell and Donald K. Grayson, eds., *Lulu Linear Punctu-
            ated: Essays in Honor of George Irving Quimby.* Ann Arbor: University of
            Michigan Press: 325–52.
    1985   "Letters." *Science* 227, no. 468: 242–44.
Mercer, Henry Chapman
    1885   *The Lenape Stone; or, the Indian and the Mammoth.* New York.
    1897   *Researches Upon the Antiquity of Man in the Delaware Valley and the
            Eastern United States.* Philadelphia.
Merrill, Elmer D.
    1949   *Index Rafinesquianus: The Plant Names Published by C. S. Rafinesque
            and a Consideration of His Methods, Objectives, and Attainments.* Bos-
            ton: Arnold Arboretum, Harvard University.
Mertz, Henriette
    1986   *The Mystic Symbol.* Global, Maryland: Global Books.
Minnesota Historical Society Museum Committee
    1915   "The Kensington Rune Stone." *Minnesota Historical Society Collections*
            15.
Monge, Alf
    1967   *Norse Medieval Cryptography in Runic Carvings.* Glendale, California:
            Norseman Press.
Moratto, Michael J.
    1984   *California Archaeology.* Orlando, Florida: Academic Press.
Morgan, William
    1980   *Prehistoric Architecture in the Eastern United States.* Cambridge, Mas-
            sachusetts: MIT Press.
Morison, Samuel Eliot
    1971   *The European Discovery of America: The Northern Voyages.* New York:
            Oxford University Press.
Mourt, G.
    1963   *A Journal of Pilgrims at Plymouth: Mourt's Relation* [1622]. Dwight
            Heath, ed. New York: Corinth Books.
Munro, Robert
    1905   *Archaeology and False Antiquities.* London: Methuen.
Natural History. "The First Americans" (series). November 1986 to July 1988.
Noble, David Grant
    1984   *New Light on Chaco Canyon.* Albuquerque: School of American Re-
            search Press.

Oliver, Chad
    1954   *Shadows in the Sun*. New York: Ballantine Books.
    1955   *Another Kind*. New York: Ballantine Books.
    1957   *The Winds of Time*. Garden City, New York: Doubleday.
    1984a *The Shores of Another Sea*. New York: Signet Books.
    1984b *Unearthly Neighbors*. New York: Crown Publishers.
Olson, Julius E., and Eben Norton Horsford
    1891   *Review of the Problem of the Northmen and the Site of Norumbega and a Reply*. Cambridge, Massachusetts.
Page, R. I.
    1987   *Runes*. Berkeley: University of California Press.
Peabody, George
    1868   "Letter of Gift" [1866]. *First Annual Report of the Trustees of the Peabody Museum of Archaeology and Ethnology* 4–28.
Pennell, Francis W.
    1942   "The Life and Writings of Rafinesque." *Transylvania College Bulletin* 15, no. 7: 10–70.
Pidgeon, William
    1858   *Traditions of De-Coo-Dah and Antiquarian Researches*. New York.
Pius XII, Pope
    1950   *Encyclical Letter: Divino Afflante Spiritu* [1943]. In John P. O'Connell, ed., *Holy Bible*. Chicago: Catholic Press: lvii.
Poirier, David
    1981   "Bibliography: Norse, Phoenecian and Other Pre-Columbian Wanderers in North America." In Renee Kra, ed., *Bulletin of Archaeological Society of Connecticut* 4: 67–73.
Powell, John W.
    1894   *12th Annual Report of the Bureau of Ethnology*. Washington, D.C.
Priest, Josiah
    1833   *American Antiquities and Discoveries in the West*. 2d edition. Albany, New York.
    1845   *Slavery, as it Relates to the Negro*. Albany, New York: Title changed to *Bible Defence of Slavery* in 1852.
Priestley, J. B.
    1949   *Delight*. New York: Harper & Bros.
Putnam, F. W.
    1890   ["Remarks on Early Man Studies"]. *Proceedings of the Boston Society of Natural History* 24: 467–69.
Radner, Daisie, and Michael Radner
    1982   *Science and Unreason*. Belmont, California: Wadsworth Publishing.
Rafinesque, Constantine S.
    1824   *Ancient Annals of Kentucky*. Frankfort, Kentucky.
    1836a *Life of Travels*. Philadelphia.
    1836b *The American Nations or Outlines of a Natural History of the Ancient and Modern Nations of North and South America*. Philadelphia.

1838   *The Ancient Monuments of North and South America.* 2d edition. Philadelphia.

Rafn, Carl C.

1834   *Antiquitatae Americanae.* Copenhagen.

Rathje, William

1977   "The Ancient Astronaut Myth." *Archaeology* 31, no. 1: 4–7.

Read, Matthew Canfield

1879   "Inscribed Stone of Grave Creek Mound." *American Antiquarian* 50, no. 2: 139–49.

Reith, Adolf

1970   *Archaeological Fakes.* New York: Praeger Publishers.

Rogers, Malcolm

1939   "Early Lithic Industries of the Lower Colorado River and Adjacent Desert Areas." *San Diego Museum of Man, Papers* 3.

Sabloff, Jeremy

1982   *Archaeology: Myth and Reality. Scientific American.* San Francisco: W. H. Freeman.

Sagan, Carl

1987   "The Fine Art of Baloney." *Parade.* February 1: 12–13.

Sayles, E. B.

1968   "Lead Crosses." *Fantasies of Gold.* Tucson: University of Arizona Press: 103–12.

Schoolcraft, Henry Rowe

1845   "Observations Respecting the Grave Creek Mound." *Transactions of American Ethnological Society,* vol. 1. New York: 369–424.

1851–57   *Historical and Statistical Information Respecting the History, Conditions and Prospects of the Indian Tribes of the United States.* 6 vols. Philadelphia.

Schwartz, Stephan

1978   *The Secret Vaults of Time.* New York: Grosset & Dunlap.

1983   *The Alexandria Project.* New York: Dell Publications.

Shafer, Harry J.

1986   *Ancient Texans: Rock Art and Lifeways Along the Lower Pecos.* San Antonio: Witte Museum.

Sharer, Robert, and Wendy Ashmore

1979   *Fundamentals of Archaeology.* Reading, Massachusetts: Benjamin/Cummings Publishing.

Shaw, George Bernard

1906   *The Devil's Disciple* [1897]. In *Three Plays for Puritans.* New York: Brentano's Publishers.

Shefler, Laura

1990   "Linguistic Sleuth [Sally Thomason]." *Pitt Magazine* 5, no. 1: 44–45.

Sillito, Linda, and Allen Roberts

1988   *Salamander: The Story of the Mormon Forgery Murders.* Salt Lake City: Signature Books.

Silverberg, Robert
   1968   *Moundbuilders of Ancient America*. Greenwich, Connecticut: New York Graphic Society.
Snow, Dean
   1976   *The Archaeology of North America*. London: Thames & Hudson.
   1981   "Martians and Vikings, Madoc and Runes." *American Heritage* 32, no. 6: 102–8.
Spooner, A. L.
   1953   "Michigan's Controversial Finds." Unpublished paper, presented to the Michigan Archaeological Society, Aboriginal Research Club. Detroit, Michigan: April 18.
Squier, Ephraim G.
   1848   "Observations on the Aboriginal Monuments of the Mississippi Valley." *Transactions of the American Ethnological Society,* vol. 2: 131–207.
   1849   "Historical and Mythological Traditions of the Algonquins." *American Review,* no. 14 (February).
Squier, Ephraim G., and Edwin H. Davis
   1848   *Ancient Monuments of the Mississippi Valley*. Washington, D.C.: Smithsonian Institution.
Stanford, Dennis
   1981   "Who's on First?" *SCIENCE 81* (June): 91–92.
Stanton, William
   1960   *The Leopard's Spots*. Chicago: University of Chicago Press.
Stearn, Jess
   1967   *Edgar Cayce: The Sleeping Prophet*. Garden City, New York: Garden City Historical Society.
   1974   *A Prophet in His Own Country: The Story of the Young Edgar Cayce*. New York: William Morrow.
Steibing, William
   1984   *Ancient Astronauts, Cosmic Collisions and Other Popular Theories About Man's Past*. Buffalo, New York: Prometheus Books.
Talmadge, James E.
   1911   "The Michigan Relics: A Story of Forgery and Deception." *Deseret Museum Bulletin* no. 2.
Taylor, R. E., L. A. Payen, C. A. Prior, et al.
   1985   "Major Revisions in the Pleistocene Age Assignments for North American Human Skeletons. . . ." *American Antiquity* 50, no. 1: 136–40.
Thalbitzer, William
   1951   "Two Runic Stones from Greenland & America." *Smithsonian Miscellaneous Collections,* vol. 116, no. 3.
Thomas, Cyrus
   1894   "Report on the Mound Explorations of the Bureau of Ethnology." In Powell 1894: 1–730.
Thomas, David Hurst
   1979   *Archaeology*. New York: Holt, Rinehart & Winston.

Thomas, Dylan
    1971   *Collected Poems: 1934–1952*. New York: New Directions.
Tompkins, Peter
    1976   *Mysteries of the Mexican Pyramids*. New York: Harper & Row.
Totten, Norman
    1981   "Archaeology and Epigraphy: Confrontation in America." *Epigraphic Society Occasional Publications* 9, no. 209: 15–22.
Trillin, Calvin
    1977   *Runestruck*. Boston: Little, Brown.
Tushingham, A. D.
    1966   *The Beardmore Relics*. Royal Ontario Museum, Booklet 1.
Van Sertima, Ivan
    1976   *They Came Before Columbus: The African Presence in Ancient America*. New York: Random House.
Vescelius, Gary S.
    1956   "Excavations at Pattee's Caves." *Bulletin of the Eastern States Archaeological Federation* 15, January: 13–14.
    1982–83   "The Antiquity of Pattee's Caves (3 Parts)." *NEARA Journal* 17, no. 1: 1–16; 17, no. 2: 25–42; 18, no. 3: 57–67. With Introductions by Richard V. Humphrey.
Vogel, Dan
    1986   *Indian Origins and the Book of Mormon*. Salt Lake City: Signature Books.
Wahlgren, Erik
    1950   *The Kensington Stone: A Mystery Solved*. Madison: University of Wisconsin Press.
    1986   *The Vikings and America*. London: Thames & Hudson.
Wallace, Brigitta L.
    1971   "Some Points of Controversy." In Geoffrey Ashe, ed., *The Quest for America*. New York: Praeger Publishers: 155–74.
Walthall John
    1980   *Prehistoric Indians of the Southeast: Archaeology of Alabama and the Middle South*. Tuscaloosa: University of Alabama Press.
Wauchope, Robert
    1962   *Lost Tribes and Sunken Continents: Myth and Method in the Study of American Indians*. Chicago: University of Chicago Press.
Webb, George E.
    1983   *Tree Rings and Telescopes: The Scientific Career of A. E. Douglass*. Tucson: University of Arizona Press.
Wells, Gary, and Elizabeth F. Loftus
    1984   *Eyewitness Testimony: Psychological Perspectives*. New York: Cambridge University Press.
Weslager, C. A.
    1944   *Delaware's Buried Past*. Philadelphia: University of Pennsylvania Press.
    1972   *Delaware Indians: A History*. New Brunswick, New Jersey: Rutgers University Press.

Wheaton, Henry
    1831   *History of the Norsemen*. London and Philadelphia.
White, Peter
    1974   *The Past Is Human*. New York: Taplinger Publishing.
Whittall, James P., Jr.
    1990   *Myth Makers: Epigraphic Illusion in America*. ESRS Epigraphic Series
            no. 1. Rowley, Massachusetts: Early Sites Research Society.
Whittlesey, Charles
    1872   "Archaeological Frauds: Inscriptions Attributed to the Moundbuild-
            ers—Three Remarkable Forgeries." *Western Reserve Historical Soci-
            ety—Historical and Archaeological Tract*, no. 9.
    1876   "Archaeological Frauds." *Western Reserve and Northern Ohio Historical
            Society*, tract 33.
    1879   "The Grave Creek Inscribed Stone." *Western Reserve and Northern
            Ohio Historical Society*, tract 44.
    1881   "Inscribed Stones, Licking County, Ohio." *Western Reserve and North-
            ern Ohio Historical Society*, tract 53.
Wiener, Leo
    1920–22   *Africa and the Discovery of America*. 3 vols. Philadelphia: Innes &
            Sons.
    1926   *Maya and Mexican Origins*. New Haven: Yale University Press.
Wilcox, Elizabeth G.
    1963   *Mu: Fact or Fiction*. New York: Pageant Press.
Willey, Gordon, and Jeremy Sabloff
    1980   *A History of American Archaeology*. 2d edition. San Francisco: W. H.
            Freeman.
Williams, Stephen
    1987   "Fantastic Archaeology: What Should We Do About It?" In Harrold
            and Eve 1987: 124–33.
    1988   "Some Fantastic Messages from the Past." *Archaeology* 41, no. 5: 62–70.
Winsor, Justin
    1889   *Critical and Narrative History of America*, vol. 1. Boston.
Witthoft, John
    1955   "Brief Note." *International Journal of American Linguistics* 2: 194.
    1960   "Of Forgeries and Fantasies." *Oklahoma Archaeological Society Newslet-
            ter* 8, no. 9: 2–19.
Wuthenau, Alexander von
    1975   *Unexpected Faces in Ancient America*. New York: Crown Publishers.
Wyl, W.
    1886   *Mormon Portraits: or The Truth about Mormon Leaders from 1830–1886*.
            Salt Lake City, Utah.
Yeats, William Butler
    1960   *The Collected Poems of W. B. Yeats*. New York: Macmillan.

Sources for Illustrations

(page no.)

2. Churchward, James, *The Lost Continent of Mu* (London: Neville Spearman, 1926; reprint, Albuquerque, New Mexico, forthcoming): frontispiece. Used by permission.

3. Däniken, Erich von, *Chariots of the Gods? Unsolved Mysteries of the Past* (reprint New York: Putnam Berkley, 1984). Copyright © 1968 by Econ-Verlag GMBH, English translation copyright © 1969 by Michael Heron and Souvenir Press. Used by permission of the Putnam Publishing Group and Souvenir Press of London. Photograph by Stephen Williams.

6. LucasFilms, Ltd., publicity photograph. Courtesy of LucasFilms, Ltd.

18. Lee, Stan, and Fred Kida, "Atlantis: Legend or Truth?" *The Amazing Spider-man* (Marvel Comics Group, February 7, 1985). Courtesy of Marvel Entertainment.

29. Squier, Ephraim G., and Edwin H. Davis, *Ancient Monuments of the Mississippi Valley* (Washington, DC: Smithsonian Institution). (1848)

30. Sargent, Winthrop, "Plan of an Ancient Fortification at Marietta, Ohio," *Memoirs of the American Academy of Arts and Sciences,* new series, 5, no. 1 (1853): opposite p. 28.

36. Sargent, Charles Sprague, and Emma Worcester, *Epes Sargent of Gloucester and His Descendants* (Boston: Houghton Mifflin, 1923): opposite p. 56.

37. Williams, Stephen, ed., *The Collected Works of Antonio J. Waring, Jr.,* Papers of the Peabody Museum 58 (Cambridge, Massachusetts: Peabody Museum, 1977): 61.

39. *National Cyclopedia of American Biography,* vol. 9 (New York: James T. White, 1907): 468.

42. Atwater, Caleb, "Descriptions of the Antiquities Discovered in the State of Ohio and Other Western States," *Transactions and Collections of the American Antiquarian Society,* vol. 1 (Worcester, Massachusetts: 1820): 238.

44. *National Cyclopedia of American Biography,* vol. 4 (New York: James T. White, 1897): 79 (Davis); 319 (Squier).

46. Squier and Davis, *Ancient Monuments:* 144.

47. Squier and Davis, *Ancient Monuments:* opposite 189.

49. Winsor, Justin, *Critical and Narrative History of America,* vol. 1 (Boston, 1889): 411.

54. Pidgeon, William, *Traditions of De-Coo-Dah and Antiquarian Researches* (New York, 1858): 10.

56. Pidgeon, *Traditions:* frontispiece.

64. Winsor, *History:* 411.
66. Original photograph, courtesy of Department of Anthropology, National Museum of Natural History, Smithsonian Institution, Washington, DC.
67. *Lamb's Biographical Dictionary of the United States,* vol. 4 (Boston: James H. Lamb Publishers, 1900–1903): 129.
69. Original photograph, courtesy of Peabody Museum Archives, Peabody Museum of American Archaeology and Ethnology, Harvard University, Cambridge, Massachusetts.
79. Barnum, P. T., *The Life of P. T. Barnum* (New York: 1855): frontispiece.
81. Squier and Davis, *Ancient Monuments:* 169.
83. Youmans, William J., ed., *Pioneers of Science in America* (New York: 1896): 301.
86. Reid, M. C., "Inscribed Stone of Grave Creek Mound," *American Antiquarian* 1, no. 3 (1879): 139.
88. Original photograph, courtesy of Dr. Wesley J. Cowan, Cincinnati, Ohio.
90. (Jacob Gass photograph), Jacob Gass, "Account of the Discovery of Inscribed Tablets," *Proceedings of the Davenport Academy of Natural Sciences* II (Davenport, Iowa: 1877): 92. (Cook Farm mound sketch), Marshall McKusick, *The Davenport Conspiracy* (Iowa City: University of Iowa Press, 1970): plate 20. Copyright © University of Iowa Press, 1970. Used by permission.
91. Original photograph, courtesy of Peabody Museum Archives.
93. Original photograph, courtesy of Peabody Museum Archives.
99. Youmans, *Pioneers:* 183.
107. Squier, Ephraim G., "Historical and Mythological Traditions of the Alonquins," *American Review,* no. 14 (February 1849): 275–80.
117. (Charles C. Abbott), original photograph, courtesy of Peabody Museum Archives. (Henry Chapman Mercer), original photograph, courtesy of Spruance Library of the Bucks County Historical Society, Henry Chapman Mercer Museum, Doylestown, Pennsylvania.
119. Mercer, Henry Chapman, *The Lenape Stone; or, The Indian and the Mammoth* (New York, 1885): figures 1, 16.
122. Meltzer, David J., and William C. Strutevant, "The Holly Oak Shell Game: An Historic Archaeological Fraud," in Robert C. Dunnell and Donald K. Grayson, eds., *Lulu Linear Punctuated: Essays in Honor of George Irving Quimby* (Ann Arbor: University of Michigan Press, 1983): 330, 340.
132. *National Cyclopedia of American Biography,* vol. 1 (New York: James T. White, 1898): 397.
133. Donnelly, Ignatius, *Atlantis: The Antediluvian World* (New York, 1882): 47.
137. Donnelly, Ignatius, *Ragnarok: The Age of Fire and Gravel* (New York, 1883): 220.
141. Brochure, "H. P. Blavatsky and Her Writings " (Wheaton, Illinois: The Theosophical Publishing House). Reprinted by permission of the Theosophical Publishing House.
146. Churchward, James, *Children of Mu* (Binghampton, New York: Vail: Ballou Press, 1931): 22.
147. Churchward, *Lost Continent:* 28.
149. Churchward, *Children of Mu:* 40a.

150. Original photograph, courtesy of Peabody Museum Archives.

151. Churchward, *Children of Mu:* 24.

160. Brochure, "The Prophet Joseph Smith Testimony" (Salt Lake City, Utah: Public Communications Department, Chrush of Jesus Christ of Latter Day Saints): 14. Copyright © The Church of Jesus Christ of Latter Day Saints. Used by permission.

162. "Joseph Smith Receives Gold Plates," from the brochure, "The Prophet Joseph Smith Testimony": 13. Copyright © The Church of Jesus Christ of Latter Day Saints. Used by permission.

165. "Book of Mormon," from the brochure, "Temple Square" (Salt Lake City, Utah: Public Communications Department, Church of Jesus Christ of Latter Day Saints). Copyright © The Church of Jesus Christ of Latter Day Saints. Used by permission.

168. Beers, F. W., *Atlas of Licking County, Ohio* (New York: 1866): 37.

169. Randall, G. O., "The Mound Builders and the Lost Tribes: The Holy Stones of Newark," *Ohio Archaeological and Historical Publications* 17 (1908): 212.

173. Original photographs, courtesy of Bradley T. Lepper, Newark, Ohio.

175. Winsor, *History:* 399.

177. Etzenhouser, Ralph, *Engravings of Prehistoric Specimens from Michigan, USA* (Detroit: John Bowman & Son, 1910): frontispiece.

178. Original photograph, courtesy of Dr. Wesley J. Cowan, Cincinnati, Ohio.

186. Original photograph, personal collections of the author.

190. Winsor, *History:* 90.

195. Blegen, Theodore C., *The Kensington Rune Stone: New Light on an Old Riddle* (St. Paul: Minnesota Historical Society, 1968): 10 Used by permission of the Minnesota Historical Society.

187. Original photograph, courtesy of the Kelsey Museum of Ancient and Medieval Archaeology, University of Michigan, Ann Arbor. Museum Photo Archives 5.7963.

196. Blegen, *Kensington Rune Stone:* 76a. Used by permission of the Minnesota Historical Society.

197. (Kensington Rune Stone), original photograph, courtesy of the Minnesota Historical Society. (Runic text), Eric Wahlgren, *The Kensington Stone: A Mystery Solved* (Madison: University of Wisconsin Press, 1950): endpaper.

207. *Lamb's Biographical Dictionary of the United States,* vol. 4 (Boston: James H. Lamb, Publisher, 1900–1903): 159.

208. Horsford, Eben N., *The Discovery of the Ancient City of Norumbega* (Boston, 1890): opposite 16.

210. Horsford, Cornelia, *Vinland and Its Ruins* (New York, 1899): 14.

211. Original photographs, courtesy of the Royal Ontario Museum, Toronto, Ontario, Canada.

215. Winsor, *History:* 103.

216. Original photograph, courtesy of Peabody Museum Archives.

218. Original photograph, courtesy of Peabody Museum Archives.

221. Original photograph, courtesy of the Maine State Museum, Augusta, Maine.

225. Original photograph, courtesy of Peabody Museum Archives.

227. Haury, Emil W., and T. Jefferson Reid, "Harold Sterling Gladwin, 1883–1983," *Kiva* 50, no. 4 (1985): (Gladwin): 271, (Gila Pueblo): 276.

229. Gladwin, Harold S., *Men Out of Asia* (New York: McGraw-Hill, 1947): xii. Copyright © 1947 by McGraw-Hill Co. Used by permission of McGraw-Hill.

231. Gladwin, *Men Out of Asia:* 2. Copyright © 1947 by McGraw-Hill, Inc. Used by permission of McGraw-Hill.

233. Gladwin, *Men Out of Asia:* 222. Copyright © 1947 by McGraw-Hill, Inc. Used by permission of McGraw-Hill.

235. Gladwin, *Men Out of Asia:* 360. Copyright © 1947 by McGraw-Hill, Inc. Used by permission of McGraw-Hill.

241. Covey, Cyclone, *Calalus: A Roman Jewish Colony in America from the Time of Charlemagne Through Alfred the Great* (New York: Vantage Press, 1975): frontispiece. Original photograph, courtesy of Cyclone Covey, Winston-Salem, North Carolina.

245. Covey *Calalus:* 84, 88 Original photographs used by permission of Cyclone Covey, Winston-Salem, North Carolina.

260. Vescelius, G. S., "North Salem, N. H. Site Report" (1955): figure 2.

265. Original photograph, courtesy of Photo Archives, Museum of Contemporary Zoology, Harvard University, Cambridge, Massachusetts.

272. Fell, Barry: *America B.C.: Ancient Settlers in the New World* (New York: Quadrangle/The New York Times Book Co., 1976), copyright © 1976, used by permission of Random House, Inc.; *Saga America* (New York: Time Books, 1980), copyright © 1980, used by permission of Random House, Inc.; *Bronze Age America* (Boston: Little Brown, 1982), copyright © 1982, used by permission of Little, Brown, Inc. Photograph by Stephen Williams.

274. Original photograph, courtesy of the Ferdinand Hamburger, Jr. Archives, Johns Hopkins University, Baltimore, Maryland.

287. Schwartz, Stephan, *The Secret Vaults of Time* (New York: Grosset and Dunlop, 1978): 2.

291. Schwartz, *Secret Vaults:* 60.

292. Schwartz, *Secret Vaults:* 166.

295. Obituary of John Norman Emerson, *Canadian Journal of Archaeology* no. 3 (1979): 240.

298. Goodman, Jeffrey, *American Genesis* (New York: Summit Books, 1981): back cover.

300. Schwartz, *Secret Vaults:* back cover.

309. Jennings, Jesse D., *The Prehistory of North America* (Mountain View, California: Mayfield Publishing, 1989; 3rd. edition): 87.

311. Jennings, *Prehistory:* 101, 103.

313. Price, James E., and James J. Krakker, "Dalton Occupation of the Ozark Border," University of Missouri Museum Brief, no. 20 (1975): 14, 15, 16, 17, 19.

319. Jennings, *Prehistory:* 176.

320. Jennings, *Prehistory:* 144.

322. Webb, Clarence, *The Poverty Point Culture,* Geoscience and Man, vol. 17 (Baton Rouge: Louisiana State University, Geoscience Publications, Department of Geography and Anthropology): 17.

323. Webb, *Poverty Point Culture:* 38, 43, 59, 61, 63; 44, 47, 50, 51, 55.

325. Jennings, *Prehistory:* 232, 82.

326. Squier and Davis, *Ancient Monuments:* 144.

328. Jennings, *Prehistory:* 339, 240.

329. Jennings, *Prehistory:* 241, 242.

331. Williams, Stephen, and Jeffrey Brain, *Excavations at the Lake George Site, Yazoo Co. Miss. 1958–60,* Papers of the Peabody Museum 74 (Cambridge, Massachusetts: Peabody Museum, 1921): frontispiece.

334. Jennings, *Prehistory:* 274, 275.

336. Jennings, *Prehistory:* 296, 297, 298.

337. Guernsey, Samuel J., and Alfred V. Kidder, *Basket-Maker Caves of Northeastern Arizona,* Papers of the Peabody Museum 8, no. 2 (Cambridge, Massachusetts: Peabody Museum, 1921): figure 16; plates 24, 32, 33, 34, 39.

338. Jennings, *Prehistory:* 312.

341. Jennings, *Prehistory:* 304, 309.

Index of Names

Boldface numbers indicate pages containing illustrations

Index of Subjects

This book has been set in Linotron Galliard. Galliard was designed for Mergenthaler in 1978 by Matthew Carter. Galliard retains many of the features of a sixteenth century typeface cut by Robert Granjon but has some modifications which give it a more contemporary look.

Printed on acid-free paper.